City of Gabriels

The History of Jazz in St. Louis, 1895–1973

Dennis Owsley

REEDY PRESS

St. Louis, Missouri

This book is dedicated to my wife Rosa: best friend, lover, and saint
for putting up with 43 years of my jazz obsession;
and to Eddie Randle: the wisest man I have ever known.

City of Gabriels: The History of Jazz in St. Louis, 1895–1973 is published in conjunction with an exhibit of the same name in the History of Jazz Gallery, September 2006–June 2007, organized by
The Sheldon Art Galleries
3648 Washington Blvd.
St. Louis, MO 63108
www.sheldonconcerthall.org/galleries.asp.

The Sheldon Art Galleries present both the exhibition and this book, *City of Gabriels: The History of Jazz in St. Louis, 1895–1973* through the generous support of an anonymous donor.

Reedy Press
PO Box 5131, St. Louis, MO 63139, USA

Library of Congress Control Number: 2006926890

ISBN: 1-933370-04-1

For all information on all Reedy Press publications visit our website at www.reedypress.com.

Printed in Canada
06 07 08 09 10   5 4 3 2 1

Design by Nick Hoeing

A complete discography of jazz music recordings in St. Louis or by St. Louis musicians during the years 1895–1973 can be found on the Sheldon's website at www.sheldonconcerthall.org/galleries.asp.

Contents

Acknowledgments   iv

Foreword   v

Introduction   vi

1 The Pre-Jazz Era (1895–1919)   1

2 The Riverboats and the 1920s (1919–1929)   14

3 St. Louis in the 1930s: The Plantation Club, the Unions,
and the Decline of the Riverboats (1930–1939)   46

4 The War Years: Jimmy Blanton, Miles Davis's St. Louis Years,
and the Inception of Jazz Radio in St. Louis (1939–1949)   74

5 The Jazz Scene in St. Louis in the 1950s (1949–1960)   106

6 The Rise & Fall of Gaslight Square (1959–1967)   132

7 The Polarization of St. Louis Jazz: Traditional Jazz and BAG (1968–1973)   154

Epilogue   187

Appendix: Charter Members of the St. Louis Jazz Club   195

Index   196

Acknowledgments

Paul Reuter, Executive Director of the Sheldon Arts Foundation, and Olivia Lahs-Gonzales, Director of the Sheldon Art Galleries, thank author Dennis Owsley for his years of research, including interviews with many key musicians for his 1987 KWMU radio documentary and his dedication to bringing to light the amazing history of St. Louis jazz. St. Louis has played an important role in the development of jazz, and Dennis has captured both the facts and the feel for this vibrant art form in St. Louis.

Special thanks are due to many individuals who helped make this project possible: Baikida Carroll; Ben Cawthra; Brian Clarke; Michael Cuscuna, Mosaic Images LLC; The Miles Davis Estate; Therese Dickman, National Ragtime and Jazz Archives; Frank Driggs; Zelli Fischetti, Western Historical Manuscripts Collection, University of Missouri–St. Louis; William Gottlieb; Oliver Lake; Chuck Haddix, Marr Sound Archives, University of Missouri–Kansas City; Richard Henderson, Crusaders for Jazz; Jean Huber; Victoria Love, Director, Scott Joplin House, St. Louis; Frank Maloney of the St. Louis Jazz Club; Juanita Moore, Director, American Jazz Museum, Kansas City; Bruce Boyd Raeburn, Curator, Hogan Jazz Archive, Tulane University; Eddie Randle, Jr., and Sharon Randle Gardner; Rob Ray, Special Collections Librarian, Charlie Menees Collection, University of Missouri–Kansas City; Duncan Scheidt; Joe Schwab; Duane Sneddeker, Curator of Photographs, Missouri Historical Society, St. Louis; Chuck Steward; Trebor Tichenor; William Trumbauer, Jr.; and Patricia Wente, General Manager, KWMU Radio, St. Louis.

We also thank our research assistants: Shawn Wedel and Aaron Wilcher, graduate students in the Department of American Studies at Saint Louis University. Without their tireless work, the project would not have been completed.

We are grateful for the scholars and consultants who provided valuable insights: Professor David Baker, Chair of the Department of Jazz Studies, Distinguished Professor of Music and Adjunct Professor, African American and African Diaspora Studies Department, Indiana University, and Senior Consultant for Music, The Smithsonian Institution, Washington, D.C.; Professor Gerald Early, Merle Kling Professor of Modern Letters, Department of English, and Director of the Center for the Humanities, Washington University in St. Louis; and Donald L. Wolff, jazz historian and KMOX radio jazz DJ, St. Louis.

Dennis Owsley thanks the following individuals who served as early editors and fact checkers on the book: Rosa Owsley, Paul DeMarinis, Roscoe Crenshaw, and Paul Reuter.

A project like this could not be carried out without acknowledging those who have gone before: Dr. Bartlett D. Simms for his history of white St. Louis jazz musicians of the 1920s; John Cotter for his dissertation on black music-making in St. Louis; Irene Cortinovis and the University of Missouri Jazzman Oral History Project; Frank Driggs, Wil Warner, and Dan Havens for their interviews of St. Louis jazz pioneers; Lynn Driggs Cunningham and Jimmy Jones for their book *Sweet, Hot and Blue*; Charles Rose for his dissertation on the St. Louis musicians unions; Charlie Menees for his unflagging enthusiasm for St. Louis jazz history; Jim Wallace and Bill Bunkers of KWMU for conducting some of the interviews for the 1987 radio documentary; Kevin Powell of KWMU for his work as recording engineer and tape editor for the 1987 radio documentary; and the many musicians who gave of their time to Dennis Owsley and others in interviews that bear witness to that history.

The Sheldon Arts Foundation in St. Louis, Missouri, presents many great jazz concerts each year in the perfect acoustics of the historic Sheldon Concert Hall and important art exhibits in the Sheldon Art Galleries, including *City of Gabriels: A History of Jazz in St. Louis* being shown concurrently with the release of this book in the History of Jazz Gallery. We thank our board members, volunteers, and many donors who make possible our work in presenting jazz concerts and exhibits and building audiences for the great American art form of jazz. On this occasion we especially thank one very generous anonymous donor who made possible both the exhibit and the publication of this book.

Foreword

I am not certain of the exact reasons why my hometown of St. Louis has had such a great jazz trumpet tradition. It could have been the midwestern atmosphere or the other great musical traditions of the city—but I know that the origins of that tradition come straight from the great Mississippi River.

Some of the earliest players I know came up the river on the great paddlewheel steamboats. The center of it all was Charlie Creath, "The King of the Cornets," a flamboyant man, a wee bit egotistical, always with a string of ladies. We always said that, "As Charlie Creath went, so went St. Louis trumpet playing."

There were so many other great players who formed that tradition. Levi Madison was the most revered to us younger trumpeters. We camped outside his first-floor apartment to hear him practice. He was so crazy that he would practice for ten or fifteen minutes, then he'd laugh for half an hour! We had to take a lunch break and stay all day just to hear him play one piece.

Sleepy Tomlin was, at one time, the first trumpeter for the great Jimmy Lunceford Band. He had a way of keeping his teeth clenched so you couldn't tell whether he was smiling or grimacing. He'd call me "fuzzy." He'd say, "You'll be okay once you get rid of that fuzz in your sound."

Dewey "Squirrel" Jackson was the loudest trumpeter of those who used to play on the riverboats. He drank gin and red soda. All the parents knew when it was time to go pick up their kids because they could hear him playing all the way down the river as the boat came in.

Other great players were "Spare Ribs" Lindsay, who used to sell pigs' feet; Crack Stanley, Bruz Woods, Bill "Buff" Buffington, George Hudson, Huey Webb, Ham Davis, Amos Woodruff, Harold "Shorty" Baker (who was the lead trumpet with Duke Ellington when I joined that band), and Stanley Thomas, a good legit player who was in the navy with me at Great Lakes Naval Training Center. Trumpeter Eddie Randle had a band that used to play around town in St. Louis constantly, and that band eventually included a young Miles Davis.

In addition, I had a family connection: my older sister Ada married Sy McField, a tuba player with Dewey Jackson's Musical Ambassadors. His band used to play at the ballroom in Sauter's Park, which was for white clientele only. The only way that we kids could hear the band was to hide back in the bushes behind the bandstand. Their sound inspired us to form our own band, using makeshift instruments made from jugs, beer cups, and vacuum hoses, with drums from deteriorated ice pans that rattled like snares. My instrument was a discarded water hose coiled in the shape of a trumpet, with a kerosene funnel as a bell on one end and a lead pipe mouthpiece on the other.

In spite of the fact that there were so many other outstanding jazz creators from St. Louis during that era, trumpet players formed the tradition that shaped my early life and music. I learned so much from these early players, not by reading books by or about them, but by being with them and hearing their stories firsthand. With this book, author Dennis Owsley does a wonderful job of relating that same oral tradition, straight from the people who created the history of jazz in St. Louis.

—Clark Terry

Introduction

Trumpet players have shaped the sound and direction of St. Louis jazz from the beginning.

The sound of a St. Louis trumpet player is unmistakable, whether the trumpeter is Charles Creath, Dewey Jackson, Miles Davis, Clark Terry, Floyd LeFlore, or Lester Bowie. That unique sound is described as a clear, singing tone, with many bent notes reminiscent of the human voice.

St. Louis has made specific contributions to American music over the years. It was the first center for the ragtime music that so infectiously forms one of the roots of jazz. The first great lyrical jazz saxophone stylist, Frank Trumbauer, spent much of his early career in St. Louis. Trumbauer's virtuosity, sound, and style were the major influences on Lester Young. Young founded an entire saxophone style in the 1930s as an alternative to the prevailing style derived from Coleman Hawkins. A line of St. Louis–area trumpeters, from Charles Creath to Miles Davis and Lester Bowie, changed the way we think about music. Davis changed the course of jazz four times during his career, while Bowie was part of an avant-garde movement in the Midwest that challenged the way jazz has been played.

St. Louis is a river city and a railroad hub. Thus, many musical influences have come through the area. Its history is dominated by German and Catholic traditions. The music heard in St. Louis and in many towns north on the Mississippi River is influenced by German brass band music. According to Judge Nathan B. Young, a noted African American historian and founder of the *St. Louis American* newspaper:[1]

New Orleans and its music . . . has a French background because there you have the French opera. And all the people there, all the people went to the French opera there. And you have a delicate type of music that grew out of New Orleans. Jelly Roll Morton and his type of music has a delicacy about it that is French.

. . . in St. Louis where the Germans came after the revolution in '48—the German-Americans came here and they brought their culture and their music and the black St. Louisans were ready to listen to it and partake of it. For one thing is, the German culture [and] music was very much like what the black culture and music was: it had bottom to it. It had bass and contralto and alto and part-singing. And the first musicians in St. Louis that disseminated music were the Germans. Or, if you wanted to take a lesson in music in St. Louis, you would have to go to a German teacher. All the band instruments and all the band music were German. And so the black musicians, the early black musicians all had German teachers.

You can hear the German influence in nearly all the early midwestern brass players who grew up along the river. These brass players include trumpeters such as Bix Beiderbecke of Davenport, Iowa; Louis Metcalf of St. Louis; and Miles Davis of East Alton, Illinois.

Blues from the Mississippi Delta influences the music of St. Louis as well. It has always had a large and, at times, vibrant blues community. By contrast, the blues influence in Kansas City was from the southwestern states, such as Texas and Oklahoma. Thus, a trumpet player in St. Louis has the vocal inflections of the Mississippi Delta blues laid over the German brass tradition's singing tone. St. Louis trumpeters use many blues inflections (bent notes), with vocal effects and mutes that are not found in trumpeters from river cities further to the north.

During the 1920s, St. Louis was a major regional jazz center. Both the Okeh and Brunswick labels made field recordings here of jazz and blues bands from all over Missouri and southern Illinois. By 1929, however, the regional jazz center in Missouri had shifted to Kansas City from St. Louis. Why did this happen? What were the conditions in St. Louis and Kansas City that caused this shift? Why can it be said that it is better to be a musician from St. Louis than a musician working in St. Louis?

Because St. Louis is a river town and railroad center, influences have come and gone. No regional style of jazz has grown up here, in contrast to Kansas City or Chicago. In addition, St. Louis, in many respects, has always been a city that looked down the Mississippi rather than up the river to Minneapolis/St. Paul. Thus, much of the great black migrations of the last part of the nineteenth century and the years of World War I bypassed St. Louis and went on to Chicago.

Jazz history is much more complex than the standard "up the river from New Orleans to Chicago" legend. While it is true that New Orleans musicians such as Louis Armstrong, Pops Foster, and Henry "Red" Allen spent part of their early careers on excursion boats working out of St. Louis, most moved on to Chicago and New York by rail and did not remain in St. Louis. Before the 1920s, jazz musicians boarded trains and traveled all over the United States. New Orleans jazzmen were found in Los Angeles, San Francisco, Kansas City, Dallas, Chicago, St. Louis, and New York well before 1920.

This book is an oral history of jazz in St. Louis. It is based on interviews of major and minor jazz musicians conducted for a 1987 radio documentary on St. Louis jazz. Other sources are used as well. It is divided into chapters that cover logical divisions in the life and times of St. Louis. It examines the jazz musicians and music of the St. Louis metropolitan area up to 1973 and the particular conditions for both black and white musicians that have shaped their lives and styles. Since people are human and they forget things or tell stories that place themselves in a favorable light, the historical perspective is important to getting at the truth of a situation. Where there is a conflict between the oral history and the accepted written history, the conflict is allowed to remain, because sometimes the "people on the ground" have a better perspective than the professional historian.

Endnotes

[1] Judge Nathan Young, "Creative Aging," KWMU Radio, 1985.

1

The Pre-Jazz Era (1895–1919)

Two periods in the city's music history have produced highly original music. The first is the ragtime era at the turn of the twentieth century. The second period is the time of the Black Artists Group from 1967 to 1973. In both periods, it appears that the power structure ignored the artists. In the former period, ragtime was heard in a district informally designated as a "vice" district, where drinking, gambling, and prostitution were tolerated. In the latter case, many Black Artists Group members were speaking unpleasant truths about the lot of African Americans in the city, and were best ignored.

The vice or "sporting district" in St. Louis was known as Chestnut Valley. It was an entertainment area for African Americans who worked on the steamboats that plied the Mississippi from New Orleans to St. Paul. As a center of commerce, the levee needed many people to serve as deckhands, cabin boys, stewards, and roustabouts to operate and load and unload the packet steamers.[1] The steamboats not only brought African American workers to the levee, but they also supplied beautiful, light-skinned "Creole" women to work in such establishments as Babe Connor's brothel—known as the Castle and located at 210 South 6th Street next to the Southern Hotel.[2] According to Trebor Tichenor,[3] another factor in the development of the vice district was

> the massive black migration north in '93 and a lot of people stayed here, settled in St. Louis. There was a district that developed here and just was let alone by the city fathers and I think this was a black area and [it was] originally around Targee Street, which is long gone and was a little street that connected Market and Clark that would run through the middle of Kiel Auditorium. But that was a center for, let's say, early black activity in music around 1890s, early '90s. And then it moved out around Union Station and this became the hotbed for ragtime: a lot of the piano players going and coming through town could always be assured of finding a job at one of the places on Market or Chestnut. That's really where ragtime grew up.

Chicago was the primary destination for the black migration of the late 1800s and the Great Migration that occurred following World War I. The direct route from the South to Chicago was the Illinois Central Railroad, which bypassed St. Louis. However, a significant number of people transplanted to St. Louis from the South, but they found a situation in the city very similar to what they had left. The East St. Louis Race Riot of 1917 also hastened the migrating blacks to continue northward. Because of these and other factors to be discussed in this book, St. Louis never became a center for African American culture like Chicago and New York.

Judge Nathan B. Young described the influence of Chestnut Valley on American music of future generations.[4]

> Out of the green scum and muck grow the fairest lilies and valuable hardwood trees; out of old Chestnut Valley sprang the stock of popular American music, nurtured and flavored by Negro musicians. Many of the theme songs and radio favorites of 1937 were first played here in the '90s.

The Castle was the site of much revelry. George S. Johns,[5] editor of the *St. Louis Post-Dispatch* at the time, took the great pianist Ignace Paderewski to the Castle. He described the scene in this manner:

> Babe Connors imported the pick of the girls from Louisiana. She advertised them as "creoles," and no doubt they had the old blood of Creoles in their veins, but they were octoroons. They danced in little more than stockings, and Mammy Lou, a gnarled, black African of the purest type, sang, with her powerful voice, a great variety of indigenous songs. She was among the first to sing "Frankie and Johnny" for entertainment, and she excited hair-raising emotion when she sang the refrain of that song.

Two other songs sung by Mammy (or Mama) Lou were "There'll Be a Hot Time in the Old Town Tonight" and "Ta-Ra-

Ra-Boom-De-Ay." White American composers stole both songs. These songs became staples of the Victorian era, a period in American history of hypocritical morality. It is also ironic that "It's Howdy Doody Time," the theme song of the *Howdy Doody Show*, a popular children's television show of the 1950s, takes its melody from "Ta-Ra-Ra-Boom-De-Ay."

Chestnut Valley attracted many, including W. C. Handy, who described it in his autobiography, *Father of the Blues*.[6] "I wouldn't want to forget Targee Street as it was then . . . the high-roller Stetson hats of the men or the diamonds the girls wore in their ears. Then there were those who sat for company in little plush parlors under gaslights." A lover's quarrel between Allen (Johnny) Britt and his girlfriend Frankie Baker that ended in a Targee Street saloon was immortalized in the ballad "Frankie and Johnny." A story in the *St. Louis Post-Dispatch* on October 20, 1899, noted: "22-year-old Frankie Baker, 'an ebony-hued cake-walker' shot two-timer 'Johnnie'—17-year-old Albert Britt—at 22 Targee Street on October 15, 1899."[7]

Trebor Tichenor comments.[8]

> I think it's sort of agreed that that tune was an ancient, imported tune, you know, from Europe someplace, but it was adapted here and it became the ballad. . . . A St. Louis legend says that a piano player by the name of Dooley picked up on a local homicide case and that was the Frankie and Johnny case in 1899 and that he created it, but this is a legend, of course. But it's true that it did become famous from here. Now, I think the first publication of the tune was around 1914.

Ragtime was the first national popular music, and St. Louis was its first center. Judge Nathan Young makes a good case that Tom Turpin, owner of the Rosebud Cafe, was the first king of ragtime music.[9] "A few years ago when W. C. Handy broadcasted over a local radio station about his composing the "St. Louis Blues," he reminded his listeners that the real father of the Blues and jazz was Tom Turpin of St. Louis, the stout, somber, seldom smiling Tom Turpin." Turpin published the first ragtime piece by an African American, "Harlem Rag," in 1897,[10] at least three years before the world heard of Scott Joplin.

Turpin opened the Rosebud Cafe in 1900 at 2220–2222 Market Street. The Rosebud was a sprawling entertainment complex. It contained two bars, a gambling room, and a "hotel" upstairs. Tom Turpin was a very large man, weighing 350 pounds. As a result, the wine room where he played had a piano raised up on blocks to accommodate his size. Another room, the Hunting and Sporting Club, was for those who liked both outdoor and indoor sports. An annex to the Rosebud, called the Hurrah Club, had a piano. It was there that the legendary "cutting contests" between local pianists and out-of-town musicians occurred. Turpin sponsored formal ragtime piano contests at the Rosebud and later at the Booker T. Washington Theater. These contests often continued over several days. His last piano contest was in 1916, won by local pianist Charley Thompson. Many of the St. Louis ragtime school, including Joplin, Scott Hayden (1882–1915), Arthur Marshall (1881–1968), Joe Jordan (1882–1971), and Louis Chauvin (1881–1908), were members of the Hurrah Club.

Of all the men of the St. Louis ragtime school, Louis Chauvin's composing talent nearly equaled of Joplin's. Chauvin could not read music, but his technique made him a highly feared competitor in the Rosebud piano contests. His only published work was "Heliotrope Bouquet," a rag co-composed with Scott Joplin and two other songs that were not ragtime pieces. Sam Patterson remembered his technique in the cutting contests.[11]

> Turpin was great, but Chauvin could do things that Turpin couldn't touch. He had speed fingering and he tossed off octaves overhand. You can talk about harmony—no one could mistake those chords. Chauvin was so far ahead with his modern stuff; he would be up to date now. As a boy, I thought I was some peanuts, but I knew then that I would not be the artist Chauv was. I had lessons and he taught himself. When he was thirteen, you never heard anything like him. When he would first sit down, he

Thomas Million Turpin (c. 1873–1922)

Tom Turpin[12] was born in Georgia around 1873. He had an older brother, Charles, born in 1867. Their parents soon moved to Mississippi, and then to St. Louis in the late 1870s. The father, "Honest John" Turpin, opened a saloon, the Silver Dollar at 425 South 12th Street. During this period, Charles and Tom were prospecting in Nevada. Both returned to St. Louis in 1894.

Tom Turpin—a very large man weighing over 350 pounds—had successful careers both as a pianist and a saloonkeeper. The two careers often intertwined, as he performed at his own establishments. Turpin's career as a pianist began at The Castle, Babe Connors' bawdy house. His saloonkeeper career began sometime in the late 1890s when he opened Turpin's Saloon at 9 Targee Street.

Turpin began publishing his compositions in 1897 with "Harlem Rag," which was the first rag published by an African American composer. "Bowery Buck," his second rag, was published in 1899. "A Ragtime Nightmare" was published in 1900, and "St. Louis Rag" was released in 1903. Turpin's last rag published during his lifetime was "The Buffalo Rag" in 1904.

Tom Turpin, St. Louis, date unknown. Photographer unidentified. Copy photograph by Dennis Owsley. © The Scott Joplin House State Historic Site, St. Louis.

In 1900, Turpin opened the Rosebud Cafe at 2220–2222 Market Street. The Rosebud quickly became a center of ragtime and piano playing in St. Louis. Turpin knew how to advertise. In addition to his piano contests, other events generated publicity, including the annual Rosebud Ball, Old Rosebud whiskey, and a holiday party in 1904 that featured an "Electric Christmas Tree." The Rosebud closed its doors in 1906.

Tom opened the Eureka Club at 2208 Chestnut in 1910. His brother Charles owned the Booker T. Washington Airdrome, a vaudeville theater at 2323 Market Street. Tom was music director for this enterprise, known as the Booker T. Washington Theater after it became a permanent building in 1913. He also opened an establishment at 2333 Market in 1916. This later became the Jazzland Café. Turpin remained with the theater, publishing his World War I song, "When Sambo Goes to France," in 1918.

Tom Turpin died of peritonitis on August 13, 1922. He is buried in St. Peter's cemetery in St. Louis.

always played the same Sousa march to limber up his fingers, but it was his own arrangement with double-time contrary motion in octaves, like trombones and trumpets all up and down the keyboard. . . . And Chauv had so many tricks, my God, that boy!

A lingering question about the performance practices of ragtime goes as follows: Is there evidence that the early rags were impro-vised, or were they set pieces that musicians worked out and someone eventually wrote out? Trebor Tichenor addresses this question.[13]

> I think the earliest days of ragtime it was definitely a performer's art, and there was a lot of improvisation going on. There's one player who recorded late in life, ah, his name is Brun Campbell, known as the Ragtime Kid and he palled around with Scott Joplin. Late in life he recorded some tunes the way he played them in St. Louis and Sedalia, and there's a lot of improvisation and a surprising amount of blues influence . . . in his music and I think it evolved into a written music for the piano because the piano was the hottest instrument around at the turn of the century; everybody had a piano and there was a market for sheet music that was incredible. It's like videotapes today and records, you know, people bought sheet music in those days. So, there was a desire to buy ragtime. It was quickly mar-keted, it was quickly notated by 1897 and it became a hot item.

The music was also used in brass bands. Like the written piano music books, scores for brass bands like *The Red Back Book* were developed. Tichenor also addresses this question.[14]

> John Stark orchestrated most of the classic rags himself and put 'em out in what he called the *Red Backed Books*. These are the ones that Gunther Schuller, for ex-ample, worked with when he did the famous recording on Angel in the '70s. New Orleans bands certainly played a lot of rags and the early cake walks.

The better-known ragtime composer Scott Joplin was apparently in and out of St. Louis from around 1885 to 1894.[15] Trebor Tichenor comments on Joplin and his arrivals in St. Louis. "Scott Joplin of course was here, legend says as early as 1885. Joplin did not move here until 1900. . . . Joplin was published in 1899 in Sedalia and then he and publisher Stark moved here in 1901 and then this became the center for classic ragtime."

In any cultural history of St. Louis, the 1904 World's Fair looms large. St. Louis has forgotten many things, but the 1904 World's Fair is not one of them. At the Fair, ragtime was only heard on the Pike—a mile-long stretch of amusements, beer halls, and attractions. Joplin did not play at the Fair, although his composition, "The Cascades," was written in honor of the event and became quite popular. According to Tichenor, the 1904 World's Fair was good for the musicians.[16]

Scott Joplin, location and date unknown. Photographer unidentified. Copy photograph by Dennis Owsley. © The Scott Joplin
House State Historic Site, St. Louis.

For the ragtime players it was good because it gave them
more opportunities to work that year and most of the players
found a job on the Pike, that's a tremendous entertainment area,
a midway area of the Fair. Ragtime was not an official part of the
Fair. The legend is that the city fathers were afraid that ragtime
would overrun the fair. There persists a legend that Scott Joplin
played at the World's Fair. There is really no evidence of that, but
he did of course write *The Cascades* in commemoration of it. But
about as close to authentic ragtime got on the fair docket was, say,
Sousa playing cakewalks. That was about as close as it got. But
most of the ragtime was kind of underground. Players were all on
the Pike, the Rosebud was buzzing, it was good for the musicians
that year. . . . St. Louis was a peak here for ragtime activity, you
know. It brought in a lot of players, and there was a tremendous
contest here that Tom Turpin had, a piano competition in that
year.

On the Pike, Arthur Marshall played at the Spanish Café.
Sam Patterson and Louis Chauvin performed duo piano ragtime and songs at a beer hall called Old St. Louis. In addition
to the aforementioned "The Cascades," other compositions
were written for the Fair. "St. Louis Rag" (Turpin, 1903) was
the first. James Scott contributed "On the Pike." "St. Louis
Tickle" by Theron C. Bennet was also popular. The best-
known song of the Fair, "Meet Me in St. Louis," had lyrics by
Andrew B. Sterling and music by Frederick Allen "Kerry" Mills.
Neither man attended the Fair.[17]

It appears that 1904 was the apogee of the St. Louis ragtime school. The musicians began to drift away to Chicago as
soon as the World's Fair had ended, because there were more opportunities in that city.[18] The departure of talented musicians had a profound effect on St. Louis businesses and neighborhoods.

The closing of the Rosebud Cafe in 1906 hastened the demise of Chestnut Valley, and soon blues musicians began to
migrate to an area known as "Deep Morgan" on Biddle Street, north of the city. Trebor Tichenor comments on unsuccessful
efforts by "moralists" to close down Chestnut Valley.[19]

Well, there seems to have been just a general apathy about it. The city fathers just didn't seem to get too involved with it.
There was one priest down at a church at 16th and Pine, Father Coffey, who became very vocal about the district and he tried, he
succeeded in helping get a law passed called the "Newbury Law" in the early '90s. Part of the Newbury Law stipulated removal
of musical instruments from saloons and wine rooms. This was rarely enforced. (laughter) And Father Coffey found himself reas-
signed to another parish all of a sudden. There was a lot of power in the district, and you know, he got a little too vocal about it.

In Deep Morgan, the bars mainly had blues musicians working in them. This was the start of the blues community in St.
Louis that continues to this day. W. C. Handy also spent time in St. Louis before 1900, and his composition the "St. Louis

5

Scott Joplin (c. 1868–1917)

Scott Joplin[20] was born on a farm in the Texarkana, Texas, area in late 1867 or early 1868. Joplin's family soon left the farm and moved to Texarkana. Legend has it that Joplin taught himself to play piano in the home of a white family that employed his mother. Julius Weiss, a local German-born music teacher, gave him a thorough grounding in European music.

Joplin moved to Sedalia, Missouri, in the 1880s, attended high school, and started his musical career. Some anecdotes place him in St. Louis in 1885, but his first mention as a performer was in a Texarkana paper in 1891, when he was leading a minstrel troupe. He worked as a cornetist and bandleader outside the Chicago World's Fair in 1893. Returning to Sedalia after the fair, Joplin continued his career as an itinerant musician, with Sedalia as his home base. He published his first two songs in Syracuse, New York, in 1895.

Joplin worked as a pianist at various events and social clubs (the Maple Leaf Club was one) in Sedalia when he was not traveling. Also in Sedalia, he studied at George R. Smith College, and he published two marches and a waltz in 1896. His first ragtime composition, "Original Rags" was published in 1898, but he was forced to share credit with a staff arranger, Charles N. Daniels. Joplin then obtained the services of a lawyer who helped him gain a contract with John Starks, the owner of a Sedalia music store. This contract stipulated a one-cent royalty on each sale of his sheet mu-

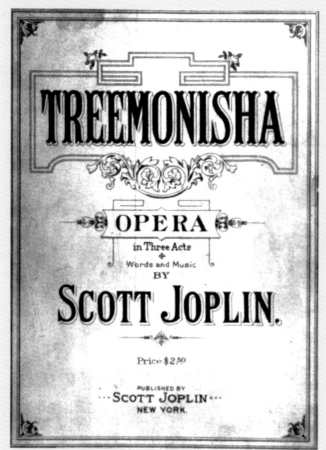

Cover of *Treemonisha by Scott Joplin—Sheet Music.* Copy photograph by Dennis Owsley. © The Scott Joplin House State Historic Site, St. Louis.

sic. While in Sedalia, Joplin completed "The Ragtime Dance" and "Swipesy," the latter a collaboration with Arthur Marshall.

Joplin moved to St. Louis in 1901 and became associated with Tom Turpin. Alfred Ernst, Director of the St. Louis Choral Symphony Society (predecessor of the St. Louis Symphony) asserted in the *St. Louis Post-Dispatch* in 1901 that Joplin was an extraordinary genius as a composer of ragtime music. He spent much of his years in St. Louis composing and not performing. Stark also moved to St. Louis. While in St. Louis in 1903, Joplin filed a copyright application for an opera, *A Guest of Honor*. He formed an opera company and took it on a disastrous tour of the Midwest. Copies of the opera were not filed with the Library of Congress and no copy of it has been found.

Joplin remained in St. Louis until 1907, when he moved to Chicago and then on to New York. Joplin went to New York to find financial support for another opera, *Treemonisha*. The final years of his life were spent composing and trying in vain to stage a production of *Treemonisha*. Joplin never succeeded in this endeavor.

The self-styled "King of the Ragtime Writers" began to experience the physical and mental debilitation due to syphilis, possibly contracted some twenty years before. He was hospitalized in January 1917 and was then moved to a mental institution, where he died on April 1, 1917.

Blues" has been an unofficial ambassador for the city. Sources claim that Biddle Street was the source of the lyrics of this composition. Trebor Tichenor comments on W. C. Handy's ties to the ragtime era.[21]

> Handy talked about coming through here and in '93 and stayed very briefly on Targee Street and then went on to Chicago as a lot of musicians did for the World's Fair that year in Chicago. Yeah, those Handy tunes were published earlier than a lot of people realized [in] 1914, "Memphis Blues" was published in 1912 and they were originally marketed as rags. . . . Of course, we don't recognize "Yellow Dog Blues" as a rag, but it was published as "Yellow Dog Rag" because this, you know, was the ragtime era. They were marketed as blue rags or ragtime blues and of course that's all forgotten today but original editions have ragtime on the cover, even "St. Louis Blues."

The "St. Louis Blues" is one of the most recorded songs in jazz and swing music. The Tom Lord Discography lists over 1,450 recordings of the composition up to approximately 1995. Notable recordings of the tune are by Bessie Smith and Louis Armstrong (1925),[22] Thomas "Fats" Waller on organ (1926),[23] Dave Brubeck (1963),[24] the Thad Jones/Mel Lewis Jazz Orchestra (1968),[25] and the Ralph Sutton/Jay McShann piano duo (1979).[26]

The Turpin brothers were greatly affected by the shift from Chestnut Valley to Deep Morgan, but the brothers were natural entrepreneurs. Charles Turpin—Tom's older brother—won an election as district constable in 1910.[27] Tom opened the Eureka Club at 2208 Chestnut the same year, but without the success of the Rosebud Cafe. Charles also owned the Booker T. Washington Airdrome, a vaudeville theater at 2323 Market Street. Tom was music director for this enterprise, later known as the Booker T. Washington Theater. Artie Matthews, a musician who worked at the Booker T. Washington Theater and served as music director before Tom Turpin, published the first blues,[28] "Baby Seal Blues," in August 1912, two months before W. C. Handy's more famous "Memphis Blues." Matthews is best known in jazz circles as the composer of "Weary Blues."

The Booker T. Washington vaudeville theater was a force in St. Louis music into the 1920s. In addition to black vaudeville, the theater hosted Tom Turpin's ragtime piano contests. In 1915, the winners were George Goins, Charles Thompson, Owen Marshall, and Raymond Hines. Mary Parker won the women's piano contest.[29] John Arnold, an important musician of the 1920s, won a blues piano contest at the Booker T. Washington in the fall of 1915.[30] The last ragtime piano contest was held at the Washington Theater in May 1916, won by Charles Thompson.[31]

By that time, classic ragtime was no longer popular and was evolving into different styles. According to Tichenor:[32]

> It didn't just vanish, it evolved into several different things. Written ragtime evolved into something called novelty piano, which was popularized after Zez Confrey published "Kitten on the Keys," in that style. And in the east it evolved into Harlem stride, which is probably the granddaddy of the piano—black piano mainstream jazz tradition, certainly. So it just didn't disappear, it just evolved with the rest of the music by the '20s.

An important event took place at the Booker T. Washington Theater in 1916. The African American patrons of the theater began to demand more "high-class" acts. According to the *St. Louis Argus*, the black acts were not changing their routines, were undependable, and were using routines that smacked of minstrelsy. Clark and Lovere was the first white act to appear at the theater.[33] This tradition of the theater hiring both black and white acts continued into the 1920s. It led to the appearance of white musicians "Pee Wee" Russell, Sonny Lee, and possibly Frank Trumbauer as part of the black Charles Creath Band around 1926.[34] Vaudeville and later blues singer Trixie Smith played at the Booker T Washington in 1917.[35]

A St. Louisan, Eva Taylor (1895–1977), was a vaudeville performer from an early age. She performed at age three at the Orpheum Theater in St. Louis. By 1904, Taylor began touring all over the world. She settled in New York in 1921 and began working with Clarence Williams. She eventually married him and recorded under both her name and as Irene Gibbons with his "Blue Five" and other bands. She performed as a vocalist with jazz musicians until 1974. Taylor died on October 31, 1977.[36]

An important pre-jazz African American vaudeville act, the Creole Band, played at various white theaters during this period. The band played St. Louis six times, including appearances at the Anheuser-Busch brewery.[37] The band played the Empress Theater (3616 Olive), Mannion's Park (an outdoor entertainment venue at 8600 South Broadway), and the Alton, Illinois, Airdrome in 1915. In addition, a special performance was held at the Keystone Café, a black St. Louis cabaret.[38] The band returned in 1916 and 1917. In 1917, they played Erber's Theater in East St. Louis, the Grand Theater, and a special engagement at the private dance hall of Sam Shepard. This performance for a black audience was described in the *Argus*.[39]

> The private dance hall of Mr. Sam Shepard's place, 3654 Pine Street, was beautifully decorated for the big banquet which was given in honor of the Creole Band by Mr. Geo. P. Dore, Tecumseh Bradshaw, Robert Anderson, Alonzo Thomas and Sam Shepard. Fifty guests were present and had the time of their lives with plenty of everything to eat and drink. The band played the sweetest music that was ever heard in St. Louis and the guests enjoyed themselves until 3 a.m. when everyone left feeling very happy.

The Creole Band personnel included trumpeter Freddie Keppard, clarinetist George Baquet, trombonist Eddie Vincent, trumpeter Jimmy Paolo, guitarist Norwood Williams, dancer and vocalist Henry Morgan Prince, and bassist Bill Johnson. Keppard was one of the great New Orleans trumpeters who went on to a career in Chicago in the 1920s. Baquet recorded with Bessie Smith and Jelly Roll Morton in the 1920s. Vincent had a short career in Chicago. Bill Johnson was an important jazzman. He had a long career with the King Oliver Creole Jazz Band, clarinetist Johnny Dodds, and many others. The Creole Jazz Band was recorded for RCA Victor on December 2, 1918.[40] The recordings were never issued.

The early music in St. Louis came out of the German brass band tradition. Judge Nathan Young stated that in the early years of St. Louis black musicians took lessons from German teachers. With the racial segregation of the times, it became apparent that African Americans needed a conservatory of their own. The Luca Conservatory for black musicians began in 1888. St. Louis has a strong tradition of having quality music teachers in the schools in the black community. Since the turn of the century, St. Louis has had the reputation as a town that sends highly trained musicians out into the world.

By the turn of the century, a number of highly trained musicians were teaching in the black schools and leading community bands. Community bands were an excellent source of instruction for up-and-coming musicians in both the white and black communities in St. Louis. They offered hands-on instruction from seasoned musicians as well as the opportunity to perform in front of audiences. Some of the bands in the black community were the Harmony Club Band and Orchestra (led by James H. Harris and Johnathan Easton),[41] the Blue and Harmony Band (William M. Blue, bandmaster, and James H. Harris, leader),[42] the Oddfellows Band, William Blue's Concert Band, and the Knights of Pythias Band. An issue of the *St. Louis Argus* shows Arville Harris and Bob Shofner in the Knights of Pythias Battle Axe Cadets.[43] They, along with trombonist Willie Austin, were the section leaders. All three young musicians became well-known professionals in the 1920s. William Blue was the father of William Thornton Blue, a well-known clarinetist in the 1920s and 1930s. P. B. Langford was also active in both community bands and cabarets. He led the Oddfellows Band. Drummer Harry Dial[44] recalls the musicians who passed through the Oddfellows Band: "There were such trumpet players in that band as Dewey Jackson, Andrew 'Big Babe' Webb, Shirley Clay, R. Q. Dickerson, and Leonard 'Ham' Davis, and trombonists Harvey Lankford, Charles Lawson, and Andrew Luper, drummers Robert 'Red' Muse, Ralph Stephenson, who was also the band's drum major, and Lawrence Madison. Eugene Sedric, Andrew Brown, and Jerome Pasquall are clarinetists who received their early training from Mr. Lankford." All of these musicians became professionals in the 1920s with Clay, Dickerson, Davis, and Sedric having long careers in New York. Dial was a drummer who played with Thomas "Fats" Waller for many years.

Musicians in the community bands played for social functions held by many social clubs and on Monday riverboat excursions. Each edition of the *St. Louis Argus* and *St. Louis Palladium* newspapers carries several notices of such functions during this period. The major dance hall in the black community was Pythian Hall, located at Lucas and Compton.[45] A major dance hall for the white community was Dreamland Ballroom, which became the Arcadia Ballroom after 1925. It was located at 3515–3523 Olive Street and was managed by Joe Ternes and Paddy Harmon.[46] On August 17, 1917, the *Argus* lists Bogg's Café (2901 Lawton), Jimmy Collins' Garden Café (at Cardinal and Lawton), the Keystone Garden (at Compton and Lawton), and the Rathskeller Garden (at Laclede and Leonard) as cabarets having musicians.[47] The Chauffeurs Club at 3125 Pine, an important after-hours club in the 1920s, was listed in the *Argus* as early as 1915.[48] Later on, from the 1930s into the 1950s, the Tom Powell American Legion Post Drum and Bugle Corps fulfilled this function. These musicians also taught in the segregated schools of St. Louis. According to Miles Davis's teacher, Elwood Buchanon,[49] the school music was the classics, the "heavy stuff." There were no stage bands or jazz ensembles then.

Other highly trained music teachers in the black schools of the St. Louis region included Major N. Clark Smith, C. Spencer Tochus, Clarence Hayden Wilson, Kenneth Billups and later George Hudson, Ernest Nashville, Vernon Nashville, Lester Bowie, Sr., Allen Ivey, Hughie Ellison, Herman Morgan, Paul Overby, Richard Overby, Charles Rose, Harold Wayne, Walter Lathen, and Ed Nicholson.

Another unlikely source of training for black St. Louis musicians was the Fate Marable Band. Marable, a pianist from Paducah, Kentucky, came to St. Louis in 1918 and led bands on the riverboats until 1940. New Orleans musicians said that playing for Marable was like going to a conservatory. Musicians were expected to be good readers and to play anything at sight. St. Louis musicians were very proud of their training and abilities. In fact, according to Kimball Dial, a musician on the riverboats, St. Louis musicians looked down on their New Orleans brethren because they could play anything in all twelve keys, while the New Orleans musicians only knew how to play in two or three keys.[50]

Before the turn of the century, excursions on steamboats were a major feature of life in St. Louis. Usually, social groups booked the excursions and most excursions, included a band for dancing and other entertainment. The excursion boats remained strictly segregated until 1969. African Americans were only allowed on the boats on Monday nights. Several examples follow from the archives of the *Palladium* and the *Argus*.

- The Madison Social Club gives a Grand Moonlight Excursion on the steamer *Corwin Spencer* on May 18, 1903.
- The Madison Social Club charters the *City of Providence* on June 26, 1905.
- A Monday night cruise on the *Grey Eagle* on July 30, 1915.
- Scullin Steel excursion on the *Grey Eagle* on June 26, 1916.

Streckfus Steamers, St. Louis, June 10, 1913. Photographer unidentified. © "Cactus" Charlie Menees Collection, Department of Special Collections, Miller Nichols Library, University of Missouri–Kansas City.

- Promoter Jesse Johnson led a moonlight excursion on the *Grey Eagle* on August 14, 1916, with music by the Western Band. That same day, the *Grey Eagle* took a Sumner High School boys excursion to Cave Springs, Missouri, with music by Louis Crenshaw's band.

The Streckfus steamers began bringing boats into St. Louis in 1911 and eventually became the dominant excursion company on the St. Louis waterfront. Before the Streckfus family was involved on the Mississippi, a boat owned by the Acme Packet Company, the *J.S. No. 1*, ran from Rock Island, Illinois, to New Orleans. Fate Marable had been leading a band of white musicians playing ragtime on this boat from 1907 until it burned in 1910. Captain John Streckfus bought the Diamond Jo Packet Company and its boats, including the *Sidney*. Marable was hired for the *Sidney* and remained on the boat leading white musicians until 1917. His experiences in New Orleans lead him to hire a black band in Paducah that he called the Kentucky Jazz Band. Captain John Streckfus then sent Marable north to St. Louis to play solo piano opposite the white Gene Rodemich Band in 1918. Marable brought an all-black New Orleans band back to St. Louis on the *St. Paul* in 1919. That band included Louis Armstrong and Norman Mason (trumpets), Davey Jones (mellophone), Paul Dominguez (violin), Sam Dutrey (clarinet), Marable (piano), George "Pops" Foster (bass), Johnny St. Cyr (banjo), and Warren "Baby" Dodds (drums). After

City Club Excursion, St. Louis, 1914. Photograph by Arthur W. Proetz. © Western Historical Manuscript Collection, St. Louis.

a tentative start on their first night, they became a sensation in St. Louis.[51] The subsequent effects of bringing these jazz musicians and the music that they played will be discussed in the following chapter.

Jesse Johnson was a promoter and champion of black music all during the next several decades. He got his start leading excursions on the riverboats. Some of his promotions will be detailed in Chapters 2 and 3 of this book.

Racial segregation on the riverboats and in other establishments led to the formation of two musicians' unions. Both black and white unions were formed on November 19, 1896. Before joining the American Federation of Musicians, each group had separate musicians associations. There were several white musicians' associations: The Musiker Untersteutzung Verein (formed February 2, 1844), The Polyhymnia Society (1860), the Musicians' Mutual Benefit Association (September 13, 1885), the Musicians' Mutual Protective Association (1886), and the National League of Musicians (1890). A black association, the Musicians Equity Association, was a branch of the Knights of Labor. The Musicians' Mutual Benefit Association, the Musicians' Mutual Protective Association, and the Polyhymnia Society merged in 1888 to become the Musicians Association of St. Louis. This group joined the National League of Musicians in 1890.[52]

The great labor organizer, Samuel L. Gompers, had tried for years to get musicians' associations to join the American Federation of Labor (AFL). He asked for all organized musicians to send delegates to a meeting in Indianapolis in October 1896. From St. Louis, three whites, Owen Miller, I. L. Schoene, and Frank Gecks represented the Musicians' Mutual Benefit Association. The blacks sent John L. Fields, who represented the Musicians Equity Association. Owen Miller became president of Local 2, and the Musicians Equity Association became Local 44.

While the majority of customers on the riverboats, in the bawdy houses, and in the circuses were white, both black and white segregated bands played for them.[53] White musicians did not play for black audiences. The white musicians' local was mostly concerned with concert bands, symphony orchestras, and theater pit bands while the black musicians' local dealt with

Fate Marable Band, S.S. St. Paul, St. Louis, 1919. Photographer unidentified. Left to right: Baby Dodds (drums), Joe Howard (trumpet), Grant Cooper (trombone), Pops Foster (bass), Johnny St. Cyr (banjo), Fate Marable (piano/calliope/leader), David Jones (melody sax/mellophone), Louis Armstrong (cornet), Sam Dutrey, Sr. (sax/clarinet). © Frank Driggs Collection.

small groups playing parties and dances. The wage scale and minimum number of musicians for jobs were the same for both groups during this period.[54]

Charles Rose remarked:[55]

> The abundance of music and musicians in St. Louis gave the city the potential for becoming one of the major music centers of the United States. The musicians' union did very little to create a working relationship between the musicians, business establishments, and local politicians. St. Louis was known to many musicians as a creative city, but a city not interested in supporting the growth of musicians socially or economically.

Fate Marable's Society Syncopators, S.S. Sidney, St. Louis, c. 1919. Photographer unidentified. Left to right: Baby Dodds (drums), Bill Ridgeley (trombone), Joe Howard (trumpet), Louis Armstrong (cornet), Fate Marable (piano), David Jones (mellophone), Captain Joe Streckfus (owner), Johnny Dodds (clarinet), Johnny St. Cyr (banjo), Pops Foster (bass). © Frank Driggs Collection.

Endnotes

1 Nathan B. Young "Your Place and Mine," excerpted in *Ain't But a Place*, Gerald Early, ed. (St. Louis: Missouri Historical Society Press, 1998), pp. 339–346.

2 Ibid.

3 Trebor Tichenor, interview with the author, 1986.

4 Young, "Your Place and Mine," pp. 339–346.

5 Gordon G. Jones, *Tom Turpin: His Life and Music* (The Tom Turpin Ragtime Festival, Inc., 1995).

6 W. C. Handy, *Father of the Blues, An Autobiography* (New York: McMillan, 1941).

7 *The African-American Heritage of St. Louis—A Guide,* http://www.umsl.edu/services/library/blackstudies/stacentc.htm.

8 Tichenor interview.

9 Young, "Your Place and Mine," pp. 339–346.

10 Jones, *Tom Turpin.*

11 Ibid.

12 Ibid.

13 Tichenor interview.

14 Ibid.

15 Edward A. Berlin, *A Biography of Scott Joplin* (c. 1867–1917) (Written for the exclusive use of the Scott Joplin International Ragtime Foundation) 1998, http://www.scottjoplin.org/biography.htm.

16 Tichenor interview.

17 Jones, *Tom Turpin.*

18 Ibid.

19 Tichenor interview.

20 Berlin, *A Biography of Scott Joplin.*

21 Tichenor interview.

22 Bessie Smith, *The Bessie Smith Collection,* Columbia CK 44441.

23 Thomas "Fats" Waller, *Fats at the Organ, Volume 3, 1926–1929,* EPM Musique 159262.

24 Dave Brubeck, *Dave Brubeck at Carnegie Hall,* Columbia C2K 61455.

25 Thad Jones/Mel Lewis, *The Complete Solid State Recordings of the Thad Jones/Mel Lewis Orchestra,* Mosaic MD5-151 (limited edition–out of print).

26 Ralph Sutton/Jay McShann, *Last of the Whorehouse Piano Players–The Original Sessions,* Chiaroscuro CR(D) 206.

27 Jones, *Tom Turpin.*

28 Ibid.

29 *St. Louis Argus,* February 19, 1915.

30 Ibid., September 29, 1915.

31 Ibid., May 12, 1916.

32 Tichenor interview.

33 *St. Louis Argus,* March 31, 1916.

34 Martin Williams, *Jazz Masters of New Orleans* (New York: Da Capo Press, 1979), p. 186.

35 *St. Louis Argus,* January 26, 1917.

36 Lynn Driggs Cunningham and Jimmy Jones, *Sweet, Hot and Blue: St. Louis Musical Heritage* (Jefferson, NC: McFarland and Company, 1989), pp. 163–164.

37 Lawrence Gushee, *Pioneers of Jazz: The Story of the Creole Band* (New York: Oxford University Press, 2005), p. 129.

38 *St. Louis Argus,* July 2, 1915.

39 Ibid., January 12, 1917.

40 *Tom Lord Discography,* version 3.3.

41 *St. Louis Palladium,* February 13, 1904.

42 Ibid., August 13, 1904.

43 *St. Louis Argus,* April 21, 1916.

44 Harry Dial, *All This Jazz About Jazz: The Autobiography of Harry Dial* (Chigwell, Essex, England: Storyville Publications and Co. Ltd, 1978).

45 Western Historical Manuscript Collection (WHMC), University of Missouri–St. Louis, UMSL Black History Project (1980–1983) Photograph Collection, http://www.umsl.edu/~whmc/guides/whm0336.htm.

46 Streetswing.com (Dance History Archives), http://www.streetswing.com/histclub/a1d.htm.

47 *St. Louis Argus,* August 17, 1917.

48 Ibid., January 3, 1915.

49 Ellwood Buchanan, interview with the author, 1986.

50 Dial interview.

51 *St. Louis Globe-Democrat,* July 22, 1945.

52 Charles E. Rose, "The American Federation of Musicians and Its Effect on Black Musicians in St. Louis in the Twentieth Century," A Thesis submitted in Partial Fulfillment of the Requirements for the Degree of Master of Music. Department of Music in the Graduate School, Southern Illinois University, Edwardsville, November 1978, pp. 8–14.

53 Ibid., p. 14.

54 Ibid., p. 16.

55 Ibid., pp. 24–25.

2
The Riverboats and the 1920s (1919–1929)

The Blues and St. Louis Jazz

The jazz music of St. Louis in the 1920s was highly influenced by the blues. In the Biddle Street area, known as Deep Morgan, blues musicians practiced their craft in the cabarets found there. Blues pianists such as Speckled Red, Roosevelt Sykes, and Wesley Wallace found work. Wallace recorded a wonderful train blues for Paramount in 1930, *No. 29,* which described a trip from Cairo, Illinois, to St. Louis.[1] Early Delta blues guitarists also performed in St. Louis during this period. These guitarists include Lonnie Johnson, who lived in St. Louis from 1920 to 1926. Johnson went on to fame in New York, recording with Duke Ellington and Louis Armstrong. He recorded with Charles Creath in 1925 and worked with Creath on the steamer *St. Paul* from 1920 to 1922. Johnson also recorded a wonderful series of duets with the white guitarist Eddie Lang (under the pseudonym Blind Willie Dunn). Other well-known blues guitarists that worked in St. Louis during this period were Sylvester Weaver and Big Joe Williams. The singer Victoria Spivey recorded in St. Louis in 1926 and worked as a staff writer for the St. Louis Publishing Company from 1926 to 1929. In addition, a thriving blues scene on the east side of the Mississippi had such well-known clubs and other establishments as the Blue Flame Club, the 9-0-5 Club, Jim's Place and Katy Red's. Boots on the Levee was a going concern because the riverboats would dock near the establishment. Apparently, whites also were in the place for "slummin' and enjoyment."[2]

Sheldon Harris, from *Blues Who's Who,* made the following observation:[3]

> For some reason St. Louis has never had its due as a centre for the blues. The city fostered piano ragtime in the early part of the century and was also a significant jazz centre where Charlie Creath's riverboat bands were based. The tragic race riot in East St. Louis of 1917 could have killed off the life of the city, and in some respects it did: sixty-odd years later it is still an ugly urban wilderness, written off by planners and administrators alike. Blues has found a home in such environments, offering both an outlet for frustrated emotions and a release for unsatisfied creative instincts.

Jazz Recording in St Louis during the 1920s

Although Scott Joplin recorded two piano rolls (*The Strenuous Life* in 1902 and *Something Doing* in 1903) in St. Louis, no jazz or dance band music was recorded in the city until 1921 when the Gene Rodemich Orchestra recorded for the Brunswick label. The discography of jazz recordings made in St. Louis during this period supports the thesis of the pervasive influence of the Delta blues on St. Louis jazz. Many of the recordings featured groups of jazz and blues artists working together.[4] The St. Louis jazz musicians of the 1920s were also influenced by ragtime. From 1921 to 1928, St. Louis was a center for field recordings of many kinds of music.

In 1923, the Okeh record label began a series of "field recordings" with a recording of Benny Moten's Kansas City Orchestra. This label recorded extensively in St. Louis with recordings by both black and white jazz and dance bands from all over the Midwest, including recordings by the Jesse Stone Blue Serenaders of St. Joseph, Missouri (1927). Some of these recordings were by the following St. Louis bands:

- The Arcadia Peacock Orchestra of St. Louis (1923, 1924)
- The Arcadian Serenaders (1924, 1925)
- Charles Creath's Jazz O'Maniacs (1925, 1926, 1927)
- The Palladeo Orchestra of St. Louis (1925)

Arcadian Serenaders, location unknown, c. 1925. Photographer unidentified. Seated, left to right: Wingy Manone, Felix Guarino, Cliff Holman. Standing, left to right: Johnny Riddick, Slim Leftwich. © The Al Rose Collection, Hogan Jazz Archive, Tulane University.

- Benny Washington's Six Aces (1925)
- The Old St. Louis Levee Band with Jelly Roll Martin (sic) (1926)
- Powell's Jazz Monarchs (1926)
- The Searcy Trio (1926)
- Blues guitarist Lonnie Johnson and singers Bertha Henderson, Victoria Spivey, Katherine McDonald, Alma Henderson, Charlie Butler, Cora Perkins, A. W. Adams, Irene Scruggs, and Helen Humes (1925, 1926, 1927)

It is interesting to note that Okeh records made by black artists carried a four-digit number, while those made by white artists were assigned five-digit numbers. Vocalist Alma Henderson was recorded in St. Louis on May 27, 1927, accompanied by DeLoise Searcy (piano) and Lonnie Johnson (guitar). *Mine's as Good as Yours* and *Soul and Body [He Belongs To Me]* were issued as Okeh 8489 while *Red Lips, Kiss My Blues Away*, and *Where the Wild, Wild Flowers Grow* were issued as Okeh 40823.[5]

The field recordings by Okeh abruptly stopped with the movement of Ralph Peer from Okeh to Victor in 1927. Peer had been Okeh's recording director and was in charge of field recordings.[6]

The Vocalion label recorded Dewey Jackson's Peacock Orchestra (1927) and blues singers Luella Miller and Bert "Snake Root" Hatton (1927). The King Oliver Dixie Syncopators also recorded for Vocalion in St. Louis (1927).

The Brunswick and Victor labels exclusively recorded white dance bands and musicians. The Gene Rodemich Orchestra (1924–1926), The David Silverman Orchestra (1923), Herbert Berger's Coronado Hotel Orchestra (1924, 1925), the Mound City Blue Blowers (1924), and Allister Wylie and his Coronado Hotel Orchestra (1928). The latter recording was the last commercial jazz or dance band recording made in St. Louis until 1946.

Two record labels originated in St. Louis during this time.[7] The Harmograph label (1922–1925) was a subsidiary of the Shapleigh Hardware Company, which manufactured phonographs until 1922. Harmograph did not press its own records but ordered them initially from a wholesale dealer in record masters in New York with the Harmograph label attached. These masters were from the Cameo label. Later, Shapleigh ordered through a Chicago wholesaler who sold Paramount and Pathe-Perfect. For the jazz record collector, some of the Harmograph records were alternate takes of Paramount's race series.

The Herwin label (1924–1930) was a subsidiary of the Artophone Corporation, a wholesaler of electrical appliances. The

Fate Marable (1890–1947)

Born in Paducah, Kentucky, on December 2, 1890, pianist, calliope player, and riverboat bandleader Fate Marable[8] led what musicians called "a floating conservatory" on the Mississippi. His mother taught him to play piano. He was also educated at Straight University in New Orleans. According to Warren "Baby" Dodds, Marable had a light complexion and red hair.[9] Marable's job was on the steamer *J. S.* that sailed from Rock Island, Illinois, to New Orleans. He played piano and a white man played violin. Gradually, the number of musicians increased to four pieces, playing "strictly ragtime." This band was unusual in that a black man led this band of white musicians. The *J. S.* burned in 1910, and the steamer *Sidney* became Marable's home base. By that time, the Streckfus family had acquired most of the small companies running excursion boats up and down the Mississippi and its tributaries.

While in New Orleans, Marable became enamored with the music there. He left his band and started his Kentucky Jazz Band in 1917 with black musicians from Paducah. The Streckfus company sent Marable alone to St. Louis in 1918 to advertise the opening of the steamer *St. Paul.* Marable played solo piano on the upper deck, while the Gene Rodemich Orchestra played in the ballroom. In 1919, Marable returned to St. Louis on the *Capitol* with a band that included Louis Armstrong, Baby Dodds, and Pops Foster. Armstrong was in and out of St. Louis with Marable until 1921. All of Marable's musicians had to be good readers because they had to learn fourteen new tunes every two weeks.[10] Each winter, Marable returned to New Orleans to work there. He initially staffed his bands with New Orleans musicians, but this practice gradually changed until most of his personnel came from St. Louis.

Marable was a hard taskmaster who had a cruel streak. When a musician was to be fired, a rehearsal was called. The musician being fired was given a time fifteen minutes later than the rest of the band. When he arrived, here was an axe lying in his chair and the band was playing "There'll Be Some Changes Made."[11]

Fate Marable led bands both on the river and in the greater St. Louis area until 1940, when entertainment on the boats was curtailed. He worked as a solo pianist at the Victorian Club on Washington Boulevard in St. Louis until his death. Many great musicians passed through his bands, including Louis Armstrong, Zutty Singleton, Baby Dodds, Johnny St. Cyr, Boyd Atkins, Eugene Sedric, Irving "Mouse" Randolph, Tab Smith, Don Stovall, and Jimmy Blanton. Marable died in St. Louis on January 16, 1947.

name "Herwin" came from the brothers Herbert and Edwin Schiele, who were the chief officers of Artophone. The Herwin label redistributed the Gennet masters. Although Herwin had gross sales between six and seven hundred thousand dollars in its best years, its records are hard to find. Herwin's business was strictly mail order to rural areas in the Midwest and South. No catalogs were issued.

Music on the Riverboats

Before discussing the history of jazz music in St. Louis during the 1920s, it needs to be stated that much of early jazz history consists of myths, romantic notions, racial agendas, and political agendas. One of these romantic notions is that jazz was played on the riverboats that plied the Mississippi and Ohio rivers. Many times, evidence contrary to a myth or romantic notion has been ignored. The following paragraphs address this notion. The interviews are with musicians and others who worked on and owned the excursion boats.

S.S. Capitol at Night, St. Louis, date unknown. Photographer unidentified. © "Cactus" Charlie Menees Collection, Department of Special Collections, Miller Nichols Library, University of Missouri–Kansas City.

The Streckfus Steamer Company played a large part in the development of jazz, operating excursion boats out of both New Orleans and St. Louis. Other companies also operated excursion boats. When Streckfus hired the Paducah, Kentucky, pianist Fate Marable in 1908, it set the stage for the arrival of jazz music in St. Louis. Marable brought a band of jazz musicians from New Orleans to St. Louis in 1919. See Chapter 1 for a description of Marable's background and the sensation that this band created. There is no question that the musicians in Marable's band were jazz musicians, but was the music played on the boats jazz?

Verne Streckfus was interviewed in 1960. He stated that "the dancers on the *Sidney* liked 'straight' music—fox trots, waltzes, and one-steps. The bands played stock arrangements, music as it was published, not distorted by arrangements. The dancers on the *Capitol* liked the same kind of music; the bands would play some rumbas and other special rhythms, but the floor wouldn't fill until the 'pretty' music was played."[12] Streckfus stated that the Streckfus brothers, not Marable, picked Louis Armstrong for the Marable Band. The Streckfus brothers went to Economy Hall, where Armstrong was playing with Kid Ory and King Oliver. He was playing a cornet owned by Ory. On the *Capitol*, he played a cornet belonging to the boat for over a year.[13] Bassist Pops Foster said,[14]

> The Streckfus people were funny to work for. You played music to suit them, not the public. As long as they were happy you had the job. You had fourteen numbers to play in an evening and you changed numbers every two weeks. The numbers were long. You'd play the whole number and maybe two or three encores, and sometimes two choruses. A lot of guys didn't like that and quit. The Streckfus people made musicians out of a whole lot of guys that way. Louis Armstrong, Johnny St. Cyr, and I didn't know nothin' about readin' when we went on the boats, but we did when we came off. That's what started us off.
>
> The Streckfus people liked to have a guy who fronted his own band. They had Fate, Charley Creath, Dewey Jackson, Eddie Allen, and a guy named Floyd Campbell; he only lasted about a year. We all got paid by the Streckfus people, not by Fate or the other guys, and they did the hiring and firing. Fate got more than us because he was hired as leader. He would call the numbers and start them off, and conduct rehearsals. You had a book of numbers and you played them for a month. Then you got another set. We played the numbers different lengths, sometimes we'd play one chorus, sometimes three, and then we'd make different endings.

Warren "Baby" Dodds played on the *Capitol* from 1919 to 1921. His recollections are important to this story.[15]

> The Marable Band was the first big band that I worked with. We had about a dozen men. It was a pleasure to work with that bunch of men. We didn't have to work hard. Of course, we worked hard but we didn't have to. We played strictly by music. And music is not so hard if you get with a bunch that's playing together. But it's an awful strain to play jazz with one fellow going this way and another fellow going another. That makes for hard work. It's like anything else. If you run an automobile and the gears are meshing easy you can run it pretty fast. But if the gears are meshing badly, they're going to hit each other. It's the same thing with music. Regardless of what the number is, if everybody's together, and if everybody knows his business, when the notes are joined they'll come out even. The music would sound so pretty, especially on the water.
>
> I knew how to spell when reading music but I didn't know how to read well and fast. We had loads of fun and had an hour-and-a-half or two-hour rehearsal almost every day, all new music. That's why we learned to be such good readers. New music every day and the same music we rehearsed in the day we played at night. And we had to be perfect with it. There were three Streckfus brothers, and they were all musicians. I think two of them played piano and one, violin. And they made Fate demand frequent rehearsals of the band. It was wonderful for me and everyone else concerned. It made us tidy up our music, it made our eyes fast and it made us fast on our instruments. That was the first place I learned what "time" was. They would hold a metronome on me, and a stop clock, and I wouldn't know anything about it. I had to be a very strict timekeeper in those days. I used to listen to everybody in the group and try to give each one what he wanted. Nobody tried to outplay the other fellow. We all played together, and Louis was the only one who took solos in the Marable Band.

Singleton Palmer, another riverboat veteran recalled, "One thing about the boats, you only played the music that the captain wanted you to play. You didn't play what you wanted to play. It was a routine on the boat, because things would run time-wise. I think there was three tunes to a set, there was certain times of night you were supposed to play, certain tempos, and waltzes set. There wasn't too much improvisation on the boats; you played strictly to the music."[16] In an interview, Sammy Long quoted John Streckfus, "Boys, always keep that rhythm going and play tunes that people can whistle while they're dancing." In that same interview, Kimball Dial stated that nobody took solos on the boats, except in 1931–32 when solos were permitted in Harvey Lankford's band. The soloists were Charles Creath (accordion) and Walter "Crack" Stanley (trumpet), Louis Eckehard (alto sax), or Andrew Webb (trumpet).[17]

Norman Mason, who was originally a trumpet player with Marable, discussed working on the riverboats.[18] He later was a clarinet player with Singleton Palmer on Gaslight Square.

> When I first started on there, we would take a trip out at 9:30 and play till six and then we'd come back on at night at eight. We'd come back to the same place. We'd take a trip out of St. Louis up to Auburn and then out to the Palisades, just above Auburn, and then we'd come back. The program for the night usually ran about thirteen or fourteen dances; I mean one-minute dance and then two encores for the dances. In other words, we'd play three dances to a set, and sometimes the people would keep on clapping so we'd keep on playing. We'd play on the average an hour and then fifteen minutes intermission and then we took an hour off for lunch.
>
> Saturday crowd was primarily a dancing crowd and other days were probably a family crowd for the kids. They would dance all the time. The kids would naturally come along with their parents. They didn't have any drinks on there either. See, they had soda and food and all that sort of thing.

Kimball Dial recalled that, by the end of the 1920s, Marable had arrangers Cecil White and Cecil Thornton taking songs and arrangements off hit records. Dial stated that Marable's band was very commercial on the boats. He had a show within the band with "clown numbers" with the musicians wearing clown costumes.[19]

John Chilton's book *Ride, Red, and Ride: The Life of Henry "Red" Allen*[20] has the following paragraph.

> Captain Joe Streckfus took a keen, if, at times, dictatorial interest in the music that was played by Fate Marable's Band, even sending away for orchestrations of tunes he felt the public wanted to hear. He also designated the tempo, insisting that the St Louis dancers liked their music faster than the New Orleans patrons. Looking back to the 1920s, he said (in 1958), "St Louis tempo was 20 beats per minute faster than New Orleans." . . . Discipline for the musicians was strict, both on and off the bandstand, and though the Streckfus Brothers were generally respected their word was law. Marable simply acquiesced to the regime. While he could rehearse a band expertly, he was not particularly interested in fostering improvisation and once an arrangement had been mastered he was happy to repeat it without variation for the rest of the season. Throughout his long career Marable only ever recorded two titles (in 1924 as Fate Marable's Society Syncopators), and the overall results illustrate that Marable led a dance band and not a jazz group.

It is apparent from these descriptions that while many of the excursion boats had Marable and others as the leader of the bands, the real bandleader was Captain John Streckfus. Streckfus dictated the tempo and duration of tunes. His crew timed tunes and counted tempos from a place above the dance floor to make certain that Streckfus's instructions were followed. Transgressions to these rules often led to the firing or the fining of musicians. This practice continued until the last Streckfus boat stopped having bands to entertain customers. It did not matter whether the band or the audience was black or white.

Fate Marable also was very strict with his musicians, often firing them for small transgressions to his rules. Nevertheless, many black musicians thought of Marable's bands as a "finishing school." Fate Marable (as Fate Marable's Society Orchestra) made only two recordings, "Pianoflage" and "Frankie and Johnny in 1924."[21] St. Louisan Harvey Lankford played trombone on these recordings, along with a group of New Orleans musicians. It is readily apparent that these recordings are not jazz recordings.

Although the riverboat bands had jazz musicians playing on them, it appears from the evidence above that the romantic notion about jazz being played on the riverboats is mainly false. The nature of these bands would be in modern parlance, "cover" or "show" bands. The jazz musicians played jazz in cabarets and dance halls on dry land, not on the riverboats. A similar notion that the big bands of the swing era were primarily jazz bands also goes against the evidence. Of the over four hun-

Fate Marable's Society Syncopators, S.S. Capitol, St. Louis, 1924. Photographer unidentified. Left to right: Zutty Singleton (drums), Norman Mason (alto sax/clarinet), Bert Bailey (tenor sax/clarinet), Fate Marable (piano), Walter Thomas (alto sax/clarinet), Willie Foster (guitar/banjo), Sidney Desvignes (trumpet), Amos White (trumpet), Harvey Lankford (trombone). © Frank Driggs Collection.

dred big bands listed in George Simon's book, *The Big Bands*, a small fraction could be called jazz bands. The remaining bands were dance bands with little jazz content.[22] Baby Dodds comments, "You see the [King] Oliver band was a real jazz band. They played nothing but jazz music. But with the band on the boat we played some semi-classics and numbers like that."[23] Trumpeter Clarence "Perch" Thornton, a veteran of the "Fats" Pichon Orchestra out of New Orleans, sums up the situation in William Howland Kenney's *Jazz on the River*,[24] "To play for Streckfus, you had to go backwards musically. The music was like Jeckyl and Hyde. . . . the same tunes that we knew, but they sure sounded different! New Orleans was supposed to be the jazz capital, and with Louis Armstrong playing on the boat, that supposedly made it Jazz, even though it wasn't."

Segregation was strictly practiced on the riverboats. Blacks were only allowed on the boats on Monday nights, a practice kept until 1969. At first, blacks were only allowed on the *Grey Eagle, Liberty, Pilgrim,* and *Majestic*, rivals to the Streckfus steamers. Jesse Johnson and Charles Creath talked the Streckfus brothers into allowing blacks onto their boats on Monday nights. The first excursion with Streckfus was on September 20, 1920.[25] The late David Hines talked with several older members of the black community and recounted this story.[26]

That was an event. That was a very, very special event. People would begin to prepare for that as early as five o'clock. I mean, immediately off from work. . . . You'd get dressed in your very, very best clothes. . . . People would walk to the boat a long distance, many, many blocks. If you don't have enough to ride the bus, you don't have enough to go on the boat. But the point was at that time, you didn't have polyester or permanent press. And if you were on a crowded streetcar or anything, your shoes were shined and somebody might step on your shoes. Also if you sat down and it was very hot and humid, you would wrinkle the pants. You didn't want to ruin the crease in your pants. So, you'd neatly fold your coat across your arm and you'd walk to the boat.

Jazz and Dance Music in St. Louis during the 1920s

Charlie Menees—longtime jazz disc jockey, critic, teacher, and observer of the St. Louis scene—talked about the importance of St. Louis in American jazz: "We are important as Frank Driggs and others have said who are writing about the national scene. They say that St. Louis is more important than we recognize and certainly more important than a lot of outsiders recognize."[27]

Menees also commented on the lack of a regional St. Louis jazz style.[28]

I wasn't the originator of the idea or the theory or the conception, but there was a general agreement on it. That St. Louis being the railroad and river transportation center that it was brought musicians here and carried musicians from here. . . . And the musicians that came here on the train, they'd learn from our people here; our people learned from them. As you know, a good many of our people moved from here and became internationally famous jazz people.

In addition to the riverboats, St. Louis had many cabarets and dance halls during this period. Because this was the Roaring Twenties and prohibition was the law, St. Louis entertainment institutions were afflicted by the lawlessness caused by prohibition. Of course, as in other cities, prohibition gave rise to organized crime. All of the speakeasies, ballrooms, and clubs had mob connections, whether they wanted them or not. Pee Wee Russell told a funny story of Sterling Bose and the mob. During an engagement at the Arcadia Ballroom as members of the Frank Trumbauer Orchestra, Pee Wee and trumpeter Sterling Bose (a member of the Arcadian Serenaders, the house band at the Arcadia) hung out at Joe Hardaway's speakeasy near the Arcadia. This story is told in a letter to an English jazz fan.[29]

Bosie was about five foot five and weighed less than a sparrow. Those were the days when gangs were infesting this country, and St. Louis had the toughest ones. As bad, if not worse, than Chicago. These kids used to own planes and pilots, and they would think nothing of going out and bombing each other. That's on the level. I'm not exaggerating at all. Every speak had its silent partners. Hoodlums who simply declared themselves in.

One Saturday night after work, Bix [Beiderbecke], Bosie and I went to Hardaway's for our usual before bed snorts. We were all pretty stiff, but Bosie was just about out. Quietly out. He was a good boy and no trouble. He sat on a chair with his feet up against an old fashioned pot-bellied stove when three hard characters came in.

They bellied up to the bar, and one of them said out of the side of his mouth, "Give everybody a drink." Joe turned green. He knew this was the mob, and he knew that this was the beginning of their part ownership. So everybody got a drink. Then they repeated it, and everybody got another drink. That is everybody but Bosie. He seemed to be quietly dozing. Then the third time.

With that, Bosie seemed to come to. He pulled himself up, walked over to the three and said to the leader, "Get the hell out, you son of a bitch."

The guy looked down on Bosie, who was no bigger than a minute and said nothing. What the hell was there to say? Bosie repeated himself. Bix and I were weak with fright. Let me add that Bosie accompanied his request with a little finger poking at the guy's middle. . . .

Pee Wee Russell (1906–1969)

Clarinetist Charles Elsworth "Pee Wee" Russell[30] was born in Maplewood, Missouri, on March 27, 1906. His parents moved to Muskogee, Oklahoma, where he took his first music lessons on a number of instruments. He eventually settled on clarinet and played his first professional job at age thirteen. As a youngster and throughout his career, he was always an incorrigible, willful person. As a result of this willfulness, he was sent to Western Military Academy, where he played in the band from 1920 to 1921. The following year, his military school career was terminated.

In 1922, he and his parents moved back to St. Louis, living on Goodfellow. Pee Wee worked afternoons on the riverboats *St. Paul* and *J. S.* and traveled upriver to Davenport and Keokuk, Iowa. He heard and played with many black musicians, including making an appearance with a Charles Creath group at the Booker T. Washington Theater in 1925 or 1926. Pee Wee traveled through Kansas, the Dakotas, and Iowa with the Allen Brothers tent show. While in Iowa, he got a telegram to join the Herbert Berger Orchestra in Laredo, Mexico. This band eventually worked its way back to St. Louis. The Berger Orchestra recorded in both New York and St. Louis. Pee Wee is audible on two notes on the coda of the "Fuzzy Wuzzy" Bird.[31]

Pee Wee moved to Texas to play in the pianist Peck Kelly's

Pee Wee Russell at Nick's, New York, c. June 1946. Photograph by William Gottlieb. © William Gottlieb from the Library of Congress Collection.

band with Jack Teagarden. He later returned to St. Louis to play in Frank Trumbauer's band with Bix Beiderbecke at the Arcadia Ballroom (1925–1926). When the Arcadia Ballroom job ended, Russell went to Hudson Lake, Michigan, for a summer engagement with Bix Beiderbecke and Frank Trumbauer. Pee Wee moved to New York in 1927 and recorded with Red Nichols and many others, including St. Louisan Red McKenzie and the Mound City Blue Blowers. This record date produced *Hello, Lola* (named for a girlfriend of Pee Wee's) and *If I Could Be With You One Hour Tonight*, two of the most famous jazz recordings of the 1930s.[32] From 1937 on, he worked with Eddie Condon units and in various Dixieland/mainstream groups. One of his best clarinet solos is *Wailin' D.A. Blues* on Commodore.[33]

Pee Wee nearly died from the effects of alcohol in the early 1950s, but his marriage to his wife Mary saved his life. Although the public thought of Pee Wee as a traditional jazz player, he had a great ear and could play with anybody. He recorded with Thelonious Monk at the 1963 Newport Jazz Festival.[34] His later recordings featured tunes by John Coltrane and Ornette Coleman.[35] Pee Wee also showed remarkable skills as an abstract painter later in his life. When his wife died, he seemed to give up and died in Alexandria, Virginia, on February 15, 1969.

The tough guy hesitated, looked around and said to his buddies, "Come on." And they walked out. He must have thought that this little guy who was not afraid of him and obviously not armed must have powerful connections . . . he had to be one of the boys. The very big boys.

The next day, we had a matinee and made it to Hardaway's first for our usual pickup. Bosie walked in full of the shakes and hoping that Joe will let him add a couple to his tab.

First thing Joe says to him was, "Have a drink on me." Bosie was a little startled. This wasn't according to Hoyle. And Joe wasn't known for his generosity. Meanwhile, we said nothing to Bosie. Joe poured the drinks himself. The second, the third, the fourth. Bosie had a foolish look on his face. He knew something was going on, but he couldn't figure it out. . . .

Then Joe told him. He couldn't believe it. At first he thought it was a rib. But Bix and I leveled with him, and he knew it was true. The kid had drawn a complete blank about the night before.

Well, his shakes came back worse than ever. A half hour later he was on a train to Chicago and never came back to the Arcadia ballroom.

White Dance Bands and Cabarets during the 1920s

Because of the segregation that existed in St. Louis, there are two parallel histories of black and white jazz and dance band musicians that intersect only occasionally. Each history will be treated separately. The histories will be presented with the white jazz musicians first, simply because they recorded first. This will keep the histories roughly in chronological order. The first intersection is the friendship between the two band bookers in St. Louis during the 1920s, Ted Jansen (white) and Charles Creath (black). They had friendly band battles at Creve Coeur Lake and Marigold Gardens on the South Side of St. Louis.[36] This intersection had important consequences (see below).

Elmer Schoebel, a pianist from East St. Louis, played in theaters and moved to Chicago in 1920. He made his first recordings with the New Orleans Rhythm Kings in 1922.[37] Schoebel was one of the first important arrangers in jazz and was also an electrical engineer. He invented a radio manufactured in the 1930s in his own shop.

The first major dance band in St. Louis during this period was that led by Gene Rodemich. Rodemich first recorded in 1919. He worked often at both the Arcadia Ballroom and the Coronado Hotel, both popular white dance venues. Rodemich brought both Frank Trumbauer and Red McKenzie to national prominence. Another member of the orchestra, drummer Paul Sporleder, owned a drum shop in St. Louis for many years. A white musician from the Rodemich Orchestra, Sonny Lee, recorded with Charles Creath. When Rodemich left St. Louis for Boston in 1926, the Conley–Silverman and David Silverman orchestras were subsequently formed. Trombonist Larry Conley later became a popular music composer. His best-known composition is "A Cottage for Sale," made popular by Billy Eckstine and others. Conley and Rodemich co-composed both "Tia Juana" (recorded by Jelly Roll Morton) and *Shanghai Shuffle* (recorded by the Fletcher Henderson Orchestra and others).

Other white dance orchestras that featured white jazzmen in the early 1920s were the Herbert Berger Coronado Hotel Orchestra (Pee Wee Russell—clarinet), the Les Carlbach Orchestra,[38] the Joe Gill Orchestra, the Joe Kayser Orchestra, and the Ted Jansen Orchestra (the latter two had Frank Trumbauer on saxophone). The Ambassador Bellhops worked at Trimp's Ambassador Ballroom (Freddie Laufkoetter—trumpet, Vernon Brown—trombone) and recorded in Chicago in 1926. The Allister Wylie Coronado Hotel Orchestra recorded in 1928 for Victor.

According to Dr. Bartlett D. Simms, a very enthusiastic chronicler of the white jazz scene in St. Louis, the Ted Jansen Orchestra with Frank Trumbauer was very influential.[39]

Gene Rodemich (1890–1934)

Gene Rodemich was born in St. Louis on April 13, 1890. He was the son of Dr. Henry Rodemich, a dentist, who studied violin as a young man. Gene studied piano with Louis Hammerstein, organist at Temple Israel. Like all young musicians of his day, he was schooled in the classics. At the 1904 St. Louis World's Fair, the ragtime music played on the Pike turned his thinking around. He began to play his interpretations of popular music. At age nineteen, he was the pianist on the Governor's boat in President William Howard Taft's 1909 tour down the Mississippi River. This led to work at private parties, social events, and various country clubs.

Rodemich went to New York in 1913 and initially had difficulties finding work. He was the accompanist for vaudevillian Elise Janis, touring the front lines in France in 1917 during World War I. He returned to St. Louis in 1918, led several small groups and finally fronted his own twenty-two-piece orchestra at the Liberty Theater. Rodemich from that point on was recognized as one of St. Louis's best bandleaders. His orchestra had a national hit in his 1919 recording of "Swanee" for the Brunswick label. Rodemich recorded for Brunswick during this period with contributions from such musicians as Frank Trumbauer, Porter Brown, and Larry Conley.

Rodemich played at all the major venues in St. Louis up until his departure for Boston in 1926 to open the Metropolitan Theater, where he had a two-year contract. He hired musicians from the Boston area. Apparently, some of his St. Louis musicians went to New York; some may have rejoined his orchestra when he left Boston for New York around 1927.

He began to work at the CBS radio studios, playing for radio shows. He wrote the music for the "Manhattan Merry-Go-Round" show. Rodemich died on February 27, 1934, as he was getting into motion picture work on Long Island at the Amity-Van Buren Sound Studios, composing and arranging music for the *Aesop's Fables* cartoons and Frank Eaton's Sports Travelogues.[40]

Not until 1920 did the Jansen & Trumbauer band appear, really called *Ted Jansen's Jazz Band*. Ted Jansen was a good booker and manager who could get lots of billings around this town. He was also a very capable drummer. But Trumbauer was the backbone of the band and was and is St. Louis' musicians' musician. Whenever Trumbauer played, musicians, white and black, were around learning phrases and copying his hot style, which was many years in advance of the Chicago style.

. . . The original band opened the very exclusive Coronado Hotel Ballroom. His line-up was Frank Papila, hot accordion; Frankie Trumbauer, sax; Norman Rathert, banjo; Charlie Mischner, piano, and Clarence Forster, trumpet. But the height and the heyday of the Jansen Band followed several years later and reached its peak at the Marigold Gardens on the South Side. Jansen, as was said before, was a good drummer but also a good businessman and he had as many as five bands operating in Missouri under his name. The real Ted Jansen jazz band, however, played some really fine hot music. Tunes like *Sugar Foot Stomp, San, Strut Your Stuff, Cry Baby Blues* were stomped off in a manner that would please the most ardent hot fan. In fact, Trumbauer's solo on *San* became the standard for sax players to measure up to. Nobody in this town was considered a sax player unless he could take off on *San* somewhat in Frankie's interpretation. The closest were Often Sepp and Rolla Bierman. Trumbauer was the fair-haired boy of the hot musicians in St. Louis [and] was as well known in the colored local as in the white.

. . . Besides those mentioned, who comprised the original Ted Jansen band, the following men later came through the personnel ranks and many later attained considerable fame in their own right: Paul Ashenbrenner, better known later as Paul Ash, Al Sarli, Gus Henschen, Allister Wylie, Gordon Jenkins on piano, Bob Casey, bass; Art Wamser, Fud Livingston, clarinet; Ray Ludwig, Clarence Forster, Herbert Berger, Wingy Manone, trumpet; Charles Schmott, Jack Teagarden, Sonny Lee, trombone.

Trumbauer was in and out of St. Louis during the early 1920s with Joe Kayser's band, the Gene Rodemich Orchestra, and the Ray Miller Band. His saxophone playing attracted a lot of notice, even in the early days of his career. While with Kayser's band, he began to take advantage of that notice.[41]

One night as we were riding the train to our next stop, Bob Chaudet and I hit upon an idea. It seemed that wherever we played, musicians would gather after the dance, and ask about my saxophone, as to the tone, etc. Bob and I purchased as many

Frank Trumbauer (1901–1956)

Born in Carbondale, Illinois, on May 30, 1901, Frank Trumbauer was raised in St. Louis from 1907 on. His mother was a theater pianist and organist. Trumbauer started musical lessons on violin and moved on to the trombone but was taken with the saxophone when he saw Ray Reynolds play at the Arcadia Ballroom. He obtained a C-melody saxophone and worked out the various fingerings by ear as his mother played chords for him on the piano. Trumbauer then realized that he would have to learn to read and spent the next nine months practicing reading music for the saxophone.

Trumbauer joined the navy at the end of World War I, playing in the band at the Great Lakes Naval Training Center. He received more musical training during his military service. Discharged in 1919, he returned to St. Louis and joined Local 2. During this period, he had a number of jobs, and in 1920, met the booker Ted Jansen. He was on the road with the Joe Kayser Band in 1921 when he was called by Jansen to join his band at Forest Park Highlands. Soon after, he and Jansen became partners. For a time they had all of the major hotel and ballroom jobs sewed up. He made his first recordings in 1921 with the Gene Rodemich Orchestra, traveling to New York with Rodemich. In these recordings, he was the only St. Louisan who played with a studio orchestra presented as a St. Louis dance band. Trumbauer worked in Chicago and recorded with the Benson Orchestra in 1923.

Trumbauer returned to St. Louis and worked with both Jansen and Rodemich. He later recorded *San* with the Mound City Blue Blowers in St. Louis in 1924.[42] His C-melody saxophone solo on that recording was widely admired by saxophone players, black and white. Joining the Ray Miller Orchestra, he worked his way east and played at the White House in 1925.

The Arcadia Ballroom offered Trumbauer a job as a bandleader. He accepted the offer and opened in St. Louis on September 8, 1925. When the Arcadia closed for the summer in May 1926, Trumbauer and fellow band members Bix Beiderbecke and Pee Wee Russell headed for Hudson Lake, Michigan, for a summer engagement. Trumbauer and Beiderbecke joined the Jean Goldkette Orchestra in the fall. On February 24, 1927, Trumbauer and Beiderbecke made one of the most influential jazz recordings of all time, "Singin' the Blues."[43]

Trumbauer and Beiderbecke joined the Paul Whiteman band when the Goldkette band broke up. He remained with Whiteman until 1936 and led his own band until 1939. He retired from music in 1940 to join the civil aeronautics authority and work in Kansas City. He only played sporadically after World War II. Trumbauer continued to write music and sit in with friends in Kansas City until his death on June 11, 1956.

reeds as we could locate, and then sandpapered the manufacturer's name off of them, and rubber-stamped "Trumbauer" on each one. We told the musicians that the reason for my tone was the secret in these reeds, and we promptly sold them for a dollar each! It was a good thing we were only doing one-nighters.

Trumbauer made a famous recording with Gene Rodemich and a studio orchestra in 1921. "By the Pyramids"[44] had the first two-part, harmonized saxophone break, played with Bernie Kreuger.[45] In 1925, after leaving Ray Miller, Trumbauer brought a very famous band—the Trumbauer Band—into the Arcadia Ballroom. Simms describes the band, its personnel, and its effect on listeners.[46]

I heard the band on numerous occasions and everybody else who has heard this band says this, "It is the most hell-for-leather band they have ever heard." Ken Farmer, secretary of the St Louis local, intimate friend of Bix's, speaking of the band said with a sigh: "That was a band to conjure with. Some of the men have become leaders, some have become famous side men, some have

Red McKenzie (1899–1948)

A former jockey, Red McKenzie[47] was born in St. Louis on October 14, 1899. He formed his original Mound City Blue Blowers in 1923. (The Mound City was one of St. Louis's nicknames.) McKenzie was working at the Claridge Hotel at the time as a bellhop. The Butler Brothers Soda Shop across the street had a soda jerk name Dick Slevin. McKenzie and Slevin started making music together in the soda shop, accompanied by the rhythm of a shoeshine boy. McKenzie played a tissue paper–covered comb in a style he called "blue blowing." Slevin was a kazoo player. They soon met banjo player Jack Bland and began jamming at his apartment. Their first job was at Turner Hall as a relief band, where Frank Trumbauer heard them. Simms gives us an account of this discovery, "It all happened at the North St. Louis Turner Hall, when the three came on during intermission. There was Jack Bland, banjo, Dick Slevin, kazoo, and Red McKenzie, comb and tissue paper, or kazoo. They tore out on *Tiger Rag* and were so good that one of the boys in the band [Trumbauer] who played the Grand Central Theatre show where Rodemich was playing persuaded Rodemich to put them in the stage presentation as a novelty act."[48]

Trumbauer brought them to the attention of Gene Rodemich, with whom they began making a national name for themselves. The first Mound City Blue Blowers record, *Arkansaw Blues* (1924), sold more than a million copies. A subsequent record, *San* (1924), with Frank Trumbauer on C-melody saxophone, was very influential with saxophone players, both black and white. The group traveled to England in 1925.

By 1927, McKenzie began a second career as a promoter and band booker in New York. In 1929, McKenzie made one of the great recordings in jazz history. The recording session produced *Hello, Lola* and *If I Could Be With You One Hour Tonight*. For this date, the Mound City Blue Blowers had a front line of McKenzie, Pee Wee Russell, Glenn Miller, and Coleman Hawkins. All of the Mound City Blue Blowers records are now on CD.[49]

In the 1930s, McKenzie was better known as a vocalist, recording under his own name and with such leaders as Paul Whiteman, Adrian Rollini, and Victor Young. By 1937, the jazz revivalist movement was underway and McKenzie played an important part. He sang at Nick's, a favorite hangout of traditional jazz fans and musicians. Red recorded for Commodore records. He was also a participant in many of the Eddie Condon Town Hall and Ritz Theater concerts in the 1940s. His last recorded performance was on a live radio broadcast of the WNYC jazz festival in February 1947. He died a year later on February 7, 1948, of cirrhosis of the liver.

gone into other business, but that unit produced more hot music than I have ever heard, before or since." It was a happy band and happy bands play happy music and happy music is always good hot music. Money was plentiful; the boys were putting everything they had into their music. There was Frankie [Trumbauer] on sax; Bix Beiderbecke, cornet; Pee Wee Russell, clarinet and sax; Ray Ludwig, trumpet; Doc Girard, sax; Russ Toedtman, tuba; Wayne Jacobson, banjo; Marty Gardner, drums; Bud Hassler, violin and sax; Louis Feldman, piano; Often Sepp, sax; and Walter Stovall, sax.

There were some changes in this band during the year but this was the main aggregation that carried this band to fame. They alternated on the same floor at the Arcadia Ballroom with a group called the "Arcadian Serenaders" who recorded for Okeh, which included Wingy Manone, trumpet; Norman Rathert, banjo; Sonny Lee, trombone; Avery Lopez, trombone; Slim Hill, banjo; Johnny Riddick, piano; Cliff Holman sax; O. C. Duncan, clarinet and sax; Marty Livingston, vocal; and Felix Guarina, drums. Sometimes Peewee Russell doubled in both bands and was heard on clarinet with the Arcadian Serenaders. Later Sterling Boze [sic] came in and played trumpet when Wingy left.

Trumbauer's autobiography gives the following personnel for the band: Bix Beiderbecke (cornet); Ray Thurston, later Vernon Brown (trombone); Charles "Pee Wee" Russell (clarinet/alto sax); Damon "Bud" Hassler (tenor sax/arranger); Frank Trumbauer (alto sax/C-melody sax/leader); Louis Feldman (piano); Dan Gaebe (bass); Wayne Jacobson (banjo); Dee Orr

Frankie Trumbauer Orchestra, Arcadia Ballroom, St. Louis, September 1925. Photographer unidentified. Left to right: Ray Thurston (trombone), Marty Livingston (trumpet), Pee Wee Russell (clarinet/alto sax), Frankie Trumbauer (melody sax), Dee Orr (drums), Bix Beiderbecke (cornet), Bud Hassler (tenor sax), Louis Feldman (piano), Dan Gaebe (bass), Wayne Jacobson (banjo). © Frank Driggs Collection.

(drums); Marty Livingston (vocalist).[50] According to Richard Sudhalter, the Arcadian Serenaders played opposite the Trumbauer Band on Wednesday, Saturday, and Sunday. Sudhalter also lists other bands playing opposite the Trumbauer Band at the Arcadia. These were the Les Carlbach, the Joe Lechner, Ted Jansen, and Conley–Silverman bands, along with the Missouri Cottonpickers and the Frisco Ramblers.[51]

The Trumbauer Band also played at the Racquet Club near Forest Park after the Arcadia Ballroom closed. They also played for Elks Club dances in Carbondale, Illinois, for the St. Louis University Prom at the Statler Hotel, and at Indiana University in Bloomington, Indiana. The group tried to recruit trombonist Jack Teagarden and the legendary Texas pianist Peck Kelly but was thwarted by union rules in each case.[52] For a short while, Bix, Kelly, Teagarden, Pee Wee Russell, and a drummer played as the intermission band at the Arcadia. Pee Wee said that was the greatest band he had ever played in.[53] When the Arcadia engagement ended on May 3, 1926, Beiderbecke, Russell, and Trumbauer went to a job at Hudson Lake,

Michigan. Trumbauer and Beiderbecke then joined the Goldkette Orchestra in Detroit.

Sudhalter also noted that Beiderbecke, Russell, and Trumbauer played at after-hours jam sessions with black musicians at the Chauffeurs Club at 3133 Pine. John Estes owned the establishment at the time. Bud Hassler was quoted by Sudhalter: "St. Louis was pretty segregated at this time, but the common interest in jazz that we had with the negro musicians dissolved many social barriers. We wouldn't have dared played in public with them, but after hours was another story."[54] A recording led by the saxophonist Jimmy Powell titled "The Chauffeur's Shuffle" was said to commemorate such events.[55] According to Harry Dial,[56] this Jimmy Powell was an older man, not the Jimmie Powell who was born in New York in 1914, who played with many of the swing era bands.

Beiderbecke and Russell rented an apartment in Granite City. Pops Foster, the black New Orleans bassist, recalled,[57]

> On Mondays all the musicians had the day off and we used to all go over there to see who could burn up the most barbecue. They didn't have a regular barbecue; we just dug a hole in the ground, put rocks in, then some wood and got a fire going. We'd cook the barbecue, eat it, and drink a lot of corn whiskey. We never played or jammed together in those days, that all started in New York. We just got together for kicks. The colored and white musicians were just one. We'd stay out all night, drink out of the same bottle, and go out with the same girls. We used to all pile in Bix's car and go over to Kattie Red's in East St. Louis and drink a lot of bad whiskey. It was green whiskey, man, they sure had bad stuff, but none of us ever got sick on it.

Zutty Singleton also tells of another intersection between these two parallel histories.[58] We knew Frankie Trumbauer, Bix Beiderbecke, Pee Wee Russell and those fellows. We used to jam with them at the Westlake Dance Pavilion, where they played with Ted Jansen's band every Wednesday night. I remember once the Creath musicians were to play a benefit at the Booker T. Washington Theater and we got the idea to ask them to join us on the stage. They just about screamed with delight.

Bud Hassler was also a symphony musician, and Sudhalter also noted that Beiderbecke took a few lessons with Joseph Gustat,[59] principal trumpet with the St. Louis Symphony. Pee Wee Russell described Beiderbecke attending the Friday St. Louis Symphony matinees. Others, including Dr. Bartlett Simms have noted the maturation of Beiderbecke's playing from before and after the Arcadia engagement.[60] While the symphony contacts were important, Trumbauer brings another facet to Beiderbecke's playing during their stay in St. Louis.[61]

> It was here that Bix and I got to know each other. When I hired him, he told me that he was a poor reader and he hesitated taking the job. Bix had a screwy way of picking out notes from a violin part, playing them in the key of "C" on a "B flat" cornet. It was confusing to everyone, even Bix! We fixed up a book of regular trumpet parts and for hours on end, I would work with Bix. I would teach him a tune, note for note, and then hand him the part and we would follow it. Bix was a brilliant boy and it wasn't long before he could follow new parts. No one but Bix and I shall ever know the hard work and patience it took to accomplish this. We would take down some of Bix's choruses, note for note, and then hand them to him to play in an ensemble. He would take one look at the notes and say, "man, this is impossible!"
>
> Many nights we sat in the back room of a little cafe with an old upright piano, going over things we both loved. Contrary to the belief of most people, Bix didn't care much for other bands. Oh, we both loved Louis Armstrong. But, our favorites were: Delius, Debussy, Ravel and Stravinsky.
>
> . . . By now, Bix and I were thinking alike. I could stop on any note and Bix could pick it up and finish the phrase perfectly, and he could do the same with me. We could play simultaneous choruses and never clash. I want to say, right here, for the record, that this was the happiest and healthiest period in our lives. I made him assistant leader of the band. We played golf, rode horses, and he didn't have a drink for months at a time.

There is a very interesting recording by the Palladeo Orchestra for Okeh on October 25, 1925, called the "What-Cha-

Call-Em Blues."[62] No one knows the personnel. There is no record of a "Palladeo" dance hall in St. Louis. This recording features a trumpet player who has listened very closely to Bix Beiderbecke. The Arcadia engagement of the Trumbauer Band started September 8, 1925.

Another musician who was a member of the Trumbauer Arcadia Band was trombonist Vernon Brown. In addition, Brown played with the Ambassador Bellhops before playing part of the 1925–1926 season with Trumbauer. He was born in Venice, Illinois, on January 6, 1907. He worked with Goldkette in 1928 and then freelanced for ten years before joining Benny Goodman (1937–1939). During his stay with Goodman, he was an integral part of the band with several warm-toned solos at the famous Carnegie Hall concert.[63] After Goodman, he worked with Artie Shaw (1940) and Muggsy Spanier (1941–1942). He spent the rest of his career as a studio musician, dying in Los Angeles on May 18, 1979.[64]

Most other white musicians in St. Louis worked in either the silent film theater orchestras or in the symphony. Because most of the musical work was divided between both white and black unions, an uneasy truce existed between them until 1927. In 1927, the first talking picture, Al Jolson's *The Jazz Singer*, was released. The advent of talking movies soon caused the loss of theater music jobs among the white musicians. Although there was always friction between the two Locals, from this point on this friction broke out into open warfare on the part of the whites in the early days of the Depression. The story of the unions will be detailed in Chapter 3.

Although both black and white musicians worked on the riverboats, their work was segregated. Black musicians played for both black and white patrons, while white musicians played for only white patrons.

Black Musicians and Venues in St. Louis during the 1920s

St. Louis's reputation in the jazz history of the 1920s rests almost exclusively on the black musicians that worked the riverboats and cabarets. The white history has not been gathered in one place. The best-known of the black musicians during this period were trumpeters who worked on the riverboats and who became nationally known. Charlie Menees tells of the origin of the title of this book.[65]

> About the trumpet name . . . I questioned him [Jeff Leopold of the Jazz Club] about that and he told me that he thought it went back to the jazz archives at Tulane. His name was Dick Allen. And Allen had gotten touch with Leopold one time and he said we ought to call St. Louis the Cradle of the Gabriels because you have so many trumpet players from here. . . . And Leopold took that and he has sort of carried the banner.

Black St. Louis musicians left the city at various times during the 1920s, but a band originally organized by Wilson Robinson took quite a few St. Louis and Kansas City musicians. Harry Dial remembers the band.

> In the spring of 1923, Wilson Robinson, a violinist, organized a band and called it Robinson's Syncopators. The personnel I remember were: R.Q. Dickerson on trumpet; DePriest Wheeler [Kansas City] on trombone; Earres Prince on piano; Andrew Brown on clarinet; Eli Logan of Kansas City on sax; Davey Jones on sax; Jimmie Smith on bass; and Benny Washington on drums. Benny was soon replaced by Leroy Maxey, also of Kansas City, who was one of the great sensational drummers of that era. That band played the Pantages vaudeville circuit on the West Coast for a season and then the Orpheum circuit in the east for a season and wound up in the Cotton Club in New York and became famous as the Cotton Club band for two years before Duke Ellington began playing there. By the time they reached New York, Wilson had been disposed of as the leader and Jimmie Smith and R.Q.

Dickerson had become leader and manager. It was said that the break with Robinson came about because he failed to pay the men a raise that had been given them.

Louis Metcalf also left St. Louis with Robinson. Violinist Andrew Preer eventually became the leader of the group. They recorded as the Cotton Club Orchestra in 1925 and later as the Missourians in 1929. St. Louis clarinetist William Thornton Blue also recorded with the Missourians in 1929. The Missourians became the Cab Calloway Band in 1930.

The most popular nightspot in St. Louis's black community was the Chauffeurs Club, according to drummer Harry Dial.[66]

> The Chauffeurs Club was right next door to the Pythian Hall in the 3100 block on Pine Street. It was operated by John Estes. It was a large private house, what we call in New York a brownstone. Some eight or ten chauffeurs paid Estes a monthly fee for the privilege of having two telephones installed in the downstairs hall to receive calls from folks who wished to hire their cars. At that time the white cab lines did not carry blacks and we had no cab fleet of our own.
> There were so many guys hanging around all day that John began preparing lunch and dinner for them. Soon his meals, pies and cakes brought in many of the neighborhood residents to the extent that it wasn't long before the entire first floor was turned into a dining room. Later, he converted the second floor into four private rooms for dining, each being decorated in different colors. Still later, the back yard, which was very spacious, was turned into a summer garden. He put a small band in the garden and a piano player in the downstairs dining room. I don't know who his first band were [sic], but that piano player was "Egghead" Charlie Thompson; he stayed there for a number of years. The last addition Estes made was a dance floor in the garden and a roof over it, making it a year-round place, and he prospered there for years.

Kimball Dial, Sammy Long, and Elijah "Lige" Shaw mentioned other clubs and cabarets in St. Louis in the 1920s.[67] The Hummingbird was at Compton & Lucas. Sammy Long, Dewey Jackson, William Luper, and Harry Dial worked there in 1926. Jazzland (later known as the Bohemia) was two blocks from the Booker T. Washington Theater. The Wedge Club was across the street from the Arcadia Ballroom (3600 Olive). Shaw worked there with Joe Hardaway during that period. The Piccadilly was at 6th and Chestnut.[68] Other clubs and dance halls were the Paradise Dance Palace (930 Sarah), Pythian Hall (3137 Pine), and the Argus Hall (2312–2316 Market).[69]

According to Dial, the best-known combos around St. Louis in 1921 were those of Charles Creath and Jimmy Harris. Creath's band had Grant Cooper (trombone), Jerome Pasquall (clarinet), Creath's sister Marge (piano), and Robert "Red" Muse (drums) and, of course, Creath on trumpet. Violinist Jimmy Harris had his sister Marie (piano), his brother Arville (clarinet), Guy Williams (banjo), and Beverly Sexton (drums). Jimmy Harris belonged to a musical family. His brother, Leroy Harris, Sr., (born 1900) was a banjo and guitar player and flutist who played on the riverboats in the early 1920s and then went to New York. Harris played with Fletcher Henderson, Clarence Wiliams, Jesse Stone, Horace Henderson, and Willie Bryant. He was later involved in rhythm and blues. Leroy Harris, Sr., died in St. Louis in 1969.[70] His son, Leroy Harris, Jr., worked with Earl Hines in the 1930s and had a long career in St. Louis with Singleton Palmer. (see Chapter 3 and subsequent chapters).

Fate Marable supplanted Harris's position when he decided to spend the winters in St. Louis. Trumpeter Dewey Jackson's first combo, known as the Gold Melody Band in 1922 had Janie Hemingway (piano), Boyd Atkins (violin, reeds), Sammy Long (tenor sax), William Luper (trombone), and Harry Dial (drums).[71]

In clubs, a common practice then and through the 1970s was "job knocking." A musician would come to a club, ask to sit in, and if he did well, try to convince the management to hire him and replace the working band. Marable's musicians were trained well and could play in nearly all the keys. When the musician called a tune, he was asked for the key he liked. The

Floyd Campbell and His Synco-Seven, People's Finance Company Building, St. Louis, 1927. Photographer unidentified. Left to right: Nat Story (trombone), Irving "Mouse" Randolph (trumpet), Floyd Campbell (drums/vocals), Armand "Red" Brown (banjo), Janie Hemingway (piano), Cliff Cochran (alto sax), Sammy Long (tenor sax). © Frank Driggs Collection.

Marable Band would then deliberately play the tune a half-step higher or lower than the requested key. Thus, if the musician liked the key of B-flat, the band would play in either the key of B or the key of A. When the musician struggled, he was told that the piano was out of tune. Only the best of musicians could play well under those circumstances.[72]

The Floyd Campbell Singing Synco Seven Orchestra worked in St. Louis in 1927 both on land and on the river. They traveled to Cincinnati and worked there for four weeks.[73] The personnel of the band included Irving "Mouse" Randolph (trumpet), Nat Story (trombone), Clifton Cochane and Sammy Long (reeds), Janie Hemingway (piano), Armand "Red" Brown (banjo), and Campbell (drums and vocals). Gus Perryman (piano) and William Calloway (banjo) replaced Hemingway and Brown, and Winston Walker (tuba) was added. In May 1928, Promoter Jesse Johnson put together a battle of the bands between the Alphonso Trent Orchestra and the Campbell Band fronted by Louis Armstrong on the *St. Paul.* According to Campbell,[74] Johnson made no attempt to limit the number of tickets. Five thousand people were on the boat, which overloaded it. The captain returned very quickly to shore, averting a disaster. In 1929, Campbell toured the Midwest with a band that included Walter "Crack" Stanley (trumpet), Harvey Lankford (trombone), Sammy Long, Clifton Byrdlong and Cecil Thornton (reeds), Perryman, Calloway, and James Barlow (bass).

Jelly Roll Morton visited St. Louis in 1926 to play a job with another pianist.[75] As Jelly Roll Martin, he recorded "Soapsuds" for Okeh.[76] The band is unknown and sounds like amateurs.

Because of its position as a river and rail transportation center, a musician stranded in St. Louis or in a close-by town could find work with bands as they traveled through the city. The 1927 edition of the King Oliver Dixie Syncopators Band was formed in St. Louis in April. This edition of the Syncopators played their initial jobs in St. Louis on the *Capitol* before moving to New York. This band recorded *Black Snake Blues*[77] in St. Louis before it left for New York and later declined a job offer from New York's Cotton Club. Duke Ellington got that job. This decision provided the opportunity for Ellington to begin his rise to the top echelon of his profession. It also precipitated the fall of Joe "King" Oliver into obscurity.

A very advanced band from western Missouri, the Jesse Stone Blues Serenaders, recorded in St. Louis in 1927. The group recorded four titles and only "Starvation Blues" and "Boot to Boot" survive on CD.[78] This group included trombonist Druie Bess, who had, according to Gunther Schuller, "a style and technical fluency that only Snub Moseley and Miff Mole had attained by 1927."[79] Schuller also asserted that very little jazz in 1927 could match the depth of feeling of Stone's band. This band is clearly playing in jazz time and not ragtime and the horns and arranging do not sound as rhythmically stiff as the black St. Louis bands up until this point. Druie Bess moved to St. Louis in 1931. His career will be described in Chapter 3.

St. Louis Trumpeters

St. Louis trumpeters were apparently very territorial and did not treat strangers kindly. Roy Eldridge was stranded in St. Louis in 1926 or 1927. He was working with a pianist at the Grand Central Hotel on Pine Street and ran into the St. Louis trumpet school at jam sessions on Sundays.[80]

> Every Sunday five trumpet players came down and tore me apart. I was about 16 and I was playing smooth. They played with a guttural kind of sound. They were more or less on a Louis Armstrong kick, the way Louis used to play, but more guttural. I was playing what could be called cool then, and I wasn't familiar with that other style. I couldn't understand how they got around to playing like that—the lip vibrato, trills, etc.

The St. Louis trumpet sound is described as a clear, singing tone, with many bent notes reminiscent of the human voice. Many black St. Louis trumpeters were also experts in the use of mutes. St. Louis trumpeter David Hines remarked that a lot of these trumpeters sounded very similar, with a big fat vocal sound common to St. Louis trumpeters.[81] It is interesting to note the evolution of trumpet sound and conception that stretches back from Charles Creath up to Lester Bowie. Judge Nathan B. Young attributes the sound to a tradition of German brass band music that dates from the 1840s. David Hines recounts a conversation with Young.[82]

> I talked to Judge Nathan Young, who took me back 150 years to a trumpet player by the name of Tyler, George Tyler. . . . And he said that this guy worked, he was a slave who worked as an entertainer, playing for dances and things like that. And even after slavery, he continued to work in that field.

The list of these trumpet players in the 1920s includes Charles Creath, Dewey Jackson, Bob Shofner, R. Q. Dickerson, Louis Metcalf, Joe Thomas, Ed Allen, Irving "Mouse" Randolph, Andrew "Big Babe" Webb, Leonard "Ham" Davis, Benny Starks and Oliver Cobb. All but Creath, Jackson, Webb, and Cobb left St. Louis and achieved wider reputations. It is interesting that many of these men went through the Knights of Pythias and Oddfellows bands as young musicians (see Chapter 1). Both Hines and Clark Terry think the St. Louis trumpet sound goes back to Charles Creath.[83]

Charles Creath (1896–1951)

Charles Creath[84] came from a musical family. He was born in Ironton, Missouri, on December 30, 1896, and by the time Charles was fourteen, the Creath family was living in East St. Louis. He played clarinet in the East St. Louis Lincoln High School Band. He later played alto saxophone and finally cornet. Creath also played in the St. Louis Odd Fellows Band. At seventeen, he left home to travel with the Ringling Bros. Circus. He returned to St. Louis to live with his family in 1919. Creath was now living at home and working as a professional musician. Creath was an excellent musician, able to read and interpret many styles of music. He was an excellent blues player and was proficient on piano, organ, accordion, and alto sax.

Creath organized his band, the Jazz-O-Maniacs around 1919.

This band played in cabarets around St. Louis and worked regularly on the Streckfus steamers on the St. Louis to New Orleans run. Creath was the first black band booker in St. Louis, with an office on Market Street.[85] Often, Creath would book several bands around the city. He would visit each site in his Marmon car and play a few tunes with each band.

By 1928, Charles Creath had contracted tuberculosis. When he recovered, he had to give up his horn. He continued leading bands on the riverboats until 1938, when he moved to Chicago. He ran a nightclub for a time and was an aircraft inspector during World War II. His health began to fail in the late 1940s, and he eventually took his own life on October 23, 1951.

That [sound] goes all the way back to Charlie Creath. And I think he was sort of responsible for that, in a sense. And another thing that was kind of responsible in a sense was Gustaf (*sic*) [Gustat]. You know the first trumpet of the St. Louis symphony? He used to . . . all of the people that he taught, he would insist on them using Hime mouthpieces. It's a very thin, very deep trumpet mouthpiece. And all the guys around town used to hear this sound (*makes instrument sound*) with this Hime mouthpiece and most of them, if they couldn't come by a Hime mouthpiece; they got something as close to it as they probably could. And they all shot for that particular sound, and I think possibly, Gustaf [Gustat] and Charlie Creath, way back in those days, were totally responsible for that sound that most of the trumpeters in St. Louis sort of, you know, started to get.

Creath organized his band to work on the Streckfus steamer *J. S.* The band also worked at the Jazzland Café on Market Street, the Chauffeurs Club, and the Coliseum at Washington and Jefferson. Trumpeter Dewey Jackson worked with Creath on the *J. S.* in 1919 and also recorded with him in 1927. He worked again with him in 1932. Other trumpeters who worked with Creath were Ed Allen, Bob Shoffner (beginning of the 1920s), Tommy Ladnier (1921), Leonard "Ham" Davis (1924–1925), and Benny Starks (1926). Ladnier introduced the Harmon mute to St. Louis in 1921.[86] The Harmon mute became an important component of Miles Davis's sound.

Unfortunately, Creath was also a gambler who played with his sidemen's salaries. If you worked for him you might not be paid or have your salary doubled, depending on how successful his gambling was on that night. Benny Starks recounted, "Charlie was well liked down on Dago Hill. He had all the dances out there, all the weddings. Dagoes have a lot of weddings. We used to play battles of music against Frank Trumbauer. He was great, man. We'd play Creve Coeur Lake, he'd be on one side and we'd be on the other."[87] Henry "Red" Allen described Creath's magnetism,[88] "When Dewey Jackson, a great blues player, ran over his horn to warm it up, the people would start screaming. Then Charlie Creath would hit just one note and draw attention—his tone was so big and wide that he would pull everything together, I thought that both were great trumpeters."

Charlie Creath's Jazz-o-Maniacs, St. Louis, 1924. Photographer unidentified. Left to right: Sammy Long (alto sax), Willie Rollins (tenor sax), Marge Creath (piano), Grant Cooper (trombone), Charlie Creath (cornet), Alexander Lewis (drums). © Frank Driggs Collection.

Garvin Bushell described Creath's playing.[89]

Creath had a Joe Smith-like tone, but with more blues feeling and drive. He had beautiful sound and soul, and his forte was the blues. He had command of the high register too; most New Orleans players could not go above B-flat. . . . He went up to C and D and later to F and G whenever he wanted to. Creath was a phenomenon. I once heard Tommy Ladnier say: "When Charlie used to hit certain notes, the whores would just fall out and throw up their legs." He made his biggest impression on women—not so much for his looks as his playing. The way he played the blues mellowed you; people threw their glasses in the air. He'd hit a seventh chord and sustain it, and the people fell out.

Charles Creath's grandson lives in St. Louis and works in the gospel music field both in the United States and in Europe. The following paragraphs shed some light on Creath's motivations and character in becoming a musician.[90]

He was a big gambler, obviously he didn't leave a whole bunch of money; I didn't inherit any. He made it all and then gambled it away. The guy didn't really get rich. He just wanted to live the life. . . . They say he drove a big Marmon car from job to job and made one appearance at one job and then he would make an appearance at the next job, all in the name of Charles Creath and the Jazz-o-Maniacs.

There was a story where he was supposedly working with somebody, I don't know his name . . . but he had heard from another friend of his the reputation of that person for not paying. So what he did was stand all night at the box office and got his money as it came in.

Listening to his music, I have the feeling that the trumpet was not just an instrument that he placed on his lips and started fingering. It was sort of an extension of his personality. The melodies, I mean, he would cry on the trumpet (*makes instrumental sounds*). So he would kind of play around with the trumpet. He never even tuned, pulled the tuning shank on the trumpet. He would just lick the mouthpiece and blow it in tune if it was out of tune, just adjusted it with his lips. The trumpet was just a

Dewey Jackson (1900–1963)

Trumpeter Dewey Jackson[91] was born in St. Louis on June 21, 1900. As a teenager, he played in the Odd Fellows Band, where he got his first musical instruction. His first professional job was at age sixteen in the Tommy Evans Band. Later, he played with the George Reynolds Band at the Keystone Café on Compton and Lawton. He led his own bands on land and on the riverboats. He also worked with Charles Creath and Fate Marable. On the boats, he traveled to Pittsburgh and New Orleans. He spent four months in New York with Andrew Preer's Cotton Club Orchestra.

During the Depression, Jackson led bands both on the riverboats and on land, occasionally at places such as the Castle Ballroom in St. Louis. In 1934, he rejoined Creath, and worked on the riverboats, going up the Ohio River to Pittsburgh. In 1936, an experiment to have a band co-led by Creath, Fate Marable, and Dewey Jackson on the riverboat was imposed by the Streckfus steamers and Local 2. Clark Terry and Jimmy Blanton passed through his band in the late 1930s. Jackson continued to play until 1941, when he left music to manage a hotel.

His career was resurrected in 1950, when he played and recorded with Singleton Palmer's band. He worked and recorded with Don Ewell in 1951 (Delmark—unissued) and continued to work and lead his own groups into the 1960s. The last years of his life were spent working in church. Dewey Jackson died around 1963.

means to express himself.

In fact, the first blues recording made with a male vocalist was on the Okeh label with Charles Creath. Floyd Campbell was his vocalist [and drummer] for years. He did "My Daddy Rocks Me with One Steady Roll" ["Market Street Blues," "I Woke Up Cold In Hand" and others].

This is speculation. There is no record as to why he didn't leave. From all accounts, he enjoyed his stature in St. Louis. I mean there was no need to go anywhere else if you were Charles Creath.

A lot of musicians, . . . they're workin' for the fame, they're workin' for the recognition, the money, so they can make investments with the money and so forth, or to outdo the competition, whereas Charles Creath stood above the competition. I don't think he was competing with anyone. He just lived the life. He played the trumpet because it afforded him the lifestyle that he wanted to live, which was not about money. Money was the means by which he could do all the other things he wanted to do, because he was more than a musician. He was a riverboat gambler.

Charles Creath and his Jazz-O-Maniacs made four recording sessions for the Okeh label.[92] The first session was on December 2, 1924. Accompanying Creath were Leonard "Ham" Davis (trumpet), Charlie Lawson (trombone), Sam Long (alto sax), William Thornton Blue (clarinet, alto sax), William Rollins (tenor sax), Cranston Hamilton (piano), Pete Patterson (banjo), Pops Foster (bass), and Floyd Campbell (drums, vocal). The tunes were "Pleasure Mad" and "Market Street Blues" (Campbell, vocal). On each of these tunes, there is only one audible trumpet. Sammy Long claims that "Ham" Davis recorded the solo on "Market Street Blues" because Creath became ill.[93] In March 1925, the same personnel recorded "I Woke Up Cold In Hand" (Campbell, vocal), "King Porter Stomp," "Every Man That Wears Bell-Bottom Britches (Ain't No Monkey Man)" (Campbell, vocal), and "My Daddy Rocks Me (With One Steady Roll)" (Campbell, vocal).

On November 2, 1925, Creath recorded with Blue, Rollins, Hamilton, Patterson, Sonny Lee (a white trombonist), Horace Eubanks (clarinet, alto sax), and Zutty Singleton (drums). The tunes were "Market Street Stomp," "Way Down In Lover's Lane," "Grandpa's Spells," and "Won't Don't Blues" (with Lonnie Johnson added on vocals and guitar). There is an uncredited violin on "Won't Don't Blues." Lonnie Johnson is listed as having played violin on other recordings.

The final Charles Creath recording was on May 2, 1927, with Creath and Dewey Jackson (trumpet), Albert Wynn (trom-

Dewey Jackson's Gold Melody Orchestra, St. Louis, 1921. Photographer unidentified. Left to right: Sammy Rollins (tenor sax), Boyd Atkins (alto sax/soprano sax/clarinet/violin), Janie Hemingway (piano), William Luper (trombone), Dewey Jackson (trumpet), Harry Dial (drums). © Collection of Duncan Schiedt.

bone), Blue, Eubanks, Rollins, Patterson, Burroughs Lovingood (piano), probably Cecil White (tuba), and either Singleton or Campbell. This ten-piece band recorded two tunes: "Butter Finger Blues" and "Crazy Quilt."

In these last recordings, there is a rhythmic stiffness with archaic harmonies in the reeds' ensemble playing throughout that was characteristic of jazz bands in 1922–1924, but not of most jazz bands by 1927. All of Creath's recordings feature him using various mutes, but a few bars of a very powerful open trumpet player different in conception from Creath (Dewey Jackson) are heard on "Butterfinger Blues." The extensive use of mutes may have been a consequence of the recording equipment available at the studio. This is unfortunate, because we will never have the chance to hear his open horn. The solo work of William Thornton Blue on clarinet on all the Creath sides is exemplary for the time. Blue's career will be discussed later in this chapter.

Dewey Jackson was another major trumpeter and bandleader in St. Louis. In 1919, Jackson played with the Charles Creath Band on the riverboat *J. S.* He led his own band, the Golden Melody Band, from 1920 to 1923. By 1924, he returned to Creath on the *S.S. Capitol*. He joined Andrew Preer's Cotton Club Orchestra in New York in 1927, staying for four months. In 1927, he went to New Orleans and joined Fate Marable, returning to St. Louis. That same year, he recorded with his own Peacock Orchestra. During the rest of the 1920s, he either led his own bands or worked with Fate Marable on the riverboats.

Dewey Jackson's nickname was Squirrel.[94] Musicians described Jackson as one of the loudest trumpet players they had ever heard. Singleton Palmer described him. "He was wonderful. One hell of a trumpet player. Yeah. And swing. Strong and powerful. Never had no lip troubles that I know of. If he did he never said anything about it. But he was . . . and a good bandleader. A good man on trumpet."[95] Vertna Saunders described his trumpet style as "very forceful. Anything he played, it looked like it was the last thing he was ever going to do. . . . He put heart and soul in it. He was a very, very good, a good trumpet player, a good jazzman, good swing."[96]

Singleton Palmer played with Dewey Jackson in the 1930s.[97] "Sometimes we would leave right from one job and go to another. You know. Like that all night long. Yeah, he had things pretty well sewed up at one time. Well he . . . Charlie Creath and Fate Marable practically had everything sewed up around here at one time."

Dewey Jackson recorded with his own Peacock Orchestra in 1926. All three tunes feature the vocals of drummer Floyd Campbell. The personnel included Dewey Jackson (cornet), Albert Snaer (trumpet), William Luper (trombone), William Thornton Blue (alto sax, clarinet), Burroughs Lovinghood (trumpet), Pete Robinson (banjo), Pops Foster (tuba), and Floyd Campbell (drums and vocal). They recorded "She's Crying for Me," "Capitol Blues" and "Going to Town." Jackson uses a mute on the first two numbers and plays open horn on "Going to Town." William Luper is featured on some mournful solos on all three and William Thornton Blue is heard on three very powerful clarinet solos. The reed ensembles in these recordings sound less stiff than any of the Creath recordings. Dewey Jackson also recorded with blues vocalists Missouri Anderson (1926) and Luella Miller (1926?), all on Vocalion Records.[98] Jackson's subsequent career will be discussed in following chapters.

Andrew "Big Babe" Webb was another trumpeter who never left St. Louis. Webb recorded with bluesman Bert "Snake Root" Hatton (1927) on Vocalion. He also recorded "Compton Avenue Blues" with Bennie Washington's Six Aces on November 4, 1925. The rest of the band included Harvey Lankford (trombone), William "Weedy" Harris (clarinet, alto sax), Harold Este (clarinet, tenor sax), John Arnold (piano), Pete Patterson (banjo), and Benny Washington (drums). John Arnold plays a very tasty piano solo, as does Lankford. Webb uses a mute to play his solo. The saxophone solos all are in the "slap tongued" style in vogue in some jazz recordings in 1925. These stiffen the rhythm during these sections. The brass and rhythm section players seem to be playing in jazz time while the reeds are in ragtime. The Benny Washington band was popular in St. Louis throughout the mid- to late 1920s. They played on the *St. Paul* for five seasons.[99] Patterson (known as "Banjo Pete") worked with many musicians in St. Louis into the 1970s.

Trumpeter Joe Thomas (1909–1984) was born in Webster Groves, Missouri.[100] Thomas left St. Louis in 1927 at age eighteen to go on the road with Cecil Scott and other midwestern territory bands. Arriving in New York in 1934, he soon found work with such luminaries as Fats Waller and Fletcher Henderson. He eventually became a top studio musician in the 1940s, making recordings with many players, including Art Tatum. He led his own groups for Keynote and for the Hot Record Society. His most famous recording was "Black Butterfly"[101] on Keynote. Thomas continued to work throughout the 1950s and gradually fell into obscurity, spending his last years in society bands.

Although he was born in Nashville, Tennessee, trumpeter Ed Allen (1897–1974) was raised in St. Louis. While in St. Louis, he played with Fate Marable–led bands on the riverboats. He also led the Whispering Gold Band while in New Orleans

(1922) that featured the first saxophone section on the riverboats. By 1924, Allen was in Chicago working with Earl Hines. The next year, he went to New York and recorded with Clarence Williams and Bessie Smith.[102] Allen was active throughout the 1930s, but, by 1945, was playing in taxi-dance halls in New York.

Louis Metcalf (1905–1981), a minister's son,[103] was born in Webster Groves. He was taught cornet by P. B. Langford and played in Warner Long's "kid band."[104] He worked with Charles Creath on the *J. S.*, leaving for New York in 1923 at age eighteen to tour with Wilson Robinson's Syncopators. There, he worked with Willie "the Lion" Smith, Andrew Preer and the Cotton Club Orchestra, and the Charlie Johnson Orchestra, among others. Metcalf made his name for his work with Duke Ellington (1926–1928).[105] He was the predecessor of Freddie Jenkins, whose major role in the band was that of a hot, modern trumpet soloist. Clark Terry played that role during his tenure with Ellington. Leaving Ellington, Metcalf worked with Jelly Roll Morton, many singers, and the Luis Russell Orchestra. Henry "Red" Allen eventually took his place after he had a falling out with Russell. During the Depression, Metcalf bounced between Montreal, Chicago, St. Louis (1935 on the *St. Paul* with Dewey Jackson), and New York, eventually leading small groups in New York clubs until his death in 1981.

St. Louis trumpeter Leonard "Ham" Davis (1905–1957) played and recorded with Charles Creath from 1924 to 1925. He recorded "Jamboree" with blues singer Bertha Henderson in 1926. Davis moved to New York in that year and worked with many well-known musicians, including Edgar Hayes, Charlie Johnson, Eddie Condon, Elmer Snowden, Don Redman, Benny Carter, and Sidney Bechet during the late 1920s and 1930s. While he was mostly a section player rather than a soloist, Davis's reputation is based on two solos with an Eddie Condon group that featured Jack Teagarden in 1929: "That's a Serious Thing" and "I'm Gonna Stomp Mr. Henry Lee."[106] Davis was only a part-time player by the mid-1940s.

R. Q. Dickerson (1888–1951) was born in Paducah, Kentucky, but grew up in St. Louis.[107] He played trumpet in theaters from 1918 to 1920 before leaving to tour with the Wilson Robinson's Syncopators. This band eventually went into New York's Cotton Club. Violinist Andrew Preer then had the band, which had several St. Louis musicians. This band became known as the Missourians. Dickerson's best-known solo is on "Ozark Mountain Blues" (1929).[108] Dickerson left music in 1931.

Bob Shofner (1900–1983) was born in Bessie, Tennessee, but was brought up in St. Louis. He was both a ragtime pianist and trumpeter. After working with various bands, he joined Creath in 1919. He moved to Chicago in 1921, where he worked with Honore Dutrey, King Oliver, Freddie Keppard, Tommy Ladnier, and Lovie Austin. Shofner recorded regularly with Austin and with Luis Russell. He also worked with Charlie Elgar, Erskine Tate, and the McKinney's Cotton Pickers Band. After working as a freelancer in New York and Chicago, Shofner left music until 1957, when he joined Franz Jackson, playing until 1965.[109]

Trumpeter Irving "Mouse" Randolph (1909–1997) was born in St. Louis. He played in the bands of Walt Farrington (1924), Willie Austin (1925–1926), Art Sims (1926), Norman Mason (1926), Fate Marable (1927), and Floyd Campbell (1927–1928) while in St. Louis. He then worked with the Alphonso Trent Orchestra (1928) and Andy Kirk (1931–1933) in Kansas City. Mouse worked with most of the major black big bands during the swing era, most notably with Fletcher Henderson, Cab Calloway, and Ella Fitzgerald. Randolph then worked with small groups in New York in the 1940s and toured with a Latin band in the 1950s. From 1958 into the mid-1970s, he played with Chick Morrison in New York. He died in 1997. Frank Driggs thinks his early conception resembled that of Henry "Red" Allen.[110]

Benny Starks was another St. Louis trumpet artist who had an interesting and varied career. He is the brother of saxophonist Thomas Starks. Benny worked with Marable and Creath on both the riverboats and on land. He remained with

Creath until 1928. Starks and Creath trombonist Albert Wynn then went to Winnipeg, Canada, and joined a band led by Cle Harris. Harris went to Paris and took Wynn, but Starks stayed in Winnipeg for the next seven years because there was not much prejudice. He moved to Montreal and eventually led an all-white band at the St. Charles Hotel. Starks returned to St. Louis in 1937 because he was homesick. In contrast to Canada, Starks commented, "Here, much prejudice." He worked with Eddie Randle and was in the Jeter–Pillars Orchestra in 1939 with Jimmy Blanton. He also worked in Eddie Johnson's and George Hudson's bands.[111] In later years, he was heard with Singleton Palmer.

A trumpet player named Oliver Cobb patterned himself after Louis Armstrong and had a band called the Oliver Cobb Rhythm Kings. Singleton Palmer made his first recordings with Cobb. Here, Palmer recalls why he took up the tuba and his path into the Oliver Cobb Band.[112]

> I was born in St. Louis here, on November the 13th, 1912. I really was inspired by music from the time I was 5 or 6 six years old. Because there used to be a church two doors from where we lived. . . . They had a band that would play out in front of the church before the services. And they had a trombone, a trumpet, a banjo and a clarinet I believe. Well, anyhow they would play gospel tunes like you know and I would stand out there and listen to 'em and then we would go inside while we were in there. So I was just musically inclined. . . . It fascinated me you know? And then from there I talked my father . . . my stepfather really into buying me a trumpet. And I started taking trumpet lessons when I was eleven. And I played trumpet from the time I was eleven until I was fourteen and I switched over to the tuba. And during that time when I was playing the trumpet I was in junior high, and in high school at Sumner. And I was playing with a band by the name Mose Wiley. . . . I was playing second trumpet in the band and so times were hard so he decided to cut down. And me being the trumpet player, the second trumpet player I was the one to go. So he asked me. He said "Can you play bass horn?" I said, "I don't know." I said, "I never even tried you know." He said, "So, if you can play a bass horn I can keep you," 'cause he didn't have a bass. So I went home and told my old man about it and. . . . So back in those days it was . . . you know money was kind of rough, so he did, he scraped up got me an old Sousaphone for I think it didn't cost a hundred and twenty five dollars for. . . . It was my Christmas present. So I switched right on over from trumpet to the tuba because the fingering on the double Bb trumpet...I mean double Bb tuba and trumpet, the Bb trumpet is the same, only you play in . . . the bass clef see. And in the meantime I was taking trumpet lessons from Mr. Langford. P. B. Langford. He was the head of the Oddfellows Band. And he showed me how to transpose the part you know, to the tuba. So then I would just take second trumpet parts and just play 'em right . . . you know, on the tuba with the rest of the . . . rest of the brass you know?
>
> I was in Sumner then. And he [Oliver Cobb] was a trumpet player. . . . He was a good trumpet player. Good. In fact he, he . . . played in the style of Louie back in those . . . even sang like him. And I know one time when Louie came here and played at the . . . Coliseum. Years ago. And we played . . . it was on the same bill with him. And . . . Louie was so impressed with Oliver that he wanted to take Oliver with . . . you know, in his band. But Oliver wouldn't go.

Oliver Cobb and his Rhythm Kings recorded in Chicago for Brunswick on August 15, 1929. The band was Oliver Cobb (cornet, vocal), Freddy Martin (clarinet, alto sax), Walter Martin (alto sax), Ernest "Chick" Franklin (tenor sax), Edith Johnson (piano), Benny Jackson (banjo), Singleton Palmer (tuba), and Lester Nichols (drums). They recorded "The Duck's Yas Yas Yas" and "Hot Stuff."[113] "The Duck's Yas Yas Yas" was written by "Stump" Johnson, brother of promoter Jesse Johnson. Cobb recorded again for Paramount in Grafton, Wisconsin, in August 1930 in a duet with Edith Johnson on the two-part "Cornet Pleadin' Blues." The latter recording is not available on CD.

Edith Johnson (1903–1988), also known as Hattie North or Edith North Johnson, the band's pianist, was born in St. Louis in 1905.[114] She was also a blues singer who had recorded with Clarence Williams and others in 1928.[115] In 1929, Count Basie in Kansas City accompanied her on a blues called *Lovin' That Man Blues*.[116] Edith North Johnson also recorded in St. Louis in 1961. Johnson married promoter Jesse Johnson in 1928 and operated the Johnson's Deluxe Café from the time of his death in

1946. The Deluxe will figure prominently in the history found in Chapter 4.

In late 1929, Eddie Johnson became the pianist in the Rhythm Kings. In 1930, in Davenport, Iowa, Cobb drowned in the Mississippi. According to Singleton Palmer,[117] Cobb was an epileptic. He could have suffered a seizure while swimming. The leadership of the Rhythm Kings was then co-opted by Eddie Johnson. This band became the St. Louis Crackerjacks. Its history will be covered in Chapter 3.

St. Louis Reed Players

Clarinetist Norman Mason was born in Canada and lived in the Bahamas for a time as a teenager. His original instrument was the trumpet. [118]

> My people took me to Nassau, Bahamas when I was a kid around about 1911 and I was there for four or five years. They had music down there with the same beat. They use to have a guy down there that use to play guitar. There was another guy that used to play the trombone and they played the same thing that you hear now. That was the real stuff, the swing. They played rhythm and then some people played like Spanish type.
>
> I started on a riverboat, with Fate Marable, in 1920. We were out of St. Louis. Apart from playing on the riverboat we played quite a few of the most exclusive nightclubs in St. Louis. When I first got started on the road we were getting fifty dollars a week which was quite a bit of money. Shortly after that, when we went to jazz, we made around a hundred dollars.
>
> After being recommended to Fate Marable I started playing on the riverboat. Louis Armstrong played with him but there was no second trumpet. Louis and I played the trumpet and David Jones played the mellophone, Mingus (?) played the violin, Johnny St. Cyr played the guitar. A fellow by the name of Kimble played the bass fiddle and Baby Dodds played the drums. The music was what you might say in transition from what they called the New Orleans jazz.

Mason became a reed player in 1921 and played in the sax section of the Ed Allen Whispering Gold Band on the *Capitol*.[119]

> The saxophone came in about two years after I played my first engagement on the boat. They had been playing around but as far as being used in orchestras they were not. As a matter of fact, there were not too many saxophone players around. So on the riverboat, I played the saxophone and I doubled on the saxophone and trumpet. I think after I practiced up on it a few months I was able to play it.
>
> I started the clarinet a long time after that, maybe about eight or nine years after. I brought a clarinet from a fellow, you know, and the first lesson that I tried to take from this fellow I found that he didn't even know anything about the clarinet. So I just decided to try to teach myself. That was about 1929. The funny thing about it, I didn't play much clarinet. I just played mostly saxophone and the baritone and soprano and alto and an E-flat soprano. That kept me pretty busy.

Mason started his group known as the Carolina Melodists. The band was heard on WIL and KMOX. With this group, Mason played throughout the Midwest and South and in New York. He came off the road in 1939 in St. Louis.[120] During World War II, he worked at Scullin Steel and played in their band. His last musical jobs were with Singleton Palmer on Gaslight Square in the 1960s.

William Thornton Blue (1902–1938) was the son of bandleader William Blue. He was born in Cape Girardeau, Missouri.[121] Blue first left St. Louis with Wilson Robinson in 1923, but soon returned. He recorded with Charles Creath and Dewey Jackson in St. Louis (1924–1927). On the strength of these recordings, Paul DeMarinis, director of jazz studies at Webster Univer-

Ed Allen's Whispering Serenaders, S.S. Capitol, St. Louis, c. 1921–1922. Left to right: Harvey Lankford (trombone), Sidney Desvigne (trumpet), Unidentified (drums), Ed Allen (trumpet), Johnny St. Cyr (banjo), Unidentified (alto sax), David Jones (alto sax), Norman Mason (alto sax), Pops Foster (tuba, bass), Gene Sedric (tenor sax, clarinet). © Frank Driggs Collection.

sity in St. Louis, believes he was in the same league with Johnny Dodds as a soloist.[122] He left St. Louis again to play with the Cotton Club Orchestra and to tour Europe with Noble Sissle (1928). Blue returned to New York in 1929 and recorded with the Missourians. He also recorded with Louis Armstrong and Cab Calloway through 1936. Blue also played with Luis Russell. By this time, his health began to fail. Blue spent the last years of his life in a New York sanatorium. He is buried in St. Louis.[123]

Horace Eubanks (born 1900) was born in St. Louis. At some point, he moved to Chicago. While in Chicago, he recorded with Jelly Roll Morton (1923). That same year Charles Creath brought Eubanks and Bob Shofner back to St. Louis. He recorded with Creath in 1925 and 1927. Eubanks then moved back to Chicago and worked with Wilson Robinson and in Europe with Benny Payton. He returned to Chicago in 1934, joined Carroll Dickerson's band, and recorded with Zutty Singleton the same year. Eubanks then returned to St. Louis to work with Fate Marable and Charles Creath. The St. Louis musicians thought that he sounded old-fashioned when he returned.[124] At some point in his life, he suffered a mental breakdown and spent some years in the Missouri state mental hospital (1940s).[125]

William Rollins (1901–1971)[126] was born in St. Louis. Rollins played in the Odd Fellows Band (1918). He worked with Charles Creath and played in various bands on the riverboats from 1920 to 1930. In the 1940s, Rollins worked with George Hudson and Buggs Roberts. Rollins organized the Scullin Steel Band in 1941. That band included St. Louis musicians Kimball "Cabbage" Dial, Singleton Palmer, and Norman Mason. He organized and led the Local 197 Concert Band and was on the board of directors of the musicians union for thirty years.

Alto and tenor saxophonist Samuel H. "Sammy" Long (born c. 1901 in St. Louis)[127] worked and recorded with Charles Creath (1920–1925). Long played with the Dewey Jackson Peacock Orchestra (1925–1926) but did not record with him. He then worked with Floyd Campbell (1928–1930). When Campbell left for Chicago, Harvey Lankford took over the band. Long remained with the band until 1934, working on the *Capitol* and the *St. Paul*. He worked with Eddie Randle, Eddie Johnson, and others from 1934 to 1936. He then joined the W.P.A. Music Project and remained with it until 1942. In 1943, he joined George Hudson's band and remained until 1945, when he became a member of the Buggs Roberts Band at the West End Waiters' Club and stayed until Roberts died. He and William Rollins took over the band and kept it until 1955. This was his last steady musical job.

Jerome Pasquall (1902–1971) was a saxophonist who spent much of his career as a section player who occasionally soloed.[128] Although his birthplace is unknown, he grew up in St. Louis, playing mellophone in the Odd Fellows Band under the direction of P. B. Langford. Pasquall was in the army by 1918, playing mellophone with the 10th Cavalry Band. He switched to clarinet while in the service and played with the Ed Allen Band (1919) upon discharge from the service. In St. Louis, Pasquall played with Creath and Marable on the riverboats. Then, Pasquall moved to Chicago to attend the American Conservatory and to play with Doc Cook's Dreamland Orchestra on tenor saxophone. He then studied at the New England Conservatory and played alto saxophone with Fletcher Henderson (1927–1928). Moving back to Chicago, Pasquall led his own groups and also played with Freddie Keppard, Dave Peyton, Jabbo Smith (1931), Fess Williams, Eddie South, and Noble Sissle's Orchestra (1937–1944). He toured Europe with the *Blackbirds of 1934* review. Pasquall left Sissle and freelanced in New York, worked with the Tony Ambrose Orchestra, and faded from music.

The Fats Waller Connection to St. Louis

Over the course of his career, six St. Louis musicians worked or recorded with Thomas "Fats" Waller. Trumpeter Leonard "Ham" Davis recorded with Waller as members of McKinney's Cotton Pickers and the Chocolate Dandies in 1929 as well as on a 1929 recording with Waller as a leader.[129]

Arville Harris (1904–1954) was a reed player who recorded *Minor Drag* and *Harlem Fuss* with Waller and Eddie Condon in 1929.[130] His nephew was Leroy Harris, Jr. (see Chapter 3). He was born in St. Louis and worked both on the riverboats and in a band led by reed player Hershal Brassfield. Harris recorded with Clarence Wiliams and went to Europe with the Cab Calloway Orchestra. Harris also worked with Claude Hopkins and Maurice Rocco and led the band at the Majestic Ballroom in New York until his death.[131]

Trumpeter John "Bugs" Hamilton (1911–1947) was a St. Louis native who moved to New York at age nineteen. Hamilton performed briefly with Chick Webb and with Kaiser Marshall in 1935. He worked with Waller from 1938–1942 and with Eddie South in 1943. That same year he contracted tuberculosis and eventually died in St. Louis.[132]

Saxophonist Emmett Mathews (born 1902) was born in St. Louis.[133] He worked with St. Louis bands early in his career, leaving with Louis Metcalf on the Wilson Robinson's Bostonians vaudeville tour. By 1928, he was in New York. Mathews was working with Bill Benford's band in 1931 when that band became Fats Waller's Rhythm. He continued to accompany Waller until 1937. Mathews then began working in theater orchestras through the 1950s.

Tenor saxophonist/clarinetist Eugene (Gene) "Honey Bear" Sedric (1906–1963) got his nickname when he wore a camelhair coat in 1930. He was the son of ragtime pianist Paul "Con Con" Sedric. Sedric started playing with the Knight of Pythias Band (see Chapter 1) and in 1922, played his first professional job with Charles Creath. He later worked with Fate Marable and Dewey Jackson. In 1923, he went to New York and worked with Ed Allen and later joined Sam Wooding. Sedric was with Wooding when he brought jazz to Europe in 1925. He remained there until 1931. Sedric then worked with Alex Hill and, briefly, with Fletcher Henderson. In 1934, Sedric joined Waller. The association lasted until 1942. During the rest of the decade, he worked in New York with his own band and Hazel Scott or Phil Moore. He returned to Europe in 1953. Returning to New York, Sedric worked with Conrad Janis and freelanced until 1961, when his health began to fail.

Drummer Harry Dial (1907–1987) was born in Birmingham, Alabama, and moved to St. Louis when he was two.[134] Irving "Mouse" Randolph was his first musical inspiration. A friend's sister had a set of drums and Dial started playing them. He started practicing drums with the Odd Fellows Band under the direction of P. B. Langford. At age twelve, Dial began unloading riverboats on Saturdays to pick up some spare change. The Marable Band rehearsed on the riverboat, and Dial went on the boat and stood next to the bandstand. He recounted some conversations,[135] "Way back then, I heard those fellows talking about 'swing' and 'soul,' ya know, who had it and who didn't, and to this day I haven't heard what I consider a correct or good definition of 'swing.' I know it was promoted as a style of music; I will give my own idea about it later on. As for 'soul,' the guys praised Charlie Creath as a trumpet player with soul; they had great admiration for a white trombone player by the name of Larry Conley, whom they spoke of as being a guy with 'soul,' but today they have made 'soul' strictly a Negroid or black possession, which it is not." His maternal grandmother bought him a set of drums on the stipulation that[136] "if I didn't learn to beat it right, she was gonna beat me to death and she wanted every nickel of her money back."

Dial's first job was at the Manchester Café at Manchester and Kingshighway in 1921. Dial mentions that Robert "Red" Muse was thought to be the best drummer in St. Louis at the time. Muse died in 1923. In April 1922, Dial worked at the Manhattan Café (Newstead and Finney) until 3 A.M. and went to school during the day. Later that summer, Dial worked at the Marigold Gardens and at the Almac Hotel at 14th and Locust, a job that continued until he joined Fate Marable on the *J. S.* He played jobs all over St. Louis with Creath, Dewey Jackson, Norman Mason, and Jimmy Powell until 1928, when he went first to Chicago and then to New York in 1933. He worked and recorded with Louis Armstrong and from 1934 to 1935 was a member of Fats Waller's Rhythm. He worked in New York, leading his own bands and as a sideman until he retired around 1980.

By the end of the 1920s, the stock market had crashed and the economy foundered. The dark days of the Great Depression will be detailed in Chapter 3.

Endnotes

[1] Various Artists, *The Riverside History of Classic Jazz,* Riverside 3-RBCD-005-2, Fantasy, Inc., 1994.

[2] *St. Louis Blues Musicians,* http://www.bluesworld.com/OTHERPRE.html.

[3] Sheldon Harris, *Blues Who's Who,* quoted in *St. Louis Blues Musicians,* http://www.bluesworld.com/OTHERPRE.html.

[4] Dennis Owsley, "Discography of St. Louis Jazz Recordings," unpublished.

[5] *Tom Lord Discography,* version 3.3.

[6] Chuck Haddix, Director, Marr Sound Archives, private communication, 2003.

[7] This information on the Harmograph and Herwin labels is compiled from John Randolph, "The St. Louis Labels Harmograph and Herwin," *Playback* (August 1, 1949): 3–4, 6.

[8] *St. Louis Globe-Democrat,* July 22, 1945.

[9] Warren "Baby" Dodds, *The Baby Dodds Story,* as told to Larry Gara, revised edition (Baton Rouge: Louisiana State University Press, 1992), pp. 21–32.

[10] Tom Stoddard, *Pops Foster: The Autobiography of a New Orleans Jazzman* (Berkeley: University of California Press, 1971), pp. 106–115.

[11] Clark Terry, interview with the author, 1986.

[12] Verne Streckfuss interview, September 22, 1960, Hogan Jazz Archives, Tulane University.

[13] Ibid.

[14] Stoddard, *Pops Foster.*

[15] Dodds, *The Baby Dodds Story.*

[16] Singleton Palmer interview with Bob Rusch, *Cadence Magazine* (February 1987): 5.

[17] Kimball "Cabbage" Dial, Sammy Long, and Elijah "Lige" Shaw, interview with Frank Driggs, September 24, 1978. Frank Driggs Archives, University of Missouri–Kansas City.

[18] Norman Mason, interview with Don Hill, 1960, *Cadence Magazine,* 13(4) April 1987: 17–20.

[19] Kimball "Cabbage" Dial, interview with Frank Driggs, May 5, 1986. Frank Driggs Archives, University of Missouri–Kansas City.

[20] John Chilton, *Ride, Red, Ride: The Life Henry Red Allen* (New York: Cassell Academic Press, 1999), pp. 31–33.

[21] *Tom Lord Discography.*

[22] George T. Simon, *The Big Bands* (New York: Macmillan, 1971).

[23] Warren "Baby" Dodds, *loc. cit.*

[24] William Howland Kenney, *Jazz on the River* (Chicago: The University of Chicago Press, 2005), p. 63.

[25] William Howland Kenney, "Just Before Miles: Jazz in St. Louis, 1926–1944," in *Miles Davis and American Culture*, Gerald Early, ed. (St. Louis: Missouri Historical Society Press, 2001), pp. 24–39.

[26] David Hines, interview with the author, January 24, 1986.

[27] Charlie Menees, interview with the author, October 1986.

[28] Ibid.

[29] Robert Hilbert, *Pee Wee Russell: The Life of A Jazzman* (New York: Oxford University Press, 1993), pp. 35–37.

[30] Condensed from Hilbert, *Pee Wee Russell.*

[31] Owsley, "Discography of St. Louis Jazz Recordings."

[32] Coleman Hawkins, *Retrospective (1029–1963),* RCA Bluebird, 1995.

[33] Pee Wee Russell, *Jazz Original,* Commodore MVCJ-19073.

[34] Miles Davis, *Miles and Monk at Newport,* Columbia C2K 53585.

[35] Pee Wee Russell, *Ask Me Now!* Impulse! 0247557422.

[36] Dial interview.

[37] *New Orleans Rhythm Kings and Jelly Roll Morton,* Milestone MCD-47020-2.

[38] Phillip R. Evans, Larry F. Kiner, and William Trumbauer, *Tram: The Frank Trumbauer Story* (Metuchen, NJ: Scarecrow Press, Inc., 1994), pp. 26–29.

[39] Dr. Bartlett D. Simms, "White Jazz in St. Louis," *Jazz Record,* July 1946, pp. 4–6.

[40] Ibid.

[41] Evans, Kiner, and Trumbauer, *Tram,* p. 23.

[42] Mound City Blue Blowers, *Hot Comb & Tin Can (1924–1931),* Vintage Music Productions VMP 0151.

[43] Bix Beiderbecke, *Singin' the Blues,* Columbia CK 45450.

[44] Gene Rodemich's Orchestra 1921 (Compact Disc), Starlight Productions, St. Louis.

[45] Evans, Kiner, and Trumbauer, *Tram,* p. 23.

[46] Simms, "White Jazz in St. Louis."

[47] (a) Frederic Ramsey, Jr., and Charles Edward Smith, *Jazzmen* (New York: Harcourt, Brace & Company, 1939); (b) Red Hot Jazz website: http://www.redhotjazz.com/mound.html.

[48] Simms, "White Jazz in St. Louis."

[49] See Note 34.

[50] Evans, Kiner, and Trumbauer, *Tram,* pp. 51–56.

[51] Richard M. Sudhalter and Phillip R. Evans, *Bix: Man and Legend* (New York: Schirmer Books, 1975).

[52] Hilbert, *Pee Wee Russell.*

[53] Jean Pierre Lion, *Bix: The Definitive Biography of a Jazz Legend,* translated from the French by Gabriella Page-Fort with the assistance of Michael B. Heckman and Norman Field (New York: Continuum Press, 2005), p. 106.

[54] Sudhalter and Evans, *Bix,* p. 148.

[55] *Tom Lord Discography.*

[56] Harry Dial, *All This Jazz About Jazz: The Autobiography of Harry Dial* (Chigwell, Essex, England: Storyville Publications and Co. Ltd, 1978).

[57] Stoddard, *Pops Foster.*

[58] Martin Williams, *Jazz Masters of New Orleans* (New York: Da Capo Press, 1979), p. 186.

[59] Sudhalter and Evans, *Bix,* p. 152.

[60] Simms, "White Jazz in St. Louis."

[61] Evans, Kiner, and Trumbauer, *Tram,* pp. 51–56.

[62] *Tom Lord Discography.*

[63] Benny Goodman, *Live at Carnegie Hall,* Complete, Columbia C3K 65143.

[64] Ian Carr, Digby Fairweather, and Brian Priestley, *Jazz: The Essential Companion* (New York: Prentice Hall, 1987).

[65] Menees interview.

[66] Dial, *All This About Jazz.*

[67] Dial, Long, and Shaw interview.

[68] Dial interview.

[69] Kenney, *Jazz on the River,* p. 101.

[70] Barry Kernfield, ed., *The New Grove Dictionary of Jazz* (New York: St. Martin's Press, 1995), p. 497.

[71] John Cotter, "The Negro in Music in St. Louis," Master's Thesis, Washington University, St. Louis, 1959, p. 327.

[72] Dial interview.

[73] Floyd Campbell, "The Floyd Campbell Story as Told to Bertrand Demeusy," *Storyville Magazine, 74,* December 1977–January 1978: 63–66.

[74] Floyd Campbell quoted in Dempsey Travis, *An Autobiography of Black Jazz* (Chicago: The Urban Research Institute, Inc., 1983), pp. 239–240.

[75] Mason, *Cadence Magazine.*

[76] Various Artists, *Jazz in St. Louis 1924–1927,* Timeless Historical CBC 1-036 Jazz.

[77] Joe "King" Oliver and His Dixie Syncopators, *Sugarfoot Stomp,* Decca GRD-616.

[78] Various Artists, *Jazz in St. Louis.*

[79] Gunther Schuller, *Early Jazz* (New York: Oxford University Press Paperback, 1986).

[80] John Chilton, *Roy Eldridge-Little Jazz Giant* (New York: Continuum, 2002), pp. 19–20.

[81] Hines interview.

[82] Hines interview.

[83] Clark Terry, interview with the author, 1986.

[84] Compiled from a private letter from Dan Vernhettes, Paris, France, who is researching a book on Charles Creath.

[85] Kenney, *Jazz on the River,* p. 100.

[86] Dial, *All This About Jazz.*

[87] Benny Starks, interview with Frank Driggs, September 25, 1978. Frank Driggs Archives, University of Missouri–Kansas City.

[88] Chilton, *Ride, Red, Ride.*

[89] Garvin Bushell, *Jazz from the Beginning* (Ann Arbor: University of Michigan Press, 1988).

[90] Charles Creath V, interview with Jim Wallace, KWMU Radio, 1986.

[91] Lynn Driggs Cunningham and Jimmy Jones, *Sweet, Hot and Blue: St. Louis Musical Heritage* (Jefferson, NC: McFarland and Company, 1989), pp. 89–90.

[92] All of Charles Creath's Okeh recordings are collected on the CD *Jazz in St. Louis 1924–1927,* Timeless Historical CBC 1-036 Jazz.

[93] Dial, Long, and Shaw interview.

[94] Terry interview.

[95] Singleton Palmer, interview with the author, 1986.

[96] Vertna Saunders, interview with Dan Havens, April 5, 1982, National Ragtime and Jazz Archive, Southern Illinois University at Edwardsville.

[97] Palmer interview.

[98] Many of the blues recordings made in St. Louis during this time may be found on the Document Records website: www.document-records.com.

[99] Joseph "Pete" Patterson interview with Pat Immekus, April 3, 1974, Western Historical Manuscript Collection, University of Missouri–St. Louis.

[100] Frank Driggs, *The New Grove Dictionary of Jazz,* Barry Kernfield, ed. (New York: St. Martin's Press, 1995), p. 1200.

[101] *The Complete Keynote Collection,* Emarcy Records 830 121-1

[102] *Nobody Knows You When You're Down and Out,* on the CD set *The Essential Bessie Smith,* Columbia C2K 64922.

[103] Len Kunstadt, "Lewis [sic] Metcalf," *Record Research,* no. 86, 1967, pp. 3–4.

[104] Cunningham and Jones, *Sweet, Hot and Blue.* pp. 122–123.

[105] Duke Ellington, *The Okeh Ellington,* Columbia C2K 46177.

[106] Jack Teagarden, *The Indispensable Jack Teagarden,* RCA (France) 6606-2.

[107] Kernfield, *The New Grove Dictionary of Jazz,* p. 288.

[108] Various Artists, RCA Victor 80th Anniversary, Vol. 1 1917–1929. RCA Victor 09026 68777-2.

[109] Kernfield, *The New Grove Dictionary of Jazz,* pp. 1114–1115.

[110] Driggs, *The New Grove Dictionary of Jazz,* pp. 1016–1017.

[111] Benny Starks, interview with Frank Driggs, September 25, 1978. Frank Driggs Archives, University of Missouri– Kansas City.

[112] Singleton Palmer interview with the author

[113] Various Artists, *Black Chicago Big Bands 1922–29,* Frog Records, DGF28, 1999.

[114] (a) *St. Louis Blues Musicians, loc. cit.* (b) *St. Louis Post-Dispatch,* March 3, 1988.

[115] *Tom Lord Discography.*

[116] Various Artists, *Kansas City Hot Jazz,* Australian Broadcasting Corporation, ABC 846 222-2.

[117] Palmer interview.

[118] Mason, *Cadence Magazine.*

[119] Mason, *Cadence Magazine.*

[120] Kenney, *Jazz on the River,* p. 111.

[121] Jazz @ The Ten Spot 2005 Calendar, http://www.ncpr.org/tenspot/pages/05Cal/05jacal.htm.

[122] Paul DeMarinis, private communication.

[123] Eugene Chadbourne, *William Thornton Blue,* All Music Guide, http://Allmusic.com.

[124] Dial interview.

[125] Cunningham and Jones, *Sweet, Hot and Blue.* p. 34.

[126] Mrs. William Rollins, interview with Frank Driggs, Charlie Menees, and Jeff Leopold, September 28, 1978. Frank Driggs Archives, University of Missouri–Kansas City.

[127] Bertrand Demeusy, The Musical Career of Samuel H. "Sammy" Long, http://www.dtrance.ch/jazzdoc/longsam.htm.

[128] Scott Yanow, *Jerome Pasquall,* All Music Guide. http://www.allmusic.com.

[129] *Tom Lord Discography.*

[130] *Tom Lord Discography.*

[131] Kernfield, *The New Grove Dictionary of Jazz,* p. 497.

[132] Cunningham and Jones, *Sweet, Hot and Blue.* p. 73.

[133] Cunningham and Jones, *Sweet, Hot and Blue.* p. 118.

[134] This information was compiled from Dial, *All This Jazz About Jazz.*

[135] Ibid.

[136] Ibid.

3

St. Louis in the 1930s:
The Plantation Club, the Unions,
and the Decline of the Riverboats
(1930–1939)

In St. Louis, the music scene began to fade by 1929. The field recordings by the major recording companies were no longer made in St. Louis, but they were made in Kansas City. The rise of the Pendergast mob in Kansas City by late 1925 led to his complete control over the city for the next decade and a half. This control was complete enough that Kansas City became very prosperous, with as many as fifty clubs and bars featuring jazz music by the mid-1930s. According to Ross Russell,[1] the Great Depression did not exist in Kansas City. In St. Louis, however, there was very little prosperity for anyone during the Depression. Statistics show that recovery in St. Louis was slower than in almost any similar-sized American City.[2] For example, by 1939, St. Louis manufacturing output had dropped to 57 percent of the 1929 level, while the comparable number for the nation was 84 percent of the 1929 level. In 1930, unemployment in St. Louis represented 9.7 percent (8.4 percent for whites, 13.2 percent for blacks) of the workforce, while the national unemployment level was 8.4 percent. By 1933, St. Louis unemployment was over 30 percent (24.9 percent nationally), with 80 percent of black workers unemployed or underemployed. Blacks were fired and replaced by whites. In some cases, whites were granted pay increases while blacks were not. The labor unions totally excluded blacks from most skilled trades and building trades except the hod carriers. The same process happened to black musicians. White musicians were able to obtain jobs at the Arcadia and other ballrooms in the city as well as in theater and radio orchestras. The black musicians Local 44 had its charter revoked by the American Federation of Musicians in 1931 as part of this effort to disenfranchise minorities.

Walter "Tiny" Dixon, a music fan who worked for Jesse Johnson and others during this period, remarked on how music got him through.[3] "During that time, I met a lot of musicians. And St. Louis, which is polarized now, but not as bad as it was then, because they had these police districts and every white policeman in the Negro area hated Negroes. And we had a lot of discrepancies, things that are unmentionable. But, anyway, I kept my mind on music so much that I lifted myself above those bad thoughts."

Despite tensions heightened by the unions, African American jazz musicians found work in St. Louis. The Plantation Club was a primary venue, and the leading bands of the 1930s included Eddie Randle's St. Louis Blue Devils, the Crackerjacks, and the Jeter-Pillars Orchestra. Young black musicians still got their training through schools and such community bands as the Tom Powell American Post Drum and Bugle Corps. Many musicians refined their skills under the leadership of Dewey Jackson, Eddie Randle, Eddie Johnson, and Fate Marable. Others found recognition playing for Duke Ellington and other bandleaders on the national and international stage.

Also, this decade witnessed a drastic decline of dance music on the riverboats. The significance of this decline is that the riverboats were another source of work and tutelage for St. Louis jazz musicians. As discussed, the strictness of the Streckfus owners on their musicians prepared them for future challenges in the music world.

Two Musicians Unions: A Legacy of Conflict and Injustice (1896–1971)[4]

One reason that black musicians came to St. Louis in the early part of the twentieth century was the presence of the first black musicians union, Local 44. Before the unions were formed, a number of musicians associations were in existence. Several white associations merged in 1888 and became the Musicians Association of St. Louis. This group joined the National League of Musicians in 1890. Black musicians belonged to the Musicians Equity Association, a branch of the Knights of Labor. The white association became part of the American Federation of Labor (AFL) as American Federation of Musicians (AFM) Local 2 on November 6, 1896, with Owen Miller as president. The black musicians followed soon after and became

Local 44, with John L. Fields as president.

The majority of customers on the riverboats, bawdy houses, and circuses were white, but both black and white bands played for them. Local 2 was mainly concerned with concert bands, symphony orchestras, and theater pit bands, while Local 44 played at parties, in some cabarets, and at dances. The wage scale was the same for both groups.

While Fate Marable, Charles Creath, and Dewey Jackson played for both black and white audiences on the Streckfus riverboats, racial segregation and competition between black and white musicians led to bitterness and mistrust. Neither union would do anything to ease the tension.

In the 1920s, when jazz-influenced music became the popular style, Local 2 musicians began to form jazz groups. Members of Local 2 began a systematic campaign to stop white clubs from hiring black musicians. Because gangsters owned most of the clubs during prohibition, this strategy did not succeed. With the coming of talking pictures, white musicians playing in pit orchestras began to lose their jobs. Local 2 sought ways to revoke Local 44's charter. By the 1930s, there was open warfare on the part of Local 2.

The charges against Local 44 were working under scale, working overtime without extra pay, and not having the minimum number of musicians required for a job.[5] Two stories of chicanery by Local 2 illustrate the depths to which the white musicians union would sink to provide backing for their charges against Local 44.

Hayes Pillars recalled in 1975,[6] "We were playing for a radio station in the Coronado Hotel. The band normally played for an hour. One night, because the next group was not ready yet, we played one more number, to give them more time. When we got through, a member of Local No. 2 appeared to tell us that a charge was going to be filed against us for working overtime."

Jimmie Harris was president of Local 44. He had a group playing at the Bismark Hotel on 12th and Washington Streets. After the musicians were in the Bismark, Local 2 musicians put up a picket line around the hotel. When the black musicians finished playing, they had no choice but to cross the line to go home. A charge was filed to the National Office of the American Federation of Musicians against the entire membership of Local 44, stating that its members were not living up to the rules and bylaws of the American Federation of Musicians.[7]

Local 44's charter was revoked in 1931. The national office of the AFM did not officially notify Local 44 that its charter was revoked until 1933. Members of Local 44 were told that they could become subsidiary members of Local 2. The conditions were[8]:

- Subsidiary members could contract no jobs without the consent of Local 2.
- Work dues were to be paid to Local 2.
- No member of the subsidiary would be allowed to collect money from employers.
- All monies due members of the subsidiary would first go to Local 2 officials and be distributed to the members of the subsidiary through Local 2 officials.
- Members of the subsidiary would not be allowed to attend any official meetings of Local 2.
- A representative of the subsidiary would be selected by the members of that organization to come to the office of Local 2 to pick up the money to be distributed to the members of the subsidiary.
- The members of the subsidiary would have no voice in any elections or proceedings of Local 2.

Elijah "Lige" Shaw (born 1900)

Elijah "Lige" Shaw[9] was born in Jackson, Tennessee. As a child he worked as a dancer in amateur shows and became fascinated with drums. In 1918, he joined the Alabama Minstrels and began touring as a drummer, even though he was taught the rudiments of drumming while on tour. In Memphis that same year, he found work shining shoes in a barbershop and later as a janitor with Dr. W. D. Howland. His curiosity and aptitude led Dr. Howland to teach him how to make false teeth. Shaw then worked for another dentist making false teeth and used his salary to buy a drum set. He also spent two weeks with a carnival.

Shaw came to St. Louis with a minstrel show in 1917, just after the East St. Louis Race Riot. Shaw was clearly an autodidact. By the time he arrived in St. Louis, he had taught himself to play all percussion instruments by buying instruction books and practicing with them. He worked at the Manhattan Cabaret at Newstead and Finney and at the Pendleton Theater with a violinist named Grant. Joining Local 44 in 1918, he soon became business manager and vice president by 1921. He also worked at the Booker T. Washington Theater in 1922 and played drums and an electronic keyboard (nickelodeon) for silent movies. Shaw spent most of the 1920s touring in vaudeville with various shows, including Wilson Robinson's Bostonians before they got to New York. He and Fate Marable played a gig at the Coliseum for a walk-a-thon in 1928. They played continuously for more than twelve hours, only getting up from their instruments to go to the restroom.

After Shaw returned to St. Louis for good, he played on the *St. Paul* with Creath in 1934. In the late 1930s and early 1940s, he played for three years with Eddie Johnson at the Showboat at Delmar and Taylor and then led the band in that establishment for one and a half years. Despite all the setbacks, Shaw remained steadfastly pro-union and worked tirelessly to get the charter back for the black musicians local. His efforts were rewarded in 1944, when the black musicians were granted a charter for Local 197.

Shaw was vice president and president of Local 197, and during the 1940s, he began to drift out of regular performing and into piano tuning. He became one of the top piano tuners in St. Louis and was tuning a piano in University City in 1949 when the owner asked him to bring a group of veteran riverboat musicians over for a party. The musicians had such a good time that they then played parties in this neighborhood one Sunday a month until they got involved at the Barrel leading Dixieland jam sessions. This was the beginning of the Jazz Club and the Singleton Palmer Dixieland 6 by 1950.

Shaw continued to play with Palmer into 1963 at Gaslight Square. He also played with him again in the 1970s (see Chapter 5). He taught St. Louis drummer Kenny Rice and the New Orleans drummer Wilbert Kirk (with Noble Sissle in the 1940s). Although known as a jazz drummer, Shaw confessed to preferring symphonic music. He played with the Gateway Arch Professional Symphony and the Maplewood/Richmond Heights Symphony.

According to William Howland Kinney, similar actions were taken against black musicians locals in Kansas City and Denver. The Kansas City musicians refused to accept the decree. In San Francisco, the black musicians local took the white local to court to prevent it from barring black musicians from all venues.[10] A question needs to be raised as to why St. Louis black musicians did not fight back. The only way most fought back was to play jobs at non-union scale. One man, Elijah "Lige" Shaw, led the fight to get a separate black union charter back, going to all national AFM conventions, often at his own expense, to appeal for fairness.

Shaw was eventually successful, and Local 197, a black musicians local, was chartered in 1944. Segregation continued for black and white union musicians in St. Louis until 1971. In 1970, the American Federation of Labor ordered the merger of all segregated unions. In St. Louis, a series of meetings were held with both unions. At the conclusion of the meetings, both unions voted against a merger. The merger of the two unions was ordered in 1971 by the AFM, but, according to David Hines,[11] the new union (Local 2-197) would not compel its members to stop discriminatory hiring practices. Informational picketing led to auditions for theater orchestras held with musicians playing behind curtains.

The Streckfus Steamboat Company also played a part in the union situation. With the concurrence of the New Orleans black local, the Streckfus Company began cutting salaries of the black musicians that worked for them. In 1934, Streckfus tried to cut the salaries of the white musicians, asking a "concession price." Elijah Shaw remembered[12]:

> I played on the *St. Paul.* I played on there one year with Charlie Creath. And I tell you the funniest situation about that. The Streckfus people had requested, had [a] concession price, and the employment of the musicians on the river at that time, and the Local No. 2 didn't see fit to grant such [a] concession. So Captain Joe had decided that instead of using three white bands on the two boats that they ran out of here at that time, that they were going to use four colored bands. So Charlie Creath, Fate Marable and Dewey Jackson and . . . [Burroughs] Lovingood. They suppose to have a band; one on the boat in the daytime on the two boats and each one of the leaders was suppose to have a band on the boat at night. So before No. 2 would have this come about, they formed a special committee which was headed by a fellow name Harry Lang, who use to have a band at the Castle Ballroom and he use to play the summer engagement at the Forest Park Highlands, to wait on Cap'n Joe about this crisis. So when the final analysis came about, instead of having four colored bands on the boat, we just had one colored band and three white bands. And that resulted with Charlie being on the boat together with Fate, Dewey, and Lovingood. So all four of those leaders were on that boat that year at the same time.

According to both Elijah Shaw and Eddie Randle in the same interview, Harry Lang, Ted Jansen, and Lou Chortcot were the only working white dance bands in St. Louis during this period. Blacks still had most of the dance jobs sewed up. Saxophonist Harry Winn led a black "sweet" dance band that was popular until the 1950s.

Radio Broadcasts and St. Louis Jazz

Although outside the scope of the present work, radio stations hired black musicians as early as 1926.[13] Benny Washington and his Six Aces were heard on WIL in 1926, when it was broadcasting from the Mayfair Hotel. Cecil White played on KWK in 1927, The Paul Whiteman Orchestra broadcast from the Washington University Fieldhouse on KMOX in 1928.[14] Harvey Lankford was on KMOX in 1932. Initially, Oliver Cobb's Rhythm Kings broadcast on KMOX in 1930, and after Cobb died, Eddie Johnson's Crackerjacks became the staff orchestra for a while. Johnson would broadcast at 7 A.M. He also broadcast at noon and had a show three days a week called *Shades of Blue.*[15] The music educator Major N. Clark Smith had a show on KMOX called *The St. Louis Blues.*[16] Benny Goodman made a "Camel Caravan" broadcast from the Fox Theater in 1939.[17] Other notable radio broadcasts by jazz musicians will be mentioned during the course of this book.

The Plantation Club (1931–1947)

The place that offered the best wages and working conditions for black musicians was the Plantation Club, the first venue in the city to offer top black entertainment for whites in St. Louis. While white patrons danced to black bands on

Souvenir Menu from the Plantation Club, c. 1940. The Sheldon Art Galleries Collection. The front of this menu (not shown) has a ghastly image of a pickaninny. This image was seen on billboards throughout St. Louis advertising the Plantation.

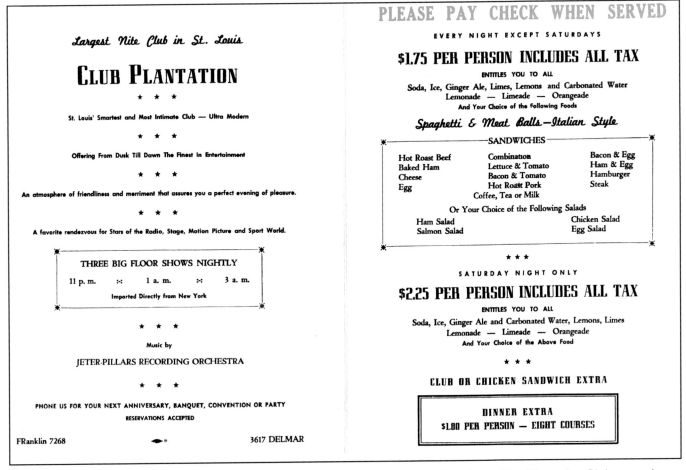

the riverboats, the Plantation was a lavish affair with a chorus line and elaborate floorshows. The Plantation Club opened at Vandeventer and Enright in 1931. In 1940, it moved to 3617 Delmar. Throughout its history, the nightclub was owned and managed by Tony and James Scarpelli. It was a whites-only establishment, featuring black bands and arrangers. Surprisingly, Kimball Dial claimed that the Scarpellis originally wanted a racially mixed establishment, but the police put down an ultimatum against the idea.[18] The first band to work at the Plantation was the Rupe Floyd Band out of Kerry Mills, Illinois. Eddie Johnson's Crackerjacks came next. Trumpeter Walter "Crack" Stanley led a band at the Plantation in 1933 that included Sleepy Tomlin (trumpet), Kimball Dial (alto sax), Albert "Pee Wee" Claybrooks and Horace Millinder (tenor sax), Robert Bell (guitar), Albert "Peanuts" Butler (piano), Vernon King (bass), and Elijah "Lige" Shaw (drums). This band lasted for a year, used mostly head (non-written) arrangements, and broadcast over KWK.[19] In 1934, the Jeter-Pillars Orchestra played at the club until 1944. George Hudson's band replaced them. The Buggs Roberts Orchestra replaced Hudson and stayed until 1947. Eddie Johnson brought his band back into the Plantation and remained until it closed that same year.

Oliver Cobb's Rhythm Kings, St. Louis, 1930. Photographer unidentified. Left to right: Ernest "Chick" Franklin (tenor sax), Walter Martin (alto sax), Freddy Martin (alto sax), Eddie Johnson (piano), Lester Nicholas (drums), Benny Jackson (banjo), Singleton Palmer (tuba), Oliver Cobb (trumpet/leader). © Collection of Duncan Schiedt.

The Crackerjacks: A Tale of Two Bands

Pianist Eddie Johnson (1912–1996) was born in East St. Louis. He joined the Oliver Cobb Rhythm Kings in 1929, replacing Edith North Johnson.[20] After Oliver Cobb's death, Johnson took over the Rhythm Kings. He renamed the band Eddie Johnson's Crackerjacks, after the popular popcorn snack of the time. This band recorded two titles for Victor in Atlanta in 1932: "The Duck's Yas Yas Yas" (a remake of their 1929 recording) and "Good Old Bosom Bread." The personnel were Harold "Shorty" Baker and James Telphy (trumpet), Winfield Baker (trombone), Singleton Palmer (tuba), Eddie Johnson (piano), Walter and Freddie Martin (alto sax), Ernest "Chick" Franklin (tenor sax), Benny Jackson (guitar, banjo, vocal), and Lester Nichols (drums). This is the first recording by Harold "Shorty" Baker, who went on to fame with Duke Ellington and was one of the major St. Louis trumpeters. Shortly after the recording, Eddie Johnson changed the name of the band to Eddie Johnson and the Victor Recording Orchestra. According to Eddie Johnson, Jesse Johnson was responsible for the recording date.

In 1931, Eddie Johnson's Crackerjacks played at the Plantation Club. Johnson played for over a year at this establishment. Singleton Palmer remembered working at the Plantation.

Oh . . . it was a good place to work. It just had long hours. Nine o'clock to . . . nine-thirty to 4 in the morning. Yeah. And then you had to play three shows a night for the chorus girls . . . and play for different acts that would come in. Mae Johnson . . . she was a singer. And then they had comedians. A guy named Strange Man. . . . Those shows were real good back in those days. It's too bad it couldn't have been on TV. But it was a hard job.

Johnson's band then played at the Greystone Ballroom in Detroit for a while and returned to St. Louis. By this time, Tab Smith had come into St. Louis to work with Fate Marable. He was working with Dewey Jackson when Eddie Johnson became interested in him for the Crackerjacks. Dewey Jackson had most of the work in those days. Jackson was apparently a somewhat cutthroat businessman. Johnson recounted what happened.[21]

And he got most of the work, until my band got popular. What I had to do, I had to break his band up. That's what happened. I took Tab out of the band, Donald Stovall out of his band, different ones out of his band. I took a trumpet player named King, and a trombone player, his brother, named Leon King. I broke his band up. He was working Sauter's Park, and then I took his band over, and they put me in Sauter's Park.

According to Freddie Martin, "Eddie Johnson broke that band up because he wanted to be the leader and we wouldn't let him be the leader. . . ."[22]

Breaking up the Dewey Jackson Band also broke up Eddie Johnson's Crackerjacks. Depending on the source, Shorty and Winfield Baker, along with the Martin twins and Chick Franklin left the band in anger or were let go by Eddie Johnson. Kimball Dial joined the band in 1934, replacing Harold Arnold. Johnson's new band had the following personnel: James Telphy, Vertna Saunders, Louis Eckehard, and Clifford King (trumpet); Buster Scott (trombone), Tab Smith and Don Stovall (alto sax), Kimball Dial (tenor sax), Benny Jackson (guitar) later replaced by Floyd Smith, Singleton Palmer (bass), and Lester Nichols (drums). While in this band, Singleton Palmer learned how to play string bass.

Tab Smith was really the cause of me playing the string bass. . . . By then, the tubas were going . . . going out of the bands . . . so I think we played somewhere in Poplar Bluff. Some guy come up asked did anyone want to buy a fiddle . . . you know a bass fiddle. So, I didn't have no money. So Tab said, "I'll get if for you and you pay me back when we get back to St. Louis." I think I paid about fifteen dollars for it. But it didn't have but three strings on it. The E-string was missing off of it, you know. And so, I played on that. I played on that fiddle. . . . In fact, it was a half-size fiddle. And I played on it for about three years with just the three strings, without the E. Until I finally scraped up enough money, you know, to get me the full size one. . . . I taught myself to play it. In fact, when I first got it, I couldn't play nothin' but the St. Louis Blues because you didn't have to do nothing but use the G and D strings, practically . . . you know.

When he was in St. Louis, Johnson's band played three years on the steamer *Idlewild*, which was not owned by the Streckfus family, but by the Meyer family out of Alton, Illinois. He also worked at a place called the Showboat for two and a half years during the late 1930s. Eddie Johnson remembers Jesse Johnson promotions for the band.[23]

Jesse Johnson was my promoter. He was my booking agent, Jesse Johnson was. He was the one that took me all out east. All around. And introduced me to Jimmy Lunceford; he put me with Jimmy Lunceford's band in Cincinnati. I was able to get the job because I said we had a good appearance. We were all very young, and they hired me over Lunceford's band. We had a pretty fair, together band, but what is great is we had a better style of dressing and put on a better show. . . . I started in St. Louis; I was starting from Kansas City. Denver, Kansas City, then Pittsburgh, all of North Carolina, South Carolina, Virginia, up and down the coastline of Virginia, up to Philadelphia.

According to Kimball Dial, this was a band to be reckoned with. In a battle of bands, the reed section would cut an

Jesse Johnson (died 1947)

Jesse Johnson[24] was a dance instructor. Ads in several 1915 *St. Louis Argus* papers place him in cabarets, leading dances and teaching dance steps. This activity was continued in 1916 when he started promoting excursions on the steamboat *Grey Eagle*. On Monday, August 14, 1916, he ran a moonlight excursion on the *Grey Eagle* with music by the Great Western Band.[25] That same day, he was in charge of a Sumner High boy's excursion on the same boat to Cave Springs with music by Lewis Crenshaw's orchestra.[26] Johnson's excursions usually had him as MC, promoting a new dance step and mixing well with the crowd. He also ran his excursions by negotiating directly with the captain and hiring the bands for each excursion. He promoted excursions on the *Grey Eagle* until 1918.

Johnson was also an entrepreneur, selling records by black artists in the community. He eventually owned a record store, a cab company, and other businesses. His record store was behind the Booker T. Washington Theater on 22nd Street.[27] This store was later moved up to Jefferson Avenue. By 1919, Johnson began promoting Monday excursions with Charles Creath on the *Liberty*, the *Pilgrim*, and the *Majestic*, direct competitors with the Streckfus steamers. Their success led Streckfus to offer Monday cruises for blacks by Labor Day of 1920. For the summer of 1921, Johnson promoted Creath on the *Majestic*. The *Majestic* burned during the winter of 1922. In the summer season of 1922, Creath and Johnson were in charge of all but one Monday cruise on the *St. Paul*. He also began promoting African American cruises four nights a week on the *Pilgrim*. The draft of the *Pilgrim* proved to be too deep for the river and it was towed downriver.

On May 14, 1926, Johnson promoted a cruise on the *City of Cairo* featuring Fate Marable and his band. He later advertised nightly cruises on this boat. Apparently this boat sank during the winter. By this time, any African American organization that wanted to have a cruise on a Streckfus boat had to negotiate with Johnson first. Bandleader Eddie Johnson said that Jesse Johnson had control of booking black bands on the riverboats.

In addition, Jesse Johnson brought to St. Louis such nationally known artists through the years as Louis Armstrong, Duke Ellington, Fletcher Henderson, Cab Calloway, Thomas "Fats" Waller, Claude Hopkins, Jimmie Lunceford, and the International Sweethearts of Rhythm. He showcased the local musical talent by having the nationally known bands "battle" the local bands. For example, in 1926, he brought the Fletcher Henderson Orchestra into St. Louis at the Coliseum and had the Charles Creath, Dewey Jackson, and Fate Marable bands on the same bill. On February 5, 1928, Johnson brought Louis Armstrong to St. Louis to play two dances. The Alphonso Trent Band backed Armstrong at the Paradise Dance Palace (930 N. Sarah) in the afternoon and at the Capitol Palace in the evening. Later that spring, Armstrong and the Trent Band played the infamous battle of the bands on the *St. Paul* that was vastly oversold. The boat did not sink because the captain became concerned and would not leave the dock. Thousands of lives would have been lost if the boat had sunk in the middle of the Mississippi.

In the early 1930s, Johnson promoted shows by Duke Ellington and Cab Calloway by dropping leaflets from airplanes over St. Louis and East St. Louis. Walter "Tiny" Dixon, a former Jesse Johnson employee, remembers the dance at the Arena:[28]

> During the time I was working for Jesse Johnson, Jesse brought Cab Calloway to St. Louis and drew the biggest dance crowd in the arena that's ever been there, over 18,000 people. . . . I don't know where he got that from, but he knew how to promote a dance. He had an airplane to fly over St. Louis and drop out free tickets. . . . Anyway, he drew so many people, Cab Calloway was so damn amazed and he said, "Where in the hell did you get all these people?" He had never played before a crowd that big. And, anytime that Jesse Johnson wanted Cab to come to St. Louis, he came, because he had brought in the biggest promotion he had ever seen in his life.

Forest Park Highlands was closed to black St. Louis musicians until Johnson began bringing in national acts and added St. Louis bands to the bills. He also promoted dances at the Coliseum, Sauter's Park, at the Harlem Night Club in Lovejoy, Illinois, and at Huffs Summer Gardens.

Jesse Johnson began promoting Eddie Johnson's Crackerjacks on tours with Fats Waller, Earl Hines, and the Mills brothers. He also secured a recording date for the band with RCA Victor in Atlanta in 1932. Eddie Johnson remarked, "I had a band, but without Jesse Johnson. . . . He put me through the limelights. He put me with every name. If someone was coming to St. Louis, I say, Duke Ellington, he say, 'Well Eddie you're going to play against Duke Ellington's band. You're going to play Count Basie, Lucky Millinder.' My name would be almost as big as the attraction. By him doing that, people all over the United States and Europe began to know me."

Original St. Louis Crackerjacks, St. Louis, 1935. Photograph by Young Studio–St. Louis. Seated, left to right: William "Bede" Baskerville (guitar/arranger), Freddie Martin (alto sax), Austin Wright (vocals), Chick Finney (piano/leader). Standing, left to right: Elmer Ming (trumpet), Levi Madison (trumpet), Nick Haywood (drums), Kermit Haynes (bass), Unidentified, Walter Martin (alto sax). © Collection of Duncan Schiedt.

opposing band before it had a chance to warm up. The reed arrangements were very difficult.[29] However, the band ran up against the Oklahoma Blue Devils out of Kansas City in St. Louis in 1933 at the Finance Building at Jefferson and Market. George Hudson, who was with the Blue Devils at the time, said that Johnson's band "sneaked out of the hall."[30]

Since the Streckfus family did not own the *Idlewild*, Johnson's band was free to play what he wanted. "On the *Idlewild*, I could play like I was playing for regular dance music. We went up and down the river, and we lived on the boat about six months out of the year, playing different towns, during the day, during the night. There were quite some times."[31]

Jesse Johnson also booked the Eddie Johnson Band as an opening act with Thomas "Fats" Waller, the Ink Spots, and the Earl Hines Orchestra.[32] Johnson remembered Fats Waller, who broadcast from WLW in Cincinnati. He also toured around the immediate area with Waller.

When we played . . . he used my band to fill in. He'd play for a half-hour, and I would play the rest of the time, and he made

Eddie Johnson and Famous Orchestra Ad, St. Louis, c. 1935. Photographer unidentified. © Western Historical Manuscript Collection–St. Louis.

most of all the money [laughs]. . . . One thing about it, he drank heavy. We had to have our uniforms in a little suitcase; he had a suitcase full of whiskey in it. Half-pints we called them then. That's what he'd take along—no clothes hardly at all. But he still could do his job. He was great.

Johnson worked around St. Louis until 1947, when his band closed the Plantation and moved to New York. At one time or other, Leonard "Ham" Davis, Jimmy Forrest, Jimmy Blanton, Eugene Porter, and Levi Madison all played with him. See Chapters 4, 5, and 6 for more of Johnson's activities. It is interesting that even though Johnson called his band the Victor Recording Orchestra after the 1932 Atlanta recordings, he never made another recording.

Meanwhile, after the breakup of the Crackerjacks, the Baker Brothers, the Martin Twins, and Chick Franklin continued to play as the Original St. Louis Crackerjacks. For a short time, there were two bands with the name "Crackerjacks" playing in St. Louis. As the 1930s wore on, they added a number of musicians to the core of the band. The 1934 edition of the band had Irving "Bruz" Woods, Joe Anderson, and Harold "Shorty" Baker (trumpet), Winfield Baker (trombone), Freddie and Walter Martin (alto sax), Chick Franklin (tenor sax), Earl Euinberg (piano), Sid Todd (bass), William "Bede" Baskerville (guitar, arranger), and Paul Commers (drums).[33] Shorty Baker continued with the band until early 1936.

The Original St. Louis Crackerjacks recorded for Decca in 1937 with Elmer Ming, George Smith, Levi Madison (trumpet); Robert Scott, Walter Martin, Freddie Martin, Chick Franklin (reeds); Chick Finney (piano); William "Bede" Baskerville (guitar); Kermit Hayes (bass); Nicholas Haywood (drums); and Austin Wright (vocal). The tunes were "Echo in the Dark," "Crackerjack Stomp," "Blue Thinking of You," "Fussin'," "Good Old Bosom Bread" (from earlier Rhythm Kings and Crackerjack recordings), "Swing Jackson," "Chasing the Blues Away," and "Lonesome Moments." The author believes the beautiful trumpet solo on "Echo in the Dark" is by Levi Madison. Unfortunately, none of these titles are currently available on CD. Clark Terry said that Madison played one of the most beautiful trumpets he ever heard.[34] Madison was an early influence on Miles Davis.

By now, the leadership of the band had passed to Chick Finney. Despite the fact that the band had recorded for a major label, it never could break into the big time. But the band soldiered on, playing on small riverboats until it came to an end for financial reasons. Finney remembered one engagement in Little Rock when the band made $0.15 per man for an entire night.[35]

Harold "Shorty" Baker (1914–1966)

Harold "Shorty" Baker[36] was a native St. Louisan who studied with P. B. Langford. Originally a drummer, he soon switched to trumpet and played in the band of his older brother, Winfield. While in St. Louis, he worked with Fate Marable in 1930. He then went to Chicago to play with the Erskine Tate Orchestra, returning to St. Louis in 1932 to play and record with Eddie Johnson's Crackerjacks. When Johnson brought in new band members in 1933, Baker remained with the Crackerjacks under his brother Winfield's and then Chick Finney's leadership until early 1936.

"Shorty" left St. Louis for good in early 1936 to join the Don Redman Orchestra, remaining until 1938. He was in the Duke Ellington Band for a short time in 1938 and then joined the Teddy Wilson Band in 1939. Baker moved to the Andy Kirk Orchestra in 1940 and eventually married the band's pianist, Mary Lou Williams. A good measure of his work is the Andy Kirk version of Ellington's "Ring Dem Bells."[37] The two musicians co-led a sextet during this period. He then joined Duke Ellington in 1942 and remained with him until 1944, when he entered the service. During this period, he took part in an Ellington Carnegie Hall concert, playing an especially expressive solo on "Black Beauty."[38] After his service in the armed forces, he rejoined Ellington and played with him regularly until 1952.

Baker freelanced around New York from the time he left Ellington until his death from throat cancer on November 8, 1966. During this period, he led his own groups and played with Teddy Wilson, Johnny Hodges, Ben Webster, Claude Hopkins, and others. One of his best recordings is *Shorty and Doc*,[39] recorded for the Swingville label in 1961.

Although Louis Armstrong originally influenced him, Baker developed his own style and tone based on St. Louis trumpet players of the 1920s. He is one in a long line of major St. Louis trumpet players to make an impact on jazz.

Eddie Randle and the St. Louis Blue Devils

Eddie Randle came from a musical family. His grandfather raised seventeen children and taught them all how to play music. He was affected early by music on the Ohio River.[40]

> Well when I was a kid, see. Fate is out of Paducah, Kentucky and I'm across the river on the Illinois side. And back in those days there were not so many machines and what not, and you actually . . . well people use to cross the river on the ferry and they would even call across the river, they would say "hey" and you could hear the voice echoing back softly and they would call for the ferry. Well when Fate would come down the river on the famous steam calliope, way before they had orchestras, when I was a little fellow; we use to listen to Fate then. Not knowing that some day I would be associated with him as a musician.

Randle's uncle taught Eddie music. His family moved to St. Louis in 1923, and Eddie went to Sumner High School. He and his father had a combination barbershop, tailor shop, and shoeshine parlor across from the skating rink on Vashon and Lucas. Many of the musicians left their instruments there.[41]

> And all the bands practiced over there, and they'd leave the instruments there in my tailor shop. And we just practiced. We would buy stocks. We'd buy what they call big sheets, and we'd just have a bunch of guys in rehearsin'. So the only band I ever played with really was with Warner Long and his band. And by being the type [of] fella I am, I used to get the work for Warner and his band. So in 1932, Karl George came to town. . . . And when he came to town, he was friends with some of the musicians in Long's band, and they wanted him. So Mr. Long wouldn't get rid of me because he knew I was doing all the work for him. I was doing the booking and everything. But the fellas started acting a little funny. And I says to Warner, I says, "Warner, what's wrong with the guys?" And he says, "Karl George is in town," and he's had a lot of experience. They wanted Karl. And I says, "Well, use Karl!" I says, "It doesn't matter to me." So he started using Karl George, and he played several places that I had booked. And the

people began to ask him, "Where's the other trumpet player?" So they told them I was sick for a while, but after I was sick so long and hadn't died [laughs], some of them says, "Well, look. If you can't bring that other trumpet player back. . . ." [He] says, "I'm sorry, we can't hire you."

Joe Jernigan—a musician playing with Warner Long—asked Randle to start a band in the fall of 1932. Describing this occasion, Randle said,[42]

"Joe, I don't know if I should or not," I says. Of course, I was in the restaurant business, and I needed to start something because I was going broke [laughs]. And I says, "Y'all are working plenty hard," and he says, "Naw," he says, "Everywhere we go they say, 'Where's your other trumpet player?'" And then he says, "If you start a band, I'll help you, Eddie." He says, "These people want you! They want you direct! They want you! And they like your sound!" And I say, "Oh, you got to be kidding."

The name "Blue Devils" came about in this way.[43]

I was out here on what they call the Hill. . . . I had heard they were gonna have a dance, and I was always out there hustling work. And while I was talking to this guy, he say, "How many of ya are there in the band?" And I say, "Seven." He say, "What's the name of the band?" Well, I always liked the Oklahoma Blue Devils. And so I just said, "Seven Blue Devils." And that's how I named the band the Seven Blue Devils, and that stayed with us. Even after I had more, I just dropped "Seven" and went by the St. Louis Blue Devils.

When I started the band, the drummer was Jessie Brazier; Joe Jernigan was the main one that helped me get the band started. And there was a fellow by the name of John Arnold, played piano. And there's a fellow by the name of Thieron Slaughter. . . . He played saxophone. I had two sax. And then there was Banjo Pete, Pete Patterson. . . . That was it. Three rhythm, two sax, and myself. Four rhythm. That's right. Piano, drum, and Banjo Pete, and three horns: Thieron Slaughter on alto, Joe Jernigan on tenor, and myself on trumpet. To make it sound like three sax, I used to put the bell of my horn in an old felt hat, and . . . it sounded real good.

The St. Louis Blue Devils traveled a lot. Randle was not only the leader but also the booker, and he booked one-nighters one year ahead.[44] He recalled how his band played.

I always like to play soft and sweet. In fact, they called my band the band of sophisticated rhythms, because we played rhythms but it wasn't noisy, it wasn't loud. We played real soft. Nobody on my bandstand could pat their foot. I would stop them right away. That's the drummer's job. You know guys would make all that noise. That's the drummer's job. And when we would get started, nobody would make any noise, everything was just smooth.[45]

Most of our work was in little towns. At that time, I started playing over at WEW every day—twice a week, rather—Tuesdays and Thursdays at 12:00. And then the letters would come in, and I would go ride around through these little towns and tell them to listen to the programs. I started getting a lot of work. See, I played so many one-nighters until we just wouldn't accept a regular job. Because at that time, we were making more than you could make on a regular job. In fact, I've had people leave regular jobs to play with me later on when I added men.

. . . The farthest from St. Louis was Sodus Point, New York. I was there a couple of summers on a regular job there [1939 and 1941]. That was a place on Lake Ontario and Sodus Bay; they called it Sodus Point, New York. I played up there. That's up above Alton, NY. You go up through Rochester and then I think Alton is about 40 miles out and then down on the lake. I played there a couple of years. Other than that, I never accepted regular work. In the summertime, here in the city, there was a lot of club dances, and I didn't have to worry about it with my one-nighters. I made a nice living.[46]

We were very popular. When Count Basie was appearing in Columbia, Missouri, and we were appearing in Moberly, an hour away, we outdrew Basie.[47]

Other towns with extended stays for the band were at Stephens Point, Wisconsin, in 1936 and Dubuque, Iowa, in 1937. Randle remembers the reception the band received in Stephens Point initially and how it changed as the summer went on. "We used to go up to the radio station or into a club and they'd carry instruments for us and everything after they got used to us. But

Eddie Randle (1905–1997)

Eddie Randle[48] was born in Villa Ridge in Pulaski County, Illinois. He came to St. Louis in 1923. His grandfather was a musician, minister, and schoolteacher. He raised seventeen children, all of whom learned to read music. Eddie's uncle taught him music, but it was in an older form of notation called "shape notes." He got his first trumpet at age seventeen and was largely self-taught.

Eddie's only musical job before he founded the St. Louis Blue Devils was with Warner Long. He was the one who booked Long's band. The demand for his playing with Long's band led to forming his own band in 1932. When he was asked what the name of his band was, the words "Seven Blue Devils" just popped out. He later called the band "The St. Louis Blue Devils." The original seven-piece band worked all over the Midwest because they found that they could make more money playing one-nighters than location jobs, such as in a club like the Plantation in St. Louis. He started playing on WEW radio twice a week at noon. The Blue Devils ranged as far as Sodus Point, New York (1939 and 1941), Stevens Point Wisconsin (1936), and Dubuque, Iowa (1937). They were a precise band that rehearsed all the time. The Blue Devils large band book was a mixture of popular and original tunes. Before beginning a job, Randle said that he would look at the records on the jukebox in the venue

Eddie Randle Studio Portrait, Chicago, 1938. Photograph by Woodards Studio–Chicago. Photo restoration by Dennis Owsley. Courtesy of the Randle Family.

and would tailor the music to what he found.

In 1932, Randle also worked with Major N. Clark Smith's Sumner High School and community bands as a brass coach. He and his father were instrumental in starting the Tom Powell American Legion Post Drum and Bugle Corps. Many black St. Louis musicians played in that corps. Miles Davis's first job in music was with the Blue Devils in 1942. Home recordings of the St. Louis Blue Devils were made in 1941.

During the war, the ration of gasoline and other shortages led to the Blue Devils becoming resident in St. Louis. Eddie took a day job at the munitions plant, eventually rising to foreman. Although Randle stopped playing music full time in 1943, he continued to front bands until 1964. He eventually became a funeral director. He remained in that job full time almost up to his death. In addition to being a musician and businessman, Eddie was a philosopher and teacher. The Reverend William Gillespie spoke at his funeral and said that he always looked forward to being able to ride to the cemetery with Eddie because he learned more theology on those rides than he learned in books.

Many well-known St. Louis musicians passed through Randle's ranks or were helped by him. In addition to Miles Davis, these include Clark Terry, Ernie Wilkins, Jimmy Forrest, Oliver Nelson, Jimmy Blanton, "Sleepy" Tomlin, Druie Bess, Tommy Dean, Charles Pillars, David Hines, and Willie Akins.

Eddie Randle's St. Louis Blue Devils, Forest Park, 1938. Photographer unidentified. Photo restoration by Dennis Owsley. Courtesy of the Randle Family.

when I first went there it was terrible."[49] Randle remembers an engagement at the Club Villa Valencia in Springfield, Illinois.

> I played . . . with one trumpet for the long time. Eddie Randle and his Blue Devils. That's how I made my name. But in 1936 I had a large band. I went into Club Villa Valencia in Springfield, Illinois. And there were two other trumpets: one, Vertna Saunders and a fellow by the name of Cliff King. And when I got in that fast company, I picked up. I always played the first book because I always had a good sound, good tone, whatever you'd say. And then the next two guys I worked with were Sleepy Tomlin and Vertna Saunders.[50]
>
> I was a fast trumpet player until I used Sleepy Tomlin. After Sleepy left my band. Sleepy played so much horn until I had to play because I was the boss, you know. And it made me actually play. Then the guys that I had played with before, when they come back and played with me, well I had advanced so just by being in fast company. And I often say that Sleepy made a musician out of me. Because he was one of the first to play with Lunceford when Lunceford first started his band, but by some reason on his own he didn't stay in fast company. But he was terrific; he was a fine trumpet player.[51]
>
> Ernie Wilkins was one of my arrangers [1939]. He was in the band along with Sleepy, and he had arrangements where after we would play he would tell Sleepy to play his solo. So one night I didn't realize that I was still advancing at my age, and Sleepy says, "Ernie, when we get through with the section, stop giving me a solo." He says, "Give me a solo following the reeds." He says, "'Cause when Randle gets through," he says, "I don't know what I'm gonna do" [laughs].

The St. Louis Blue Devils band at the Villa Valencia engagement had the following personnel: Eddie Randle, Vertna Saunders, and Clifford King (trumpet); Druie Bess (trombone); Cecil Thornton (alto sax); Pee Wee Claybrooks (tenor sax) and one other (alto sax); Robert "Bunky" Parker (piano); George Brazier (bass); and Jesse brazier (drums).[52] Cecil Thornton was the arranger and he was trying to take over the band. Vertna Saunders remembers how he was going to do it.[53]

So he was trying to take the band away from Eddie Randle. He was going to take the band. So when he would make arrangements, he would write all real high parts. . . . On the first part he would, we would have about four important notes that would be F and above. We tried it down at rehearsal and Eddie couldn't play it. Well he knew Eddie couldn't. He wasn't that type of trumpet player because you have to be, you have to get used to playing high for one thing. . . . They would hear Cecil Thornton stop the band and holler at Eddie and tell him "Man, you're supposed to play that note, that's an important note." So he fussed at Eddie about the notes and it would only be maybe from two to four high notes in a number that Cecil would fix for the band. . . . Well in doing so he would always give it to Eddie Randle and he would have one or two of the notes way up high. (laughter) So what we did, Cliff and I, we didn't make any commotion about it at all, because we begged Thornton not to do this. So what we would do, is just give Eddie one of our notes. If I was going to play Eddie's note, then I would just give him my note, I'd put his note on my paper. So then the band would play on down. When we'd get to the high notes, I would either make it or King would make it. So the music was smooth and no one would ever notice. Well Thornton noticed it but there wasn't anything . . . he didn't have the nerve to say anything about it.

The band at Sodus Point in 1939 was nearly the same with Sykes Smith on trumpet in place of King and Edgar Hayes on alto in place of Thornton. Vertna Saunders remembered the impact that the band had at the Sodus Point engagement.[54] The band was originally contracted for two weeks and was held over for eight.

All the people liked the band so very, very much and there were several fellas, booking agencies, that came and wanted the band to go into New York City, but the guys didn't want to go and wanted to get back home and I believe Eddie went over to New York City to talk with the fellas. A couple of times, but the guys wouldn't leave, so we came on back in St. Louis. . . . We had two bookings because coming back we had a job in Cleveland, then a job in Indianapolis. Then on into St. Louis.

Eddie Randle recounted how the musicians in his band faired when visiting bands battled the Blue Devils or when visiting musicians played in jam sessions with his musicians.

Cab [Calloway] was coming this way, and Rex [Stewart] was there at the local hall in New York. And Rex told our guys, "Now, when you hit the road, there's a band called the Sunset Royals. If you come across out this way, they gonna out clown Cab." He says, "When you get to St. Louis, don't depend on "Hi-De-Hi-De-Ho" to get you through there, 'cause the little band that plays just above a whisper, man, before you know it, they'll blow you out that back window."[55]
I tell you one thing. I have clarinet players that when Benny Goodman would come to the Fox Theater, that when he would leave the Fox he would be standing around in front of the band... And he would always set in with us, Benny Goodman. And we would have these jam sessions and what was his name, Ziggy Elman, they would run him off the bandstand.[56]

In the late 1930s, arranger-saxophonist Ernie Wilkins was in the band. He describes how Eddie Randle gave him his start as an arranger.[57]

I had begun writing for Eddie Randle's' band; the older guys would say to Eddie, "Oh, don't give that kid paper, waste that paper (manuscript paper) on him". My first arrangement was "Mean to Me" and it was kind of sad, I couldn't handle those chord progressions. Of course the older guys said, "I told you so, I told you so," but Eddie kept giving me paper and each arrangement kept getting better and better.

Jimmy Forrest also sat in with the band during this period. Even though the band had arrangements for three saxophones, Randle said that Forrest always could improvise a superb fourth part.[58] The story of the St. Louis Blue Devils will continue in Chapter 4.

The Jeter-Pillars Orchestra

The Jeter-Pillars Orchestra was formed out of the remnants of the great Alphonso Trent Orchestra. Gunther Schuller called the Trent band the most idolized and advanced band of the Southwest.[59] Budd Johnson said of the band, "We used to idolize those guys. . . . You have no idea just how fabulous that band was! They were years ahead of their time."[60] Buddy Tate also talked about this band.

> It was about the sharpest band I'd ever seen. I mean, like, when I say sharp, I mean appearance, you know. They, they stayed with my auntie in Dallas during the time they were workin' at the Adolphus Hotel. And they used to go on that engagement and stay a year. . . . When they'd go to work, I'd sneak in their rooms and look at their suits (laughs) and those beautiful uniforms and things and I used to listen to that beautiful band. And Hayes Pillars was in the band and he was so, one of the most, he was, played like crazy.[61]

Pianist Alphonso Trent took over a territory band called Gene Crooke's Synco Six around 1923. The Adolphus Hotel in Dallas became their base for a year and a half, a surprising turn of events considering the facts. Considering that the hotel was one of the most exclusive hotels in the South, a black band would have been uncommon. The band broadcast over a Dallas radio station. Each musician made a salary of $150 per week as they toured through the South and Midwest. The Trent Band recorded in 1928 for Gennett. The orchestra had twelve musicians by 1928. During this time tenor saxophonist Hayes Pillars joined the band on tenor sax and Stuff Smith was heard on violin. According to Gunther Schuller, the band "played with more polish than any other Negro orchestra, including Henderson's, and also featured remarkable soloists."[62] The entire recorded output of the Trent Band is available on Timeless Records.[63] Both "The Nightmare" and "Ebony Rhapsody," recorded in 1928, are remarkable pieces ahead of their time. The advanced trombone soloist Leo "Snub" Mosley is also featured in these recordings.

Trumpeter George Hudson, leader of the George Hudson Orchestra in St. Louis in the 1940s until the 1980s, was a member of the Trent Orchestra by 1929. How he joined Trent is an interesting story. He was working with Zack White at the time and was staying in Pittsburgh.[64]

> . . . we were staying at a hotel. Sterling hotel [is] the name of the hotel. All the musicians stayed there when they came into town. That was a hot town. They come in and played there. . . . And most of the guys' bands would work out of there and go play West Virginia, and Virginia and all the places like that. . . . And those ballrooms were popular all through that part of the country and had nice work. While, this Hotel Sterling . . . his name was Carter and he ran the elevator. And we were in town. And Trent called Rich [Carter], they were very familiar with Rich, everybody was familiar with him. Anyway he called him and then they sent a [telegram]. I need a trumpet player. Send me. I'll send you money and send me Roy Eldridge. Well, Roy and I grew up together in Pittsburgh. I knew Roy, and Roy wasn't in town. He was with the band called Speed Web. . . . Rich did just what Trent told him to do. . . . He came looking for me said, "I got a job for ya, and Trent wants you." And he said, "In the morning I'll have your fare waitin' for ya. So you play tonight and be ready to move." And he got a ticket and everything. And I left. 'Cause I had gotten tired of playin' with Zack, anyway. So I went up to . . . Hotdog! . . . what's the name of that New York town I went to. I'll think of it. Pillars met me at the station.

Hayes Pillars confirms the story with a few different details.[65]

> Now you see, George Hudson joined the band in 1929. See, George Hudson was in Cincinnati, Ohio, and we sent a telegram with transportation, railroad transportation, for Roy Eldridge . . . for Roy Eldridge to join us in Wilkes Barre, Pennsylvania. And we sent the telegram to a fellow named Rich Carpenter. . . . And Rich Carpenter gave this telegram to George Hudson, who was playing down there in Cincinnati with Zack Whyte's band. And so what happened was George Hudson came to Wilkes Barre,

Pennsylvania. Of course I was one of the ones that went down to meet him. And when I saw him, I'd never known him before, you know.

The Alphonso Trent Band survived a number of reversals until 1933, when the band broke up in Albany, New York.[66] James Jeter, Hayes, and Charles Pillars went to Cleveland to join Chester Clark (ex-Trent trumpeter) and his band, opening in September of that year. Jeter and the Pillars brothers formed their band on January 6, 1934, to work at a club called "The Furnace."[67] That band included the young trumpeter Harry "Sweets" Edison, who had been with Chester Clark's orchestra. The Jeter-Pillars Orchestra came to St. Louis on July 4, 1934, to play the Plantation.[68] Eddie Randle tells this part of the story,

> . . . Pillars came here to work for Tony at the Club Plantation. And in the summertime, they was running a place called the Gingham Inn. And the Gingham Inn burned down. By being treasurer of the local, they came to the local, and I went around these little towns where I go and asked them to use this band. And when Pillars sees me . . . every time he sees my wife, he says, "I never will forget this man. I would not be here today if it were not for him."[69]

Hayes Pillars continues the story of the summer of 1934.

> So we toured Kansas, Iowa, all through there. I think I got George Hudson then. [Hudson had left Trent and made his way to Kansas City, where he played for the Oklahoma Blue Devils and Benny Moten bands.] Bus fare from KC then was $2.75. We traveled in a seven-passenger MacFarlane car. They were big fine, handmade cars and that's how we traveled then. I remember that was the hottest summer I ever witnessed in my life. We were in Manhattan, Kansas and Walter Page was showing us how good condition he was in. He was jogging around a roadside track and he fell out. It was about 110 out there. He stayed with us about a year, left us in late 1935 to join Count Basie's band.[70]

George Hudson and his wife came to come to St. Louis, and he joined the band as lead trumpet in 1934. Hudson left the band in late 1937 to play with Dewey Jackson on the riverboats. In the administration of the band, Hayes Pillars was the director in charge of the music and personnel, while Jeter was the accountant and paymaster.

At various times, some of the sidemen of the Jeter-Pillars Orchestra included guitarists Charlie Christian and Floyd Smith; drummers Kenny Clarke, "Big" Sid Catlett, and Jo Jones; tenor saxophonist Jimmy Forrest; and bassists Walter Page and Carl Pruitt. Trumpeter Harry "Sweets" Edison met his first wife in St. Louis[71] and left in 1936 to go to New York. Hayes Pillars recalls how he got Sid Catlett in the Jeter-Pillars Orchestra, "We first got Kenny Clarke. We brought him here from Pittsburgh. Kenny, he stayed a week. We had been trying to get Sidney and we couldn't get him, but he wired us and told us he was ready to come. So we paid him (Kenny Clarke) off and sent him back."[72] Pillars recalled that during Catlett's tenure the chorus girls would take a bow and would then turn and bow to Catlett.[73] He also recalled Smith: "Floyd Smith joined us in 1936, we took him down to the music store and got him a real good guitar; he stayed with us until 1938."[74]

The Jeter-Pillars Band had a number of arrangers. Gus Wilson (Teddy Wilson's brother) was with the band early in its stay at the Plantation. Ernie Wilkins wrote for the band in the 1940s. According to Pillars, Tadd Dameron "made his first arrangements for us in 1938. And he made a lot of mistakes. He made a lot of mistakes. He was trying to write for a big band. I paid him, and I never criticized him, and I thanked him. And he never forgot it. He came out here with Billy Eckstine and he wrote four or five tunes—later."[75] Buggs Roberts was another arranger who later led a band at the Plantation and in a long engagement at the West End Waiters Club that lasted into the 1950s.

James Jeter and Hayes Pillars, Co-Leaders of Jeter-Pillars Orchestra, St. Louis, c. 1937. Photograph by Young Studio–St. Louis. © Collection of Duncan Schiedt.

I brought Buggs [Roberts] here in 1937, just to write. All he had to do was write two arrangements a week. First week, he wrote two; second week, he wrote two. Buggs had left us, gone to Chicago and was writing for Andy Kirk. When we got to Chicago to record our theme song, it wasn't even ready. We got down to the Columbia recording studio and Buggs started writing and, in about two hours he had finished our theme song.[76]

The Jeter-Pillars Orchestra recorded four titles for Vocalion in Chicago on August 25 and 26, 1937. The personnel of the band on these sides included: Ralph Porter, Walter "Crack" Stanley, and George Hudson (trumpet); Ike Covington and John "Bones" Orange (trombone); James Jeter and Charles Pillars (alto sax); Hayes Pillars (tenor sax and vocal); Chester Lane (piano); Floyd Smith (guitar); Vernon King (bass); Henry Ross (drums), and Ted Smith (vocal). The tunes included three vocals, "Make Believe," "I'll Always Be In Love With You," and "I Like Pie, I Like Cake." Its theme, "Lazy Rhythm" was also recorded as an instrumental. Gunther Schuller assesses these recordings. "It is a band quite difficult to assess fairly, for it only recorded four sides, which, considering their appalling quality make one hope fervently that these are not representative of their general work."[77]

Hayes Pillars remarked on the band's style in an interview with Bob Rusch. In comparing conservatism of his band to that of the Trent Band, Pillars maintained,[78]

Trent had one of the sweetest bands you ever heard. They played in them dining rooms, man, and they played beautifully. We were brought up under that philosophy and that's what we did with our band. We played hot music, then we played sweet tunes and we played soothing tunes, we played soft. Once in a while we'd blast off, on a Saturday night when the house was full of people we would play to please the musicians. You cannot have a band . . . just to please the musicians because they'll run crazy.

That was my decision. . . . It was my decision according to those arrangements. But we had some fine soloists in the band that we never exploited them and it's an unfortunate thing that we didn't. We had Gus Wilson, brother of Teddy Wilson, fine arranger. We never did have a chance to play his stuff like we wanted to do. A lot of stuff we wanted to do we didn't have time to get ready for it. . . . All we had to do at the Club Plantation was play current music, because that's what the public was asking for.

Pillars described the hard work he and he Jeter-Pillars Band put in during their stay at the Plantation.

Tom Powell Drum and Bugle Corps, St. Louis, 1936. Photographer unidentified. © Western Historical Manuscript Collection–St. Louis.

At one time we broadcast every night, just local. First started broadcasting on WIL, then moved up to KMOX. Frankly speaking, it was an injustice for the band to be broadcasting every night because the band had so much work to do. We had no nights off, understand this, seven nights a week.

Through the week it was a $1.50 admission. With that dollar and a half you got a strip steak, a plate of spaghetti, and all the beer you could drink. Now back in those days when we first came here beer was 10 cents a bottle. On Saturday night it was $2.00; they had to turn them away. The place wasn't big enough.

The story of the Jeter-Pillars Orchestra will continue in Chapter 4.

The Tom Powell American Post Drum and Bugle Corps

Around 1935, the Tom Powell American Legion Post sponsored a drum and bugle corps. Many well-known St. Louis musicians trained in that corps, including Clark Terry, Charles Fox, and Arvell Shaw in the 1930s. Eddie Randle's father helped start the drum and bugle corps and Eddie drove the car.[79]

. . . we started that legion thing as . . . the Son of the Legions. This is before World War II. It was the Son of the Legion, and I was a Son of the Legion, and I was the oldest Son of the Legion there. And I used to have a seven-passenger car and a trailer

Dewey Jackson's Musical Ambassadors, St. Louis, 1936. Photographer unidentified. Left to right: William Rollins (baritone sax/alto sax), Bradford Nichols (tenor sax), Cliff Batchman (clarinet/baritone sax), Eugene Phillips (guitar), Earl Martin (drums), Dewey Jackson (trumpet), Wendell Black (trumpet), Robert Parker (piano), Singleton Palmer (bass). © Collection of Duncan Schiedt.

that I carried my instruments in, and when we would go to the state fairs, I was the one that furnished the transportation. That seven-passenger Chrysler that I had. I'd have maybe ten, twelve little guys in there and the instruments in my trailer, and we'd go to Salem, MO, Salem, IL, anywhere.

That Tom Powell Post was important for years. In fact, I used to practice the Tom Powell Post before we started the drum and bugle corps—try to have a band. And I used to help the guys try to get it organized. A band. And then we didn't have enough men with instruments and . . . I can't call the guy's name now . . . looking right at him. He's the one that suggested the drum and bugle corps with the Sons of the Legions. . . . In fact, my father stood for a lot of the instruments and things for the Post. And later on, when we went out of business, we had to pay for them; the company sued him. He signed. He was the one that signed when we bought the instruments.

Clark Terry fondly remembered his 1935 experience.[80]

Matter of fact, Charles Fox and I were in Tom Powell drum and bugle corps in 1935 when we won the championship. I was a bugle man; Charles was a drummer. Back in those days, in '35, I was just in high school, and I didn't have a trumpet at that particular time because Clarence Hayden Wilson, who was our band director at the time at Vashon High School, had run out of trumpets, and had given me a valve trombone, and he said, "Take this and get out of here. You can make more noise with it anyhow." So the closest I came to trumpet, at that particular point, was my bugle at Tom Powell post, you know, which was an old "G" bugle, a straight bugle without any pistons, you know. I had an opportunity to learn how to do a lot of tonguing and articulating and so forth and proper embouchure build-up with the bugle.

Modern musicians Phillip Wilson and Kenny Rice also played in the corps in the 1950s.

Riverboat Musicians and the Decline of Music on the Riverboats

Dance music continued to be heard on the riverboats during the Depression. In 1930, Fate Marable, Dewey Jackson, and Harvey Lankford's Synco High Hatters played regular jobs. Dewey Jackson's 1930 band had Don Stovall, Harold Estes, and Earl Carruthers in the reed section. Carruthers had worked in Kansas City with Benny Moten. He played with both Jackson and Fate Marable while in St. Louis. He soon joined Jimmy Lunceford and stayed with the band until Lunceford's death in

Clark Terry (born 1920)

Born in St. Louis to a poor family, Clark Terry[81] was smitten by music at an early age. His first "instrument" was a water hose with a funnel on the end that sounded like a jug when he blew into it. Clark's brother-in-law was Cy McField, a tuba player with Dewey Jackson's orchestra. After his mother died in 1926, Clark was raised by one of his sisters. He showed an early aptitude for getting sounds out of a trumpet. When he went to Vashon High School, his first instrument was a valve trombone. The teacher was Clarence Hayden Wilson, who assigned him to Leonard Smalls, one of his assistants. Although he never studied with Joseph Gustat (see Chapter 2), Terry asked him about techniques. Gustat never turned him down.

Terry, Charles Fox, and Arvell Shaw were part of the 1935 Tom Powell American Legion Post that won the district championship. Clark's first professional job was at the Lincoln Theater on Market Street with a salary of 75 cents a night. When he finished his schooling, McField got him a job under bandleader Willie Austin on the Reuben and Cherry Carnival. Clark remained with Austin for about a year, eventually backing blues singer Ida Cox. He then worked with Bennie Reed, a one-legged piano player. Clark worked in occasional gigs in St. Louis with Randle and Dewey Jackson.

Terry volunteered for the Navy in 1942 and was stationed at the Great Lakes Naval Air Station in the orchestra. Musicians like Gerald Wilson, Willie Smith, and Ernie Wilkins were in that band. At the end of the war, Clark returned home to a job with George Hudson's big band, playing lead and all the trumpet solos. He also served as the straw boss of the band. Clark then worked with Charlie Barnet (1947), Hudson, Charlie Ventura, Cleanhead Vinson, and finally joined Count Basie in 1948. Over the years, Clark was able to get St. Louisans Singleton Palmer, Bob Graf, Ernie Wilkins, and Jimmy Wilkins into the Basie organization. He remained with Basie until 1951.

Duke Ellington then beckoned. Clark was with him from November 1951 until November 1959. During his stay with Ellington, he took part in the famous 1956 Newport Jazz Festival concert that brought Ellington back to prominence. He also played in such projects as Ellington's *Drum Is a Woman* (where he played Buddy Bolden), *Such Sweet Thunder* (Ellington's impressions of Shakespeare), the film score to *Anatomy of a Murder*, and other recordings. He toured Europe with Ellington at least twice.

Leaving Ellington in 1959, Clark toured Europe again with the Quincy Jones Band in a Harold Arlen Show, "Free and Easy." When that show folded, Clark joined the NBC staff orchestra in March 1960, the first African American to be in that orchestra. He received much exposure on the *Tonight Show*. He remained with NBC until 1972, when the show moved to Los Angeles.

In addition to his trumpet playing, Clark Terry is known for his hilarious scat singing, which he calls "Mumbles," recorded first in 1964 with Oscar Peterson. He has led many small groups and big bands and continues to bring the St. Louis trumpet tradition to the world. He is one of our National Treasures.

1947.[82] "Sleepy" Tomlin played trumpet and Leon King trombone in this band. Both joined the Jimmy Lunceford Orchestra in 1933 but soon returned. King returned after two months to return to his post office job.[83]

Dewey Jackson also led bands on land. He played at both the Castle Ballroom at 29th and Ewing and at Sauter's Park in Lemay—white establishments that did not allow black musicians until Jackson. His band played an integrated dance sponsored by the Catholic magazine *Interracial Review* at the St. Louis University gymnasium. Dewey Jackson's orchestra played at a "Depression Dance" at the Finance Building on June 10, 1933, with the proceeds going to the Scottsboro Boys Defense Fund.[84] He led bands on the riverboats until 1941, once co-leading a band with Fate Marable on a trip downriver to New Orleans on the *J. S.* for the winter. From 1937 to 1941, he led his band, Dewey Jackson's Musical Ambassadors, on the riverboats. The band had such musicians as George Hudson (trumpet), Singleton Palmer (bass), Earl Martin (drums), and Robert "Bunky" Parker (piano). A young trumpeter, Clark Terry, occasionally worked for Jackson and for Eddie Randle. Terry tells how he became a musician.[85]

My older sister, Ada, was married to Cy McField, who was a tuba player and played with Dewey Jackson's Musical Ambassadors. And Ol' Squirrel was a trumpet player and had an excellent band. And this is how we happened to get involved as kids because we used to hear the band rehearse, and we wanted very much to get involved, you know. So Cy really used to turn me on to it because I was at one point, when my mother passed away, the older girl in the family had to take over and become the mother of the rest of us. And at one point, we had just about run out of older girls, and we had to sort of make it on our own. So when I got into high school, the Vashon High School, I went to live with Ada, my oldest sister, and Cy, so that put me a little closer to the music scene. And I really got involved with the jazz scene at that point.

When Dewey Jackson's band would rehearse, Cy used to let me go in, and one of the guys—I think it was Louis Lattemore—used to have a little candy store over on Leffingwell. He used to bring me pennies and candy from his store, and when they would take breaks, he would say, "Son, you can watch my horn." Up to that point, I wasn't really sure what I wanted to play, but I think he convinced me that I really wanted to be a trumpet player because he was such a nice man. I tell you, anybody who would give me candy and bring me pennies—I wanted to be like that cat, you know. So one day, while he was away on break, whatever kind of break they took those days—they returned, and I had mustered up enough courage to try to make a sound on this horn. I was huffing and puffing away, and he caught me. He said, "Ahh, son. You gonna be a trumpet player." Of course, I was stupid enough to believe it, and I stuck with it, and from that point on, that was the thing that encouraged me, I suppose, to get really involved with the trumpet. Then Cy, of course, my brother-in-law, he helped encourage me, and he used to take me on little gigs, and, you know, turned me on. And [I] started making a few little bucks at it, and that really encouraged me, you know.

Because of the circumstances of the Depression, the black union began allowing pay cuts for the bands in 1932.[86] Trombonist Harvey Lankford had taken over the Floyd Campbell Synco High Hatters when Campbell left St. Louis to play first in Cincinnati and then Chicago. The personnel of the band included Charles Creath (accordion); Lester Nichols or Earl Martin (drums); Andrew Webb, Walter "Crack" Stanley, or Louis Eckehardt (trumpet); Sammy Long (alto sax); James Barlow (bass); Gus Perryman (1932) or Burrowes Lovingood (1930, 1931) (piano). Creath was fronting the band and playing accordion. Solos were permitted in this band, with the main soloists being Creath, Stanley, Eckehardt, or Webb. The salaries for the musicians were $35 per week, soon cut to $30 per week. Lankford quit when the salaries were cut. He eventually joined a Works Progress Administration (WPA) band that worked everywhere in St. Louis. This band had a symphony orchestra, entertainers, and some of the best musicians in St. Louis. Even rehearsals were paid.[87]

Fate Marable was not on the riverboats in 1931. His band included Crack Stanley and "Sleepy" Tomlin (trumpet); Willie Austin (trombone); Earl Carruthers, Kimball Dial, and Horace Millinder (alto sax); Joe Neville (tenor sax); Robert Bell (piano); John Young (banjo); Vernon King (bass); and A. G. Godley or Pete Suggs (drums).[88] Marable led units that played all around Missouri and Illinois, including a gig at the Soho Club in Springfield, Illinois. The band for this engagement included James Beard (trombone), Clifford King (trumpet), Leon King (trombone), John Young (banjo), Vernon King (bass), and George Spotts (drums). He took this band to New Orleans on the *J. S.* in 1933.

In 1936, the *St. Paul* was rechristened as the *Senator* and ran from Louisville to Pittsburgh.[89] Dewey Jackson had the band on the boat in 1936. Charles Creath was sometimes the co-leader on this job. Marable led the band on this boat in 1937–1939. Trombonist Robert Carter played on this boat in both bands. Vertna Saunders recounted an interesting incident in Pittsburgh.[90]

Dewey Jackson, St. Louis, c. 1941. Photographer unidentified. © Collection of Duncan Schiedt.

Fate had tooth trouble or something of the sort and he wasn't able to play on the boat that day. So they asked the union to send somebody to take Fate's place. So they sent a young fella down. He didn't favor him much and didn't act like he knew much about what he was doing, and Charlie Creath asked him, if he wanted to rehearse any and he said, "No." Just give him all of the guitar parts. He didn't want the piano parts because he couldn't read piano music. So on the boat we would play the introduction, and a couple of choruses, a solo. Then modulate because the last chorus was always in a different key. We'd make the modulation on the music and go into the last chorus. So everything was marked like that, with the modulation marked off, and then go into the arrows pointing to the last chorus. So they explained that to this guy, and so he said, "Well, no problem." There wasn't. There was no problem. I don't care what key you wanted to play in. I don't care what key it was, you just called the key. He played and he sounded as though he played with the band another time. After the first day, the guys found out that it was a fella named Erroll Garner.

Saunders also recounted life and rehearsals with the Marable Orchestra.[91]

We used to have trouble. There was Clifford King, myself and James Telphy, the trumpet section. So when we would go over our music, we would go over it in sections, rhythm section, reed section, the brass section. Well it just so happened, well we could read very well and the reed section, well everyone in the band was fairly good musicians. But the reed section had more trouble with their parts, and so of course that took a little extra practice. So the brass section could just walk off the stand, because when we're getting a new piece of music we'd go over it the first time, it would be perfect. So then Charlie [Creath] would say, "Okay the reed section take it from the top." Well, the brass would just leave the stand. We'd get a Coke or walk around, smoke and so on. On several occasions, Fate would come up to us and say, "You know you all are really lucky that you can read so well. You never have any trouble." But he tried all he could to find music that would stick us. (laughter) Oh, we could have been stuck. But it just so happened that they never did bring any music that we couldn't play with ease.

. . . during that time, there was in nearly every number, there was a part for a clarinet part. The saxophonist they had a little spot right where they kept the clarinet on. Then when it come to the part where they pick up the clarinets, they put their saxophones down and play clarinet part. Well the clarinet is more difficult, I guess. The majority of guys that they got to play on the boat in the reed section was saxophonists, and they played the clarinet because the part called for it, but they weren't good clarinetists. So they picked up the clarinet and when they started off do, do, do, squeak. (laughter) Oh, Fate would give them the devil. Mostly from the clarinet parts. The little squeaks that they would did on clarinet and then their fingers were a little slow for clarinet and they'd kind of slur some of the notes and he'd call them down on it, things like that.

Jeter-Pillars Orchestra, St. Louis, c. 1937. Photograph by Young Studio–St. Louis. Upper row, left to right: Floyd Smith (guitar), Vernon "Buck" King (bass), Robert Ross (drums), Ike Covington (trombone). Lower row, left to right: Chester Lane (piano), Ted Smith (vocals), Hayes Pillars (tenor sax), Charles Pillars (alto sax), James Jeter (alto sax), Ralph Porter (trumpet), Walter "Crack" Stanley (trumpet), George Hudson (trumpet). © Collection of Duncan Schiedt.

Trombonist Robert Carter worked with Eddie Johnson on the *Idlewild* to Pittsburgh in 1937. Although he worked with Dewey Jackson and Marable during the summer season, he worked with Eddie Johnson on land. In 1937, the Johnson band had James Telphy, Merrill Tarrant, and Benny Starks (trumpet); Robert Carter (trombone); Leon "Foots" Goodson and Thomas Starks (alto sax); Kimball "Cabbage" (tenor sax); Eddie Johnson (piano); Ed Hardman (guitar); Singleton Palmer (bass); and Lester Nichols (drums).[92] Benny Starks had recently returned from Canada and worked with Eddie Randle and the Jeter-Pillars Orchestra when Jimmy Blanton was in the band.

By the end of this period, dance music on the riverboats was being phased out by the Streckfus family for economic reasons. The costs of new safety regulations and replacement of old, rotting wooden boats were prohibitive. By 1940, the Streckfus steamers empire had shrunk to two steel boats, the *President* and the *Admiral*. Marable retired from the boats in 1940, and Dewey Jackson played his last riverboat job in 1941. The *Admiral* remained in St. Louis while the *President* was moored in New Orleans.

Other St. Louis Musicians from This Period

Trombonist Druie Bess[93] was born in Montgomery City, Missouri, around 1901. His father and one of his friends started him on trombone. As a young child he played in carnival bands and minstrel shows that traveled around Missouri. His parents sent him to high school at Lane Tech in Chicago, where he played in the orchestra. He went back to touring with minstrel shows after high school. After touring, Bess worked in a club in Cicero, Illinois, that was owned by gangsters. He then worked with the New Way Jazz Hounds Bill Lewis and Dixie Ramblers. Bess went to St. Joseph, Missouri, in 1925, where he joined Jesse Stone and was featured on both sweet and jazz pieces. He heard some recordings of Miff Mole, a well-known white trombonist of the 1920s.

> I heard a record one day with Miff Mole on it. I sounded so good to me because he used good tone. He used good tone and he moved on his horn fast. . . . Now I copied him. At that time he was quite a trombone player. Played with Paul Whiteman and all of them. Well, I looked, I studied music quite a bit, I knew what he was playing. He was playing thirds, a lot of thirds. It was easy to copy. But it sounded good. It was good swing but it was good sound. I played it for a long time and they called me "Miff," nicknamed me "Miff" all the time I was playing with the Oklahoma Blue Devils. I said, "Well, from now on I ain't gonna copy nobody, all the way. I'll just take a piece of somebody." And then probably I'd make a style of my own.

His only two recorded solos were with Jesse Stone in St. Louis in 1927. By late 1927, Bess had moved to Kansas City and worked with Chauncey Downs. He joined the Oklahoma Blue Devils (now based in Kansas City) in 1929 and remained with them until 1933. Eddie Randle brought him to St. Louis to play with his band in 1935. He remained with Randle until 1938 and subsequently worked with Eddie Johnson, Dewey Jackson, Cecil Scott, and Fate Marable before joining the Jeter-Pillars Orchestra at the Plantation in 1942. When the Earl Hines Band came through St. Louis in 1944, he joined and remained with the band until 1946. By 1948, he was playing with the Ringling Brothers Circus. In the 1950s, he worked with drummer Joe Smith in St. Louis and played with Singleton Palmer. Bess was a father figure to many St. Louis musicians.

Alto saxophonist Don Stovall (1913–1970) was born in St. Louis.[94] He worked with Dewey Jackson (1930–1931), Fate Marable (1932–1933), and then Eddie Johnson (1933–1936), where he was part of the saxophone section with Kimball Dial and Tab Smith. He moved to Chicago and worked with Lil Armstrong (1936) and Peanuts Holland (1936–1938) and then moved to New York. He recorded with Pete Johnson with a solo on *627 Stomp*.[95] He worked with a number of groups before joining Henry "Red" Allen in 1942. He played and recorded with Allen until 1949. Stovall left music in 1951.

Floyd Smith (1917–1942), nicknamed "Wonderful," was born in St. Louis.[96] Smith was a pioneer electric guitarist who occasionally used a Hawaiian steel guitar. He played both acoustic guitar and ukulele with Dewey Jackson, Charles Creath, and Eddie Johnson. His first electric guitar recordings were with the Jeter-Pillars Orchestra in 1937, preceding Charlie Christian's work by nearly two years. Smith then joined Andy Kirk and recorded *Floyd's Guitar Blues*,[97] one of the first blues solos on the electric guitar. He led his own groups and worked with such people as Horace Henderson and Wild Bill Davis in Chicago, New York, and St. Louis before settling in Indianapolis in 1964.

St. Louisan Karl George (1913–?) played with the Warner Long band in 1931–1932 before moving on to Detroit with McKinney's Cotton Pickers. George returned to St. Louis to play with the Jeter-Pillars Orchestra (c. 1938) and then moved on to the Teddy Wilson Band (1939–1940) and Lionel Hampton. He went to the West Coast after military service. George was the first African American to play with Stan Kenton (1945). He also worked with Count Basie and Benny Carter that same year. He worked and recorded with a number of groups in 1946 before returning to St. Louis, where he retired due to health problems.

Forrest Crawford (1908–?) was born in St. Louis. He worked with the Joe Gillis Band in 1934 and then moved to New York, where he worked and recorded with Dick Robertson, Red McKenzie, the Mound City Blue Blowers, Harry Richman, and Bunny Berigan (1935–1937). After contracting tuberculosis in 1937, he returned to St. Louis. By 1939, he was leading a band at the Showboat Ballroom.[98]

Leroy Harris, Jr., (born 1908) is the son of Leroy Harris, Sr., and nephew of Arville and Jimmie Harris (see Chapters 1 and 2). His first musical instrument was the violin. He started playing clarinet and alto sax in 1929. He worked with Chick Finney in 1939 and then moved to Chicago to work with ragtime pianist Brun Campbell. He then worked with Ray Nance (1932–1936) and Eddie Cole (1937) and was the lead alto player with Earl Hines (1938–1943). During World War II, he served as a navy bandsman (1943–1944). He recorded with Sarah Vaughan (1946) and with Wynonie Harris (1949). During the early 1950s, he worked with Bill Martin, Bill Dogget, Ben Thigpen, and Earl Hines. He worked in St. Louis with drummer Archie Burnside (1957–1959) and was with Eddie Johnson (1960–1971) at the King Brothers Motel at Lindbergh and Clayton. He later worked in Singleton Palmer's band.

Alto and soprano saxophonist Talmadge "Tab" Smith[99] (1909–1971) was born in Kinston, North Carolina. He led bands in the South and eventually came to St. Louis to work with Fate Marable. He was with Dewey Jackson's band in 1933 when Eddie Johnson brought him into the Crackerjacks, prompting the breakup of the band (see previous discussion in this chapter). He remained with Johnson until 1936, when Lucky Millinder came through St. Louis and took him to New York. From 1937 to 1944, he worked with Millinder, the Mills Blue Rhythm Band, Eddie Durham, and Count Basie. He led his own groups into the early 1960s, recording with small labels that featured a rhythm and blues sound. He then retired to St. Louis to become involved in real estate and played for fun. He also taught music in St. Louis. Smith's best-known and musically successful album is *Jump Time* on Delmark.[100]

Composer-arranger Gordon Jenkins (1910–1984) was born in Webster Groves. He worked in the orchestra at Wildwood Springs Lodge in Steelville, Missouri, during the summers of 1926 through 1929.[101] He worked as a pianist and arranger with Isham Jones in the early 1930s and later moved into theater and radio composing. Jenkins composed Benny Goodman's theme song, *Goodbye*. Later, he wrote and arranged for films and vocalists in Hollywood.[102]

Billy Banks (1908–1967) was a vocalist and female impersonator born in Alton, Illinois. There is no record of any work in St. Louis, although he did record with Pee Wee Russell and other jazz musicians. He is outside the scope of the present work.[103]

Endnotes

[1] Ross Russell, *Jazz Style in Kansas City and the Southwest* (New York: Da Capo, 1997), pp. 6–10.

[2] James Neal Pimm, *Lion of the Valley* (Boulder, CO: Pruett Publishing Co., 1981), pp. 467–472.

[3] Walter Dixon, interview with the author, 1986.

[4] The information in this section was compiled from Charles E. Rose, "The American Federation of Musicians and Its Effect on Black Musicians in St. Louis in the Twentieth Century," A Thesis submitted in Partial Fulfillment of the Requirements for the Degree of Master of Music. Department of Music in the Graduate School, Southern Illinois University, Edwardsville, November 1978.

[5] Ibid., p. 34.

[6] Hayes Pillars, quoted in Rose, ibid., p. 43.

[7] Eddie Randle, interviewed by Rose, ibid., pp. 43–44.

[8] Rose, "The American Federation of Musicians," p. 44.

[9] Information for this biography was compiled from Irene Cortinovis, interview with Eddie Johnson, Elijah Shaw, Chick Finney and Eddie Randle, August 20, 1971. University of Missouri–St. Louis Historical Manuscript Collection No. T-010; Irene Cortinovis,

interview with Elijah Shaw and Vivian Oswald, May 3, 1972. University of Missouri–St. Louis Historical Manuscript Collection No. T-109; and Kimball "Cabbage" Dial, Sammy Long and Elijah "Lige" Shaw, interview with Frank Driggs, September 24, 1978. Frank Driggs Archives, University of Missouri–Kansas City.

[10] William Howland Kenney, "Just Before Miles: Jazz in St. Louis, 1926–1944," in *Miles Davis and American Culture*, Gerald Early, ed. (St. Louis: Missouri Historical Society Press, 2001), pp. 24–39.

[11] David Hines, interview in Rose, "The American Federation of Musicians," pp. 70–72.

[12] Cortinovis, interview with Johnson, Shaw, Finney and Randle.

[13] Ibid.

[14] Richard M. Sudhalter and Phillip R. Evans, *Bix: Man and Legend* (New York: Schirmer Books, 1975).

[15] Ibid.

[16] Chuck Haddix, Director, Marr Sound Archives, University of Missouri–Kansas City, private communication.

[17] *Tom Lord Discography*, version 3.3.

[18] Kimball "Cabbage" Dial, interview by Frank Driggs, May 5, 1986. Frank Driggs Archives, University of Missouri–Kansas City.

[19] Dial interview.

[20] Eddie Johnson, interview with the author, June 27, 1986.

[21] Johnson interview.

[22] Lynn Driggs Cunningham and Jimmy Jones, *Sweet, Hot and Blue: St. Louis Musical Heritage* (Jefferson, NC: McFarland and Company, 1989), pp. 113–115.

[23] Ibid.

[24] Compiled from Cortinovis, interview with Johnson, Shaw, Finney and Randle; William Howland Kenney, "Just Before Miles"; Dixon interview.

[25] *St. Louis Argus*, August 4, 1916.

[26] Ibid., August 11, 1916.

[27] Dixon interview.

[28] Ibid.

[29] Dial interview.

[30] George Hudson, interview with Will Warner for Frank Driggs, July 26, 1978. Frank Driggs Archives, University of Missouri–Kansas City.

[31] Johnson interview.

[32] Ibid.

[33] John Cotter, "The Negro in Music in St. Louis," Master's Thesis, Washington University, St. Louis, 1959, p. 336.

[34] Stanley Dance, *The World of Duke Ellington*, 2nd ed. (New York: Da Capo Press, 1970), p. 184.

[35] Cortinovis, interview with Johnson, Shaw, Finney and Randle.

[36] Dance, *The World of Duke Ellington*, pp. 164–168.

[37] Andy Kirk/Mary Lou Williams, *Mary's Idea*, Decca GRD-622.

[38] Duke Ellington, *The Duke Ellington Carnegie Hall Concerts, January 1943*, Prestige PCD-34004.

[39] Harold "Shorty" Baker and Adolphus "Doc" Cheatham, *Shorty and Doc*, Swingville OJCCD-839-2 (1961).

[40] Cortinovis, interview with Johnson, Shaw, Finney, and Randle.

[41] Randle interview, 1986.

[42] Private conversations between Eddie Randle and the author, 1986–1997.

[43] Private conversations between Eddie Randle and the author, 1986–1997.

[44] Cortinovis, *Interview with Johnson, Shaw, Finney, and Randle, loc. cit*

[45] Ibid.

[46] Private conversations between Eddie Randle and the author, 1986–1997.

[47] Doris A Wesley, Wiley Price, and Ann Morris, eds., *Lift Every Voice and Sing—St. Louis African Americans in the Twentieth Century* (Columbia: University of Missouri Press, 1999), p. 67.

[48] Compiled from Randle interview, 1986; Paul DeMarinis, "Eddie Randle and the St. Louis Blue Devils," *Black Music Research Bulletin* 10(2), 1998; Private conversations between Eddie Randle and the author, 1986–1997.

[49] Private conversations between Eddie Randle and the author, 1986–1997.

[50] Ibid.

[51] Cortinovis, interview with Johnson, Shaw, Finney and Randle.

[52] Vertna Saunders interview by Dan Havens, April 5, 1982. National Ragtime and Jazz Archive, Southern Illinois University at Edwardsville.

[53] Saunders interview.

[54] Ibid.

[55] Private conversations between Eddie Randle and the author, 1986–1997.

[56] Cortinovis, interview with Johnson, Shaw, Finney and Randle.

[57] Ernie Wilkins, interview with Bob Rusch, *Cadence Magazine*, May 1977.

[58] Private conversations between Eddie Randle and the author, 1986–1997.

[59] Gunther Schuller, *Early Jazz* (New York: Oxford University, 1986), p. 299.

[60] Frank Driggs, "Budd Johnson, An Ageless Jazzman," *The Jazz Review* (November 1960): p. 6.

[61] Buddy Tate interview with the author, September 1986.

[62] Schuller, *Early Jazz*. p. 300.

[63] Various artists, *Richmond Rarities, 1927–31*, Timeless Records BDW 8008.

[64] George Hudson interview with the author, June 1986.

[65] Hayes Pillars interview by Wil Warner for Frank Driggs, Frank Driggs Archives, University of Missouri–Kansas City, unknown date.

[66] Hayes Pillars interview by Bob Rusch, *Cadence Magazine*, December 1986.

[67] Pillars interview by Warner.

[68] Ibid.

[69] Private conversations between Eddie Randle and the author, 1986–1997.

[70] Hayes Pillars Interview by Frank Driggs, Frank Driggs Archives, University of Missouri, Kansas City, unknown date.

[71] Harry "Sweets" Edison, conversation with the author, Denver, 1986.

[72] Pillars interview by Driggs.

[73] Pillars interview by Warner.

[74] Pillars interview by Driggs.

[75] Pillars interview by Warner.

[76] Pillars interview by Driggs.

[77] Gunther Schuller, *The Swing Era* (New York: Oxford University Press, 1986), p. 785.

[78] Pillars interview by Rusch.

[79] Private conversations between Eddie Randle and the author, 1986–1997.

[80] Clark Terry interview with the author, 1986.

[81] Compiled from information in Terry interview; Dempsey Travis, *An Autobiography of Black Jazz* (Chicago: The Urban Research Institute, Inc., 1983), p. 457; Dance, *The World of Duke Ellington*.

[82] Eddie Lambert, "Earl Carruthers," *The New Grove Dictionary of Jazz*, Barry Kernfield, ed. (New York: St. Martin's Press, 1995), p 189.

[83] Leon King interview by Dan Havens, August 1981. National Ragtime and Jazz Archive, Southern Illinois University at Edwardsville.

[84] Kenney, "Just Before Miles."

[85] Terry interview.

[86] Dial interview.

[87] Kimball "Cabbage" Dial, Sammy Long, and Elijah "Lyge" Shaw interview with Frank Driggs, *loc. cit.*

[88] Dial interview.

[89] Ibid.

[90] Saunders interview.

[91] Ibid.

[92] Benny Starks, interview with Frank Driggs, September 25, 1978. Frank Driggs Archives, University of Missouri–Kansas City.

[93] Compiled from Druie Bess interview by Irene Cortinovis and Peter Etzkorn, November 5, 1971. Western Historical Manuscript Collection, University of Missouri–St. Louis, T-033; Randle interview; Eugene Chadbourne, *Druie Bess*, All Music Guide, http://www.allmusic.com.

[94] Frank Driggs, "Don Stovall," *The New Grove Dictionary of Jazz*, Barry Kernfield, ed. (New York: St. Martin's Press, 1995), pp. 1164–1165.

[95] Pete Johnson, *The Chronological Pete Johnson 1939–1941*, Classics 665.

[96] *The New Grove Dictionary of Jazz*, Barry Kernfield, ed.(New York: St. Martin's Press, 1995), pp. 1137–1138.

[97] Various Artists, *Jazz Anthology 1939*, EPM Musique.

[98] Cunningham and Jones, *Sweet, Hot and Blue*, pp. 35–36.

[99] Compiled from Frank Driggs, "Tab Smith," *The New Grove Dictionary of Jazz*, Barry Kernfield, ed. (New York: St. Martin's Press, 1995), pp. 1142–1143. (b) Ian Carr, Digby Fairweather, and Brian Priestley, *Jazz: The Essential Companion* (New York: Prentice Hall Press, 1987), p. 465.

[100] Tab Smith, *Jump Time*, Delmark Records DD-447 (CD).

[101] http://www.wildwoodspringslodge.com/concert/Hall_of_Fame/jenkins.html

[102] American Big Bands Database, http://nfo.net/usa/j1.html

[103] Cunningham and Jones, *Sweet, Hot and Blue*, pp. 5–6.

4 The War Years: Jimmy Blanton, Miles Davis's St. Louis Years, and the Inception of Jazz Radio in St. Louis (1939–1949)

Although the riverboats declined as a music venue in the late 1930s, there still remained many outlets for musicians and bands in St. Louis in the decade to come. Venues to hear or dance to the music of the national and local big bands included the Chase Hotel, the Coronado Hotel, Forest Park Highlands, Sauter's Park, the Fox Theater, the Grand Central Theater, the Lynn Theater, the Castle Ballroom, the Arcadia Ballroom, the Showboat, the Casa Loma Ballroom, the West End Waiters' Club, and the Westminster and Imperial Ballrooms.

The Stan Kenton Orchestra had an engagement at the Casa Loma in December 1942. During the set, the St. Louis–born and Belleville-raised trumpeter Buddy Childers auditioned with the band at age seventeen and took over the lead trumpet chair. The Arcadia Ballroom became Tunetown (1942–1947). Louis Armstrong married his fourth wife, Lucille, on October 7, 1942, in the backyard of the mother of his band's female vocalist, Velma Middleton, while he was at Tunetown with his big band.[1] Charlie Menees remembered Kenton's Tunetown engagements.[2]

> Tunetown was the emporium of the swing bands when I first came to St. Louis in '42 and it lasted until a couple of years after the War. . . . It was the bastion for the swing bands. The sweet bands mostly went down to Casa Loma Ballroom on the South Side. . . . Stan Kenton set attendance records there in his first engagements at Tunetown. And Stan celebrated by going back to the Claridge Hotel with the band and taking off his pants, dropping his trousers and doing a celebration dance in some polka dot underwear shorts. . . . Charlie Wells was the promoter. Doyle Markham was the owner.

Politician Jordan Chambers reopened the Showboat as the Club Riviera on June 23, 1944. This club was a black alternative to the Club Plantation, with similar floor shows featuring the top black bands, comedians, and dancers.

Eddie Randle's St. Louis Blue Devils, the Jeter-Pillars Orchestra, and the George Hudson Orchestra were the major proving grounds for black St. Louis musicians. Many local musicians learned their trade with these bands before moving on to the national stage, including the incomparable Miles Davis and Jimmy Blanton, who had an indelible impact on jazz despite a career cut far too short.

During World War II, another training ground for St. Louis musicians was the U.S. Navy. Local musicians enlisted for every branch of the armed forces, but a multitude of musicians found themselves at the Great Lakes Naval Station in Chicago, including Clark Terry and Ernie Wilkins.

The Discovery of Jimmy Blanton

Jimmy Blanton (1918–1942) was born in Chattanooga, Tennessee. Initially a violinist who was taught by his uncle, he played locally in bands led by his mother, a pianist. He attended Tennessee State College for a short time and visited St. Louis during his summer vacation of 1939 and astounded all of the musicians with his bass playing. During that summer, Blanton worked or sat in with the Jeter-Pillars Orchestra, Eddie Randle, Dewey Jackson, Eddie Johnson, and Fate Marable. Hayes Pillars remembers when Blanton arrived.[3]

> Well, Jimmy Blanton was visiting here one summer, and he came over. We were playing up in Brooklyn, Illinois, and he came over to hear the band, and he started playing the bass, you know, and he was just so, he was so exciting, you know.
> Everybody just fell in love with him, you know. So he went on back to school. He was 17, I think, 17 or 18. So I offered him a job. I said, "You wanna work, you've gotta job," you know. At that time, he had a really small bass. It looked like, looked just like

Jimmy Blanton and Billy Taylor with Duke Ellington Band, Savoy Ballroom, New York City, 1940. Photographer unidentified. After hearing Blanton, Ellington hired him immediately, despite Taylor's presence in the band. Instead of firing Taylor, Ellington chose instead to use both bassists simultaneously. Taylor, however, eventually left the band. © Frank Driggs Collection.

a cello. And I took him down to St. Louis Music store, and we picked out a bass, you know. I just—we paid for it, you know. And that's when he got his first full-sized bass. And he started working with us. I mean he was a sensation.

Blanton initially had trouble working because of his talent and the jealousy of other musicians. Singleton Palmer remembers his troubles.

I remember when Jimmy hit town. He was a sensation. In fact, Jimmy was so good; he was so far ahead of bass players not only here but all over the country. The musicians here . . . a lot of them didn't like him, because he was just that far ahead. He was a pacemaker because of what he was doing with the bass violin. Nobody . . . not even I had heard of it before.

Blanton's cousin, Wendell Marshall, recounts how far ahead Blanton was musically in a *Downbeat* interview in 1955.[4]

"It was Jimmy, you know," emphasized Marshall, "who really revolutionized jazz bass. His rhythmic line was more melodic than most bassists had thought of playing, and his solos had the mark of his tremendous individuality. He used the bass like a horn for his solos, and he made the bass come to the front as any other solo instrument would. He could do that because he had an extensive musical background. Jimmy played other instruments as well as bass, and he arranged. And the Uncle who had originally taught him in Chattanooga played all instruments.

Jimmy had been playing the small violin since he was about ten and at about the same age, he also began arranging for piano and violin. Another fact that isn't well known about Jimmy is that he played nice alto. He really liked that instrument, probably played it just for kicks. I heard him blow alto once. His intervals were very different from any I'd heard at the time. They were wider and weren't the usual 1-3, 5 or 6 patterns that were common then. I didn't know what they were at that time, but now I realize they were more along the lines the men are playing today. Jimmy also played piano—he played things harmonically. I seldom hear men play that way even now. He was way out there musically, period.

Jimmy was very quiet and he was a perfectionist. He loved music intensely and he was studying and thinking about it constantly. I remember that at that time, he particularly liked Lunceford and wanted to play with him.

Those people who heard Jimmy only on records never really get to hear what he could do, as good as the records were. You had to catch him at a session. It was something almost unbelievable! When he had a chance to play at a session for an hour running, he really turned loose.

Walter Dixon[5] also remembered Jimmy Blanton and where he lived. "Jimmy Blanton at that time was going with a girl . . . they both lived in the same building. Jimmy lived upstairs and she lived on the first floor. I think it was on the 2700 block of Stoddard [Avenue]. And Jimmy was always practicin' his bass fiddle. Now, he could play a whole damn solo and knock you out any time you wanted to hear it, just playin' the bass, no instrumental [accompaniment], nothin' else, just the bass."

Duke Ellington came to St. Louis for an extended engagement at the Club Caprice in the Coronado Hotel from October 20 through November 2, 1939.[6] It was during this engagement that Jimmy Blanton was discovered. There are six stories on how Blanton was discovered. Rather than favor one story over another, we will present all six for the reader to decide the truth of the matter. Most of the stories involve Jesse Johnson's Deluxe Café at 10 North Jefferson and Club 49, which was upstairs. J. Von Chapman, writing "Town Chatter" for the *Argus,* related, "Duke Ellington has been frequenting Club 49 these nites while in town . . . we wonder if the maestro is planning to add Jimmy Blanton, bass fiddler with Fate Marable's band, to the aggregation."[7]

Milt Hinton had a version that is different from all the others. [8] "Ivy Anderson, the vocalist with Duke Ellington, came through and heard Jimmy Blanton and she, she's recommended him to Duke. And Duke hired, got him that way, and that's the way I heard it. And Ivy was from Chicago and I'm from Chicago and I knew her very well. I do know that he joined him in 1939."

George Hudson, St. Louis bandleader, gave the following information.[9] "Johnny Hodges and I were close friends. . . . So I came in and Johnny was there before Blanton got there that night. And he came down there after I got there and Johnny and I went in, sittin around 'cause I didn't drink nothing that night. He is the one who went down. Right down the street from there was a big hotel. Booker Washington Hotel. That's where all the bands stayed. So Duke Ellington never did hear him in this town. He went back . . . tried to get Duke to come there and Duke wouldn't. Well, . . . he [Ellington] said, 'You listen to him and you tell me.' And I was right there and heard it. Johnny Hodges was responsible for getting that boy with Duke."

Wendell Marshall said in his 1955 *Downbeat* interview,[10] "It was when he was jamming like that at a Saint Louis club that Johnny Hodges heard him. Billy Strayhorn came around too and they sent someone to get Duke. The story goes that Duke didn't want to come at first and finally arrived in his pajamas with his coat over them. After Duke heard him, he started featuring Jimmy with the band the next night.

Duke Ellington recounted the following in his autobiography, *Music Is My Mistress.*[11]

In 1939 we were playing the Coronado Hotel in St. Louis. After the gig one night, the cats in the band went out jumpin' in the after-hours joints. They landed up in a hot spot on the second floor of Jesse Johnson's restaurant, where they heard and jammed with a young bass player—Jimmy Blanton. Billy Strayhorn and Ben Webster dashed over to my hotel and came into my room raving about him. I had to get up and go with them to hear him, and I flipped like everybody else. It seemed that Jimmy had done most of his playing with his mother, a pianist, and his big band experience was limited. But we didn't care about his experience. All we wanted was that sound, that beat, and those precision notes in the right places, so that we could float out on the great and adventurous sea of expectancy with his pulse and foundation behind us.

We talked him into coming down to the hotel the next night to play a few things with us. He was a sensation, and that settled it. We had to have him, and he joined the band, although our bass man at the time was Billy Taylor, one of the ace foundation-and-beat men on the instrument. So there I was with two basses! It went along fine until we got to Boston, where we were playing the Southland Cafe. Right in the middle of a set, Billy Taylor packed up his bass and said, "I'm not going to stand up here next to that young boy playing all that bass and be embarrassed." He left the stand, left us with Jimmy Blanton, and went on out the front door.

Duke Ellington at Forest Park Highlands Amusement Park, St. Louis, 1940. Photograph by Arthur Witman. © Western Historical Manuscript Collection–St. Louis.

Eddie Randle also has a different story.[12]

    Back in those days, there was a lot of prejudice, and we had to find places for the musicians to stay. That's just the way it was. Rex [Stewart] and Lawrence Brown, I always looked out for them, and we were out together. . . . Blanton has played with me. He played with Pillars. You know, he played one-nighters with different ones. . . . Anyway, we went by the Deluxe. When Rex heard him play, Rex says, "Wait a minute! Wait a minute! Let me go call Duke." And he called Duke, and Duke got out of bed to come down there that night. But Rex, Brown and I, we were out on the town, and we happened to go by Jessie Johnson's, which had a night spot restaurant, and upstairs he had night hours. And now somebody else might call Duke, too, but Rex called Duke that night we were together and when I carried him in there, and he had him to come down. Then the next night, Jimmy Blanton was down at the Coronado Hotel in a white suit with Duke the first night! No rehearsal, just right there! He was that type of musician.

Walter Dixon was an employee of Jesse Johnson from time to time. Here he recounts his remembrances about the occasion.[13]

> So, Duke and them were in town. . . . and we were all in the Deluxe Restaurant. And his brother had an after-hours club upstairs over the restaurant called Club 49. . . . And he liked jazz; he was crazy about jazz. So Jesse Johnson owned the club. He rented the Club 49 to his brother Stump. . . . There was a bunch of us up there that night. They'd been in the restaurant; 'cause that's what we all did, tanked up in the restaurant, prepared ourselves. Then, we'd go upstairs and drink the alcohol.
>
> And so, Johnny Hodges had his saxophone and he had a damn quart of whiskey down in the bell, and you know [was] walkin' around playin'. . . . Fate was playin' the piano. . . . And Shorty Baker came through . . . and his brother Winfield, the trombone player, he was there. When Fate came in, he brought Jimmy Blanton with him. . . . Johnny said, "Walter . . . go down there and get Sweetpea [Billy Strayhorn]. . . . And he heard Jimmy playin' with Fate and said, "Oh, my God!" Well, see, Jimmy was doin' then what Slam Stewart started doin', [he] was singin' through the bass, right through the strings. . . . Sweetpea said, "Go down there and get Duke out of bed." I said, "Man, get on the phone and call." He said, "I don't want no phones, go down and tell him I said come up here."
>
> So, I went down there and I said, "Duke . . . Sweetpea says get up outta the bed and come down to the Club 49." Duke said, "Sheeit, you know I'm not getting' up outta my bed." So I said, "Sweetpea said for you to bring your ass up there." . . . Sweetpea told me not to say nothin', so I didn't. . . . Duke was still in his pajamas. It was in the fall; it hadn't got real cold yet, but it was cool enough for you to have a topcoat on if you didn't have sufficient clothes. So, Duke just put the topcoat over his pajamas and put on his shoes and socks and came on up there. And so Sweetpea says, "Duke, I want you to hear something." So Duke took a table and sat down. Johnny said, "You never heard nothin' like this in your life." . . . And so, Fate was still playin' and Sweetpea sat down on the bench beside him and they started playin' together. And Duke says, "What in the hell is this?" And Sweetpea looked around at him and winked his eye, you know, and Sweetpea says, "Do you know *Sophisticated Lady*?" He [Blanton] said, "Yes." He [Strayhorn] said, "Can you bow it?" He took out his bow and started playin' "Sophisticated Lady" and you might think I'm lyin', but [it] brought tears to Duke's eyes. He said, "I ain't heard nothin' like this in my life. . . . Walter, who is this boy?" I say, "His name is Jimmy Blanton." So, Fate was laughin', saying, "I know you never heard nothin' like this, Ed." (He called him Ed, you know, his name was Edward.) And Duke says, "Are you working?" He [Blanton] says, "Yes, I play with Fate." Duke said, "How much do you want for his contract? I'll buy it right now." He [Duke] gave him a hundred dollars for Jimmy Blanton's contract and that was it.

In addition to the stories above, we know that Ben Webster joined Duke's band in December 1939. Billy Strayhorn did not come fully into Ellington's orbit until February 1939. Were either Webster or Strayhorn traveling with the Ellington Band? An article in the *Indianapolis Recorder* has a description of Blanton with Ellington. "It was interesting to hear Johnny [Hodges] tell me how he found Jimmie Blanton in St. Louis and how when Jimmie plays Body and Soul—he plays more changes than any horn tooter."[14]

Blanton revolutionized jazz bass playing. According to the *New Grove Dictionary of Jazz*,[15] "he possessed great dexterity, roundness of tone, accurate intonation and an unprecedented sense of swing." He recorded the first fully realized solos on bass and changed the sound of the Ellington Orchestra, leading to Duke's greatest creative period as a composer. Blanton was also active in jam sessions at Minton's playhouse in New York during his tenure with Ellington. These sessions were pivotal in the development of the next style of jazz: bebop.

Apparently, Blanton was so consumed with music that he did not take care of himself. He contracted tuberculosis in 1941 and was left by the Ellington Band in Los Angeles at a sanatorium to recover. Bassist Milt Hinton recounts Blanton's last days in Los Angeles.

Duke Ellington's band was leaving California to come back east and Cab Calloway's band was goin' in the same nightclub, the ballroom that Duke Ellington left. And Ben Webster came over to me and said, "Look, the guy is pretty sick. He got sick and we have to leave him here," and what do you call it, in an asylum or a rest home. And he says, "Please go over and see him. And that's because he's very lonesome and sad. California, in those days, before commercial airlines was like bein' in Nairobi or some place. You're just way the hell away from everything and here he was twenty-two years old at the peak of his life, just joined Duke's band in '39 like, I guess this was about '41, and here he was, the band was leaving him there because he had gotten sick. And they put him in this rest home. So Ben Webster and I were good friends and I knew Blanton very well. I'd met him. And I said, "Sure!" So, we, every night from the, from the ballroom we were playing in, Cab Calloway had a radio show and he had a special spot for what he called the "Cab Jivers," four musicians out of his band, patterned them after Benny Goodman's. And there was Chu Berry, uh, Cozy Cole, Danny Barker, guitar and myself. And we had a spot in the show every night, in the radio show. And I would concoct some little blues, somethin' and dedicate it to Jimmy.

And then every other day, I would get a guy with a car and drive me out to this rest home to see him. And he was in this little cottage, a very clean, nice little cottage. But they're lonely. . . . There were no penicillin drugs or no sulfa drugs in those days, you know. And the only thing they did for tuberculosis was what they called a rest cure. Just get fresh air and sit there. Hell, this poor kid was sittin' there and all by himself, so very lonesome. . . . We would sit and talk and he would talk about the changes, and we'd discuss the changes and what we'd played that night. He was just more heartbroken than anything else. That's the thing that got me so worried. The mere fact that he was so heartbroken, you know, bein' twenty-one years old or twenty-two. And havin' that band leavin' him way out there and he didn't know anybody out there. And I felt so bad about it, I didn't have any idea what to do to, to help him, you know. And one of my friends in the band, Walter Thomas, "Foots" Thomas was a Christian Scientist, so I asked Foots would he come along with me and talk to him. And we would take some scriptures and read to him. Yeah, it was just too late, and he was just too far gone for us to be able to do any savin' the day I went out there, was the day he passed before his mother got there. Lee Young, Lester Young's brother, was out there. He was very helpful in going to see Blanton and being with him. He was a great, great artist and revolutionized bass playing, as far as I'm concerned.

Blanton never recovered and died on July 30, 1941.

Harlem Rhythm: Ralph Sutton and Miles Davis

Two nationally known St. Louis jazz musicians were born on opposite sides of the Mississippi River. One, Ralph Sutton, was born in Hamburg, Missouri, in 1922. The other, Miles Davis, was born in Alton, Illinois, in 1926. Both musicians were listening to the radio program *Harlem Rhythm* on radio station WIL. Sutton was enamored with the piano playing of Thomas "Fats" Waller on this show and became one of the foremost stride pianists of the second half of the twentieth century. The black instrumentalists and bands that played on the program attracted Miles Davis. Miles became a trend-setting trumpeter who changed the course of jazz four times.

Ralph Sutton: Stride Pianist[16]

Apparently, a phonograph was played regularly in Ralph Sutton's boyhood home, and he could hum tunes he heard at the age of two. At age nine, Sutton began piano lessons. At the same time, he began listening to *Harlem Rhythm* on WIL radio and fell in love with the music of pianist Fats Waller. While he was in high school, Sutton began working local dances and became the organist at his church.

Ralph enrolled in Northeast Missouri State College in Kirksville, but left in 1942 when he joined the Jack Teagarden Band. He was drafted into the army in 1943 and discharged in 1945. Returning home, Sutton soon found work playing piano at Roy Bowman's casino in East St. Louis. Sutton then joined guitarist Joe Schermer's trio at the Chase Hotel, remaining with the group until 1947. Leaving St. Louis, he moved to New York, appeared on a radio show, *This is Jazz*, and became the inter-mission pianist at Condon's and led groups there until 1956, when he moved to San Francisco to work with Bob Scobey.

Leaving Scobey in 1957, Sutton worked at the Hangover Club and other venues in San Francisco. Ralph began playing Dick Gibson's Colorado jazz parties in 1963 and moved to Colorado in 1965. He was a founding member of "The World's Greatest Jazz" Band in 1968. Sutton recorded piano duets with Jay McShann on a series of recordings called *The Last of the Whorehouse Piano Players* in 1978 and 1988[17] and continued to work all over the world until his death in the winter of 2001. Gaslight Records recorded Sutton twice in St. Louis in his later years at The Bistro in St. Louis in both a trio format and in piano duets with his sister Barbara.[18]

Miles Davis in St. Louis

There are six complete biographies of Miles Davis written in the English language. Clearly, Davis is one of the major mu-sicians of the twentieth century. This section will attempt to detail Miles's life and work in St. Louis until he left in 1944 to attend the Juilliard School of Music in New York. He was born in Alton, Illinois, and his family soon moved to an integrated neighborhood at 14th and Broadway in East St. Louis, behind his father's dental practice. Miles had a sister, Dorothy, and a brother, Vernon. Miles's father, Miles Dewey Davis, II, was a graduate of Lincoln University and the Northwestern University School of Dentistry. His mother was Cleota Henry Davis, and Miles thought his artistic side came from her. Living in East St. Louis, Miles heard stories about the 1917 Race Riot and these stories shaped his thinking.[19] He related the following in his autobiography.

> That's what the East St. Louis race riot in 1917 was supposed to be about: black workers replacing white workers in the packing houses. So, the white workers got mad and went on a rampage, killing all them black people. That same year black men were fighting World War I to help the United States save the world for democracy. They sent us to fight and die for them over there; killed us like nothing over here. And it's still like that today. Now, ain't that a bitch. Anyway, some of remembering that is in my personality comes out in the way I look at most white people. Not all, because there are some great white people. . . . Anyway, black people there who survived used to talk about it. When I was coming up in East St. Louis, black people never forgot what sick white people had done to them back in 1917.

Miles's father leaned toward the black nationalist and separatist politics of Marcus Garvey rather than the NAACP. This created one of many conflicts between his parents. Miles thought his attitude and race pride came from his father. Apparently, there were many conflicts in the Davis household and Miles's parents divorced in 1944. Because his father was part of the black bourgeoisie, Miles and his family were treated differently. Miles's childhood was typical of children in those days, but he soon heard some things that would shape him. His parents sent him to his grandfather's farm in Arkansas, where he heard music from Saturday night church services. "We'd be walking on these dark country roads at night and all of a sudden this music would seem to come out of nowhere, out of them spooky-looking trees that everybody said ghosts lived in."[20] At about the same age, Davis began listening to *Harlem Rhythm* on WIL that featured music by Louis Armstrong, Fats Waller, and other giants of black music. These two experiences pushed him in the direction of music. "When I got into music I went all the way into music; I didn't have no time after that for nothing else."[21] Miles Davis began taking private music lessons at the age of nine or ten.

Miles went to John Robinson Elementary School in East St. Louis. He was interested in sports and was apparently fairly headstrong as a child. The interest in sports began to fall away as he was drawn into music. He went to Crispus Attucks Ju-

Miles Davis (1926–1991)

Without a doubt, Miles Davis is the most significant jazz musician to come out of St. Louis. No other jazzman in the history of the music can lay claim to changing the course of the music more than once in his career. Miles did it four times. He was never satisfied with his music, changing the style and personnel when he became bored.

Miles was born in Alton, Illinois. His trumpet teacher was Elwood Buchanan, and his first professional experience began with the Eddie Randle Blue Devils in 1942. From all accounts, Miles was a painfully shy person, who used a gruff exterior to put a distance between him and the public. He was particularly difficult with journalists who tried to interview him as he was preparing to go on stage. Unfortunately, he has not gotten the credit he deserves among the general public in St. Louis because some people preferred to listen to what he said rather than what he played.

Miles Davis moved to New York in 1944 to attend the Juilliard School of Music and eventually ended up playing with Charlie Parker. His first recording as a leader[22] was with Parker playing tenor sax. Miles changed the course of jazz history the first time in 1949 with the album *Birth of the Cool*,[23] with arrangements by Gil Evans, Gerry Mulligan, John Lewis, and others. This style was known as the "cool style" and set the stage for the popular "West Coast Jazz" style of the 1950s. Miles changed the course of jazz a second time toward the blues and into the style called "hard bop," with the recording "Walkin'"[24] in 1954.

Following a triumphant performance of "'Round Midnight" at the 1955 Newport Jazz Festival,[25] Davis formed a quintet with John Coltrane on tenor sax, Red Garland on piano, Paul Chambers on bass, and Philly Joe Jones on drums. This group changed rhythm section playing with its very sophisticated interactions between the section and Miles's use of space in his music. Part of the sound of that group was derived from the early 1950s recordings of the Ahmad Jamal Trio.[26]

Miles began to leave hard bop orthodoxy and move into the use of modes (scales) with the recording of "Milestones,"[27] the first truly workable modal composition in jazz. It was played by the Miles Davis Sextet with John Coltrane and Cannonball Adderley. The classic album *Kind of Blue*[28] followed the album named *Milestones* in 1959 with Bill Evans on piano.[29] He also recorded three beautifully realized orchestral works, *Miles Ahead*, *Porgy and Bess*, and *Sketches of Spain*, as a soloist with the Gil Evans Orchestra during this period.[30]

By mid-1960, Coltrane, Adderley, and Evans had left Davis to begin successful careers on their own. Miles then worked for about two years with Hank Mobley on tenor sax and the Wynton Kelly, Paul Chambers, Jimmy Cobb rhythm section—his second great rhythm section. By late 1962, that rhythm section had left. Miles founded another quintet featuring a third great rhythm section. That rhythm section of Herbie Hancock (piano), Ron Carter (bass), and Tony Williams (drums) again changed the course of jazz history and revolutionized the role of the rhythm section with its highly interactive playing. The style that evolved from this group is called "free bop" and is the major mainstream style of today.

As Miles's groups played a piece, it became more abstract or faster with each performance. Some tunes became so abstract that only a few notes of the theme were sounded. The music that the Miles Davis Quintet made in the mid-1960s on records like *ESP, Miles Smiles*, and *Sorcerer* was some of the most adventurous rhythmically of the period.[31] By the time he recorded *Filles De Kilimanjaro*, Miles had begun to move toward the use of rock rhythms and electronic instruments, which became very overt in the *In A Silent Way* album (1968).[32] The album *Bitches Brew*[33] (1969) broke away from jazz rhythms into very freely improvised jazz-rock.

Following *Bitches Brew*, Miles led a series of bands that played wildly experimental electronic music until he retired in 1975, saying that he just could not hear the music anymore. He returned to performing in 1981, leaving his record company of over thirty years, Columbia, for Warner Bros. Miles continued to tour until his death, playing some classic Gil Evans scores directed by Quincy Jones at the Montreux Jazz Festival in July of 1991. He died on September 28 that same year.

nior High. While he was twelve or thirteen, Miles went to a Boy Scout camp and got the job of playing "Taps" and "Reveille." While at Attucks, he began taking lessons with Elwood Buchanan.[34]

> Oh, he's just a natural. He just had it. That's all I can say. . . . See, a lot of the people wanted to . . . play music, but they didn't have it. You got to have it, just like you become a outstandin' architect, that's just in you. You know you get some special training but if you don't have that talent you don't get anywhere, you know what I mean sir.

Walter Lathan, long-time music teacher in Webster Groves, remembered a visit to Attucks.[35]

> So, on my way from Cairo to St. Louis for the weekend, I stopped by the junior high school in East St. Louis. A good friend of mine, an alumni of the University of Illinois, Ellwood Buchanan, taught instrumental music there. So I sat in on his rehearsal. After he got through, he said, "I want you to hear a little fellow play." So he calls this fellow, and he says, "Go get your trumpet, I want you to play for Mr. Lathan." So this little fellow, junior high school age and small in size, went and got his trumpet. And he put his trumpet up to his mouth, put the mute in there, and played the trumpet solo to "Tuxedo Junction," by Erskine Hawkins. Didn't miss a note. I said, "Who is this?" He said, "This is Miles Davis." That's when I first met Miles.

Davis continued under Buchanan when he graduated to Lincoln High School. Buchanan taught "the heavy music," the classics and marches.[36] Davis liked Harry James's tone and vibrato, but Buchanan told him to play with a straight tone because he would soon get old and shake. Buchanan said of this episode, "Oh, yeah, that's my expression. You know, and to play the true tones. Just like some people sing and have a [makes whinnying sound], you know when they have that, well, see that doesn't sound good. You know what I mean."[37] Later in his high school career, Davis also studied with Joseph Gustat of the St. Louis Symphony, who recommended the Heim mouthpiece to him. He used that mouthpiece for the rest of his career.

High school bands enter contests, and the Lincoln High School band was no different. There are two views as to how Miles fared in these contests. First, from his father, "In high school competitions, he was always the best but the blue-eyed boys always won first and second prizes. Miles had always to settle for third. The officials, Miles and everybody else knew he should have had first prize. You can't treat a kid like that and tell him to come out and say the water wasn't dirty."[38] Buchanan tells a different story about how his star pupil faired in a letter to David Breskin. "He was one of the best musicians I ever taught in instrumental music. He received all first awards with my band groups that competed in the Illinois State High School Music Association contests."[39]

When Miles was playing in Carbondale with the Lincoln band, he met Clark Terry for the first time. Clark was working in Carbondale with the Benny Reed Band at the time.

> So there was an interscholastic, May-Day sports event in Southern Illinois, and Miles' school came down to participate, and each school brought their athletic team and the band. So Miles' band came down, under Buchanan's leadership, and it just so happened that Benny Reed's band . . . had been hired to play in the pavilion in the park for the kids that day, you know. And while we were playing, this little timid kid comes up and he asks me [imitating Miles with softened, timid voice], "Hey mister, show me, tell me about such a thing," and of course I was very young, and ambitious in those days, and was very much interested in young ladies, and then there were so many of those fine, little ladies around from all the high schools, and I was like a one-eyed cat looking in the seafood store. So I said to him, "Man, I don't wanna talk about no music right now. I wanna look at these pretty little girls." So, he says, "OK." So I sort of fluffed him off.
> And about a year or so later, there was a club on Cardinal, I think it was, just off of Olive Street—the Elks Club. . . . Well, Eddie Randle's band was playing up there, and I was falling by to sit in on the session, and I was climbing this long flight of stairs, I heard this horn, which I hadn't heard before, you know. He was wailing away. And I hurriedly got to the top and walked in, and

looked to see this same little timid character with his leg crossed, and he was blasting away. So I said, "Hey, man aren't you the . . ." and he said, "Yeah, I'm the guy you fluffed off in Carbondale." And we got a big laugh about it. We often laughed about that. But at the particular time, he wanted to talk about trumpet; I wasn't interested in it.

When World War II broke out, opportunities opened for musicians who were draft eligible. In 1942, Miles started playing in a little group with pianist "Duke" Brooks and drummer Nick Haywood at Huff's Beer Garden, social club dances, and church affairs. He also became friends with trumpeter Bobby Danzig, known to St. Louis musicians as Bobby Danzie.[40]

> Miles and I worked with Eddie [Randle] when I was in high school . . . Eddie had a group that was really worth joining as far as things was happenin' in that era and a lot of the things that they were doing would sound good now.
> I never was a learned musician, but Miles and I . . . came up together and his concept and mine was similar anyway. It wasn't a copy thing, it was just that we felt music somewhat alike and I thought I always had a good sound on trumpet, man, and I don't know why, but everybody would think so.
> Miles and I used to go out on the [*garbled*] and practice all day long, and he'd get an idea and he's call me on the telephone so I could hear his and he'd play something and . . . I'd call him up, you know and play it over the telephone.

According to Danzig, he and Miles went all along Olive Street to find clubs to play in. The best rhythm sections were in the white clubs, so the two young musicians went in through the back door. Danzig was born in 1926 in Arkansas. His parents moved to Venice, Illinois, when he was five, eventually settling there. According to Miles Davis, Danzig was also an expert pickpocket.[41]

Apparently, Miles soaked up musical knowledge whenever and wherever he could. Vertna Saunders was playing with Buggs Roberts at the West End Waiters Club and Miles came in each night.[42]

> So Miles Davis would stand right by that closest table, between the table and the bandstand really and look over my shoulder at the music because Buggs Roberts arranged everything. He didn't play anything by head as they call it. He had music for everything. If it was "Mary Had a Little Lamb," he had it written. . . . Miles used to stand behind me every night or anytime he was off and he would always say, "I been waiting for you to miss a note. You never miss a note do you?" (Laughter) I said, "He's got them down there for you to play," and he just laughed.

Miles was also under the spell of trumpeter Levi Madison. Clark Terry believed that Madison played the prettiest trumpet he had ever heard.[43] Madison apparently laughed all the time and no one knew what he was laughing at. He later was institutionalized.[44]

According to Eddie Randle, Miles never forgot anything.[45] Miles also learned and remembered lessons on the job.[46]

> When I was about fifteen, a drummer I was playing a number with at the Castle Ballroom in Saint Louis—we had a ten-piece band, three trumpets, four saxophones, you know—and he asked me, "Little Davis, why don't you play what you played last night?" I said, "What, what do you mean?" He said, "You don't know what it is?" I said, "No, what is it?" He said, "You were playing something coming out of the middle of the tune, and play it again." I said, "I don't know what I played. He said, "If you don't know what you're playing, then you ain't doing nothing."
> Well that hit me. Like bammm. So I went and got every thing, every book that I could get. To learn about theory. To this day, I know what he's talking about. I know what note he was talking about.

When Miles was seventeen, he was urged by either Buchanan or his girlfriend, Irene Birth (mother of his first child, Cheryl), to audition for Eddie Randle's St. Louis Blue Devils in 1943.[47]

Eddie Randle's Rhumboogie Orchestra, Rhumboogie Club, St. Louis, 1944. Photographer unidentified. Miles Davis at right end of trumpet section. Back row, left to right: Unidentified (drums), Tommy Dean (piano), Irvin "Broz" Woods (trumpet), Davis. Front row, left to right: Unidentified (tenor sax), Unidentified (alto sax), Walter Martin (alto sax), Unidentified (tenor sax). Standing: Eddie Randle (trumpet/leader). © Frank Driggs Collection.

Miles got his start between Buchanan and I. Miles had a beautiful sound. When I hired Miles, there was another fella that had a lot of experience looking for a job. So when I hired Miles, most of the guys says, "Why are you hiring that kid for? You can hire this guy here!" I forget his name now, but he taught school, taught music somewhere out West, and he's dead though now. And I says to him, I says, "The sky's the limit for this kid!" I didn't know he was going as far as he went [laughs]! But this other guy was just a musician like me. I says, "He's a good musician," I says, "but I can see this fellow needs a chance." So I hired Miles. So one day this guy comes back to St. Louis to visit his family, and he called me up, and he says, "You know, I kind of feel hard at you for hiring that kid and not hiring me." He says, "But you knew what you were doing. The sky's the limit for that youngster!" I says, "Well, I couldn't tell how far he was going, but I could tell he needed a chance."

Fella by the name of Jimmy Carew had this club, Rhumboogie, and it was sponsored by Joe Louis. Joe Louis did all he could to help a whole lot of fellas. And of course this was during the war; this is where Miles worked with me, at the club Rhumboogie. It was on Cardinal, right off of Olive Street. And he used to bring shows in, you know. That was during the war. It was during World War II. . . . That's where they used to have these fine jam sessions.

They both were playing with me at the same time, and Bobby [Danzig] was a fine musician also. Miles was fine. I remember once we had what the guys down here call a jam session. And then they brought Howard McGee down. Miles and Howard tied up. Miles didn't need any drum. He was so young; he was so scared his knees was making the noise [laughs]. Boy, did I always laugh about that [laughs]. Miles was eating him up all the way, but he was scared, you know.

Anyway, Miles showed promise in all the ways of going to be a good musician, but he was always a little shy. He wasn't an outgoing person like Clark Terry. In fact, there was a lady that came by here to ask me questions about him, and I told her—I was real busy as I was today, and she didn't stay long. Right away she says, "They tell me Miles doesn't like people." And that was an insult to me. And I said right away, "He doesn't develop his sound for hogs and pigs and cows. He develops his sound for people. He likes people. He's different. I skin 'em back when I smile, but when Miles was with me, when he was happy, I could tell from his eyes. We all smile different; we all are different. I wouldn't say that he doesn't like people. Then I got busy and pretty soon she left. I didn't get to finish the interview.

Miles stayed with Randle until 1944, eventually becoming the music director. Well-known musicians such as Benny Carter and Roy Eldridge came to hear the St. Louis Blue Devils. Kenny Dorham came all the way from Austin, Texas, to hear the band while he was still in high school.[48] Sonny Stitt came through with Tiny Bradshaw's band and was so impressed with Miles that he talked Bradshaw into offering Miles a job. His mother would not let him go. He got other offers from Illinois Jacquet and from A. J. Suliman, manager of the McKinney's Cotton Pickers.[49]

When he graduated from high school, Davis played a stint in Springfield, Illinois, with Adam Lambert's Six Brown Cats. When he returned, the Billy Eckstine Band had been transferred from the Plantation Club to the Riviera (more on this engagement later), and Miles auditioned as a replacement for trumpeter Buddy Anderson, who had contracted tuberculosis. Both Dizzy Gillespie and Charlie Parker were playing in the band at the time. Miles recounted in *Downbeat*, "This guy runs up to me and says, 'Kid, do you have a union card?' It was Dizzy. I didn't even know him. I said, 'Sure.' 'We need a trumpet player. Come on.' I wanted to hear him; I could always read, so I got on the bandstand and started playing. I couldn't read from listening to Diz and Bird."[50] Davis played out the remainder of the engagement at the Riviera. When the band went on to Chicago, Marion Hazel came in on trumpet in Miles's place.[51]

Two jarring notes about this engagement complicate the picture of the young Miles Davis in St. Louis. Billy Eckstine remembered in a *Melody Maker* interview, "When I first heard Miles, I let him sit in so as to not hurt his feelings; but he sounded terrible; he couldn't play at all."[52] Bobby Danzig recounted that the musicians around St. Louis and the Eckstine band laughed at Miles.[53] How can these observations be reconciled? Eckstine's description of Miles playing certainly fits his playing on his first recordings with Charlie Parker ("Now's the Time" and "Billie's Bounce" on November 26, 1945).[54] There seem to be two possibilities: (1) all of the people in St. Louis are looking back on Miles with rose-colored glasses; or, (2) Miles's shyness prevented him from performing at his top level at crucial periods in his early career.

Another part of Miles's character was respect for his father. In an interview with Ben Sidran, he recounted the time he decided to leave Juilliard and follow Charlie Parker.[55]

But I found that I could go my own way. I said to my friend Freddie Webster, I said, "Freddie, I'm going back to St. Louis," and he was one of those who said, "Man, you know if you go to St. Louis, back to St. Louis and them hooges and crackers there, you're going to get mad and blah blah blah . . . you know, you might get killed." So I said, "No, I have to go tell my father that I'm gonna leave Juilliard." He said, "Why don't you call him up?" I said, "Uh uh, not my father. I can't call him up and say I'm going with Bird and they do this and Dizzy is this."

What can we learn about Miles Davis's childhood and early musical experiences in St. Louis from the data that is available in public sources, from those musicians who witnessed his growth, and from his own words?

- It is apparent that from an early age Miles was obsessed with music. Single-minded obsessions can cause problems in other parts of one's persona.

Eddie Randle Playing Harmon Muted Trumpet with the Stem Removed, location unknown, c. 1946. Photographer unidentified. Copy photograph and photo restoration by Dennis Owsley. Courtesy of the Randle Family.

- Miles was shy and did not like people bothering him when he was not performing. This shyness probably led him to erect walls between him and the public, even though he was a very public performer. He especially did not want journalists or other people bothering him just as he was about to go on stage.
- In his early performing years, it is possible that Miles could be so overcome by performance anxieties that his talent would desert him at crucial periods.
- Miles never forgot anything and so the smallest slight could affect him for years.
- He had great respect for his father, who he said gave him his desire to succeed.
- In his career away from St. Louis, Miles soon became bored with a musical style and would have to change his working methods every three or four years. Like his band mate, John Coltrane, he was never satisfied with anything he had accomplished.
- The use of mutes was common among St. Louis trumpeters, including the Harmon mute that was introduced to St. Louis by Tommy Ladnier in 1921. Miles is credited with popularizing the sound of the Harmon mute with the stem removed, but the picture of Eddie Randle taken around 1946 shows that this technique was in use in St. Louis before Miles used it on recordings in the 1950s.

The seeds for all his personal and musical traits are found in his early years in St. Louis. See the sidebar for the remainder of his long and productive career.

The St. Louis Blue Devils in the 1940s

Eddie Randle's St. Louis Blue Devils Band continued as the incubator for many St. Louis musicians who went on to national and international careers. A partial list of his musicians includes trumpeters Clifford King, Vertna Saunders, Sykes Smith, Willie Moore, Bob Johnson, "Sleepy" Tomlin, Charles Young, "Bruz" Woods, Miles Davis, and Bobby Danzig. Some of the reed players who worked with Randle during this period include Eugene Porter, Clyde Higgins, Edgar Hayes, Grady Rice, Jimmy Forrest, and Charles Pillars. Ernie Wilkins, Cecil Thornton, and in the 1950s, Oliver Nelson played saxophone and arranged. Robert "Bunky" Parker and Tommy Dean were pianists who both played and arranged for the band. George Brazier and Raymond Eldridge, Sr., played bass, with Jesse Brazier and Fred "Horsecollar" Lee playing drums. Jimmy Blanton played bass occasionally as a substitute, as did alto saxophonist Tab Smith. Trombonist Buster Scott also arranged. In the late 1950s, saxophonist Willie Akins played in the band.[56] Dean, originally from Texas, went on to a bandleading career in St. Louis and Chicago in the late 1940s through the late 1950s. He used St. Louis saxophonist Chris Woods, and others from the Randle band on some of his early recordings.[57]

After the band spent part of the summer season at Sodus Point, New York, in 1941, the onset of World War II brought the band back into a more or less permanent residency in St. Louis. They had extended engagements at the Club Rhumboogie, the Castle Ballroom, and the Club 400.[58] A private recording of the band was made in October 1941 which included the following band personnel:[59] Eddie Randle (trumpet and vocal on "Hey Little Girl"); Willie Moore and Robert Johnson (trumpet); Eugene Porter and Edgar Hayes (alto sax, clarinet); Grady Rice (tenor sax, clarinet); Tommy Dean (piano); Raymond Eldridge, Sr. (bass); Fred Lee (drums); and Movel Bohlen (vocal). The tunes were "Scammon Boogie" (the band's theme song), "Cozy Corner Boogie," "Refugee," "Vandeventer Junction," "A Buzzy Clarinet," "Someone to Watch Over Me" (Bohlen, vocal), "Try When High," "Out of Nowhere" (Bohlen, vocal), "So Long," and "Hey Little Girl." Listening to this music, it is apparent that the Blue Devils were a band that could play a wide variety of music and were not just a blues band, as some writers had suggested.

During the late 1930s and early 1940s, Eddie Randle was also treasurer of the black musicians union, first as a subsidiary to Local 2 and then as Local 197. He stopped playing music full time in 1943 and worked at a munitions plant in St. Louis, rising to foreman. Randle eventually became a full-time funeral director but continued to lead bands and play until 1964. Walter Lathan remembers playing with the Blue Devils,[60] "Eddie had an excellent band, six or seven pieces. We would leave on Friday and play a town in Illinois Friday night and another little town in Illinois Saturday night and another one Sunday night. Then we would come back." Eddie Randle continued his second career as a funeral director until his death in 1997.

The Continuing Saga of the Jeter-Pillars Band

The Jeter-Pillars Band continued its long engagement at the Plantation Club until 1944, when they moved to the Club Riviera for a year. In 1942, the band played on the *Fitch Bandwagon* radio show. Hayes Pillars recounted this period and an offer that the band had from Joe Glaser.[61]

Ernie Wilkins (1922–1999)

Ernie Wilkins was born in St. Louis. He started music lessons on violin when he was about ten years old. His family had jazz recordings of bands like Fletcher Henderson, McKinney's Cotton Pickers, and others. Ernie was a friend of saxophonist Jimmy Forrest and started saxophone in high school, learning the rudiments of the instrument from him. He became fascinated by the big band arrangements he heard on the radio with the Lunceford Band. Later, he heard remote broadcasts that featured Duke Ellington, Earl Hines, and Count Basie. Ernie became a professional musician after he graduated from high school.

Wilkins joined Eddie Randle's Blue Devils around 1938. He remained with Randle, writing arrangements and playing saxophone until he went to Wilberforce University in Ohio on a music scholarship. Ernie remained there until June 1942, when he joined the Navy as a musician. He was stationed at the Great Lakes Naval Station in Chicago and played in the band with Clark Terry, Al Grey, and other well-known musicians. After the war, he returned to St. Louis and worked around town until he got a call to join Earl Hines in 1947. Later that year, he joined George Hudson's band and stayed until Hudson stopped touring. He is the composer of Hudson's theme, "Applejack Boogie."

Clark Terry was also instrumental in getting Ernie Wilkins into the Basie Band in 1951. Ernie's 1954 arrangement of "Every Day I Have the Blues," featuring Joe Williams, put the Basie Band back into the public eye. It never left that position until Basie's death. Following his playing stint with Basie, he continued to arrange for the band and worked as a freelance arranger for many others, such as Oscar Peterson, Sarah Vaughan, Cannonball Adderley, and Ray Charles. He moved to Denmark in the late 1970s. Ernie led a band there called the Almost Big Band, featuring the best of Scandinavian and expatriate American musicians. He continued his writing and band-leading career until his death on June 5, 1999, from complications of a stroke.

> In 1942, we had a chance to be on *Fitch Bandwagon*. We actually won it outright, but we had to share it with a white band. The man would give us a little raise so we would add on a man in the band. We were just dedicated. We never did make the money we should have made; it was a form of exploitation. Joe Glaser offered us a job, but the guys who ran the place [the Plantation]; they didn't want to let us out. It was one of the best jobs in the country for a band to have at that time. It was the depression. The only other one was Earl Hines at the Grand Terrace. We didn't have any trouble getting the very best musicians, because we paid $40-45 a week and that was very good money.

The Jeter-Pillars Orchestra opened the Club Riviera in June 1944[62] and stayed until January of 1945, with an exception of two weeks at the Plantation for the Billy Eckstine Band (see below). The group moved on to Chicago for a ten-week stay at the Rhumboogie Club in Chicago. They left the Rhumboogie as part of a package show with Louis Jordan. This show played New York's Apollo Theater for a week following Good Friday in 1945. This show continued in theaters in Washington, D.C., Detroit, and Chicago.[63] Returning to St. Louis in May 1945, the band played at the Plantation until September, when they left St. Louis for a USO tour with a show called *Red Hot and Blues*. The show first toured New England military bases for three months, and then toured the Philippines and Japan for six months. According to John Cotter, the band personnel were Walter "Crack" Stanley, Sam Massenburg, and Wimpy Mosby (trumpets); Warren Scott, Nat Story, and Edward Weston (trombones); Hayes Pillars, Charles Pillars, James Jeter, James Taylor, and Louis Transue (saxophones); John Cotter (piano); Carl Pruitt (bass); and "Razz" Mitchell (drums). This was the largest USO show in the Pacific at the time.[64]

The orchestra returned to St. Louis in June 1946 to reorganize with all local musicians for an engagement at the Club Riviera. This engagement continued until November 1946, when they left for an engagement at the Apollo. The band played one more engagement at the Apollo in June 1947.

Eddie Johnson Winds Down His Career as a Bandleader

Eddie Johnson continued to lead his bands in St. Louis during the 1940s until the Plantation Club closed in 1947. He also had a gift shop at 1008 North Vandeventer during this period.[65] The final engagement of the club featured Johnson with the Ink Spots. Johnson then moved to New York and remained an entrepreneur.

> Then I went on to New York for two or three years. At first I couldn't get no work because nobody had ever heard of me much in New York. So what I'd done, I opened me a booking office in the Apollo Theatre building and advertised [when] people would call in for bands and singers. They'd call in, and I'd play the job myself, and I stayed there until I came back to St. Louis to play an engagement for two weeks, and it lasted six months. And I've been [in St. Louis] ever since.
>
> I went to New York University and took up theory and music while I was there. I had a lot of time on my hands before I could go to work. You had to be in that town six months before the union would let you go out and take some gigs. That's one reason I opened my own booking office. Plus, I got a job in a hospital for two or three months. Most of the work I got there, people would call in. They didn't exactly want me; they wanted some music for a part of the show. And that's where I got the work in the New York area.

Johnson returned to St. Louis in 1950 and continued working as a musician. See Chapter 5 on the rest of his career.

Billy Eckstine's Band Visits St. Louis

The Plantation Club was a whites-only club that featured black musicians and entertainers in St. Louis since 1931. The Jeter-Pillars Band backed many acts in the years 1933–1944 before they moved to the Club Riviera, a club for blacks with a similar entertainment policy. In fact, groups playing at the Plantation might be found playing at the Riviera a few months later. The Plantation Club floorshows featured such well-known national acts as the Mills Brothers, the Step Brothers, the Ink Spots, the Deep River Boys, Cook and Brown, the Nicholas Brothers, the Luis Russell Band, the Fletcher Henderson Orchestra, the International Sweethearts of Rhythm, the Noble Sissle Orchestra, and the Tiny Bradshaw Band.[66] One of these engagements featured the Billy Eckstine Orchestra in July 1944.[67] Eckstine opened on Saturday, July 7, for a three-week run. This all-star band had such forward thinking and playing musicians as alto saxophonists Charlie Parker and trumpeter Dizzy Gillespie. The advertisement in the *Globe-Democrat* featured Eckstine, vocalist Sarah Vaughan, and Gillespie. By Monday, July 16, the ad for the Plantation did not mention Eckstine, and by July 18, the Jeter-Pillars Orchestra was the featured band with the same floorshow.[68] Dizzy recalled that the band ran into trouble with the management of the club.[69]

> I was playing with Billy Eckstine, and a cat took me to the basement one time in St. Louis, at the Plantation Club, and says, "I want you to turn on the light, now. When I give you the signal, turn on the light." He say, "O.K., turn it on!" He took out his gun and a big rat ran across the basement, "Pow!" He shot that rat dead.

The Plantation club in St. Louis was a white club. They fired Billy Eckstine's band because we came in through the front door and they wanted us to come in through the back. We just walked in with our horns, in front. And the gangsters—St. Louis was a stronghold for gangsterism—said, "Them guys got to go."

The drummer Art Blakey joined the band in St. Louis. His story adds more to the lore surrounding this engagement.[70]

Billy Eckstine was forming his band and Dizzy said to him, "There's a guy in Boston; this guy can play." . . . But he sent for me, and I came down to St. Louis, and there I met Bird, Billy, Sarah, Dizzy, the rest. We were playing in a prejudiced club: Billie Holiday, Billy Eckstine, Bird, Dizzy. The man told us all to come in through the back door that night and these damn fools, they got together and they came in the front door. The guy is wigged. They all come in the front door havin' a ball. He said, "I don't want you to fraternize with the customers." When Charlie got to the intermission, they all sat at the tables and the guy was about to wig. He told someone, "You gotta get this band the hell outta here." The guys were carrying on something fierce despite the fact that gangsters were walking around with big guns up on their hips. They didn't scare Bird or anyone. Tadd Dameron was drinking a glass of water. Out of one of the beautiful glasses they had to serve the customers. Bird walked over to him saying, "Did you drink out of this, Tadd?" Tadd says "Yeah." Bam! He smashes it, "It's contaminated. Did you drink out of this one?" "Yeah," Tadd says. Bam! "It's contaminated." He broke about two dozen glasses. A guy was glaring at Bird; he just looked back coolly. "What do you want? Am I bothering you?" Bird asks him. "Are you crazy?" the guy asks. "Well, if you want to call me crazy," Bird replies. Then once again he turns to Tadd, "Did you drink out of this glass?" Bam! "It's contaminated." They put us out. They put Jeter-Pillows [sic] in our place at the Plantation and they sent us to the Riviera, which was a colored club.

The Eckstine Band went to the Riviera, and the Jeter-Pillars Orchestra replaced them for the remainder of the run in St. Louis. That was when Miles Davis played with the band. The above stories have become part of jazz lore, but are they part of jazz history? Hayes Pillars told a different story about this event.[71]

Eckstine came in here to work the Plantation, he had Charlie Parker, Sonny Stitt, he had Lucky Thompson, Dizzy, Art Blakey, Tadd Dameron. Tadd made his first big band arrangement for us, made it for us in Cincy and it was all messed up. But I paid him, and he never forgot it. And he gave us a lot of scores. The band played and it was a failure with this great array of musicians. I called him and said, "Billy, why don't you get some stocks, and open with them, play one or two stocks just the way they're written and then close with one of the numbers your band likes to play. In this way you'll be able to compromise and, hold an audience." He didn't do it' and he stayed there one week, they bought his contract out. We were playing the Club Riviera and they switched us and put us back in the Plantation and put him in the Riviera.

What is the truth about the Eckstine Band in St. Louis? The *St. Louis Globe-Democrat*[72] carried advertisements for the Eckstine Band at the Plantation from July 7 through July 14 (Saturday). On July 15 and 16, no mention of the band was made in the advertisements. By July 17, the Plantation advertisement shows the Jeter-Pillars Orchestra backing the same floor-show, which ran until July 28. The *Argus* (a weekly) began carrying advertisements on July 21 for Eckstine at the Club Riviera.[73] On that date, the "Town Chatter" column by J. von Chapman stated that the Eckstine band had opened at the Riviera the Saturday night before the paper's date. The *Argus, Globe-Democrat*, and *Post-Dispatch* give no reason for the change during this period and for the first two weeks in August. Did the Eckstine Band come in through the front door, cause a ruckus, and get sent to the Riviera for those racial infractions, or were they sent there because of the uncompromising music that they played? We will never know because all of the principals are gone.

The George Hudson Orchestra

Several factors led to the formation of the George Hudson Orchestra. In 1942, the Hudson Orchestra made its debut at the "Y" Circus, an annual event to raise money for the Pine Street YMCA. Although it was not strictly a jazz event, the "Y" Circus presented many of the area's black musicians in the band led by such people as Buggs Roberts and John Cotter. The first half of the program featured local talent, with the second half having national talent. In its heyday, the "Y" Circus ran for six days at Kiel Auditorium. The "Y" Circus ran annually from 1935–1955.

Hudson had been in the trumpet section of the Alphonso Trent band for a year before it broke up. He then moved on to Oklahoma City, where he joined the Oklahoma Blue Devils, who took him to Kansas City. In Kansas City, he played with several bands, including that of Benny Moten. Hudson recalled how he got to St. Louis, along with a few members of the Moten Band.[74]

> And they found out I was over there and they . . . asked me if I would I come over there. They told me they had a regular job so that's good ya know. Salary was beautiful, $25 a week. So I said, "Yeah I'll come over." Sent me the ticket, two tickets. So I went and came over here. And after that, . . . Pillars sent for Walter Page. He sent for Dan Minor, the trombone player. He sent for him. He came over.

When Count Basie left Kansas City, Page, Jo Jones, and Minor left the Jeter-Pillars Band and began touring with Basie. Hudson stayed in St. Louis. He then moved to the Dewey Jackson Band in 1938.[75]

> When I asked him give me some more money. Not that he wouldn't but the boss . . . he wouldn't give us, give the band a raise. . . . We doin' three shows a night. You're kiddin'. And I'm playin most of the first. You've got to be kidding. I got to have some more money. So a trumpet [player] lives around here, his name is Dewey Jackson and he had a band so he came by my house one night after I got through playin' the Plantation . . . and he asked me come go up on the river with him. Where I really wanted to go cause . . . he told he was gonna give me fifty dollars a week on that boat and all my food and everything, room and board. Yeah, so I said, "good you got a horn player." So that's how I got out of Pillars band. Cause I normally wouldn't have left I would have stayed with Pillars. I . . . had a child comin' on and havin' larger quarters to live in.

By 1942, Hudson wanted to start his own band. One of the musicians he wanted was pianist Robert "Bunky" Parker. Along with Singleton Palmer (bass) and Earl Martin (drums), Parker led one of the tightest rhythm sections in St. Louis.[76]

> I wanted Singleton, Earl Martin, and we call him Bunky I didn't call him Parker I call him Bunky. And I wanted him to start my band. And I'll never forget the words that Bunky said to me. He came by the union one night and I was in there. He said, "Skinny (that's just way he said) Skinny, do you really think you can start a 16 piece band in this town and make it go?" I said "yeah" and you know, "Dewey got the town sewed up how you gonna get any work?" I said, "I can do it." And so about 3 or 4 days later he came by and said "Skinny", I said "What." "No we gonna stay with Dewey." I said "Nothing wrong with that; do what you wanna do, I'm gonna do what I wanna do, and so I did.

The original George Hudson Band consisted of Leon "Foots" Goodson, Clifford Batchman, Irvin Williams, Lloyd Smith, and Eugene Porter (reeds); Walter "Crack" Stanley, George Hudson, Cyrus Stoner, and Sykes Smith (trumpets); Robert Horne and Len Bowden (trombone); Julius Wright (piano); James Underwood (bass); and Charles Carter, Sr. (drums).[77] His band began working at Tunetown and had an engagement at the Comet Theater at Sarah and Finney with the Mills Brothers. The band became quite popular in St. Louis, also playing at the American Negro Music Festival held in St. Louis at Sportsman's Park in July 1944. A wide variety of music was presented at this meeting, including a performance by violinist Eddie South, accompanied by pianist Billy Taylor.

By 1944, the band had been both decimated by the draft and hired to replace the Jeter-Pillars Orchestra at the Plantation. Hudson recalled working there and at the Riviera.

> I enjoyed working at the Plantation. The only thing about it just wasn't a lot of money involved. But we had all the best of working conditions to work under but the finance wasn't as good. But you had a good year 'round job and the place was air-conditioned during that time. And you always had a good crowd. Both clubs were air-conditioned and you worked with the best performers. . . . But the Plantation and the Riviera, you couldn't have worked at a better place.
>
> That club [Plantation] was owned by some of the boys; you know what I'm sayin'? Do your job and they were so nice to you during the holidays with nice presents and things. Beautiful. It was just enjoyable to work. No problems with the owners at all. See I did all the emceeing at the shows that actually came in. And I would emcee then. That's about all I can tell you. Beautiful to me and to all the guys.

Apparently, performers at the two clubs spread the word about the quality of the Hudson Orchestra. When World War II ended, Hudson was able to get the cream of the crop of the St. Louis musicians, many of them from the Great Lakes Naval Band in Chicago.

> That's how I got great musicians, when they all got out of the navy. They came runnin' and one at a time, I took them; the ones that I knew that could really hump. So, we had some good musicians.[78]
>
> So that's the way I got out of there but I had some good boys. And they wanted to play and everything so it was just beautiful. I didn't have to do a lot of discipline because there's just certain things I'm not gonna put up with anyway. . . . See, they had been in that navy and had that and they had been disciplined, well disciplined, and they were crazy about the band. We'd play all night from 9 till 4 in the morning and get up, up the next day. Two o'clock rehearsal. And we had to rehearse. If I had new music we'd rehearse. Well, the guys did the discipline.[79]

After the war, the Hudson Band employed the following: Clark Terry, Paul Guydner Campbell, Cy Stoner, and Edwin Bachman (trumpet); John "Bones" Orange and Robert Horne (trombone); William "Weasel" Parker, Thomas Starks, Clifford Batchman, Charles Pillars, and William Rollins (reeds); Robert Parker (piano); Singleton Palmer (bass); and Earl Martin (drums). Terry fondly remembered the George Hudson Band. It was his first job with a major civilian band.

> George I usually refer to as my "musical daddy," my "jazz daddy," 'cause that was really the first band that I really get into, became an integral part of the band. George elected me to rehearse the band, played lead trumpet and played solos, so I was chief, cook and bottle washer in the George Hudson Band. And my sort-of a copartner, in the woodwind section, was Weasel, Willie Parker.

The Hudson Band played a year at the Plantation and went on the road to New York, based on his reputation from the Plantation. His band played the Savoy Ballroom and the Apollo Theater in New York. At the Apollo, Weasel Parker had a solo on "Body and Soul."[80]

> I got a little short guy. Guy's name was Willie Parker. . . . We did an arrangement of "Body and Soul" on the stage of the Apollo. And Willie did the solo on the tenor. And we had a brass chorus on the trumpets. And they stood up and played every note from memory before Willie would come back in and finish the arrangement. Now, I'll tell you who was the star on the show. It was Illinois Jacquet, when he had his band, small band. That boy Willie ran Jacquet off the stage.
>
> And it got to the point that after the first show at the Apollo, Schiffman [the manager] comes back and sit down . . . and says either cut . . . you did this show too long or uh I don't like that tune that you're playing and blah blah blah. That's where he and I had a big run in. People were raisin' so much Cain in the theatre standin' all up in the seats and everything when Parker got

George Hudson (1910–1996)

George Hudson was born in Stonewall, Mississippi, and spent his early years in Birmingham, Alabama. He was inducted into the Alabama Jazz Hall of Fame in 1982. He began playing piano at age six and was introduced to trumpet at an early age. His family moved to Pittsburgh, where he attended Westinghouse High School and the Pittsburgh Musical Institute. After freelancing around Pittsburgh, he joined Zack White's Chocolate Beau Brummels, a well-known territory band. Hudson joined the Alphonso Trent Band in 1930. The Trent Band was the forerunner of the Jeter-Pillars Orchestra in St. Louis and had many entertaining features later copied by the Jimmy Lunceford Orchestra.

Leaving the Trent Band in Little Rock, Arkansas, Hudson traveled first to Oklahoma City and then to Kansas City, working with the Oklahoma Blue Devils and then Benny Moten. He came to St. Louis to work with the Jeter-Pillars Orchestra in 1934 as the lead trumpeter. The Jeter-Pillars Orchestra recorded four titles for Decca in 1937. In 1938, Hudson left the Jeter-Pillars

George Hudson, St. Louis, c. 1940. Photographer unidentified. © Western Historical Manuscript Collection–St. Louis.

Orchestra to work with Dewey Jackson.

In 1942, Hudson left Dewey Jackson and organized his first band. The Hudson Band was featured at the "Y" Circus, an annual event to raise money for the Pine Street YMCA. By 1944, the Hudson Orchestra had replaced the Jeter-Pillars Orchestra as the house band at the Plantation. After the war, musicians like Clark Terry and Ernie Wilkins joined the band. They toured the East and Midwest. The band recorded four titles for King records in 1949. Hudson also recorded with Dinah Washington that same year. Ahmad Jamal, then known as Fritz Jones, had his first road job with Hudson.

With the decline in popularity of big bands, the George Hudson Orchestra came off the road in 1951 and remained only a local band from then on. Hudson began a second career, teaching music at Lovejoy High School until 1985. One of his students was Hamiet Bluiett, one of the great baritone saxophonists in jazz.

through playing that "Body And Soul." And they wouldn't let Illinois on the stage. Wouldn't let him on you know? And that Schiffman, his speech was that he wanted me to take that number out of the show. And I refused to. I said I came to make a name for myself. I didn't come here to bow down for somebody else. And I won't do it. I'll take it out if you insist, but I'm taking my band out of this theatre with it.

Hudson's band was mainly on the road until 1950, playing theaters, dance halls, and backing Louis Jordan, Ella Fitzgerald, Dinah Washington, the Mills Brothers, and the Ink Spots.

Trumpeter Cy Stoner remarked on the Hudson Band: "It was on the commercial side until we got fellows like Weasel Parker and Clark Terry." Stoner also stated that Buggs Roberts did most of the arranging, but George had gotten a lot of arrangements from white bands.[81] Hudson said that Kenton gave him thirty-five scores when he played Tunetown.[82] Theodore Bibb stated, "I think Basie give him a hell of a lot of arrangements. They say Basie give him a lot of arrangements. They were friends."[83] This practice led to the George Hudson Band's largest problem—no identifiable sound.

In 1948, Hudson added Ernie Wilkins, who played saxophone and arranged, and his brother, trombonist Jimmy Wilkins.

Ernie Wilkins remembered his experiences with Hudson.[84]

> . . . And he had a very, very good band. In fact the band was too good, according to certain promoters in New York. We played in tune; we played with precision; and we had great arrangements, things that a colored band was not supposed to do unless it was Duke Ellington. I learned very much being in the band. And, by that time, I was really writing well. I'd learned a whole lot [during] the time I was in the navy. I learned from Gerald Wilson and a few of the heavy guys that were in the navy then. So, playing with George Hudson was a great experience and it was a very good band. Everybody that ever heard the band, even Dizzy Gillespie's band, when they heard the band, they flipped. . . . And Dizzy liked the band, too. We made a few tours with Dinah Washington and the Ravens. . . . But, unfortunately, things never happened for George Hudson and his excellent band.

During the late 1940s, Fritz Jones, a pianist later known as Ahmad Jamal played with the band.[85] This was his first road job. The band recorded in 1949 for the King label. The personnel of the band for the recording was George Hudson, Tommy Turrentine, Sykes Smith, Cyrus L. Stoner, Paul Campbell (trumpets); William Seals, Robert Home, and Elisha "Bartley" Dabney (trombones); Frank Domageux and Cyrus L. Stoner, Jr. (alto sax); Ernie Wilkins and William Adkins (tenor sax); Wallace Brodie (baritone sax); Robert "Bunky" Parker (piano); James Royal (bass); Earl Martin (drums); and Danny Knight (vocal). The tunes were "It's Love," "No One Sweeter Than You," "Applejack Boogie," and "Put It On The Cuff." It is clear from these recordings that the band had no identifiable sound or style. None of these recordings have been reissued on compact disc. The band's style ranged from Count Basie ("Applejack Boogie") to Stan Kenton ("Put It On the Cuff"). Hudson also recorded with Dinah Washington for Mercury without his band in 1949.[86]

Hudson came off the road in 1950 and started teaching at Lovejoy High School in Brooklyn, Illinois. He maintained his band until the late 1980s, playing one-nighters in and around St. Louis. Walter Lathan, music instructor for Webster Groves High School, played bass in these bands. He recalled these experiences in 1999.[87]

> George Hudson's Orchestra was well done. It was known all over the East. It was the most popular band in St. Louis. They called it the society band. When fraternities or sororities wanted to have some sort of pageantry or processional marches, we could play those things. It made the affairs very fine. We played at Tan Tara, Notre Dame University; we played at Sangamon University; we played the Military Ball at Lincoln University; we played a lot of political events; we played for the opening of the Hawks professional basketball season; we played the All-Star game in St. Louis. George had an excellent bunch of musicians. About half of them were instrumental music teachers in the St. Louis school system. Others worked in the post office, and one or two worked out at McDonnell Douglas. His musicians did St. Louis proud.

St. Louis Jazz Musicians in the Service during World War II

Quite a few St. Louis jazz musicians, white and black, served in various branches of the military. Harold "Shorty" Baker, James Boyd, Jr., Sammy Gardner, George Votaw, Vertna Saunders, Bruz Woods, Foots Goodson, Wendell Marshall, Theodore Bibb, and Ralph Sutton served in the army. Charles Fox and Muggsy Sprecher served in the air force. A number served in the navy: Clark Terry, Ernie Wilkins, Jimmy Wilkins, Charles Pillars, Sykes Smith, Cliff and Ed Batchman, Len Bowden, Arvelle Shaw, Leroy Harris, Jr., Jim Bolen, Jimmy Kennedy, Dudley Brooks, Richard Haley, Raymond Eldridge, Sr., Arvelle Shaw, and Robert Carter. The Great Lakes Naval Training Center near Chicago served as a training ground for many black and white military bandsmen. These trainees included many well-known musicians. Ernie Wilkins recalls why he served in the navy.[88]

World War II was going on then and the navy decided to let people in as musicians, so recruiters began recruiting black musicians, prior to that the Navy was very Jim Crow. So we were recruited and I'm sure 99% of us went to the navy to keep from going into the army, I know I did (laughter). And that's when I met [in the Navy] such great guys as Gerald Wilson, Willie Smith, Marshall and Ernie Royal, Jerome Richardson, Jimmy Nottingham, Al Grey. We all met together in the Great Lakes Boot Camp and then were shipped out with different bands from there.

Clark Terry also served at Great Lakes and remembers how so many black St. Louis musicians ended up there and what their duties were.[89]

As a matter of fact, . . . Len Bowden was the leader of the group. He used to have a band around St. Louis; the Melody Masters, I think it was called. So he recruited an enormous amount of guys out in St. Louis. We went in as ship's company band, you know, the band that stays on the base, and we prepared other bands, and sent other bands out to other naval bases while we stayed right there. We had an awful lot of excellent musicians; some names escape me at the moment, but it was a great band.

Robert Carter's experiences in the navy shed light on the segregated nature of the military until President Truman's administration.[90]

When the war came I went into the navy. This was in 1942. At that time, the only thing that blacks did in the navy was handle the food. They were stewards. This was during Roosevelt's administration, and his wife, Eleanor, was a good liberal. She recommended that blacks in the navy have duties other than being stewards. So they recruited twenty or more bands. A chief petty officer came to St. Louis to recruit musicians, and he recruited most of us from the union. There were thirty or forty musicians who left from St. Louis.

I was stationed at Lambert Field. The navy was conducting flight training for cadets from England for the RAF at Lambert Field. Of course, segregation was still bad. All our band did was play music. We played for bond rallies, we played for the cadets when they paraded, and we played concerts. There was a white band stationed here, and, since they were regular seamen, they had to do other duties, like scrubbing floors and handling the food. The white seamen figured that the blacks, who were rehearsing and playing for bond rallies and concerts could do some of the other work, like cleaning up the rec hall and the johns. Then in the summer of '44 they built a swimming pool, but the only day the blacks could use the pool was the day they were going to drain the pool and put fresh water in it. There were a lot of little things that piled up and became a conflict. When they ordered us to clean the johns, we refused to do it. They put us all under house arrest, and they broke the band up. All of us were sent out as replacements to other bands scattered all over the world.

I was sent to Hawaii. My son was only four months old when I shipped out, and I was bitter and lonesome and homesick. I played in a big band over there, until they dropped the bomb on Japan. I wonder if they would have dropped the bomb on the Germans, since they are white. But I think Truman was one of our better presidents. He integrated the armed services, and things started improving for blacks from then on.

Most musicians that lived in St. Louis worked at day jobs to support their families. During the war, quite a few black musicians worked at Scullin Steel (an essential industry), among them Singleton Palmer. Palmer's hours were 8:00 A.M. to 5:00 P.M. as a janitor, followed by work at the Plantation or other clubs from 9:00 P.M. to 4:00 A.M. Scullin Steel also attracted musicians because it sponsored a band that played in parades. Singleton Palmer remembers the band.[91]

I played in the band in . . . '40, '41, '42, '43, '44. 'Cause I . . . worked out there. And it was under the leadership of a fella named William Rollins. And we had a good band. . . . You know 45 or 50 pieces. And practically all of George's [Hudson] band played in the [Scullin] band. Let's see. George . . . the fellow playing piano we called Bunky he played the cymbals. And . . . we had about four tubas. And you know . . . it was a good band.

The Beginnings of Jazz Radio in St. Louis

During the war, two national broadcasts by big bands originated in St. Louis. The Glenn Miller Orchestra did a "Chester-field Show" from St. Louis on July 9, 1941. The second broadcast featured the Jimmy Lunceford Orchestra on the "Spotlight Bands" program from Jefferson Barracks.[92] Although the radio broadcast live jazz and dance band programs in St. Louis, there was no one acting as a jazz disc jockey until Charlie Menees (1916–1993).[93]

> The year was 1945 and we had a friend who was a secretary to Shorty Enright who was the Program Director at WTMV at the Broadview Hotel in East St. Louis. So, she said, "Would you like to do an all night request show?" And I said, "Well, yes I would. I'd like to break into that." And so I carried two grips of records to East St. Louis every Saturday night on the bus from over near the zoo in Forest Park. . . . And we clogged the telephone lines under the Mississippi River to the point where the government called and said, We're not getting war messages, telephone messages through on Saturday night. You will have to cease and desist." And they did; they turned it over to me and I brought jazz records and I played jazz records from 12:00 midnight to 7:00 in the morning, just able to get home and get to church on time." And that was the first jazz program in St. Louis.

When Menees played the first bebop recordings on the air, the reaction was so strong that he got hate letters.[94]

> I got vociferous reactions from a lot of people and I did play the first bebop [on the air] in St. Louis; the Dizzy and the Parker, but I also got reactions to playing people like George Shearing and Sarah Vaughan and Andre Previn, and people like that. Erroll Garner, even people like that were so new that James Deakin [a self-styled "moldy fig"] wrote me several caustic letters criticizing me and so did a lot of other people. Yes, it was too much for their ears, and, of course, this was a town of traditional jazz tastes. . . . Deakin said that I would "fry in Hades for playing music that people weren't ready for and that people couldn't understand."

Another jazz disc jockey came on the air in 1947. Menees remembers Jesse "Spider" Burks (died 1975) and where he started.

> Spider began out in Clayton there on a KXLW call letter station on January 1, 1947. I remember it well. Blaine Cornwell was doing the commercial stuff, popular stuff; Spider was doing jazz. And Spider would borrow records from me because he didn't have a library. Spider was articulate, he talked well, and he would come and borrow records of Bessie Smith and others of the pio-neers so that he could play those by request or by just trying to do a chronological, historical job. But he got away from that and swung into the modern jazz field rather strongly and did a lot for modern jazz here in St. Louis.

Spider also worked for KSTL, KADY/KDAI-FM, and KATZ, leaving radio in 1969.[95] From 1946 to 1949, Menees had his show on WIL, called "Jazz at Lindell."

> And simultaneously here, a fellow named Harry Tutwell, who later became King Tut and later became Harry Frost . . . [was] the first white person in St. Louis to get into modern jazz on the air. When I had my program "Jazz at Lindell" on WIL in '46, '47, and '48, Harry Tuthill used to come down and watch through the glass, like somebody would be watching us. And his interests grew, he had a record store and he would call me and say, "Richard Twardzik's album will never be reissued and I've got one copy, so you'd better come and get it." And I did.[96]

Frost was on KXLW with a program called "Fresh Air" in the 1950s and later moved to KADY in 1962.

Charlie Menees, hosting radio show on KWMU in St. Louis, c. 1970s. Photographer unidentified. © "Cactus" Charlie Menees Collection, Department of Special Collections, Miller Nichols Library, University of Missouri–Kansas City.

Jazz Recordings by St. Louis Musicians during the 1940s

In addition to the private recording made by the St. Louis Blue Devils in 1941 and the George Hudson Orchestra in 1949, there were a number of recordings made by St. Louis musicians. The first of these was a solo piano recording by Russ David of "Body and Soul" backed by "Rose Room" for an unknown label in 1944.[97] David later went on to become a society bandleader, studio musician, and commercial jingle author.

Jimmy Forrest made a recording in a St. Louis club in 1946 for the very obscure Town label. The group consisted of Forrest (tenor sax), Charles Fox (piano), James Royal (bass), James Thompson (drums), and Freddie Jackson (bongo). The tunes were "Bolo Blues" and "Puffy." "Bolo Blues" was recorded again for Delmark in 1951.[98] "Bolo Blues" was apparently a regional hit, because advertisements for Forrest in various clubs mentioned it.

Another very obscure label was the Town and Country label that made private pressings and a few commercial recordings of other forms of music. Wendell Marshall made his recording debut as part of the Stuff Smith Quartet in December 1946. The personnel included Stuff Smith (violin, vocal), Charles Fox (piano), Bill Jennings (guitar), and Wendell Marshall (bass). Two tunes were recorded and issued: "Night Falls Again" and "Up Jumped the Devil." The Town and Country label also recorded Tommy Dean in late 1947 as Tommy Dean and His St. Louisans.[99] The personnel were Tommy Dean (piano), Gene Easton (alto sax), Chris Woods (clarinet), James

Clark Terry Featured with George Hudson and His Orchestra, St. Louis, 1947. Photographer unidentified. © Western Historical Manuscript Collection–St. Louis.

Taylor (tenor sax), Buck Underwood (bass), and Nathaniel "Pee Wee" Jernigan (drums). Two tunes were issued, both Dean compositions: "Just before Day" and "Rock Easy." This was apparently the first commercial recording for both Dean and Chris Woods. See Chapter 5 for more details on these two musicians.

Clark Terry made two recordings during this period that are of interest. A group led by Clark called his "Section Eights" made one recording in New York in February 1947. Section eight is a military term for people having mental difficulties. The group consisted of Clark Terry (trumpet), Willard "Weasel" Parker (tenor sax), Robert "Bunky" Parker (piano), Singleton Palmer (bass), and Earl Martin (drums). The tunes were "Phalanges," "Sleep," and "Billie's Bounce," all issued on V-discs. V-discs were commercial recordings that were distributed only to military personnel to build morale. "Flat 5 on the Avenue," "Terry's Tune," and "On the Sunny Side of the Street" were also recorded but not issued. The personnel on these recordings came from the George Hudson Orchestra. Eddie "Cleanhead" Vinson made the second recording with his band in St. Louis on April 29, 1947. Clark Terry was part of that band for the recording.

The Further Adventures of Clark Terry in the 1940s

Following his travels with the Hudson Band, Clark joined Charlie Barnet for a year in 1947. He remained friends with Barnet his whole life. There are very few recordings of the Barnet Band featuring Terry. In 1948, Terry joined the Count Basie Orchestra. He stayed with Basie through the breakup of the band and was with the Basie Sextet and Septet in 1950. He played with and helped recruit members of the Basie "New Testament" band that was started in 1951. One of the musicians Clark recruited was Singleton Palmer. Singleton remembers the 1948 phone call.[100]

> I was living over on Delmar at the time and the phone rang and I answered and he called me Singletoe. He said, "Singletoe!" I said, "Hi Terry." "Fine. How would you like to play with Basie?" He was in Basie's band at that time. Well you always count on so much foolishness you know, and stuff. . . . I said, "You're kidding, fella." He said "No I'm not kidding. . . . He said Basie . . . needs a bass player. And he said you get on the train and come on up here. I said. "No don't." . . . He said, "I'm not kidding. I mean it." And so I got my fiddle together and got my few clothes I had and caught the train and went on to New York. Let's see . . . I think our first gig was at [the Royal] Roost I believe. I had one rehearsal before the gig. But his music wasn't too complicated. It was real easy. . . . Not easy either, but I fit pretty well in there, I think, until I did run into some little difficulty. Once he pulled out an arrangement arranged by George Duvivier. He's a bass player and I had to go to school on it, you know, because he had stuff all wrote. But other than that, I had a wonderful time with Basie. And he was a good guy to work for. He was a wonderful fella to work for. All the guys in the band were great, you know, to work with. Paul Gonzalves, Sweets Edison, Earl Warren and let's see . . . George Mathews on trombone. Naturally, Freddie Green. And . . . he had . . . another fella that used to play with George, Weasel, . . . Willie Parker, from here. He played with George. He was in the band too. So it was good, it was a good thing.
>
> I left Basie in '50. I came home for the holidays and actually, we weren't going too good, because we'd work a week or two and be off three weeks. And it took me all practically two and a half, three years to find out that when they had a layoff it was cheaper for me to come home until the next couple of weeks then it would have to stay in New York. But, you know that's the way it was. The money was good when you made it. . . . When you go to join a band like that, well, back then, you're excited. Well, if you work two nights a week this week its *x* amount of dollars and then you'll work no more for a couple of weeks . . . all that's money gone. And it was a hard time for big band back in those days.

Palmer recorded with Basie for RCA Victor in 1949. He sang on "St. Louis Baby" with Terry and Weasel Parker.[101] Terry was also instrumental in getting saxophonist Bob Graf into the Basie Septet in 1950. That will be discussed in the next chapter.

The Decline of Entertainment in St. Louis Following the War

By 1947, the entertainment tax began to cause the decline of the big band genre. According to Cotter,[102] St. Louis and Missouri laws were passed restricting the operating hours for nightclubs. Dance halls that hired musicians were forced to close. The above factors led to the disbanding of the Jeter-Pillars Orchestra in the summer of 1947. The Plantation Club also closed that year. On January 24, 1947, the *Argus* stated that the Riviera was in dire financial straits.[103] It closed May 29, 1947, and reopened on a much-reduced schedule later in the summer. Most engagements were three days or less and happened sporadically.[104] These included appearances by nationally known white bands such as those led by Woody Herman and Georgie Auld. The *Argus* advertisements during the years 1947 to 1950 show that a shift in popular tastes toward rhythm and blues had occurred, which was reflected in the bookings at the Riviera and small clubs in the city. The West End Waiters Club with the Buggs Roberts Orchestra continued through the end of the decade on a weekly basis. The Castle Ballroom also continued to bring in nationally known acts for one-night engagements through the end of the decade.

National jazz acts were increasingly appearing at Kiel Auditorium. Jazz At the Philharmonic appeared yearly and sometimes twice yearly at Kiel through the end of the decade. The Glass Bar in the Midtown Hotel opened on March 11, 1944 and occasionally had local musicians playing there. The Tommy Dean Band was a favorite at this venue, along with rhythm and blues acts through 1950. In November 1948, drummer Ben Thigpen brought a group called his "Interracial Combo" into the Glass Bar. Tenor saxophonist Bob Graf and trumpeter Bob Burton were identified as white in the advertisement.[105] An interesting set of appearances at the Glass Bar in 1948 and early 1949 were by the all-female combos led by trumpeter "Tiny" Davis and tenor saxophonist Vi Burnside.

Other lounges that featured local jazz musicians during the last part of the decade were the Palace Gardens, the Blue Flame Club, Club Bolo, Club 211, the Cozy Corner Tavern, the 12 Oaks, "Biscuit's" Place, the Amvets Club, the 20th Century Lounge, The Renaissance, the Casbah Lounge, and the Stage Bar.

Lloyd Smith and the Musician's Club

Multi-instrumentalist Lloyd Smith (1914–1999) was born in Lexington, Mississippi. He and his family moved to St. Louis in 1919. A graduate of Sumner High School, Smith began taking violin lessons from a St. Louis Symphony musician and moved on to saxophone. He also played clarinet, oboe, and French horn. He was also trained at Juilliard, the Boston Conservatory, and Roosevelt College.[106]

> I played with most of the major bands. I was in and out. Whoever paid the most money, that's where I went. I started with Eddie Randle. We played all the small towns in Missouri, Illinois, Iowa, and Wisconsin. We broadcast every Tuesday and Thursday on the radio. That was 1932, '33, '34. I played all the major clubs. I played the Club Plantation. It was a segregated club. We played white clubs, the Castle Ballroom, the Dance Box, the Pigeon Hole, East St. Louis, Brooklyn, Illinois. I played the Cotton Club in Harlem. There were all kinds of fine musicians during that time. The bands I stayed with the longest were Earl Hines, Eddie Randle, and Dewey Jackson, a local band. But I played with Fate Marable, Louis Armstrong, Fats Waller, Cab Calloway, Billie Holiday, Paul Whiteman, Duke Ellington, Count Basie, Jeter Pillars, Josephine Baker. . . . Let me see . . . Cecil Scott, Mose Wiler [sic], Nat King Cole. Nat Cole was my friend. I played with everybody.

Smith recorded with Hines in 1944, 1945, and 1946.[107] He opened the Musicians Club in 1947.[108]

> I had an "after-hours club" from 1947 to 1955, the Musicians Club, on Delmar. It was half a block east of the Club Riviera on the south side of Delmar, 4414 Delmar. After-hours clubs were kind of outlawed, because they were open after the curfew, when they were supposed to be closed. All the celebrities who came to town came to my club. Movie stars like Frank Sinatra and Ava Gardner came there. Everybody who was somebody came there . . . Dinah Shore, Dinah Washington, Spider Burks. I had a big sign by the door that told who would appear that night: Duke Ellington, Louis Jordan, Andy Kirk, Count Basie, Earl Hines. Benny Goodman passed through on a double nighter.

Smith was a financial sponsor of the NAACP Youth Council as well as for other civil rights groups, but apparently he wanted to remain in the background. Later, in the late 1950s and 1960s, Smith helped many blacks to be hired by several major St. Louis employers. He was also public relations director at Colonial Bakery for twenty-seven years, and he operated his own music studio, providing music instruction for many young St. Louis musicians, including Dwayne and Dwight Bosman, Chad Evans, Gerald DeClue, Butch Thomas, and Hamiett Bluiett. He also was a mentor to Oliver Nelson.[109]

Other Important St. Louis Musicians from the 1940s

Bassist Wendell Marshall (1920–2002) was born in St. Louis. Wendell went to Sumner High School and Lincoln University. In 1942, he took time out to play with Lionel Hampton before returning to Lincoln. He was in the army from 1943–1946. After the army, Wendell played with Jimmy Forrest, Buggs Roberts, and had his own trio in St. Louis in 1947.[110] He worked with Stuff Smith for a short time before he joined Mercer Ellington's band. After four months, Wendell joined Duke Ellington in September 1948. He made his debut at Carnegie Hall with the band on November 13, 1948. Marshall made a number of important recordings with Ellington during his tenure with the band. Among these recordings, two stand out. *Ellington Uptown* featuring "A Tone Parallel to Harlem" was recorded in 1951–1952 for Columbia,[111] and he recorded "Piano Reflections," a series of piano duos and trios with Ellington in 1953.[112] Wendell left Ellington in 1955 and freelanced in New York, playing in music studios and in the pit bands of Broadway. Between 1955 and 1956, Hank Jones, Wendell Marshall, and Kenny Clarke were the house rhythm section for Savoy Records.[113] Wendell played on 370 record dates and was probably the busiest bass player in New York from the mid-1950s to the mid-1960s. He made one record as a leader, *Wendell Marshall with the Billy Byers Orchestra*,[114] in 1955. Marshall retired to St. Louis in 1968, where he taught occasionally and worked at non-musical pursuits.

Bassist Arvell Shaw (1923–1992) was born in St. Louis. He played both bass and tuba in high school. He also played in the Tom Powell American Legion Post Drum and Bugle Corps. He learned to play bass with Fate Marable's band in 1942. After navy service, he played with Louis Armstrong's big band and All-Stars for long periods up to Armstrong's death. Shaw's specialty with Armstrong was a bass solo on "Dark Eyes." He studied composition and harmony in Geneva, Switzerland, in 1951. He toured Europe with Benny Goodman in 1958 and played and recorded with Teddy Wilson and Sidney Bechet, among others. He continued to work as a freelance musician and tour with various groups until his death.[115]

St. Louis–born vocalist Velma Middleton (1917–1961) began her career singing in local clubs in the 1930's.[116] She sang and toured with Louis Armstrong's big band and small groups from 1942 until her death in Freetown, Sierra Leone. Her best work with Armstrong can be found on *Satch Plays Fats* and *Louis Armstrong Plays W. C. Handy*.[117] Middleton was a large, very agile woman who often performed splits during her performances with Armstrong. Velma made two recordings as a leader with the obscure Dootone label in Los Angeles in 1948 and 1951.[118] She became ill and died while on tour with Armstrong in Africa.

Sumner High graduate Charles Fox had played piano professionally since age 13. Fox and his good friend Clark Terry both played in the Tom Powell American Legion Post Drum and Bugle Corps, where Fox played cymbals. He worked with Forrest, Thomas Starks (alto sax), Jimmy Blanton and Joe Smith at the Capitol lounge in the late 1930's. Fox recorded with Jimmy Forrest in St. Louis in 1946 (see above) and in Chicago in 1952.[119] He moved to the West Coast in 1947. There, he recorded with Dexter Gordon,[120] Sonny Criss and Wardell Gray[121] and played in a trio with Charles Mingus and Irving Ashby. Fox also worked with Charlie Parker, Stuff Smith, Ben Webster, Ray Nance and Sonny Greer in New York during the 1950s. As part of the Count Basie All-Stars, Fox went to the French Riviera in 1984. He toured with Clark Terry throughout his career, touring 12 countries in Africa with Clark and Chris Woods in 1980.[122] Fox made his last recording with Clark Terry in 1994.[123] Fox died in the summer of 2001.

Floyd "Candy" Johnson (1922–1981) was born in Madison County, Illinois. Originally a drummer, he changed to alto and tenor sax. After his student days at Wilberforce College, he played with Ernie Fields and Tiny Bradshaw. He worked with Andy Kirk (1942–1947), Count Basie (1951–1953), and with Bill Doggett (1958–1964). Johnson quit playing until 1971, when he began working with Milt Buckner, Jay McShann, and others.[124]

Eddie Randle Poster, c. 1940s. Photo restoration by Dennis Owsley. Courtesy of the Randle Family.

Buddy Moreno (born 1912 in Los Angeles), a former guitarist/vocalist with Griff Williams, Dick Jurgens and Harry James brought a sweet band into the Casa Loma ballroom in 1947. In 1948, Harold Koplar hired his band to play for the summer at the Chase Hotel. By 1949, the big band business was collapsing and Moreno became a radio personality. He hosted a variety show on KMOX for eighteen months. He returned to music as the leader of a band at the Chase for ten years and then joined KWK as an all-night disc jockey, moving to WEW after ten years. Moreno was also music director for the Fox Theater and the Municipal Opera orchestras. He has hosted a jazz show on WSIE-FM since 1991.[125]

Endnotes

1 Laurence Bergreen, *Louis Armstrong, An Extravagant Life* (New York: Broadway Book, 1997), pp. 420–421.

2 Charlie Menees, interview with the author, 1986.

3 Hayes Pillars, interview with Wil Warner for Frank Driggs, Frank Driggs Archives, University of Missouri–Kansas City, unknown date.

4 John Cotter, "The Negro in Music in St. Louis," Master's Thesis, Washington University, St. Louis, 1959, pp. 461–462.

5 Walter Dixon, interview with the author, 1986.

6 Duke Ellington Itinerary, http://home.swipnet.se/dooji/duke.html. According to this source, Ellington was a popular figure in St. Louis, having played various venues ten times before the October engagement. In 1940, the band was in St. Louis three times.

7 *St. Louis Argus*, October 27, 1939.

8 Milt Hinton, interview with the author, September 1986.

9 George Hudson, interview with the author, June 1986.

10 Cotter, "The Negro in Music in St. Louis."

11 Duke Ellington, *Music Is My Mistress* (New York: Doubleday and Company, 1973), p. 164.

12 Eddie Randle, interview with the author, July 4, 1986.

13 Dixon interview.

14 *Indianapolis Recorder*, December 23, 1939, p. 12.

15 J. Bradford Robinson, "Jimmy Blanton," *The New Grove Dictionary of Jazz*, Barry Kernfield, ed. (New York: St. Martin's Press, 1995), p. 117.

16 Compiled mainly from James D. Schacter, *Piano Man: The Story of Ralph Sutton* (Chicago: Jaynar Press, 1975).

17 Ralph Sutton and Jay McShann, *Last of the Whorehouse Piano Players—The Original Sessions*, Chiaroscuro CR (D) 206; Ralph Sutton and Jay McShann, *Last of the Whorehouse Piano Players*, Chiaroscuro CR (D) 306.

18 Ralph Sutton, *Swings St. Louis*, Gaslight GR5001; Ralph Sutton, *The Second Set*, Gaslight GR5002; Ralph Sutton and Barbara Sutton Curtis, *Home Again*, Gaslight GSL_5003.

19 Miles Davis with Quincy Troupe, *Miles: The Autobiography* (New York: Simon and Schuster, 1989), pp. 14–15.

20 Ibid., pp. 28–29.

21 Ibid., p. 29.

22 Charlie Parker, *The Complete Savoy and Dial Studio Recordings: 1944–1948*, Savoy/Atlantic 92911-2.

23 Miles Davis, *The Complete Birth of the Cool*, Capitol CDP 4 94550-2.

24 Miles Davis All Stars, *Walkin'*, Prestige OJC-213.

25 Miles Davis, *'Round About Midnight (Legacy Edition)*, Columbia C2K 94750.

26 All of Miles Davis's Prestige Recordings are found on *Miles Davis Chronicle*, Prestige PCD-012-2.

27 Miles Davis, *Milestones*, Columbia CK 40837.

28 Miles Davis, *Kind of Blue*, Columbia CK 64935.

29 All of Davis's recordings with Coltrane are collected in Miles Davis/John Coltrane, *The Complete Studio Sessions 1955–1961*, Columbia CK 65833.

30 All of these recordings are collected on Miles Davis/Gil Evans, *The Complete Columbia Studio Recordings*, Columbia 67397.

31 All of these recordings are collected in Miles Davis, *The Complete Columbia Studio Sessions of the Miles Davis Quintet 1965—1968*, Columbia CK 46863.

32 Miles Davis, *In a Silent Way*, Columbia CK 86556.

33 Miles Davis, *Bitches Brew*, Columbia C2K 65774.

34 Elwood Buchanan, interview with the author, 1986.

35 Walter Lathan interview from *Lift Every Voice and Sing—St. Louis African Americans in the Twentieth Century*, Doris A Wesley, Wiley Price, and Ann Morris, eds. (Columbia: University of Missouri Press, 1999), p. 116.

36 Ibid.

37 Ibid.

38 Marc Crawford, *Ebony*, January 1961. Quoted in Ian Carr, *Miles Davis: The Definitive Biography* (New York: Thunder's Mouth Press, 1998), p. 6.

39 "Letter to David Breskin," quoted in Gary Carner, ed., *The Miles Davis Companion* (New York: Schirmer Books, 1996), p. 2.

40 Bobby Danzig, interview with Charles Rose. National Ragtime and Jazz Archive, Southern Illinois University at Edwardsville.

41 Davis, *Miles*, p. 33.

42 Vertna Saunders, interview with Dan Havens, April 5, 1982. National Ragtime and Jazz Archive, Southern Illinois University at Edwardsville.

43 Stanley Dance, *The World of Duke Ellington*, 2nd edition (New York: Da Capo Press, 1970), p. 184

44 Davis, *Miles*, p. 34.

45 Randle interview.

46 Miles Davis, interview with Ben Sidran, in Gary Carner, ed., *The Miles Davis Companion* (New York: Schirmer Books, 1996), p. 186.

47 Randle interview.

48 Davis, *Miles*, p. 44.

49 Carr, *Miles Davis*, p. 14.

50 Miles Davis, *Downbeat*, March 6, 1958. Quoted in Carr, *Miles Davis*, p. 16.

51 Davis, *Miles*, p. 45.

52 Billy Eckstine, *Melody Maker*, September 4, 1954.

53 Danzig interview.

54 Charlie Parker, *The Complete Savoy and Dial Studio Recordings: 1944–1948*, Savoy/Atlantic 92911-2.

55 Davis interview with Sidran, pp. 193–194.

56 Paul DeMarinis, "Eddie Randle and the St. Louis Blue Devils," *Black Music Research Bulletin* 10(2), 1998.

57 Robert L. Campbell, Armin Buettner, and Robert Pruter, *The Tommy Dean Discography*, May 16, 2005. http://hubcap.clemson.edu/~campber/deanie.html

58 Ibid.

59 Randle interview.

60 Lathan interview.

61 Hayes Pillars, interview with Frank Driggs, Frank Driggs Archives, University of Missouri–Kansas City, unknown date.

62 Cotter, "The Negro in Music in St. Louis," pp. 342–345.

63 Ibid.

64 Ibid.

65 *St. Louis Argus,* advertisements in various editions, 1944–1956.

66 Ibid., p. 340.

67 Philip Martin, "Critical Mass: 'Round about Miles," *Arkansas Democrat-Gazette,* June 14, 2005. http://www.nwanews.com/story.php?paper=adg&section=Style&storyid=1 19318

68 *St. Louis Globe-Democrat,* entertainment sections for July 7–July 31, 1944.

69 Dizzy Gillespie with Al Fraser, *To Be or Not…to Bop* (New York: Doubleday and Co., Inc., 1979), p. 188.

70 Art Blakey, quoted in Robert Riesner, *Bird: The Legend of Charlie Parker,* Da Capo Press, New York, NY, 1975. p. 51.

71 Hayes Pillars Interview by Frank Driggs, *loc cit.*

72 *St. Louis Globe-Democrat,* all editions July 1–August 15, 1944; *St. Louis Post-Dispatch,* all editions July 1–August 15, 1944.

73 *St. Louis Argus,* all editions July 7–August 11, 1944.

74 Hudson interview.

75 Ibid.

76 Ibid.

77 Cotter, "The Negro in Music in St. Louis," p. 355.

78 Hudson interview.

79 Ibid.

80 Ibid.

81 Cy Stoner interview with Frank Driggs, Frank Driggs Archives, University of Missouri–Kansas City, May 26, 1976.

82 George Hudson, interview with Wil Warner for Frank Driggs, Frank Driggs Archives, University of Missouri–Kansas City, July 26, 1978.

83 Theodore Bibb interview by Dan Havens, National Ragtime and Jazz Archives, Southern Illinois University–Edwardsville, April 19, 1982.

84 Ernie Wilkins, interview with the author, 1988.

85 Ahmad Jamal interview with Jim Wallace for KWMU radio, June 7, 1986.

86 Dinah Washington, *The Complete Dinah Washington, Vol. 5,* Mercury 823444.

87 Lathan interview.

88 Ernie Wilkins, interview by Bob Rusch, *Cadence Magazine,* May 1977.

89 Clark Terry, interview with the author, 1986.

90 Robert Carter interview from *Lift Every Voice and Sing—St. Louis African Americans in the Twentieth Century,* Doris A Wesley, Wiley Price and Ann Morris, ed. (Columbia: University of Missouri Press, 1999), p. 24.

91 Eddie Randle, conversations with the author, 1986–1997.

92 *Tom Lord Discography,* version 3.3.

93 Menees interview.

94 Ibid.

95 St. Louis Radio History, hrrp://www.stlradio.com/hof-legacy-1.htm

96 Menees interview.

97 *Tom Lord Discography,* Version 3.3.

98 Jimmy Forrest, *Night Train,* Delmark DD-435.

99 Robert L. Campbell, Armin Büttner, and Robert Pruter, *The Tommy Dean Discography,* December 2005. http://hubcap.clemson.edu/~campber/deanie.html

100 Singleton Palmer, interview with the author, June 1986.

101 Count Basie, *Count Basie and His Orchestra 1947–1949.* Classics 1107.

102 Ibid.

103 *St. Louis Argus,* January 24, 1947.

104 *St. Louis Argus,* all issues from June 4, 1947–year end, 1950.

105 *St. Louis Argus,* November 28, 1948.

106 Lloyd Smith interview from *Lift Every Voice and Sing—St. Louis African Americans in the Twentieth Century,* Doris A Wesley, Wiley Price and Ann Morris, Ed., University of Missouri Press, Columbia, MO 1999. p. 75.

107 *Tom Lord Discography,* version 3.3

108 Smith interview.

109 Paul Harris, Lloyd Smith Obituary, *St. Louis Post-Dispatch,* April 11, 1999.

110 Cotter, "The Negro in Music in St. Louis," pp. 358–359, 460–463.

111 Duke Ellington, *Ellington Uptown,* Columbia CK 40836.

112 Duke Ellington, *Piano Reflections,* Capitol CDP 7 91223.

113 *Tom Lord Discography,* version 3.3.

114 Wendell Marshall, *Wendell Marshall with the Billy Byers Orchestra,* RCA Victor LPM 1007.

115 Johnny Simmen, "Arvell Shaw," *The New Grove Dictionary of Jazz,* Barry Kernfield, ed., St. Martin's Press, New York, NY, 1995. p. 1108.

116 *The New Grove Dictionary of Jazz,* Barry Kernfield, ed. (New York: St. Martin's Press, 1995), p. 771.

117 Louis Armstrong, *Satch Plays Fats,* Columbia CK 40378; Louis Armstrong, *Louis Armstrong Plays W. C. Handy,* Columbia CK 40242.

118 *Tom Lord Discography,* version 3.3.

119 Jimmy Forrest, *Night Train,* Delmark DD-345.

120 Dexter Gordon, *Settin' the Pace,* Proper Records, Properbox 16.

121 Wardell Gray, *The Wardell Gray Story,* Proper Records, Properbox 55.

122 Charles Fox, interview with the author, July 1986.

123 Clark Terry, *Shades of Blues,* Challenge Records CHR 70007.

124 Edward Rye, "Floyd "Candy" Johnson," *The New Grove Dictionary of Jazz,* Barry Kernfield, ed. (New York: St. Martin's Press, 1995), p. 618.

125 "My Buddy: Bandleader Buddy Moreno Remains A Musical And Broadcasting Icon In The St. Louis Area", *Jazz Connection Magazine,* October 2001. http://www.jazzconnectionmag.com/buddy_moreno_article_october_2001.htm

5

The Jazz Scene
in St. Louis in the 1950s
(1949–1960)

The early 1950s were a great time for jazz in St. Louis. Bassist John Mixon recalled that there were thirty to forty clubs on both sides of the river where you could hear jazz.[1] The Glass Bar, the DeBaliviere Strip, and the Blue Note Club on the East Side were places where both black and white musicians got a lot of work. Segregation continued on most bandstands, however, and there were clubs where blacks were not welcome. The national interest in "traditional" jazz, which had been building since around 1945, was strong in St. Louis and led to work for quite a few of the older musicians.

The Beginnings of the Singleton Palmer Dixieland Six

In late 1949, Elijah "Lige" Shaw was working as a piano tuner at a home in University City. He recalled how the older surviving riverboat musicians got together again.[2]

> I was tuning a piano out in University City for a lady name Mary Ruth. At 7171 Washington. This was May 1949. She asked me if I knew the older musicians in St. Louis and did I know where they were and what instrument they played and if I thought we could get them together to see if we could revive some of the riverboat music, in St. Louis. So being president at that time of the Negro musicians, I had a roster in my pocket. So I gave her the names of the older musicians who played on the boats, and to my surprise she called every one of them up and invited them out to her house for a party. And she said, "I haven't got the money to pay you, I just want to see if we can start something." So we went out there like about 2 o'clock on a Sunday. She had bar-be-cue, hot dogs, hamburgers, beer, and whiskey if you like and all kinds of soda.
>
> So we played, some of the first ones to play we had . . . Sam Shelton and they got him, they had Dewey Jackson, and they got Janie Hemingway for the first set. And, well, we had John Orange on trombone and we got Norman Mason on clarinet, and I told her I would play on the drums until they found a better drummer. We played there from about 2 o'clock in the evening till the people next door on both sides start complaining about 2 or 3 o'clock in the morning. We had such a good time until we decided that we would do that once a month, and move it around to the different ones that present at this first party house if they had a piano. So we moved it around to quite a few places, but we had a problem of each Sunday, maybe some guy had a job and we couldn't depend on him we had to get somebody else. So we had quite a number of ones to play with us.

Pianist Ralph Sutton played a concert at Kiel Auditorium on August 30, 1949, with people from this circle. The band included Bill Martin (trumpet), Norman Mason (clarinet), John "Bones" Orange (trombone), Sutton, Walter Lathan (bass), and Lige Shaw (drums).[3] Shaw continues his narrative.[4]

> So finally when we got back to Mrs. Ruth's house, she had invited one of the tavern operators, a fellow name Ernest Shapiro. He and his brother run a place on Delmar called the Barrel. He was so impressed with the music that he decided that he would have a Dixieland band jam session at the Barrel on Saturdays from 3 'til 5:30. But at that time we had mingled so till the band had become 50 percent black and 50 percent white. We had Barbara Sutton, Ralph Sutton's sister, playing the piano by that time and a boy that used to play trumpet with Gene Krupa name[d] Norman Murphy was playing trumpet. And we had lost our trombone player John Orange to Joe Smith. . . . And we had a boy name Sid Dawson from out in Ferguson who incidentally is a residential musician of Chicago now. So we got our thing started and the place caught on so, we kept such a crowd until the man put the band on for five weeks every night. But it just wasn't a big enough place to support six musicians. So we started to play Dixieland jam sessions on a Sunday at the Universal Dance Studios right in front of DeBallivere on Delmar. The people used to pay a dollar and bring their own bottle and they get ice and soda there in the hall. So the business outgrew that place. And we went down on a boat called the *Fort Gay*, it used to be docked at the foot of Harper Street, and we star[ted] giving Dixieland jam sessions on there on a Sunday evening.
> . . . We played down there and played down there 'til this boy that was running all these stop signs and things, lived on Waterman or something, I think they called him Hot Rod Moore. He come down there once . . . weaving away from there he hit a post and wrapped his car around the post and the police come and shut down the jam sessions, cause he suppose to have gotten drunk on this

Singleton Palmer's Dixieland Six, St. Louis, 1955. Photographer unidentified. Seated, left to right: Elijah "Lige" Shaw, Dewey Jackson, Bob Carter, Norman Mason. Standing, left to right: Singleton Palmer, Gus Perryman. © Western Historical Manuscript Collection–St. Louis.

boat. But as far as I know of, nobody was selling nothing to drink on the boat, if he got drunk on there he brought his own drink.

Singleton Palmer had returned for the holidays from his job with Count Basie and recalled what happened when he was called as a substitute for bassist Vernon King, who had been working in the group.[5]

> . . . I came home for the holidays. . . . They were having jam sessions outside the Universal hall [Universal Dance Studio] out on DeBallivere and Delmar every Sunday: Dixieland sessions. And they asked if I would come out and play, you know, one of the sessions with them. So I told them "Yeah." So I got through I think it was a three-hour gig. And they gave me $50. . . . Yeah. I'm in New York and work one or two nights a week on the road. And I come home and make fifty dollars for a couple hours. So I put two and two together so when I came home that night, I sit down and sent Basie a certified letter that I wasn't, you know, rejoining the band. But then at the time, he had broken the band down to a small group anyhow.

Shaw picks up the story of how Palmer joined the group.[6]

> So he got Singleton Palmer to play in his place with the jam bunch. So Singleton had him to bring his tuba one day, he impressed everybody with the tuba so well that he decided he would bring the tuba rather than bringing the bass fiddle. So Bobby Swain who was the musical advisor for the Koplar Hotels, he came over one Sunday to hear the group and he invited Singleton Palmer over to his table to have a drink and he asked Singleton Palmer to organize a band. But he said he couldn't take a mixed band; have to have all blacks. So that's when Singleton and I got together and decided who we would get to replace the white musicians in our band. We were very hurt over the fact that they wouldn't take the band mixed because all of us was very crazy

about Barbara Sutton and I think she loved us and loves us 'til today.

Singleton Palmer recalled the musicians who went into the Snack Bar at the Forest Park Hotel.[7]

> And then I got Dewey Jackson [on trumpet] and Gus Perryman on piano, and Robert Carter on trombone. So we went in the Snack Bar for two weeks and we stayed eight months. And . . . we've been going ever since.

Others in the group were Al Guichard (clarinet) and Lige Shaw (drums). The *Argus* of August 4, 1950, confirms this engagement.[8] This band recorded in 1950 for the obscure Disco label. Bob and Vivian Oswald, who were later founding members of the St. Louis Jazz Club, financed the recording.[9] The recording included the band noted above: Dewey Jackson (trumpet), Robert Carter (trombone), Al Guichard (clarinet), Gus Perryman (piano), Singleton Palmer (tuba), and Lige Shaw (drums). The tunes were: "Washington and Lee Swing," "Waiting For the Robert E. Lee" (both issued on Disco 1087), "Tailgate Ramble," "Milenberg Joys," and "Basin Street Blues" (the last three unissued).

Later musicians in the Singleton Palmer Dixieland Six included trumpeters Benny Starks and Andrew Webb, Jr., trombonist Leon King, clarinetist Norman Mason, clarinetist/alto saxophonist Leroy Harris, Jr., pianist Robert "Bunky" Parker, and drummers Ben Thigpen and Rick O'Connor. Palmer kept working up until close to his death.

The St. Louis Jazz Club

Coincidentally, the St. Louis Jazz Club was started the month after the Palmer recordings. Jeff Leopold gives the date as October 28, 1951,[10] while Lige Shaw gives the date as the first Monday in October (October 1).[11] Charlie Menees remembers the formation of the group.[12]

> . . . I remember well when it was formed, and the people like Vivian and Bob Oswald . . . and the Dorsey Ruth's and a good many others. They . . . allowed themselves to form this club. . . . I helped them get publicity in the media here at that time. And the club began to build slowly and after trying several meeting places, as I recall, they were up at the Hamilton Hotel . . . in the basement there. They had some meetings at the Kingsway Hotel. I remember those very well. Well, they never did find a place that they could settle in full time and I always regretted that. . . . We had some outstanding musicians in St. Louis that came and played and we talked about records.

Jeff Leopold recalled that in the early days some wags referred to the Jazz Club as the Singleton Palmer Fan Club.[13] The club began to produce concerts and events. These events often featured racially mixed bands. They had a cruise called "Jazz on the River" on the *Admiral* for seven straight years. The Jazz Club put on a joint concert with the St. Louis Symphony and Jazz at Vespers at Christ Church Cathedral. On July 27, 1958, the Jazz Club cosponsored the first St. Louis Jazz Festival at Kiel Auditorium. This concert featured an all-star Dixieland band led by Singleton Palmer and a modern group led by John Cotter, which featured Hugh "Peanuts" Whalum on tenor sax. For six or seven years, the club did a jazz mass for Father Shockley at St. Bridget's Catholic Church. At their high point, the club was responsible—directly or indirectly—for approximately three hundred gigs a year for St. Louis's traditional jazz musicians. They brought in traditional jazz bands from all over the country and from Europe. The St. Louis Jazz Club continues to meet today (2006) and produces a monthly jazz concert. The focus has slowly changed from Dixieland and pre-1940s swing styles to mainly a Dixieland focus today.

Jazz Club Cruise, St. Louis, August 9, 1959. Photograph by Arthur Witman. Left to right: Norman Mason (clarinet), Unidentified (trumpet), Sid Dawson (trombone), Elijah "Lige" Shaw (drums), Singleton Palmer (tuba), "Banjo" Pete Patterson. © Western Historical Manuscript Collection–St. Louis.

Bob Koester and Delmar(k) Records

In 1950, record collector and music fan, Bob Koester, was at St. Louis University to take business courses. He began selling records he had obtained from second-hand stores out of his dormitory room.[14]

A jazz club was being organized at the time in St. Louis and I went to the founding meeting. I was a founding member of the group. I remember the first meeting where I heard a hell of a lot of good music. I later found out that some of the best musicians in town were there. Bob Graf was there. Clark Terry was there. Through the St. Louis Jazz Club I was able to do a certain amount of promotion for my business. Eventually I was chairman of the program committee; as soon as I was able to go into bars, I wasn't old enough at first. At the second meeting of the jazz club I met a guy named Ron Fister.

Singleton Palmer (1912–1993)

Singleton Palmer was born in St. Louis. His father died in 1916 during the influenza epidemic. He did not have a musical family but was interested in music early. He heard music in a sanctified church near his home on Fairfax and in street parades. A neighbor played piano and alto horn in her church and let Singleton play the alto horn. He took piano lessons for six months and, at age eleven, convinced his stepfather to buy him a cornet. At age thirteen, he played with a cousin, Duree Smith, in Metropolis, Illinois, over the Christmas holidays. He began working in the Mose Wiley Band at age fourteen, along with another trumpeter, James Talphey. Charles Creath and Dewey Jackson influenced Palmer as a cornet player. He was able to sneak into the Jazzland Café on Market Street to hear them on several occasions. His parents took him on the riverboats several times on Monday nights.

Singleton began playing tuba in 1928, when Mose Wiley decided to cut the band's size by laying off one of the cornet players. His stepfather bought him a tuba for Christmas. Palmer continued to play both tuba and cornet in his high school band. He then joined Oliver Cobb's Rhythm Kings in 1929 and made his first recordings with Cobb in 1929. Singleton remained with the band after Cobb's death in 1931. When Eddie Johnson took over the band and renamed it the St. Louis Crackerjacks, Palmer remained with the band for a time, recording with them in 1932. He switched to string bass in 1933. Palmer then joined Dewey Jackson on the riverboats in 1934, remaining with him until 1941.

During the war years, Palmer worked at Scullin Steel during the day and played in their band. He remained with Scullin Steel for ten years. He then worked as a custodian for another twenty-five years. Palmer joined George Hudson's first band in 1941. He remained with Hudson and with Jimmy Forrest until he joined Count Basie on Clark Terry's recommendation in 1947. The Basie Band was in decline at the time and Palmer left in 1950, after recording eleven sides with him.

Palmer returned to St. Louis and started his Dixieland Six in 1950, recording that same year. He was a charter member of the St. Louis Jazz Club. Palmer continued leading his group through the 1950s, and he became a star of Gaslight Square at the Opera House, recording six albums from 1960 to 1967. Singleton continued to work both public and private engagements with his group until his death.

Fister collected thirties and forties pop music, along with some jazz artists. Together, Koester and Fister started K & F sales and eventually started the Blue Note Record Shop. Soon, the two knew that they were moving in different directions and split the inventory. Koester moved to a new location on Delmar between Goodfellow and DeBaliviere and named his label Delmar Records. He began recording traditional jazz and blues groups at age twenty-one. His first recording was the Windy City Six in July 1953.[15] The personnel of this group were Muggsy Sprecher (cornet), Skip Derringer (trombone), Sammy Gardner (clarinet), Bob Dorner (piano), Wally Eckhardt (bass), and Jerry Fiscle (drums). The group recorded the following tunes: "Hangover Lament," "Jelly Roll Blues," "San Francisco Bay," "When The Saints Go Marching In," "Royal Garden Blues," and "Lonesome Road." Koester later recorded the Dixie Stompers with Don Franz (trumpet), Jimmy Haislip (trombone), Jerry Schroeder or Bob Schroeder (clarinet, vocal), John Chapman (piano), Bill Shroder or Wyatt Ruther (banjo), Ed Wilkinson (tuba), and Bob Kornacher (drums).[16] The group again recorded in 1954 with the same musicians, and in 1956 with Bill Mason (cornet), Haislip and Norman Mason (clarinet), Glen Tinterra (piano), Pete Patterson (banjo), and Kornacher (drums).[17] See the recordings section below for details of these recordings. Koester moved to Chicago in 1958 and later founded the Jazz Record Mart, a Chicago institution. The label name was changed to Delmark, apparently over copyright infringement problems. Delmark and its co-label, Nessa Records have recorded Chicago's finest musicians from traditional blues to the avant-garde music of the Association for the Advancement of Creative Musicians (AACM).

Hugh "Peanuts" Whalum, St. Louis, c. 1957. Photograph by Bernie Thrasher. Courtesy of Joe Schwab.

The DeBaliviere Strip

The DeBaliviere Strip was an area south of Delmar on DeBaliviere. Clubs along Delmar were also part of it. The Barrel was at 5614 Delmar and the Windermere Bar was across the street. By 1951, the Windemere had drummer Joe Smith's Riverboat Ramblers with Sammy Gardner working. Sorrento's was a popular spot for jam sessions. According to Jeff Leopold,[18] drummer Rick O'Connor's Saints worked at various places on the strip during this period, as did the Dixie Stompers and the Mound City Jazz Band. The Top Hat, the Spa, and Little Nero's were other clubs in the area.

Trombonist Norman Menne, who was a professional musician by age 13, was able to get into the places on the DeBaliviere Strip.[19]

I was introduced to the DeBaliviere Strip by my brother Tom, who used to take me down there after our regular gigs were over. . . . Sorrento's was one of the places we used to jam [at] and some of the other places, . . . The Barrel, The Top Hat. Very good clean, fun. There was good entertainment, good players, good players, good clean fun. It was extremely exciting to me; at the time I was between thirteen and seventeen years old. But Bill Ruler's Barrel was probably one of the neatest places.

The Barrel was the site of a recording made by Miles Davis and Jimmy Forrest in 1952.[20] In addition to Miles (trumpet) and Forrest (tenor sax, vocal), the other players were Charles Fox (piano), John Mixon (bass), Oscar Oldham (drums) and Percy James (conga). The tunes were "Our Delight," "What's New?," "Ray's Idea," "Wee Dot," "Lady Bird," "All the Things You Are," Perdido, "A Night in Tunisia," and "Lady Be Good."

The Davis recording at the Barrel was made during one of Miles's periodic visits to St. Louis to conquer his drug addic-

Album Cover for Jazz on the Right Track *Featuring the Herb Drury Trio,* Victoria Records. Recorded 1965, released 1998. Left to right: Herb Drury (piano), Jerry Cherry (bass), Phil Hulsey (drums). Courtesy of Herb Drury.

tion. John Mixon, the bassist of the group remembers that "Miles and I were, from way back, always kind of tight, with Peanuts [Hugh "Peanuts" Whalum] and, you know. . . . We were all just hangout buddies. . . . We played a lot of dates together and when we got off, we would go by his Dad's farm [in Millstadt, Illinois]. He had a little lake out in the back yard and we'd get in a rowboat and we'd just sit there and he [Miles] would teach me how to form chords and so forth."[21]

The drummer with Forrest on the "Night Train" and Barrel recordings was a very promising young player named Oscar Oldham. Mixon rated Oldham at that time as being in the same league as "Max [Roach] and those guys."[22] Mixon was working with a quartet that included Oldham, saxophonist Peanuts Whalum, and pianist John "Albino Red" Chapman. He was the only one who had a car. On May 1, 1953,[23] after leaving Chapman off on the way home, the three were hit broadside at the corner of Euclid and Highland. Oldham was killed and Whalum had one arm and hand damaged so severely that he was in the hospital for thirty-five days.[24]

Saxophonist/vocalist/pianist Hugh "Peanuts" Whalum (born 1928) was born in Wilberforce, Ohio, and was a member of the Wilberforce Collegians Orchestra. Whalum came to St. Louis in September 1949 and began working in clubs with his group "Peanuts" Whalum and His Three Nuts. He worked with the Lionel Hampton Band in the early 1950s. In St. Louis, he worked with John Mixon, George Hudson, John Cotter, and others. He has played piano and sung in many venues with his Nat Cole–styled voice as both a solo act and as a trio. He also teaches in the jazz department of Webster University.

Pianist Herb Drury and bassist Jerry Cherry began their long-term musical partnership when Cherry subbed for a bass player at French Village in East St. Louis. Drury was the pianist on the gig. Later, they had a trio, first at comedian Davey Bold's Celebrity Club at Delmar and Skinker and later at Sorrento's, at DeBaliviere and Waterman. Drummers Phil Hulsey and Art Heagle played with the group, along with TV personality Jim Bolen on vibes. Cherry and Drury played together mainly as a duo up to Cherry's death in 2000.[25] Drury remembered how Bolen started playing with them.[26]

Jimmy Forrest (1920–1980)

Tenor saxophonist Jimmy Forrest[27] was born in St. Louis. His mother, Eva Dowd, was an orchestra leader in the city. While he was still a child, he played in that orchestra. While he was in high school, he worked with Eddie Randle, the Jeter-Pillars Orchestra, the Eddie Johnson Band, and Fate Marable. Leaving home with the Texas bandleader Don Albert, Forrest eventually found his way to the Jay McShann Band, where he played with Charlie Parker (1940–1942). He played at the 400 Club in St. Louis before returning to New York and the Andy Kirk Band. He remained with Kirk until 1948, but returned home frequently. While on one of his sojourns home, he recorded "Bolo Blues" (named for a St. Louis nightclub) and "Puffy" for the Towne label in St. Louis. He also worked in St. Louis at the Blue Flame Club, the Club Bolo, the Manhattan Lounge and Rendezvous, the Renaissance, and the Glass Bar (1946–1950).[28] Jimmy Forrest spent time with the Ellington Band in 1948 but was never recorded commercially. Part of the band's repertoire was the "Deep South Suite" that featured a section called "Happy-Go-Lucky Local." In 1950, Forrest was back in St. Louis working in clubs and working part time as a clerk in the records department of the Gamen Appliance Company. While recording for a label in Chicago called United (1951–1953), he adapted the first strains of "Happy-Go-Lucky Local" and made "Night Train," a tune favored by many ecdysiasts (strippers).[29]

Forrest used St. Louis musicians Charles Fox, Bunky Parker, John Mixon, Chauncey Locke, Bart Dabney, Oscar Oldham, Hershel Harris, Bob Regan, and Percy James on these recordings. Later, Forrest went back to New York and worked with Harry "Sweets" Edison (1958–1962). He also recorded for Prestige and finally began touring again as a soloist with Count Basie (1972–1977). His solo on "Body and Soul"[30] showed many modern touches. He then relocated to Grand Rapids, Michigan, and co-led a quintet with trombonist Al Grey until his death.

Well, Jim's been with us almost as long as the trio existed. It's sort of an interesting thing, how we got together. Davey Bold, a comedian who is no longer with us, . . . had a club here. And it was called Davey Bold's Celebrity Club. It was on Delmar and Skinker. In fact, the building doesn't even exist anymore. We worked as a trio for him for a year and of course, during that year, we met a lot of "celebrities," you know, local ones, a lot of the TV personalities, which of course, Jim Bolen was one of those. He used to be Cookie on "Cookie and the Captain." . . . So anyway, he came in one night and he brought his vibes to set in. And, it turned out that he left his vibes there, because Davey Bold liked to play around on them too. Davey was a pianist. He was pretty good. He played very adequate for his dirty songs, you know and all that kind of stuff. Cute guy, really was great, very funny man. I laughed every night at him. But anyway, Jim Bolen used to come out and set in with us there. . . . And when we left Davey Bold's, we took a job at a little place called Sorrento's, which was on DeBaliviere and Waterman. Al Baker owned that place then. And we played three nights a week there, Thursday, Friday, and Saturday, and on Thursday night, we had guest night, and we'd hire a soloist. . . . We had several different players on alternate Thursday nights, you know. And we finally settled down with Jim Bolen because we seemed to play together the best with him, you know. So Jim sorta became the fourth member there, occasionally, and it's been like that ever since. Every place we've played, not every place, but several places, he's been with us at least one night a week.

Herb Drury was the major jazz piano teacher in St. Louis during the 1960s through the 1990s. He taught at the University of Missouri–St. Louis and privately. Jerry Cherry was a bass repairman until his death. The Drury Trio recorded two albums during the Gaslight Square period: *Keep Your Sunny Side Up*[31] and *On the Right Track*[32] (see Chapter 6).

John Mixon (1927–1996)

Bassist John Mixon[33] learned to play bass in the army at age twenty-one. When he left the service in 1949, Mixon studied bass in Boston for two years. He came back to his native St. Louis and joined Jimmy Forrest in 1951. He was with Forrest for about eight years and then worked around town with "Peanuts" Whalum, "Foots" Goodson, John Cotter, Bob Graf, and Tab Smith. He then was with the Lionel Hampton Band for over two years, recording on the *Golden Vibes* and *Silver Vibes* albums for Columbia (now out of print). Mixon stayed in New York after leaving Hampton and studied with Paul Chambers. He also studied cello with Oscar Pettiford. He went to Manhattan University while he was in New York. John returned to St. Louis and continued to work.

Mixon was in great demand during the Gaslight Square days, making several recordings for the VGM label. In 1965, he worked in a group with trumpeter Lester Bowie, saxophonist John Norment, pianist John "Albino Red" Chapman, and drummer Phillip Wilson. He described the group as being "kind of out, but Lester Bowie was always kind of out." In the 1970s, he had a quartet with Willie Akins (tenor saxophone), John Hicks (piano), and Sonny Hamp (drums). In 1984, he toured Europe with Lester Bowie's "Root to the Source" group. Mixon got sick a week before the group made a recording for Black Saint in Italy. He continued to work in St. Louis until his death.

Jazz Central

Davey Bold's Celebrity Club was the headquarters for another group: Jazz Central. Lee Hyde tells of how Jazz Central was formed and obtained sponsorship from KMOX.[34]

> Well, we didn't necessarily dislike that type of music [Dixieland jazz], but the group thought that type of music was a bit primitive. And we wanted something that was a little closer to what we were all digging at that time, which was the Dave Pell cool sound out of Los Angeles. He had an octet similar to ours. He used four horns instead of five and used a guitar, which we didn't use. But, we liked that sound. We got ahold of a couple of their arrangements. . . . We had to have musicians that had a jazz feel and could hopefully solo. But, it eliminated some of the musicians that we really would liked to have in there in that they had to be able to read well, too.
>
> . . . I wrote some arrangements. Harry Stone wrote some arrangements. And we got together. And we thought that instead of having, as they say, a kicks band, why not organize? So we had dues and we bought some [music] stands and frantically wrote some arrangements and got some sports coats. . . . And we decided the first thing [that] we should do would be to give a concert. . . . We put on a concert at the old Ambassador Kingsway Hotel across from the Chase. And the room was filled up. We were so surprised that that many people would show up. Someone that worked for [General Manager] Bob Hyland down at KMOX heard about the concert and how it was received. And [he] was able to convince him that if we could find a place to play on Saturday afternoons and one day a week, we'd play a school concert, [KMOX] would put the Saturday concert, at least a half an hour or an hour of it, on the air.
>
> We started right off the bat and we stayed at the Kingsway for six months. Then we eventually played at the Rose and Crown Room at Medart's (now the Cheshire Inn). We played . . . at a place on Kingshighway called the Embers. We broadcast from there for six months and we wound up our final six months on the air from the Forest Park Highlands outside bandstand. Over a two-year period, we did some fifty concerts that were sponsored jointly by KMOX and the American Federation of Musicians.

The school concerts used KMOX personalities like Jack Buck as announcers. Eventually, Jazz Central acquired a club in

1959, in the building that had been the Celebrity Club at Delmar and Skinker. They brought in such national names as Al Hirt, Cannonball Adderley, Dizzy Gillespie, Carmen McRae, Ramsey Lewis, and the Dukes of Dixieland.[35] The Herb Drury Trio also worked at the Jazz Central Club. Jazz Central also recorded an album called *Natural Habitat* in 1959 as an alternative to what the liner notes said was "straw hat Dixieland." The personnel included Lee Hyde (trumpet), Fred Del Gaudio (alto sax), Dale Billings (tenor sax), Don McRady (trombone), Bobby Swain (baritone sax), Herb Drury (piano), Ralph DeRousse or Boris Anastisoff (bass), and Harry Stone or Bud Murphy (drums). The tunes were a mixture of standard and original works: "'Round Midnight," "Centralization" (their theme song), "Blues in My Heart," "New South Wail," "Ocho Nueva," "I'll Remember April," "Stone's Throw," "Meet Mr. Gordon," "Prelude to a Kiss," "A Foggy Day," "Brother, Can You Spare a Dime?" and "Room 270."

Pianist Dave Venn was born in St. Louis.[36] He started piano lessons at age seven and played saxophone and clarinet in high school. Venn attended the St. Louis Institute of Music, and while there, he played tenor sax with Jazz Central. By then, it was obvious that there was more work for a piano player than a tenor player. Dave began his long St. Louis career on Gaslight Square. He accompanied Clea Bradford at the Trés Bien Club (see Chapter 6). Venn remains in high demand for clubs and concerts and has often accompanied nationally known musicians. He recorded *A Celebration of American Song* with guitarist Steve Schenkel in 1984,[37] and *Together* in duet with pianist Herb Drury in 1996.[38] Venn's latest recording is the CD *1, 2, 3* from Max Productions.[39]

The Tommy Dean Combos and Chris Woods

Eddie Randle's pianist in 1941 was Tommy Dean (1909–1965). Dean was born in Franklin, Louisiana.[40] He is the composer of "Scammon Boogie," the theme of the St. Louis Blue Devils during the 1940s. After he left Randle, Dean began working around St. Louis and apparently took his own band around the Midwest, reaching Chicago in 1945. His band was known in Chicago as "Tommy Dean and His St. Louisans," and he recorded in St. Louis under that name in late 1947 for the Town and Country label (See Chapter 4). Dean worked at the Glass Bar and other venues from 1946 on and was quite popular in St. Louis. Although he made St. Louis his home base, he worked in both Chicago and St. Louis for the remainder of his career, turning further into rhythm and blues by the middle of the 1950s.

Chris Woods was a saxophonist with Dean in the late 1940s and early 1950s.[41]

Tommy Dean was an excellent musician. His roots were in the blues, as you can tell, but, with his group we didn't only do R&B stuff—as you said by listening to the records, they were like jazz-oriented records—and on our personal appearances we did all kinds of things. But Tommy Dean was trying his best to get a hit record out. And that was the reason for a lot of the vocal things that he did that were kind of R&B things. He always did quite well, you know, financially. He really wanted to have a hit record so he was working in the vein of R&B things as far as his recordings were concerned. A lot of the things that we did live were not recorded, but maybe eventually we would have recorded them if he had continued to record.

Dean recorded a number of sides with various labels. The 1949 Chicago recordings that produced "Hour Past Midnight," "Scammon Boogie," "Just About Right," "Sweet And Lovely," "Jump For Joy," and "Dean's Theme" were recorded for Miracle. The first four tunes were released on Official as *Deanie Boy Plays Rhythm and Blues* (Official 6038). The personnel included

Chris Woods (1925–1985)

Multi-reed player/composer Chris Woods was born in Memphis,[42] Tennessee. After playing his first professional jobs in Memphis, Woods moved to St. Louis shortly after World War II. He worked with the Jeter-Pillars and George Hudson orchestras before beginning work with Tommy Dean. He recorded for the United label and worked around St. Louis, leading various combos after leaving Dean, but he became discouraged by audiences wanting to hear the rock and roll hits of the day.[43] He quit music for nine months and got a job as a bus driver for the city of St. Louis. He got back into music in 1955 but kept his day job until 1961, when he left for New York. He played, toured, and recorded with Carla Bley, Dizzy Gillespie, Clark Terry, Ernie Wilkins, Sy Oliver, and others during the 1960s and 1970s. He made a number of recordings in Paris in the mid-1970s. Woods joined the Count Basie Orchestra in 1983 and remained with the band until his death from cancer. Clark Terry described Woods about a year after his death, "He was one of the most beautiful people that I ever met, and one of the most underrated musicians that I've ever known. And I think I'm happier playing with him by my side than almost anybody that I know in the business. Because he was supportive, he was competent, he was articulate, and he was a marvelous, marvelous person. He could do anything. He could do anything, and when you said Chris Woods, you said it all to me."[44]

Chris Woods (alto sax), Edgar Hayes (tenor sax), Gene Easton (baritone sax), Tommy Dean (piano), unknown (bass), and Pee Wee Jernigan (drums and vocals). He recorded *Tommy Dean and His Gloom Chasers* on June 4, 1952, in Chicago with the same personnel, adding Eugene Thomas (bass) and Jewel Belle (vocals). The recordings eventually made their way to the Delmark label. The tunes recorded were "Raining," "Lonely Monday" (Jewel Belle, vocal), "Foolish," and "Cool One-Groove Two." "Just Right" was unissued.

Chris Woods recorded for United in Chicago on February 24, 1953. The album *Somebody Done Stole My Blues* was not released on the Delmark label until 1977. Chris Woods (alto sax), Arthur "Pete" Redford (trombone), Gene Wright (baritone sax), Charles Fox (piano), Gene Thomas (bass), Pee Wee Jernigan (drums), and an unknown male vocalist were on the record date. The tunes included "Brazil," "Somebody Done Stole My Blues," "Bobo," "Where or When," and "Blues for Lew." "Brazil" and "Blues for Lew" were released as a United single in 1953. The title tune is one written by Chris Woods that Sonny Stitt recorded as "Loose Walk" after hearing Woods play it at a club in St. Louis. From these recordings, it appears that quite a few black St. Louis musicians moved between St. Louis and Chicago, going where the work would take them. Ollie and Virgil Matheus booked the Dean Band, Jimmy Forrest, and Chris Woods for dances for white teenagers in south St. Louis.[45]

Eddie Johnson Returns to St. Louis

Pianist and bandleader Eddie Johnson returned from New York and obtained a job at the [Hawaiian] Roma Room on Finney in 1951. He was at the Hurricane Lounge at Compton and Lawton and the Harlem Club in Brooklyn, Illinois, for extended engagements. He later worked jobs with Tab Smith and others in various venues in St. Louis. He and Leroy Har-

Oliver Nelson (1932–1975)

Oliver Nelson[46] was born to a musical family in St. Louis. His brother worked with Cootie Williams in the 1940s while his sister played piano with a group in St. Louis. Nelson studied piano at six, saxophone at eleven, and played his first job while he was still in elementary school. He worked in St. Louis with the Jeter-Pillars and George Hudson orchestras in 1947 and 1948 and also played with Eddie Randle for a time. Leaving St. Louis, he worked with the Nat Towles Band in 1949 and with the Louis Jordan big band in 1950–1951. His musical career became part of his military service experience, playing in bands and officers clubs in 1952–1954. He studied composition and theory at Washington University from 1954 to 1957 and at Lincoln University for the 1957–1958 school year. He then moved to New York in 1958.

During his stay in New York, he worked with many artists, including Erskine Hawkins, Wild Bill Davis, Eric Dolphy, and Louis Bellson. He made his first recording as a leader for Prestige's New Jazz subsidiary in 1959. Highlights of his career in this period are the albums *Afro-American Sketches*,[47] *Blues and the Abstract Truth*,[48] and *Sound*

Oliver Nelson, location unknown, c. late 1950s. Photograph by Chuck Stewart. © Chuck Stewart.

Pieces.[49] According to St. Louis drummer Kenny Rice,[50] Nelson had become disillusioned with the New York scene and was considering returning to St. Louis to set up a record company with Leo Gooden, a lifelong friend and owner of the Blue Note Club in Centreville, Illinois. However, he had a hit recording with "Walk on the Wild Side" with organist Jimmy Smith on Verve in 1962 and continued his career in New York until 1967. He then moved to Los Angeles to work as a television and film composer.

Nelson's television credits include theme and incidental music for *Longstreet*, *The Six Million Dollar Man*, and *Matt Lincoln*. He also scored episodes of *Ironside*, *It Takes a Thief*, and *Name of the Game*. He scored the films *Death of a Gunfighter*, *Skullduggery*, *Zig Zag*, and *Trans Europe Express*. Nelson was also the author of *Patterns for Saxophone*.

Nelson visited St. Louis and Washington University in the late 1960s and early 1970s, leading jazz clinics every summer. He suffered a heart attack and died in Los Angeles at age forty-three.

ris, Jr., had the longest running gig in St. Louis at the King Brothers Motel at Clayton and Lindbergh. The gig ran for eleven years, from 1958 to 1969. In addition, he founded ELJ Records and made recordings of some St. Louis musicians as 45-rpm singles. Pianist/vocalist Joe Buckner recorded two singles in the early 1950s with his trio and Leroy Harris, Jr. (ELJ 8003/4 and ELJ 8011/12). Tab Smith made his last recording in the early 1960s on this label (ELJ 8013/4). Before that, Smith had been a hot commodity for United, with a hit rhythm and blues recording of "Because of You" in 1951.[51] Smith lived in St.

Louis and worked sporadically until his death (see Chapter 3).

Ernie Wilkins and the Basie Band

Saxophonist Ernie Wilkins and his trombonist brother Jimmy had left George Hudson's band after Hudson came off the road in 1950. In early 1951, Ernie got a call from Clark Terry.[52]

> You know, I always had a thing with Basie. He would always ask me for people to put into his band. Whenever he needed somebody, he would always call me over and say, "I need so-and-so and so-and-so," and that's how Ernie Wilkins got in the band. We were playing the Strand Theatre once. . . . Well, the band wasn't very good at this particular time because we had broken up and was starting all over again. And he said to me one day while he was . . . in the steam bath, he says, "I need an alto player and a trombone player." I said, "Well, OK." So I got to thinkin', so I got on this phone while he was in the steam bath, and I called long distance to St. Louis, and I got Ernie [Wilkins], and I said, "Hey, you wanna come and join Basie?" And it took me fifteen or twenty minutes to convince him I wasn't kidding. And finally, he agreed, and I told him to get Jimmy and bring Jimmy along, and I'd reserved a hotel room for them, and so I said to Basie after he come out the steam bath, "Yeah, Basie, I got an alto player and a trombone player for you." I knew Ernie had never played alto before in his life, but I knew he was a good enough musician that with a good enough sound, and that he could read good enough to be able to adjust to playing any woodwind. So I told Basie I had these two guys for him. He says, "OK. Good." I said, "Well, they're out of town right now. They'll be back in town tomorrow," to give them time to get into New York from St. Louis.

Ernie Wilkins continues the story.[53]

> My brother and I, we were foolin' around in St. Louis and suddenly the phone rang one day. It was Clark, "Hey, how would you and Jimmy like to come and join Count Basie?" And at first, I thought he was puttin' me on, "Oh, man, you're kidding." You know. "No, Basie wants you, he's formin' a new band and he's askin' me to get some guys for the band. So, I thought about you and Jimmy. . . . But you're gonna have to play alto." (laughter) I say, "Play alto? I'm a tenor player." "Well, what do you wanna do? Do you want to come with the band or do you want to stay there in St. Louis?" So I say, "O.K., I'll come." so I borrowed an alto from one of the members of my mother's church. . . . And we got on the train and rode the train all the way from St. Louis to New York. But one thing that Clark Terry doesn't remember [is] that when I got there, Basie remembered seeing me in George Hudson's band.

Wilkins joined the band in time for their May 6, 1951, recording date.[54] Terry remembers telling Basie of Ernie's writing skills.[55]

> So a couple days later, they came in, and I walked into the dressing room area one morning with these two guys, and I said, "Basie, this is Ernie Wilkins and his brother, Jimmy. This is your new alto player and your new trombone player." I said, "In case Buster and Jimmy get busy writing, Ernie's a good writer; he can help 'em out." So he says, "Well, yeah, OK. Alright." . . . So Ernie wrote, I think it was, "Everyday," or one of those tunes, recorded it, and it just catapulted the band right back into prominence, and it's been there ever since. Just from that lie I told on the telephone (laughter).

How "Everyday I Have the Blues" was written is an interesting story. Ernie Wilkins remembers Joe Williams coming into the Basie Band.[56]

> He joined the band Christmas Day of 1954. Then, after the holidays, we went straight down South on a tour. Joe didn't have any music and so we were just playing what we call head arrangements behind him, you know, settin' some riffs behind the blues and everything. So Basie say, "Hey, man. We're getting ready to get into the Howard Theater in Washington, D.C., and we should have an opener for Joe. So why don't you get with Joe and write something that we can play behind him for the Howard Theater."

Ernie Wilkins playing alto sax with the Count Basie Band, Savoy Ballroom, New York City, December 16, 1953. Photograph by Popsie Randolph. Left to right: Eddie Jones (bass), Frank Wess (tenor sax/flute), Wilkins, Gus Johnson (drums), Marshall Royal (lead alto sax), Freddie Green (guitar), Frank Foster (tenor sax/arranger), Reunald Jones (trumpet), Charlie Fowlkes (baritone sax), Paul Campbell (trumpet), Wendell Culley (trumpet), Henry Coker (trombone). © Frank Driggs Collection.

So, we were in Norfolk, Virginia, and I got some music paper and Charlie Fowlkes, the baritone player (he was the copyist). We sat in the hotel room and I wrote "Everyday" in one afternoon and Charlie Fowlkes was copying the parts as I was writing the score. And we played it on the gig that same night.

Not only did that arrangement propel the Basie Band back into a prominence that it never relinquished, but it also jump-started Ernie's career as a composer and arranger. Jimmy Wilkins eventually moved to Detroit and led a big band. He moved to Las Vegas in recent years and now leads a big band in that city.

The Glass Bar and Peacock Alley

The Midtown Hotel at 7935 Lawton had a club that was initially named the Glass Bar and, in 1955, was refurbished and renamed Peacock Alley. The club had featured local musicians like Tommy Dean and Jimmy Forrest sporadically in the 1940s.

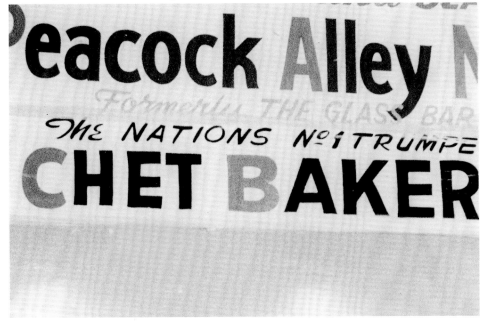

Peacock Alley Poster, Peacock Alley, St. Louis, date unknown. Photographer unidentified. © "Cactus" Charlie Menees Collection, Department of Special Collections, Miller Nichols Library, University of Missouri–Kansas City.

Peanuts Whalum worked at the Glass Bar in May and June 1950. The owners of the Glass Bar began featuring national jazz groups in May 18, 1951, with an engagement by Stan Getz.[57] Getz was so popular that he returned to the Glass Bar two more times in 1951. All of the major names in jazz played the Glass Bar, including James Moody, Dizzy Gillespie, Gene Ammons, Sonny Stitt, Lester Young, Charlie Parker, and Bud Powell. The modern jazz engagements alternated between local and nationally known rhythm and blues players.

Walter Dixon worked in that club during this period as a bouncer and valet. It featured many well-known national names of the time and local modernists. Charlie Parker worked at the club with Jimmy Forrest's band backing him from August 14–22, 1953.[58] Dixon remembers problems with Parker.[59]

> When Charlie Parker came to St. Louis, he didn't have no group, he just came himself. Well, Jimmy Forrest was the club band. . . . He's gonna play with the club band. So, everybody was there to hear the great Charlie Parker. . . . That when he was in the midst of the deepest part of his drug habit. Well, people were payin', at that time, $2 . . . and he was just comin' down there, grabbin' his horn and holdin' it and Jimmy Forrest was blowin'. So people would call me and say, "What's the story on Charlie Parker? . . . He didn't blow a f***** note." . . . So this Saturday matinee, somebody called me, said, "Walter come upstairs." I said, "What do you mean come upstairs?" He said, "Charlie Parker is layin' out here drunk. This s.o.b. can't play no matinee. . . . This s.o.b. is knocked out, layin' there in the lounge." I went up that day and he was all sprawled out in the lounge. (author's note: Walter Dixon was a large, strong man, even in his later years) I picked up this s.o.b., throwed him over my shoulder, and I had one of my friends open up his room. And he had his clothes on. I throwed that s.o.b. up under the shower, clothes and all and turned that cold water on his ass. . . . So that cold water snapped him out of it. . . . Charlie Parker got up there [on the bandstand], started blowin' and he knocked people out. People were just squealin' and hollerin'. . . . Next thing everybody knew was that Jimmy Forrest had picked up his horn, walked off the bandstand, right out the front door. . . . He didn't come back anymore.

An interesting thing also happened when Bud Powell visited the Glass Bar for an engagement that ran from October 30 to November 7, 1953.[60] Before the gig started, Powell was shown a substandard piano on the bandstand. Walter Dixon remembers this incident.[61]

> He walked in and they had one of them little spinet pianos. Bud walked in. He said. "What the hell is that? The man said, "That's your piano." He [Powell] spit on the piano, said "I don't play nothin' that looks like that. If you don't get something else, you can forget it. I'm goin' back to New York." So, the following night, he walked in and there was a big baby grand piano sittin'

there. . . . He got on that piano and ate it up.

By 1955, the Glass Bar had been renovated and renamed Peacock Alley. The first great Miles Davis quintet with John Coltrane (tenor sax), Red Garland (piano), Paul Chambers (bass), and "Philly Joe" Jones (drums) came into the club in October. His visit was eagerly awaited, but the appearance of the band members shocked the local musicians. According to drummer McClinton Rayford,[62] the rest of the group looked like bums. Although Miles was clean, the rest were all heroin users and looked like they had slept in their clothes for days. One of them had vomited over himself and didn't clean his clothes off. They all smelled badly.

Davis brought the same group back into the club in July 1956. Recordings have been issued from tapes made by Jesse "Spider" Burks, who was the emcee for the broadcasts on station KXLW.[63] Two matinee sessions were broadcast, July 14 and July 21. The repertoire in the broadcasts was as follows: "Ah-Leu-Cha," "A Foggy Day," "All of You," "Woody 'N' You," "Walkin'," "Two Bass Hit," "Well, You Needn't," "Billy Boy" (rhythm section only), "Airegin," "Oleo," and "Miles' Theme." These tunes were all in Miles's standard repertoire and had been recorded for either Prestige or Columbia within the previous year.

There is photographic evidence of Peacock Alley engagements during this time (1955–1959) by the Chet Baker Quartet; the Max Roach group with George Coleman (tenor sax), Ray Draper (tuba), and Kenny Dorham (trumpet); the Chico Hamilton Quintet with Paul Horn (reeds); the J.J. Johnson Quintet with Bobby Jaspar (reeds); Carmen McRae; and Sonny Stitt. Bob Graf was also photographed and recorded at the Glass Bar in February 1958. The personnel for this recording were Graf (tenor sax), Jimmy Williams (piano), John Mixon (bass), and Albert St. James (drums).[64] Two tunes were recorded: "Stella by

Bob Graf at Peacock Alley, St. Louis, c. 1950s. Photographer unidentified. © "Cactus" Charlie Menees Collection, Department of Special Collections, Miller Nichols Library, University of Missouri–Kansas City.

Starlight" and "Alley Blues." Both were issued on Delmar DL-401 but have not reached compact disc. A recording was also made on January 27, 1958, at Westminster College in Fulton, Missouri, with similar personnel. Ron Ruff was added on tenor sax and Bob Maisel played bass in place of Mixon.[65]

The Show Bar (formerly Club Playground) at Delmar and Taylor began bringing in name artists in 1952, and this policy apparently lasted until 1954.

Tenor saxophonist Bob Graf (1927–1981) was born and raised in St. Louis.[66] He was a friend of Clark Terry. Terry got him into the Basie small group that played at the Brass Rail in Chicago in 1950, but Graf never recorded with Basie. Wardell Gray soon replaced him, and Graf moved on to Woody Herman's band. He recorded with Herman's band in 1950–1951. Graf moved to Los Angeles and was featured on some of Chet Baker's big band recordings for Pacific Jazz in 1956.[67] Returning to St. Louis, he was recorded in 1958 at Westminster College and Peacock Alley (see above). He was recorded with vocalist Bev Kelley in the basement of a church in the Soulard District[68] in St. Louis in 1959.[69] In late 1959 and early 1960, Graf worked in St. Louis with a group that included guitarist Grant Green. Later in the 1960s, he played with Gerry Mulligan's big band but did not record with the group. Graf became an instrument repairman and continued to play around St. Louis until his death in 1981.

Organist Sam Lazar is a mysterious figure. He was apparently from St. Louis and was originally a pianist. Lazar worked around town with various musicians, most notably Grant Green and "Peanuts" Whalum. He recorded the album *Space Flight* with Green and drummer Chauncey Williams in Chicago for the Argo label in 1960.[70] Lazar continued to record for Argo and its successor label in Chicago until 1964. The trail disappears at that point. Drummer Phillip Wilson played with him.[71]

> Sam was completely nuts. Crazy. I was on the road with him for four years and he used to do the . . . wildest things. I mean he'd fire me . . . 'cause I wouldn't play a certain cymbal. . . . He'd fire me for about a half an hour or so and then I'd be hired back again. I spent six months in New York with Sam. I spent a year in Cleveland. . . . Sam was a phenomenal musician but he had quite a few problems.

Grant Green and the Holy Barbarian[72]

Guitarist Grant Green (1935–1979) was born in St. Louis. Both his father and uncle played guitar. Green was something of a child prodigy. His father bought him his first instruments. Walter Dixon remembered him as a child.[73]

> He was really a gifted musician, because when he was a little bitty boy, small boy, his father bought him a toy guitar. And he got the damndest sounds out of that toy guitar. So his father bought him a ukulele. Then he bought him a tipple [a half-sized guitar]. And, in the summertime, you know, people didn't have no air conditioning. . . . And people would be sittin' out on the front porch at night, and he'd take that damn tipple and you could hear it all over them two blocks. And people would say, "Listen to that boy play."

Green's influences were guitarist Charlie Christian and saxophonist Charlie Parker, learning his solos note for note. At thirteen, he began playing professionally. He played first in church and it was there that Richard Henderson heard him. "Why, it was the first time I had seen a guitarist playing in the church. The church where I saw him singing was kind of like a sanctified church. The church I went to was Baptist. So that (a guitar player in church) wasn't happening there."[74] Later, Green played with local rhythm-and-blues and jazz combos led by such musicians as accordionist Joe Murphy, drum legend Joe Charles, trumpeter Harry "Sweets" Edison, organist Sam Lazar, and saxophonist Jimmy Forrest. Green played in strip clubs, country-and-western clubs, and blues clubs and occasionally in jazz clubs, beginning to make a name for himself at "The Sportsman" in East St. Louis. Saxophonist Chuck Tillman was something of a mentor to Green.[75]

> I liked his concept. His concept was that of a horn player. Grant wasn't avant-garde. He was just a soulful musician that could express himself and he didn't mind being funky. He could play stank with the best. The patterns he could play were reminiscent of what I think horn players would play because of the single stroke and the way he moved it. He played things that were not basically guitar licks.

Elvin Jones heard Green in 1956 in St. Louis. On October 23 of that year, he recorded with Tommy Dean in Chicago for the Vee-Jay label, but the recordings were not issued.[76] Green recorded two albums for Delmark with Jimmy Forrest and Jones in 1959[77] and *Space Flight* with Sam Lazar in 1960. Alto saxophonist Lou Donaldson discovered Green in an East St. Louis club in 1960 and invited him to audition for Blue Note Records in New York. Before he left St. Louis, Grant was working in a strip club with organist Sam Lazar. They moved to a short-lived club at 572 DeBaliviere called the Holy Barbarian. According to Ollie Matheus, the club owner, "We had Grant and Chauncey Williams on drums, Sam Lazar on organ, and Bobby Graf on tenor. Bobby was the white boy. It was the first interracial club in the city and both of the [musicians'] unions gave me a lot of crap over that. But it was the happiest place."[78] The police closed the Holy Barbarian down after eight weeks on a charge of employing a minor as a waitress.

When he got to New York, Green's audition impressed Blue Note Records enough that he was hired as the staff guitarist for the label. His first recording was with Lou Donaldson.[79] He was a fixture in the Blue Note recording studios during the 1960s, playing on over eighty recording dates as a leader or sideman for the label. Among his recordings for Blue Note, *Feelin' the Spirit, The Complete Quartets with Sonny Clark, Idle Moments,* and *Talkin' About* stand out.[80]

Unfortunately, Green acquired a drug habit early in his career, and as the 1960s wore on, he became increasingly unreliable. His recordings became more funk oriented and he was becoming a crossover artist. In the fall of 1978, he suffered a stroke that temporarily paralyzed his left side. He also had heart problems and died at age forty-three of a heart attack.

Grant Green, at a Recording Session at Rudy Van Gelder's Studio in Englewood Cliffs, New Jersey, April 26, 1962. Green's album *The Latin Bit* was recorded that day. Photograph by Francis Wolff, © Mosaic Images LLC.

Leo Gooden and the Blue Note Club

On the East Side, the Blue Note Club was going strong from the late 1950s through 1967. That club was where most of the big names could be found after they finished their regular jobs on Gaslight Square or DeBaliviere. The late Leo Gooden owned the club. Drummer Kenny Rice recalls the scene at the Blue Note and Gooden's respect and care for the musicians.[81]

That was the place in the Midwest that you could go hear anybody at any time almost. You walk in there, sometime, Miles Davis would be at the bar. Whenever cats came through St. Louis, they went there because they knew Leo.

He'd [Gooden] always tell me that he could have anybody, but this group was hand picked. I went in there one year with Albert King and he said, "I want you to be my drummer. I'll pay you $90 a week [and all you can eat]."[82] And that was back in 1960. Then, he got Don James. We had to get Don's organ from the club he was playin' in. . . . He finally quit the place, but he didn't want to go back and get his organ. Then he got Hamiet Bluiett. . . . It was me, Hamiet [baritone sax], Charles "Little Man" Wright [alto and tenor sax], and Larry Prothro [trumpet]. He gave "Little Man," being the oldest, the assignment of bringing all the tunes and overseeing the rehearsals. If it hadn't been for him, we wouldn't have had a repertoire.

. . . We were there every night. We started at 11:00 and that's when all the places in St. Louis closed up. That's when Gaslight Square was goin'. Phillip Wilson took Dave Sanborn over when he was still in high school.

A lot of club owners think that musicians are the last ones to come along. . . . But Leo . . . believed that the musician was the most important one in the establishment.

Rice remembers a night when saxophonist Yusef Lateef came over to the Blue Note after playing his job at the Missa Luba on Natural Bridge. He became part of a jam session with Oliver Nelson. Rice remembers that they "played 'Night in Tunisia' for almost an hour. I almost died."[83]

Phillip Wilson concurred with Rice's comments about Gooden and his Blue Note Club.[84]

I really respected Leo Gooden for taking care of the musicians. . . . He took care of Kenny, took care of Don [James]. He really took care of the musicians. You know what I mean. . . . You could go over there any time and it was always happenin'.

Leo Chears described Gooden, "Basically, Leo Gooden was a 400-pound cat who struck you as being 'the Godfather.'"[85] Rice said, "Leo was a very large man and when he sang, he sounded like Billie Holiday."[86] The Blue Note group made a recording called *Spider Burks Presents Leo's Five* for L. G. Records in 1960.[87] The group included Larry Prothro (trumpet), Charles "Little Man" Wright (alto sax, tenor sax), Hamiet Bluiett (baritone sax), Don James (organ), Kenny Rice (drums), and Leo Gooden (vocal). The tunes were "Are You Real?," "Picture on the Wall," "Tippin'," "Le-o-Fa-Sa," "Mop Water," "I'll Be Seeing You" (LG-vocal), "Early Autumn," "Frederick's Dream," "You've Changed" (LG-vocal), and "Cookin' with Chezie Mae." In 1963, Gooden went to New York and recorded *Leo Sings*, a vocal album with strings and woodwinds arranged by Oliver Nelson for L. G. Records.[88] Don James played organ on that recording.

Unfortunately, Gooden died in 1965 and his dreams died with him.

Drummer Kenny Rice (born 1942) was born in St. Louis and raised in Kinloch. His father was a gospel singer. His high school band director, Vernon Nashville, spotted him in the eighth grade, and Kenny earned money to buy a snare drum by shining shoes. Rice took lessons from Elijah "Lige" Shaw. He used to walk from Kinloch to downtown St. Louis and back for his lessons. He played for a blues band and then toured with Albert King. Leo Gooden spotted him one night in the Blue Note Club and made him a member of "Leo's Five." Rice got a lot of experience at the Blue Note. He worked on the road with Grady Tate and Nat Adderley, Richard Martin, Eddie Fisher, Johnny Johnson, and the Kennedy brothers in 1976.[89]

Drummer Phillip Wilson remembered that at fourteen he was working with Don James and saxophonist Freddie Washington at the Toast of the Town at Finney and Taylor. James lived in Crystal City, Missouri, and had a radio show down there. Apparently, there was a lot of musical activity in the city park when the weather would cooperate and James was part of that.[90] Kenny Rice recalled James and how he played. Don James died in 1967, after the Blue Note Club closed.

Don played the organ like a pianist. Most organ players will comp [i.e. accompany a soloist] with block chords and stuff. A piano player, a real good piano player, [uses] mostly right hand. Don could play [the bass line] as fast as any upright bass player. He attacked the organ. Many times I played with him and his hand would be bleeding like that; knuckles would be bleeding.

Saxophonist Charles "Little Man" Wright[91] was born in Arkansas in 1927, but he was raised in East St. Louis. When he was ten years old, Jimmy Forrest lived across the street and when he touched Forrest's horn, he knew he wanted to become a saxophonist. His mother bought him a curved soprano sax from a pawnshop. He studied music until he went into the service. When he mustered out in 1945, he began taking lessons at the Ludwig School of Music. Miller Brister recommended him to Eddie Randle for a job at the Harlem Club in Brooklyn, Illinois. Wright worked with "Snookum" Russell, Tab Smith, Count Basie, B. B. King, and Ray Charles during the fifties. He was an original member of Leo's Five. He continued working at various venues through the 1980s.

Other Jazz Recordings during the 1950s

Pianist/vocalist Beverley White—with William Moore (guitar), Art Schieler (bass), and Robert Heuer (drums, vibes)—recorded four tunes for the obscure Trumpet label on June 7, 1952. The tunes were "I Waited Too Long," "I Don't Care," "Cling to Me," and "When I'm With You." These have been reissued on a CD called *Shout, Brother, Shout,* on the Alligator label.[92] According to Cy Stoner, Cecil Scott had a band in St. Louis in the early 1930s. White was known as Magnolia White then and left town with the Scott Band.[93] She recorded under the name Beverley White with Andy Kirk and Claude Hopkins.[94] White was working around St. Louis in the 1940s as Beverley. At some point in the 1950s, she left St. Louis, returning in the late 1970s to work on Laclede's Landing, passing herself off as May Tatum—Art Tatum's daughter!

Clarinetist Sammy Gardner recorded for Delmar with his own group, the Windy City Six (see above) and for his own label, Mound City Records. The *Mound City Jazz* recording[95] made in the early 1950s featured Muggsy Sprecher (cornet), Jimmy Haislip (trombone), Gardner (clarinet), Wally Eckehardt (bass), and Chuck Kreigh (drums). The repertoire included "San Francisco Bay," "Tishomingo Blues," "Just Before the Battle," "Mother," "Royal Garden Blues," "Down By the Riverside," "South Rampart Street Parade," "Wolverine Blues," "When the War Breaks Out in Mexico I'm Gonna Head for Montreal," "Windermere Blues," "Just a Closer Walk With Thee," "Black and Blue," and "At the Jazz Band Ball." Gardner recorded with the same personnel with Joe Sabatino added on banjo on an LP called *Southern Comfort* for Mound City.[96] The tunes on this recording included "Memphis Blues," "Sleepy Time Down South," "Alabama Jubilee," "Carolina in the Morning," "South," "Washington and Lee Swing," "Relax With Southern Comfort," "Is It True What They Say About Dixie," "Waitin' for the Robert E. Lee," "Bourbon Street Parade," "Little Rock Getaway," and "Milneberg [i.e., Milenberg] Joys." Gardner also recorded a 45-rpm single for Mound City (Mound City 1188) with probably the same personnel. Two sides were issued: "Little David Play on Your Harp" and "Battle Hymn of the Republic."

The Dixie Stompers recorded in Creve Coeur, Missouri, in 1952–1953 for Delmar.[97] The personnel included Don Franz (trumpet), Jim Haislip (trombone), Jerry Shroder (clarinet, vocal), John Chapman (piano), Bill Shroder (banjo), Ed Wilkinson (tuba), and Bob Kornacher (drums). They recorded the following tunes: "I Wish I Could Shimmy Like My Sister Kate," "Mecca Flat Blues," "Ice Cream," "I Can't Give You Anything But Love," "Mosley Moan," and "Rock Of Ages."

The Dixie Stompers recorded again in Creve Coeur during the same time frame.[98] In this recording, Bob Schroeder played clarinet and Wyatt Ruther played banjo and bass. Jerry Schroder, Bill Schroder, and Ed Wilkinson were not on this recording. The tunes recorded on this session were: "High Society," "At the Jazz Band Ball," "Shine," "Nobody's Fault But Mine," "Black and White Rag," "Careless Love Blues," and "Pretty Baby." The piano player on these sessions, John Chapman, is not the black John "Albino Red" Chapman who was such an important mentor to John Hicks, Freddie Washington, and others (see Chapter 6).

A racially integrated Dixie Stompers[99] recording was made in St. Louis and Fulton, Missouri, in 1956 with Bill Mason (cornet), Jim Haislip (trombone), Norman Mason (clarinet), Glen Tinterra (piano), Pete Patterson (banjo), and Bob Kornacher (drums). The tunes were: "Mahogany Hall Stomp," "Heebie Jeebies," "Dipper Mouth Blues," "Doctor Jazz," "Tishomingo Blues," "At a Georgia Camp Meeting," and "Lonesome Road." Many of the tunes recorded during this period have been recorded again and again by traditional jazz groups in St. Louis up to the present time.

Charlie Parker was recorded with the Woody Herman Orchestra in August 1951 from a broadcast from the Chase Hotel. The LP called *Bird with the Herd* appeared on Almanac. The Almanac titles listed are also on Sound Hills (Japan) 8017/34 [CD], an eighteen-CD set of Charlie Parker's music. Boogie Woogie pianist Pete Johnson was privately recorded in the fall of 1954 in solo and piano duet with either Tom Harris or Charlie Castner. Gene Krupa was recorded on a cassette called *Gene Krupa and His Men of Jazz* at the Sheraton-Jefferson Hotel in 1958 for the Starline label (SLC61006). Pianist Russ David was recorded as part of a group called the Millionaires Four for Lammert's Furniture Store on an LP called *You Don't Have to Be a Millionaire* around 1960 (Lammerts LALP-A100).[100]

Vocalist Bev Kelly recorded live in the basement of a church in the Soulard District[101] with Bob Graf (tenor sax on the last seven tunes), Jimmy Williams (piano), Lyle Moore (bass), and Henry Ettman (drums) in November 1959 by the VGM label. The LP, titled *You Go To My Head*,[102] included "My Buddy," "Ain't Misbehavin,'" "The Nearness of You," "Exactly Like You," "Delilah" (instrumental), "You Go To My Head, Gone With the Wind," "This Can't Be Love," "All Blues" (Instrumental), "Detour Ahead," and "Bye Bye, Blackbird."

Other St. Louis Musicians with National Reputations from the 1950s

The great baritone saxophonist Bobby Gordon[103] (1928–1955) left his native St. Louis after high school and played with the dance bands of Shorty Sherrock (1946), Alvino Rey (1948–1951), Billy May (1952), and Horace Heidt (1962–1963). Gordon studied at the Westlake College of Music in 1948–1949. He was a mainstay of the West Coast Jazz movement, recording with Shelly Manne, Shorty Rogers, and others. Gordon made one recording as a leader, *Meet Mr. Gordon*, for Pacific Jazz in 1954.[104] Unfortunately, Gordon was killed in Los Angeles in a car accident.

Largely self taught, trumpeter Buddy Childers (born 1926) was born in St. Louis but raised in Belleville, Illinois. While the Kenton Orchestra was at Tunetown in December 1942, he successfully auditioned for the lead trumpet spot, working on and off with the band until 1954. He also worked with the bands of Benny Carter (1944), Les Brown (1947), Woody Herman (1949), Tommy Dorsey (1951–1952), and others through 1954. He moved to Los Angeles and became a studio musician, recording with Oliver Nelson, Quincy Jones, and others. Childers also taught at Los Angeles City College and was still working in 2001.[105]

Vocalist Leon Thomas (1937–1999) was born in East St. Louis. He studied music at Tennessee State University and went to New York in 1958, working with many mainstream and avant-garde players in the 1960s and 1970s. His vocal style is unique for its use of "yodeling" for scat singing.[106]

St. Louis Clubs Presenting Jazz in the Latter Part of the 1950s

There were many clubs on both sides of the Mississippi presenting jazz. The Judges Chambers was an East Side club, as was the Harlem Club. The Harlem Club must have had an arrangement with the Glass Bar, because musicians booked at the Glass Bar would play a one nighters at the Harlem Club just before or just after their Glass Bar engagements. The Glass Bar/Peacock Alley, Club Riviera, the Show Bar, the Hurricane Lounge, and the Barrel were the best known in St. Louis. The Roma Room on Finney, the Mellow Cellar, the Paris Lounge, the Blue Flame Club, Club Manhattan, and others were less well known. By the late 1950s, El Patio at Easton (now Dr. Martin Luther King) and Taylor, the Baby Grand at Taylor and Cook, Gino's at Delmar and DeBaliviere, the Beaumont Bar (at Olive and Beaumont), Nips at Washington and Taylor, and the 20th Century Bar on Vandeventer near Enright all had modern jazz by mainly black local musicians. The Frolic Bar was just up Lawton from the Peacock Alley. Until Gaslight Square, white and black local musicians mainly played on the DeBaliviere Strip, although Gino's had modern musicians. White and some black players also worked in South St. Louis in places like the Fallen Angel on Gravois (drummer Henry Ettman worked there with reedman Ron Ruff, guitarist Bobby Caldwell, and bassist John Mixon). Grant Green was heard with Ettman at the Club Pastime at Dewey and Bates. The Playgirl on South Grand featured the twin tenors of Bob Graf and Red Anderson with Bob Ost on piano.[107] Parallel black and white jazz histories are beginning to become apparent again by the late 1950s.

Endnotes

[1] John Mixon, interview with the author, July 1986.

[2] Irene Cortinovis, interview with Eddie Johnson, Elijah Shaw, Chick Finney and Eddie Randle, August 20, 1971. University of Missouri–St. Louis Historical Manuscript Collection No. T-010.

[3] *St. Louis Argus,* September 2, 1949.

[4] Cortinovis interview.

[5] Singleton Palmer, interview with the author, June 1986.

[6] Cortinovis interview.

[7] Palmer interview.

[8] *St. Louis Argus,* August 4, 1950.

[9] Bob Koester, Delmark Records, private conversation with the author.

[10] Jeff Leopold, interview with the author, April 1986.

[11] Irene Cortinovis, interview with Elijah Shaw and Vivian Oswald, May 3, 1972. University of Missouri–St. Louis Historical Manuscript Collection No. T-109.

[12] Charlie Menees, interview with the author, 1986.

[13] Leopold interview.

[14] Sandra Pointer Jones, "Delmark History" in *Blues Revue Quarterly,* http://delmark.com/delmark.history.htm.

[15] *Tom Lord Discography,* version 3.3. (Delmar DL 101)

[16] Ibid. (Delmar DL 112 and 113)

[17] Ibid. (Delmar DL 204)

[18] Leopold interview.

[19] Norman Menne, interview with the author, July 10, 1986.

[20] Miles Davis/Jimmy Forrest, *Our Delight,* Prestige PRCD-24117-2 [CD].

[21] Mixon interview.

[22] Ibid.

[23] *St. Louis Argus,* June 6, 1953.

[24] Ibid.

[25] Herb Drury, interview with Bill Bunkers, KWMU radio, 1979.

[26] Ibid.

[27] Adapted from Peter Vacher, "Jimmy Forrest," *The New Grove Dictionary of Jazz,* Barry Kernfield, ed. (New York: St. Martin's Press, 1995), p. 400.

[28] *St. Louis Argus,* all issues from 1946 to year–end 1950.

[29] Jimmy Forrest, *Night Train,* Delmark DD-435.

[30] Count Basie, *Fun Time,* Pablo PACD-2310-945.

[31] Victoria Records VC 4332.

[32] Ibid. 4331.

[33] Compiled from Mixon interview, and Lynn Driggs Cunningham and Jimmy Jones, *Sweet, Hot and Blue: St. Louis Musical Heritage* (Jefferson, N.C.: McFarland and Company, 1989), p. 124.

[34] Lee Hyde, interview with Dennis Owsley and Jim Wallace on *Jazz Spectrum,* KWMU radio, St. Louis, 1985.

[35] Lee Hyde, interview with the author, March 24, 1986.

[36] Compiled from Dave Venn Biography on the Maxjazz website, http://www.maxjazz.com/venn/bio.htm.

[37] Steve Schenkel and Dave Venn, *A Celebration of American Song,* Generic Records GR-1.

[38] Herb Drury and Dave Venn, *Together,* MusicMasters MM-20148.

[39] Dave Venn, *1, 2, 3,* Max/Productions/Victoria Co. MM-34533.

[40] Robert L. Campbell, Armin Büttner, and Robert Pruter, *Tommy Dean Discography,* http://hubcap.clemson.edu/~campber/deanie.html.

[41] Chris Woods, interview with Bob Rusch, *Cadence* 10(6), June 1984.

[42] Peter Vacher, "Chris Woods," *The New Grove Dictionary of Jazz,* Barry Kernfield, ed. (New York: St. Martin's Press, 1995), p. 1306.

[43] Woods interview.

[44] Clark Terry, interview with the author, 1986.

[45] Campbell, et al., *Tommy Dean Discography.*

[46] Barry Kernfield, "Oliver Nelson," *The New Grove Dictionary of Jazz,* Barry Kernfield, ed. (New York: St. Martin's Press, 1995), pp. 833–834.

[47] Oliver Nelson, *Afro-American Sketches,* Prestige OJCCD-1819.

[48] Oliver Nelson, *Blues and The Abstract Truth,* Impulse! IMPD154.

[49] Oliver Nelson, *Sound Pieces,* GRP Impulse GRD-103 (Out of Print).

[50] Kenny Rice and Phillip Wilson, interview with the author, 1986.

[51] Tab Smith, *Jump Time,* Delmark DD-477.

[52] Terry interview.

[53] Ernie Wilkins, interview with the author, 1988.

[54] *Tom Lord Discography,* version 3.3.

[55] Terry interview.

[56] Wilkins interview.

[57] *St. Louis Argus,* May 18, 1951.

[58] Ibid., August 14, 1953.

[59] Walter Dixon, interview with the author, 1986

[60] *St. Louis Argus,* October 30, 1953.

[61] Dixon interview.

[62] McClinton Rayford, conversations with the author 1969–1985.

[63] Miles Davis, *The Miles Davis Quintet at Peacock Alley,* VGM-Soulard VGM-SOU-1997.

[64] *Tom Lord Discography,* version 3.3.

[65] Bob Graf, *Bob Graf at Westminster,* Delmark DD-401.

[66] Alex Henderson, *Bob Graf,* All Music Guide. http://www.allmusic.com.

[67] Chet Baker, *Chet Baker Big Band,* Pacific Jazz CDP 7 81201.

[68] Henry Ettman, telephone conversation with the author, February 1, 2006.

[69] Bev Kelly sings with the Bob Graf Quartet, *You Go to My Head,* VGM 0007.

[70] Sam Lazar, *Space Flight,* Argo LP 4002.

[71] Rice and Wilson interview.

[72] Compiled mainly from Sharony Andrews Green, *Grant Green: Rediscovering the Forgotten Genius of Jazz Guitar* (San Francisco: Miller Freeman Books, 1999).

[73] Dixon interview.

[74] Green, *Grant Green,* p. 47.

[75] Ibid., p. 60.

[76] *Tom Lord Discography,* version 3.3.

[77] Jimmy Forrest, *All the Gin Is Gone,* Delmark DD-404; *Black Forrest,* Delmark DD-427.

[78] Sharo Green, *Grant Green,* p. 69.

[79] Lou Donaldson, *Here 'Tis,* Blue Note BLP 4066.

[80] Grant Green, *Feelin' the Spirit* (Blue Note 64471), *The Complete Quartets with Sonny Clark* (Blue Note 57194), *Idle Moments* (Blue Note 99003), and *Talkin' About* (Blue Note 21958).

[81] Rice and Wilson interview.

[82] Kenny Rice, quoted in Green, *Grant Green,* p. 75.

[83] Rice and Wilson interview.

[84] Ibid.

[85] Leo Chears, quoted in Green, *Grant Green,* p. 74.

[86] Kenny Rice, quoted in Green, *Grant Green,* p. 74.

[87] Leo Gooden, *Spider Burks Presents Leo's Five,* L.G. Records #T6951.

[88] Leo Gooden, *Leo Sings,* L. G. Records.

[89] Kenny Rice–Richard Martin Quintet with Nat Adderley, *Recorded Live,* Recorded Live Records.

[90] Ibid.

[91] Cunningham and Jones, *Sweet, Hot and Blue,* pp. 206–208.

[92] Various artists, *Shout, Brother, Shout,* Alligator ALCD 2800.

[93] Cy Stoner, interview with Frank Driggs, May 26, 1976. Frank Driggs Archives, University of Missouri–Kansas City.

[94] *Tom Lord Discography,* version 3.3.

[95] Sammy Gardner, *Mound City Jazz,* Mound City Records P0687.

[96] Sammy Gardner, *Southern Comfort,* Mound City Records P-2854.

[97] The Dixie Stompers, Delmar DL-112.

[98] The Dixie Stompers, Delmar DL-113.

[99] The Dixie Stompers, Delmar DL-204.

[100] All information in this paragraph found in *Tom Lord Discography,* version 3.3.

[101] Ettman conversation.

[102] Kelly, *You Go to My Head.*

[103] Adapted from "Bob Gordon," *The New Grove Dictionary of Jazz,* Barry Kernfeld, ed. (New York: St. Martin's Press, 1995), p. 441.

[104] This session is available on Jack Montrose, *Jack Montrose Sextet,* Pacific Jazz CDP 4 93161 [CD].

[105] Robert Spencer, "Buddy Childers Biography," *All about Jazz* website, http://www.allaboutjazz.com/artists/bchilders.htm.

[106] Lee Jeske, "Leon Thomas," *The New Grove Dictionary of Jazz,* Barry Kernfeld, ed. (New York: St. Martin's Press, 1995), p. 1201.

[107] Ettman conversation.

6 The Rise & Fall of Gaslight Square (1959–1967)

An entertainment district centered on Olive and Boyle became quite popular by 1960. It happened because of a random act of nature. Before the area became known as Gaslight Square it was called Greenwich Corners, because of the clientele that frequented bars in the area like the Gaslight and the Golden Eagle. The neighborhood had interesting shops and residents that could be described as Bohemian in their outlook. That changed when a tornado struck the center of St. Louis on February 10, 1959. The Olive and Boyle neighborhood was particularly hard hit. According to Thomas Crone's book, *Gaslight Square: An Oral History*,[1] "The popular history suggests that local merchants quickly sank their insurance monies into refurbishing and renovation. Buildings that had been homes were now stripped out for restaurants or nightclubs. The fortunes of the block turned. The 4200 block of Olive became Gaslight."

A number of people began developing the area, Jay and Fran Landesman among them. The Landesmans opened the Crystal Palace at 4236–4240 Gaslight. They wrote the play, *The Nervous Set*, and brought in entertainers such as the Smothers Brothers and Barbra Streisand, who first attracted national attention on Gaslight Square. In addition to the national acts, countless local talent found work on Gaslight Square. According to Norman Menne, "I understand that Gaslight employed more musicians on a six night-a-week basis than anywhere in the country at any time."[2] Pianist Jeter Thompson, who worked with his group the Quartette Trés Bien at the Dark Side, said,[3] "Gaslight Square was the jewel of the city during that time and it had such a variety of entertainment, Dixieland jazz, straight ahead jazz, folk songs, restaurants, you name it, they had it." This chapter does not attempt to write a history of Gaslight Square, instead it attempts to delineate the part that jazz music played in it by describing the people, places, and clientele that enabled the music to flourish.

Traditional Jazz on Gaslight Square

Traditional jazz was heard with the Singleton Palmer Dixieland Six at the Opera House, Muggsy Sprecher's Gaslighters at Bustles and Bows and the Silver Dollar, Sammy Gardner at the Tiger's Den, and the St. Louis Ragtimers at the Natchez Queen and Bustles and Bows.

St. Louis always has been a weekend town, and if it had not been for the tourist trade, Gaslight Square would not have happened. Bringing in tourists looking for a good time caused problems for patrons who went there to listen. Charlie Menees recalled, "Some of those places on DeBaliviere and on Gaslight Square were somewhat difficult to appreciate jazz [in] because lots of people weren't there for jazz appreciation. They were there to have a good time. So, we would have to quiet them down frequently or go on an off night, when they wouldn't be too crowded like they would be on Fridays and Saturdays."[4] Jimmy Haislip, a fine trombonist who played with Gardner on Gaslight Square, characterized the Dixieland of that period as "rah, rah" music.[5]

Charlie Wells (1920–2002)[6] was the owner of the Tiger's Den. He was born in Maryville, Missouri, and came to St. Louis in 1941 to work in advertising first at the *Globe-Democrat* and then at the Gold Advertising Agency. He was the booker for both Tunetown and Club Plantation during this period. In the 1970s, Wells booked bands for the Heman Park Summer Concert Series in University City, using many of his favorites from Gaslight Square days. In 1981, Wells founded the Mid American Jazz Festival and ran it in late March for eighteen years. He and Charlie Menees founded the Lake of the Ozarks Jazz Festival in the early 1990s. Both festivals featured mainly traditional jazz with some jazz in the swing style.

Each venue on Gaslight Square was unique. The Dark Horse was in the style of an English Pub, while the Natchez Queen was a small room with expensive gold-on-white wallpaper and gaudy chandeliers. This room was so small that the musicians often carried on conversations with the customers, who were there to listen. Bustles and Bows was a large room with two bars and a very boisterous crowd. A club called The Roaring 20s featured dancers dressed as flapper girls, a doorman carrying a very real looking but non-working machine gun, and bartenders with toy guns in holsters. The entertainment was like a vaudeville show. Other clubs had Hawaiian décor or a Spanish theme with flamenco dancers.[7]

The Crystal Palace was described by comedian Lenny Bruce as "a church gone bad."[8]

Owner Jay Landesman called it a "cross between a church and a movie palace, without the reverence." Its walls were painted fire engine red; a backlit 50-foot stained glass mural cast a glow which was reflected in the Landesman-designed chandeliers worked of brass and crystals salvaged from Victorian structures falling to the wrecker's ball as part of the city's "progress." Stained glass, ornate wooden paneling, marble busts, and even wrought iron grilles rescued from the demolished Merchants Exchange building found new life in this transformed retail space.

Singleton Palmer was one of the stars of Gaslight Square. He talks about his experiences.[9]

It was great. I loved it over there. In fact, I don't see how I'm able to sit here talk to you now because see, I worked there from 9-1 at night and I would leave there and go on my . . . what they called a housekeeping job . . . for Chromalloy Company. I worked in the housekeeping department until 8-9 in the morning. . . . I'd get home at around 9:30 or 10 every morning. . . . Leave home at about eight. I did that for eight years. Of course I worked for them [Chromalloy] for twenty-five years. I've always had two jobs. Because in the music business it's okay for some people but a lot of guys just . . . don't want to do anything but that. And if you want to make a decent living and try to raise a family . . . unless you get on top, or something, you can't, there's no way. Not locally.

Gaslight Square Poster, date unknown. Photo montage by Edward H. Goldberger. © "Cactus" Charlie Menees Collection, Department of Special Collections, Miller Nichols Library, University of Missouri–Kansas City.

GASLIGHT SQUARE, whose nighttime brilliance is caught in the above montage, beckons visitors to St. Louis with its kaleidoscope of color and excitement. The soft gaslights which line the famed square have brightened the entertainment scene in St. Louis in thousand-foot candles of intensity. Basically built, around a re-creation of St. Louis' famed riverboat and gaslight era, the scope of the Square now includes a world-wide assortment of brilliantly designed spots. From Japanese calm to the other side of the moon, from elegant crystal Victorian to 2¢ seltzer at a turn-of-the-century delicatessen, a lone guitarist's concentration to a pre-Broadway production —GASLIGHT SQUARE offers the unusual in infinite variety for a perfect evening of fun.

Drummer Ben Thigpen (1908–1971) was born in Laurel, Mississippi. He was best known as the drummer with the Andy Kirk Clouds of Joy, a job he held for seventeen years. He moved to St. Louis in 1947 and led the first interracial jazz combo, playing at the Glass Bar (see Chapter 4). He played with Singleton Palmer on Gaslight Square and was a highly respected man who was somewhat of a father figure to the young musicians in St. Louis. Singleton Palmer remembered him.[10]

Well, he took guys under his wing . . . you know. He was a good drummer. And . . . very well versed on drums. . . . He was kind-of-sort-of a business agent in the union too. So we would have to go over on the gigs and collect taxes from them . . . you know. And, of course a lot of time they would say, "Oh my God here comes that Ben you know." But he was a good guy. . . . I was really upset when he passed.

Ben Thigpen is the father of drummers Ed Thigpen and Bensid Thigpen. Ed is most famous for his tenure with the Oscar Peterson Trio from 1959 to 1965. Bensid was important in St. Louis during BAG days (see Chapter 7). Ed Thigpen remembers his father.[11]

He had a lot of love in him for people. He was always helping, always willing to help, you know, be helpful. And he was a good listener, as well as speaking, you know. You know, I didn't spend a great deal of time with my father. . . . I was raised in California. I had a wonderful year with him, almost two years, when I moved back from California. But I think, spiritually, always carried him because my mother talked always highly of him, you know. And then the time I did spend with him here was full of quality. So, that gave me a lot to live on. . . . I think what I most appreciate is how he was . . . the respect he had of his peers, his fellow man. The respect he had for people. And by that, it gave me a very strong heritage, you know, . . . something to live, sort of, up to. That image that I had, you know.

You know, the time I was with him, he very seldom talked about what he did or what he was doing. If you asked him, he just did. He just was, you know. He wasn't one to talk about these guys he played with. I do remember, because it was a living experience . . . when he would explain to me certain things about playing. I would ask him questions, of course, "How do you do this and why?" And he would tell me. And then if he would see something that he thought I needed to know about; it wasn't a whole lot of things, but they were important, very important points to make. Like learning to accompany people. To become one with them, to float with them, to how to keep a good pulse, for instance, you know, swinging time, how to feather a bass drum, how to try to be sympathetic, yes, . . . not in a condescending way but in a cooperative way with the soloist, the lead players and the ensemble; being very supportive of the group.

Singleton Palmer at the Opera House on Gaslight Square, c. 1963. Photograph by McCue. © Western Historical Manuscript Collection–St. Louis.

He was a [union] representative in East St. Louis, you know. There he, I know personally, he helped a lot of people, even Ike and Tina Turner when they were around there. And he was all, you know, because you had to have your dues paid up, he was always helping people, a lot of musicians that way. . . . And he was going back in the backwoods of East St. Louis, which is really down home. I was scared, but boy he would just, he had a way of just floating through people. He was very people oriented, . . . and the people felt at ease and peaceful. We used to have an annual barbecue. Couple times he used to do that and entertain. A very gracious host, you know. And we would have just an odd mixture of people coming through the house all the time . . . one big spiritual family, you know. Everything from the mayor to whomever, you know. It was, so that was very good. My father was quite a man.

Drummer Lige Shaw also played with Palmer on Gaslight Square. Palmer described Shaw and his playing.[12]

He was a very well-versed musician. He could play the bells; he could play anything, xylophones. . . . And I've never heard of a drummer yet that could make a roll, a drum roll like Lige; just continuous. Just like you were tearing paper or something. And . . . he was very adept with his hands. . . . He was a showman. He wasn't too much of a swing man. But he could play, tip his hat, throw his sticks up and take his sticks and hit them on the floor and they would go up in the air and he would catch them comin' down. . . . He was quite an asset to the band.

Clarinetist Sammy Gardner led Dixieland bands from the early 1950s on the DeBaliviere Strip and in Gaslight clubs. He taught many young musicians how to play. Norman Menne worked with Gardner for a year in 1960 on the Square.

Sammy Gardner (1926–1995)

Clarinetist Sammy Gardner was born in St. Louis. He studied clarinet in the Kirkwood school system and was playing professionally during his high school years. Although known principally as a clarinetist, Gardner also played flute, oboe, saxophones, violin, trumpet, and tuba. After serving in the army from 1944 to 1947, he enrolled at the St. Louis Institute of Music, earning a Bachelor of Music Education. Gardner taught music in the St. Louis County schools in 1951–1957, while carrying on a parallel career as a traditional jazz musician. He recorded his first album with his Windy City Six for Delmar (later Delmark) Records in 1953.

Gardner appeared on the Arthur Godfrey TV show in July 1958 and had his own TV show in St. Louis for two years. After working at the Roundtable in New York, he returned to St. Louis for a long run at Charlie Wells's Tiger's Den on Gaslight Square. Gardner was a fixture on Gaslight Square and was known for his showmanship. Norman Menne said, "Every night was like New Years Eve" working with him. In addition, Gardner trained many of St. Louis's traditional jazz musicians as they passed through his group. With the collapse of Gaslight Square, he moved to Pensacola, Florida, to join his fellow St. Louis trumpet player, Don Gumpert, at Rosie O'Grady's original club in 1972. He continued working in Florida until his death.

He taught you tunes. Unfortunately, he taught you tempos. And dynamics rubbed off to a certain extent. But you're right; he taught a lot of guys. Every night was New Year's Eve with Sam. Everything was exciting. The slowest tune's tempo was so fast you couldn't believe it and that was the blues. . . . And Don Gumpert was on cornet with us. Don Summers [later a boat captain for Streckfus] was on tuba. Sammy taught you the music and [drummer] Charlie Kreigh taught you the nightlife, I guess you could say. But, he was fun.

Drummer Joe Buerger was a rock and roll drummer who went down to Gaslight Square while he was still in high school. Sammy Gardner hired him and trumpeter Bob Ceccarini at the same time. Buerger's father played bass with the group during the week as an unpaid member of the group.[13]

I was eighteen and had no idea what Dixieland was. Gaslight was really something to see back then. I went down there . . . and Sammy asked if I could play with his band. My folks said, "OK, as long as I graduated high school." So Sammy took me on and I got the Dixieland jazz training in that band, like a lot of us did. . . . Well, you had Sammy and Singleton Palmer and Jeanne Trevor. You could go down there; everybody was in that one little area. It was really neat. . . . And I actually thought I was [Gene] Krupa.

Later on, we found out that all the guys on Gaslight Square that were playing . . . had said to Sammy, "What are you doing hiring those two guys? They don't know how to play Dixieland." But we didn't find out until a couple of years later or we'd have given up the whole thing.

He [Gardner] would try some really nutty things just to get the audience involved. He used to have the front line lay down on the stage and play the last chorus and things. A lot of the Dixie bands I play with today are still using those [Gardner's] arrangements.

Bassist Pat Murphy began his career with Sammy Gardner while Joe Buerger was in the band.[14]

Well, Pat Murphy, the bass player came down to Gaslight Square . . . and he had just bought a bass. You gotta understand that Pat Murphy works for an elevator company and he had never touched a bass before. He just wanted to learn how to play one. And he [Murphy] walked and he said to Sammy Gardner, "Hey, man, I just bought a bass fiddle and I'm really looking forward to learning how to play it." And Sammy looked at him and said, "Where is it?" He [Murphy] says, "It's in my car." He [Sammy] said, "Go get it and bring it in. I wanna see it." So Murph went out and got the bass, brought it in and Sammy said, "Go ahead, put it up on the stage, we're goin' back off break right now." And he [Murphy] said, "Yeah, but who's gonna play it?" "You are. You

St. Louis Ragtimers, St. Louis, 1980. Photographer unidentified. © Don Franz. Left to right: Don Franz, Trebor Tichenor, Bill Mason, Al Stricker.

wanted to learn how to play the bass didn't ya?" So that was Pat Murphy's debut on the bass fiddle. To tell you the truth, I don't remember how he sounded, but he's been playin' ever since.

Buerger worked with Singleton Palmer and learned the difference between what he had been playing with Gardner and other bands and playing with Palmer.[15]

Actually, Singleton Palmer called me to play for him a couple of years ago and I filled in a little while in his band. Now, that is the real [traditional] Dixieland and there is a big difference between that and what we [whites] play. And I wasn't really familiar with it at all. And it was a little bit of a struggle for me at first until I got to know the style. . . . We do everything pretty quick. And the rhythm section is really not staying in two beat [two beats to the bar] very long while the bass player is walkin' four [beats to the bar], even though Single-ton does that. He can play four on the tuba, which is amazing. We play everything up-tempo, keep it bright and exciting; keep everybody a little nervous. And the traditional thing like with Singleton's band was real tasty and a little more laid back. When I first played with Singleton, I was walkin' all over the guys because I wasn't used to that feel.

Cornetist Muggsy Sprecher (1922–1999) was born in Independence, Wisconsin. Sprecher started playing cornet at age nine and played all through his service in World War II. He settled in St. Louis after the war and worked with Sammy Gardner. He formed his own group in the late 1940s and was a favorite on Gaslight Square. He also worked as an advertising salesman for the St. Louis *Suburban Journals* (1953–1983). He played occasionally in his later years for Jazz Club events. Sprecher died of cancer.

The St. Louis Ragtimers of Trebor Tichenor (piano), Bill Mason (cornet), Al Stricker (banjo, vocal), and Don Franz (tuba) started at the Natchez Queen on Labor Day 1961. The Natchez Queen was a small restaurant with expensive furnishings. According to Tichenor, the crowd was a listening crowd, but when they went to Bustles and Bows in 1964, a much larger venue, they found a different, more boisterous crowd.[16]

Jazz Vocalists on Gaslight Square

Three jazz vocalists who went on to long careers worked on Gaslight Square. Ceil Clayton, Jeanne Trevor, and Clea Bradford. Vocalist/pianist Ceil Clayton (1925–1997)[17] was born in New Bedford, Massachusetts. Clayton began singing on local radio stations when she was eight years old and later studied music at the New England Conservatory in Boston. She moved to St. Louis after World War II and was a feature performer at Mr. D's Steak House. She recorded two albums during this period (see below). Mainly a solo artist, Clayton started playing in a trio context in the 1980s and worked in Scandinavia late in her career.

Singer/actress Jeanne Trevor came to St. Louis from New Jersey to work on Gaslight Square. Some of her memories are in Crone's *Gaslight Square: An Oral History.*[18]

> The group was set when I came to town, primarily a trio with piano, bass and drums. It was pretty much the same people who'd been there and stayed together. Same piano player, bass and drummer. I was at the Black Horse for a lengthy time. The other main place I played was the Vanity Fair. We had big crowds. Definitely. Every night. There might have been different nights off for entertainers, like Sundays and some Mondays, but we worked every night.

Trevor had a wide repertoire during her sets, but because she did mostly jazz, she was called a jazz singer. She continues to do her potpourri of songs at all her performances. Trevor didn't work at the Dark Side or Jorgie's, which had a mainly black clientele. She played at Le Jazz Hot, one of the Square's white clubs., "That was a really jazzy, smoky place. It had all the ambiance of what people think about a jazz dive. A lot of colorful characters!"[19] Trevor reminisced.[20]

> I look back on it with a great joy and great pride. It was a wonderful time for entertainment. But also for brotherhood and camaraderie. With the polarized city that it was, it brought everybody together. Being a young person, I thought that's the way the whole City was! I lived around there and was amazed that others went to white clubs or to black clubs or only to the East Side. It was dismaying. That was not for me.
> The Quartette Trés Bien were attractive by themselves. But they also had a vocalist with them on some of the early Norman recordings, Clea Bradford. She later moved to the Washington, D.C., area. Clea Bradford, she was really the First Lady of Jazz, not me. She left and I took over her reign.

Clea Bradford was born in Charleston, Missouri, and went to school in St. Louis. She was a protégé of Jimmy Forrest and made her professional debut at Faust's in East St. Louis. She was on the Playboy Club circuit and worked for a long stretch on Gaslight Square from late 1962 to 1966 at the Trés Bien Club, accompanied first by the Quartette Trés Bien and later by Dave Venn (piano), with John Mixon (bass) and Gene Gammage (drums). Bradford recorded a 45-rpm single for Norman records in 1963, accompanied by the Quartette Trés Bien (see below). She left St. Louis to tour internationally.

Modern Jazz on Gaslight Square

Three clubs on Gaslight Square had a policy of modern jazz. They were the Dark Side, the Other Side, and Jorgie's Hip Intertainment in the basement of the Adams Hotel. These clubs, which attracted a black clientele because of the jazz style, were, coincidentally, on opposite ends of the 4200 block of Gaslight. The Other Side featured the Jimmy Williams group and other local musicians. The Dark Side featured the Quartette Trés Bien. Jorgie's featured national names, such as Miles Davis, Shirley Horn, Johnny Hartman, Donald Byrd and Pepper Adams, John Coltrane, and others. The house band had bassist John Mixon and drummer Gene Gammage, who accompanied several of the national name acts.

Jeanne Trevor

Singer/actress Jeanne Trevor came to St. Louis to sing on Gaslight Square. Jeanne has been a St. Louis resident since. She worked at the Dark Horse, Vanity Fair, and for a short time, Le Jazz Hot while on the Square. In the late 1960s, she recorded an album, *Pow!*, on the Mainstream label with the Quartette Trés Bien and saxophonist Peanuts Whalum.[21] In the 1970s, she was part of the St. Louis Jazz Quartet and presented her work in schools. This group recorded an album, *St. Louis Jazz Quartet* for EI Productions.[22] Jeanne works in Gaslight Square retrospectives. She has toured colleges in the United States, Canada, and Australia. Jeanne appeared at the International Festival of Jazz at San Luis, Senegal (Africa), in 1998. She has performed with the St. Louis Symphony and in the production "Women & Blues." Jeanne has also appeared at the Municipal Opera and now performs regularly with Young Audiences in schools. Trevor was awarded a Grammy from the National Academy of TV Arts and Sciences for outstanding achievement in a commercial spot announcement. She recorded a CD called *Love You Madly* for Catalyst Productions.[23] Jeanne has appeared at Jazz at the Bistro

Jeanne Trevor & the St. Louis Jazz Quartet

Jeanne Trevor, St. Louis, c. 1963. Photographer unidentified. © "Cactus" Charlie Menees Collection, Department of Special Collections, Miller Nichols Library, University of Missouri–Kansas City.

and worked at the Sheldon Concert Hall on a production for school children called "The Jazz Story" with Carolbeth True. She appeared at the U.S. Bank St. Louis Jazz Festival in 2003 and continues a busy performing schedule.

Jeter Thompson and the Quartette Trés Bien

One of the people who parlayed his success on Gaslight Square was pianist Jeter Thompson with his group the Quartette Trés Bien, which consisted of Richard Simmons (bass), Albert St. James (drums), and Percy James (congas, bongos, and percussion). The group came about in this way.[24]

I met Percy James on a television show. Spider Burks had a television show in Belleville, and I met Percy James there and we sort of hit it off together and we formed what was known back then as the Trio Trés Bien, which consisted of bass, bongos and congas. Incidentally, Percy played brushes on the conga to get the drum effect. . . . Before Richard Simmons the original trio consisted of Herschel Harris and Percy James and myself.

Both Thompson and Percy James[25] remember other bass players before Harris and Simmons. Drummer Al St. James joined the group at the Dark Side on Gaslight Square in 1959. Chuck Carter was the drummer with the group until then.[26]

We got quite a bit of recognition there. Matter of fact, it was a series of events there that sort of added to our popularity locally. The Route 66 television series came through town [and] shot a sequence at the Dark Side. And they chose Percy to do some dialog in the series, and the other members of the group were part of a background scene, playing instruments. Then Norman Wienstroer came through and heard us. And he wanted to cut an album, which we did. [We did] *Kilimanjaro* and *Boss Trés Bien.*

Clea Bradford

Clea Bradford-Silverlight[27] was born in Charleston, Missouri. She is of mixed African American/ Native American descent. She studied music with her grandfather, who taught her voice, music theory, and sight-reading. Her father was a minister. She was a neighbor of Jimmy Forrest and was soon on stage singing at her school prom. In the early 1950s, Forrest was holding jam sessions with Oliver Nelson and Clark Terry and she appeared with them. She made her professional debut at the Faust Club in East St. Louis. In 1955–1956, she toured in the Playboy Club Circuit.[28] Her first album in 1961, *These Dues*, was recorded for Tru-Sound. It was issued by Prestige as *Clea Bradford with Oliver Nelson and Clark Terry*.[29] She began working at the Trés Bien Club at 455 North Boyle in late 1962. Her second album, *Now*,[30] was recorded for Mainstream in 1965, and her third album, *Her Point of View*, for Cadet in 1968. Bradford toured the Soviet Union with Earl Hines in 1966 and toured Mexico with the 1967 Kool Jazz Festival, where St. Louisan John Hicks was her accompanist. She also was featured on a television special during the late 1960s called *Clea Bradford and Friends*, with St. Louis musicians Don Cunningham, Gene Lynn, and the John Mixon Quartet. The special aired in New York, Philadelphia, Chicago, Los Angeles, and St. Louis. She is now living in Washington, D.C., and continues performing and touring.

Clea Bradford at the Tres Bien Club, St. Louis, 1963. Photograph by *St. Louis Post-Dispatch*. Photo restoration by Dennis Owsley. © Clea Bradford from the Al Becker Collection.

Later, we transferred to Decca Records. He was instrumental in doing that for us, and that vaulted us into national popularity.[31]

The group left the Dark Side and became partners in the Club Trés Bien in an old theater at Gaslight and Boyle.[32]

We left the Dark Side and became part of the Club Trés Bien . . . and we featured our group and Clea Bradford, who was a wonderful singer at the time. I think we were there about eight months and we sold our portion of the club and hit the road in '63.[33]

The Quartette Trés Bien left St. Louis under the sponsorship of Dick Gregory.[34] The group was on the road for ten years, playing all the major venues, including the Apollo Theater in New York, one time on a bill with Dizzy Gillespie, comedian Dick Gregory, and vocalist Bill Henderson.

They wanted us to open the show with the curtain closed playing the song "I May Be Wrong, But I Think You're Wonderful." And we started playing the song and I heard this funny sound in the back and it was Dizzy Gillespie behind the other curtain

Jeter Thompson (born 1930)

Native St. Louisan Jeter Thompson's[35] father played piano, trumpet, and banjo by ear, and as a five-year-old Jeter started playing the piano. His formal training started when he was seventeen at Sumner High School. Jeter was sixteen when he had his first professional job, with saxophonist Emmett Carter at the Coconut Grove Strip Club in downtown St. Louis. He was thrown out of school a couple of times for playing boogie-woogie in the choir room, but he became president of the 100th class at Sumner. Thompson was in the army during the Korean War. While overseas, he got to play with many outstanding musicians. He returned from the army in 1954 and began working around St. Louis. The Quartette Trés Bien was formed with Richard Simmons (bass), Albert St. James (drums), and Percy James (congas, bongos, and percussion) in 1959. The group played at the Dark Side on Gaslight Square and, in 1963, became partners in the Club Trés Bien. They appeared on the television series, *Route 66*. Recordings during this period on Norman Records brought them to the attention of Decca Records. After eight months at the Club Trés Bien, the group went on the road.

The Quartette Trés Bien worked in all the major venues that presented jazz around the United States, including the Apollo Theater in New York, the Tivoli Theater in Chicago, and the It Club in Los Angeles. They played opposite Dizzy Gillespie, Ramsey Lewis, Thelonious Monk, Bill Henderson, Michael Olatunji, and many others. The Quartette Trés Bien came off the road in 1973 and ceased to be a regularly performing unit.

Thompson worked at the U.S. Geological Survey facility as a cartographer and as a real estate agent, while maintaining a performance schedule in St. Louis clubs like Gene Lynn's on Lindell. He continues to work with his twin brothers Harold Thompson (bass) and Howard Thompson (drums) and his niece, vocalist Danita Mumphard.

playin' along with us. Dizzy said he liked to play with musicians who could swing and I guess we fit that category. . . . We had a different sound and we were quite explosive at the time and that created a lot of excitement.

The group recorded thirteen albums for Decca and one for Atlantic during that time. During their travels they played the It Club in Los Angeles opposite Thelonious Monk in 1964. Columbia made the famous *Thelonious Monk Live at the "It" Club* recording during the engagement. Columbia also taped the Quartette Trés Bien, and Jeter Thompson has the master tape from that recording. It has never been released. They also recorded an album for United Artists that has never been released. The Quartette Trés Bien came off the road in 1973 because jazz clubs were closing all over the country and there was no supporting circuit to travel in.

Percussionist Percy James[36] was born in St. Louis in 1929. He went to Vashon High School and then to Tennessee State College and later Lincoln University, where he became a bongo player. James left school and played with Jimmy Houston and George Hudson. He was with Jimmy Forrest for seven years and played on Forrest's *Night Train* hit recording in 1952. Percy was part of the Quartette Trés Bien and was on the road with the group until 1973. He remains active in St. Louis and appeared at Artfair 2004.

Drummer Albert St. James (born 1934) is a Vashon High School alum as well. While he was there, he became interested in drums. St. James was inspired by a family friend, Clarence Taylor, at about sixteen; he did his first professional jobs with Taylor in burlesque houses. He played in the Vashon swing band, but not the marching band. St. James played with Charlie Parker at the Glass Bar in 1954 or 1955. St. James continued to work into the 1980s in St. Louis.

Jorgie Martinez was a jazz fan who was working around Gaslight Square. He set up and promoted jazz at a club, mainly remembered as being operated by Spider Burks, called the Other Side.[37]

> My first experience with a place there was a place called the Other Side. There was a club in front of that that was owned by a young lady by the name of Gayle Tibe. That was a place that featured the Quartette Trés Bien. They were the house band; they were there for like three or four years, every night, and they were just a fantastic jazz ensemble. Behind the building was a garage, it looked like a two-car garage and not much larger than this room. And the guy who had leased the space, a guy by the name of Marvin Gralnick, . . . didn't know what to do with it because he couldn't get a liquor license because there was a law that states you have to have visibility from the street.
>
> So he couldn't get a license for that reason and he didn't know where to go with it. So he came to me and he asked me if I had an idea and I said, "yeah," I had an idea. We could do a jazz coffeehouse. A late-night thing since we can't do liquor. We could open like at 11 o'clock and in those days they had the law where you had to close at 1 o'clock and on Saturday night you had to close at midnight because of the strong religious thing of not being able to sell alcohol on Sundays. So Sunday was legally after midnight. So at midnight everybody had two choices. They could either go to the East Side, which was what a lot of people did. There were a lot of very successful clubs in East St. Louis at that time, or they could try to find a late-night club. So we turned that into an espresso house featuring jazz, 'cause that's always been my main love is jazz. And so we put a jazz trio in there. That was a really exciting little scene. It was just packed every night. We served espresso coffee, soft drinks and pastries and that type of thing. We were only open from 10 till 3 A.M., every night but Monday.

Martinez recalled how popular DJ Jesse "Spider" Burks became involved in the Other Side.[38]

> What happened at that scene, there was a very well known DJ in town in those years by the name of Spider Burks. He had a jazz show on the radio for a few hours a day and he came down. He was a very manipulative guy, very ambitious, very greedy, and he was coming in regularly and talking to Marvin. And Marvin then announced to me that Spider was going to take over my role of overseeing the scene and because of his credentials with the jazz station that he had convinced him that he could really . . . I don't know how much more business they could have done. They were doing optimum business at the moment, but he thought that would be a good idea to have Spider mention the place on the radio daily, which he did. So they continued to operate the business. I don't know what happened, but it finally just ceased to be.

Martinez opened a second club, Jorge's Hip-Intertainment, in the Adams Hotel at 4295 Gaslight. He featured modern jazz,[39] including the only St. Louis appearance of the John Coltrane Quartet. Due to his place in the basement of the Adams Hotel, where a restaurant already had a liquor license, Martinez could not serve alcohol. Presenting jazz in a bar is difficult economically, but it is suicide without a liquor license.

> So all we had to offer was espresso coffee, desserts, sandwiches and that type of thing. So it was very difficult. But the Gaslight Square Association didn't like it anyway and they were happy to see it close because they were very racist. A very racist community at that time. St Louis is still a very racist city. But they thought that it would bring too many blacks into the area, and it really was not true, in fact, I was down on the end of the street and they'd really just come there and come into my club and they didn't really have any interest in any of the other places because it was not anything they had any interest in. So that was kind of an unfounded fear. That was just not working out at all.

Martinez had recording equipment tied into the PA system in his club.[40] These private tapes eventually made their way to VGM Records, which issued them in the 1980s. A number of recordings in that club can be found on that label (see later discussion). From the recorded evidence, Martinez had Johnny Hartman backed by the Andrew Hill Trio, the Montgomery Brothers, Nancy Wilson backed by the Three Sounds, the Donald Byrd-Pepper Adams Quintet, and the Shirley Horn Trio

all in the spring and summer of 1961. The Miles Davis Quintet played at Martinez's Jazz Villa in 1963 and its performance was also issued on VGM in the 1980s.

John Coltrane and his quartet with Elvin Jones were at Jorgie's in 1961. Phillip Wilson remembers a telephone call from Coltrane when Elvin did not come to work,[41] "I was livin' a block from there. I ran over there and Chauncey [Williams] played a set and after about two sets I think, Elvin came in and I was completely mesmerized. Elvin came in and just about destroyed everything I had done."

Popular jazz disc jockey Leo Chears[42] (1932–2006) was born in Lamar, Mississippi, and moved with his family to Brooklyn, Illinois, when he was eight years old. Two years later, they relocated to East St. Louis. Chears graduated from East St. Louis Lincoln High School. Leo was in the army from 1955 to 1957 and began work in one of the Barnes Hospital labs when he returned. He married his wife Betty in 1955. The couple had two children and five grandchildren. His radio debut was on WAMV-AM in East St. Louis. During his career, Chears worked at WBBR, KADI-FM, KSD, WMRY, WRTH, and WSIE. Because he worked during the day, Chears was a nighttime presenter of jazz. He worked from his own record, and later CD, collection and normally played jazz from the mainstream "soul music" style but was knowledgeable in all jazz styles. Chears was known as "the Man in the Red Vest," a nickname he was given by one of his sponsors when he was on KSD, Anheuser-Busch. Chears wrote a weekly jazz column for the *St. Louis Monitor* for nearly forty years. His radio show ran from midnight to 5:00 A.M., six nights a week. Illness forced him to reduce his workload to one night a week, which he produced from his home.

The Upstream Lounge

The Upstream Lounge at 7th and Pine opened in 1964. The Gayle Bell Quartet played on that bandstand and was superseded by the Eddie Fritz Quartet. Fritz and his group played there for seven years. Fritz remembers a young David Sanborn sitting in with the group. The Upstream was eventually moved to 903 West Pine around 1976. Other groups that worked at the Upstream included the Gordon Lawrence Latin Jazz Group, the Bernard Hutcherson Quartet, the Kennedy Brothers, and a quartet with organist Benny Wilson, alto saxophonist Bob Gibson, and drummer McClinton Rayford. The Upstream Lounge ceased its jazz policy around 1978.

Other Musicians Working Around St. Louis during This Period

Pianist John Chapman was a legendary player around St. Louis. He was also known as "Albino Red" among the musicians. Chapman went to Sumner High School and was in demand from the time he was young. The tenor saxophonist Freddie Washington remembered Chapman.[43]

> Oh, Yeah. That was one of the greatest . . . He was one of the first St. Louis pianists I heard that, you know, was really versed in all the masters prior . . . during that time. Thelonious Monk was a big influence on his playing. You could hear that and Bud Powell as well and some of the others. But, nevertheless, he had a sound and a style of his own. And the way his fingers go across the piano, you never think he's make anything. But his whole approach was different and interesting . . . always the element of surprise. And I think that helped the creative spirits and it really helped me to find different avenues of playing.
>
> He was a very comical guy; he had some nonverbal communications [that would] really break everybody up. He bounces when he walks. There were a whole lot of things about him that were just a treasure.

The pianist John Hicks first met Chapman when he tuned his family's piano.[44] Later he and Chapman used to hang out at El Patio in the late 1950s. Chris Woods played with Chapman a lot during this time. Hicks recalled, "John was very inspiring to a lot of other players. On the level that he played, everybody had to be up for it." Hicks remembers visiting him at his mother's house and he had the complete score for *Porgy and Bess*. Chapman was a big fan of Gershwin and had the scores to all the Gershwin piano pieces. Hicks wrote a composition for him called "For John Chapman" in 1984 on a recording called *John Hicks* that was reissued in 2003.[45] Unfortunately, Chapman was a substance abuser and froze to death during the winter of 1978.

Tenor saxophonist Freddie Washington was born in St. Louis in 1937. Although his family had no musical training, his mother played piano by ear. He and his siblings took piano lessons. Freddie took lessons from age eight to age ten. Around age twelve, he heard an alto sax on the radio and ended up taking lessons on a C-melody saxophone. He took his first lessons from a Mr. Slaughter and stayed with him two or three years. He then took music lessons at the Ludwig Music Company. By the time he was sixteen, he was playing with Jimmy Houston's band and later with George Hudson's orchestra. Freddie graduated from Sumner High School and joined the navy in 1956 as a musician and was stationed in Washington, D.C., with the navy band. He returned to St. Louis in 1959 and began working in a quintet with Bobby Danzig, John Chapman, John Mixon, and the legendary drummer Joe Charles. Washington's influences as a saxophone player are Sonny Stitt, Stan Getz, Sonny Rollins, and John Coltrane. His playing was also affected by trumpeter Vincent Pitts and by St. Louis tenor player Wilbert Hemsley, a player with harmonic concepts similar to those of Coltrane. His first recordings were for the VGM label in 1965, under Webster Young's name (see below). He has had a long career in St. Louis, recording with cornetist Nat Adderley, the Kennedy Brothers, and Kenny Rice in 1977.[46] He also recorded with vocalist Mae Wheeler in 2001.[47]

Musicians Who Left St. Louis during This Period

Pianist John Hicks (1941–2006) was born in Atlanta. His father family moved to St. Louis in 1955 when his father became the pastor of Union Memorial Methodist Church. He attended Sumner High and went to Lincoln University in 1958 for one year. He then went to New York, playing with tenor saxophonists Pharoah Sanders, Lucky Thompson, and Sonny Rol-

Freddie Washington, St. Louis, 1978. Photograph by Dennis Owsley. © Dennis Owsley Collection.

lins, drummer Art Blakey, Jr., and trumpeter Kenny Dorham. He attended Berklee College of Music during this period. In 1964, Cedar Walton recommended him to Art Blakey. He toured with Blakey for two years and learned a few things. "For one thing, I learned endurance. We used to do a lot of long sets with the three-horn format. I did some writing. . . . One of the main things about that band was that Art was encouraging you to write."[48] Hicks was in and out of St. Louis from 1965 to 1967, taking part in some VGM recordings (see above). He worked with Woody Herman in 1968 and had a long stay as Betty Carter's accompanist (1975–1980), although he had worked with her in 1966, 1973, and 1974. Hicks remembered that Carter "did these long, slow ballads. That was just great for my time."[49] John Hicks has become one of the most in-demand pianists in jazz. According to Scott Yanow, "From the early '80s on, Hicks has led his own trio and worked regularly with David Murray, Arthur Blythe, Pharoah Sanders, and others. As a leader, John Hicks has recorded for Strata East, Theresa, Limetree, DIW, Timeless, Red Baron, Concord, Evidence, Novus, Reservoir, Mapleshade, and Landmark, among others."[50]

David Sanborn was born in Tampa in 1945 and later moved to Kirkwood, Missouri, with his family. At age fourteen, he was working with Albert King. He later went to the University of Iowa and Northwestern University. Several people in St. Louis figured in his development. He heard some of his earliest jazz music at the Blue Note Club when Phillip Wilson took him there. Charlie Menees remembers taking him to clinics and J. D. Parran took him to places on Gaslight Square. He is best known as a rhythm and blues/rock player and studio musician. He now divides his time between studio work and performing. Interestingly enough, in interview after interview, Sanborn is emphatic that he is not a jazz musician. He hosted a show on jazz for top 40 radio stations and a late night TV show that featured Sun Ra, among others. In a *Downbeat* interview in August 1986, he said,[51] "I don't see myself in a direct line in the tradition of jazz. I didn't come out of that tradition . . . most of the contexts I've played in have been either blues based or R&B or straight out rock and roll. What experience I've had in playing jazz has been sporadic; most of it was with Gil Evans. . . . I don't want to misrepresent myself and I don't want to misrepresent the music." An interesting point: Sanborn still studied saxophone with jazzman George Coleman.[52] Sanborn last played in St. Louis at the First Bank Jazz Festival in June 2001.

Born in St. Louis in 1931, vocalist/saxophonist/percussionist Don Cunningham worked around St. Louis as a percussionist and was then on the road with Johnny Mathis after his army service. He returned to St. Louis and formed a quartet, working in many venues, most notably in the Playboy Club. It was there that his group recorded his album *Something for Everyone.* Cunningham left for Los Angeles in the early 1970s and married Alicia Cunningham. Both Cunninghams perform together and have an international reputation everywhere except in the United States. The Cunninghams live and work in Las Vegas.[53]

Drummer/percussionist George Marsh from Belleville began gigging when he was fifteen and sat in with Herb Drury and others during the Gaslight Square period. He moved to California in 1968, eventually teaching concurrently at the University of California–Santa Cruz and California State College at Sonoma. Marsh is the author of the book, *Intuitive Drumming*, and has recorded with John Abercrombie and others.[54]

Jazz Recordings in St. Louis during the Period (1960–1967)

Norman Wienstroer began to record St. Louis artists on his Norman Label during this period. He apparently was interested in getting the music that these people made out into the general public. He helped the Quartette Trés Bien get a Decca recording contract and also was instrumental in getting Singleton Palmer's group making records for Decca.

The VGM label recorded a number of nationally known artists in live performances on Gaslight Square in Jorgie Martinez's venues. Something must be noted about the VGM recordings: none contain statements for the national artists that were recorded by VGM that say, for example, "Donald Byrd appears courtesy of Blue Note Records," or "Miles Davis appears courtesy of Columbia Records."

Traditional Jazz Bands Recorded during the Gaslight Era

Singleton Palmer was recorded a number of times at the Opera House on Gaslight Square. The Norman Records releases *Dixie by Gaslight*[55] and *At the Opera House*[56] were apparently made at the same time in 1961 at the Opera House on Gaslight Square. The traditional jazz recordings made at Gaslight Square were quite narrow in their repertoire and, thus, song titles will not be given for the recordings. Only the personnel will be given, except where there is an exceptional performance. The personnel on the Palmer 1961 recordings is as follows: Bill Martin (trumpet), Leon King (trombone), Norman Mason (clarinet), Gus Perryman (piano), Singleton Palmer (tuba), and Lige Shaw (drums). The same personnel with Ben Thigpen in for Shaw on drums recorded in 1964 and 1967. The August 1964 recordings were *Singleton Palmer & His Dixieland Band*,[57] *Singleton Palmer*,[58] and *The Best Dixieland Band*.[59] A recording with the same personnel made for the Japanese label Paddlewheel Records in 1967 also was called *Singleton Palmer and His Dixieland Band*.[60]

Muggsy Sprecher recorded four albums during the Gaslight Square period. The first of these was *Ah-gah-boo*, which was recorded sometime in the early 1960s. The personnel included Sprecher (cornet), Tom Harrison (trombone), Bob Schroeder (clarinet), Paul Stanis (piano), Jerry Cherry (bass), and Rick O'Connor (drums).[61] Sprecher recorded three more albums with a different personnel: Muggsy Sprecher (cornet), Joe Sabatino (banjo, electric bass), Chuck Kreigh (drums), Bob Lush Dorries (piano), Russ Reno (clarinet), and Smith "Skip" Derringer (trombone). The following albums were recorded in 1962: *At Bustles and Bows with Muggsy's Gaslighters*,[62] *Silver Dollar Dixie* (with Art Buechler replacing Dorries),[63] and *Silver Dollar Dixie, Vol. 2*.[64]

Clarinetist Sammy Gardner recorded two albums in 1962. We know that one was recorded at the Tigers Den. There is a good chance that the second one was also recorded in that venue. The personnel included Gardner (clarinet, vocal), Jim Haislip (trombone), Don Gumpert (trumpet), Alfred Ware (piano), Don Summers (tuba), and Ralph Pellegrino (drums). The albums were titled *Sammy Gardner*,[65] and *Circa 1962*.[66]

Pianist Henry Brown and vocalist Edith North Johnson were recorded in St. Louis in May 1961 on an LP called *Barrelhouse Piano & Classic Blues* for the Folkways label.[67]

The St. Louis Ragtimers made two recordings in St. Louis for the Atlanta-based George H. Buck label during the period 1963–1964. The personnel included Bill Mason (cornet, washboard), Trebor Jay Tichenor (piano), Al Stricker (banjo, vocal), and Don Franz (tuba). The following tunes are on a CD titled *Honky Tonk Piano*:[68] "Cake-Walking Babies from Home," "Riverside Blues," "Georgia Swing," "Moving Day," "Black Mountain Rag," "Dead Man Blues," "Chestnut Valley Rag" (piano solo), "By and By," "I Ain't Rough," "Tank Town Bump," "When Ragtime Rosie Ragged the Rosary," "Bucksnort Stomp," "Eli Green's Cakewalk," and "They Gotta Quit Kickin' My Dawg Around." Drummer Ed Freund joined the group to fill out the CD on "Shake That Thing," "Lulu White," "Sailing Down Chesapeake Bay," "Up Jumped the Devil," "Mahogany Hall Stomp," "Steamboat Stomp," and "King Chanticleer." This repertoire is a bit different from the traditional jazz repertoire in that it dates from the 1890s up to the mid-1920s. The usual traditional jazz repertoire includes tunes mostly from the early 1920s through the Chicago-style period in the mid-1920s to the Bob Crosby Band of the 1930s.

St. Louis Ragtimers, Vol. 1,[69] a second George H. Buck CD, featured the group with Ed Freund and had the following tunes: "Waiting for the Robert E. Lee," "Gatemouth," "Canal Street Blues," "Ice Cream," "Maple Leaf Rag," "Chattanooga Stomp," "Gut Bucket Blues," and "Deep Ellum Blues." These tunes are again mainly from the ragtime era and the early 1920s.

Trebor Jay Tichenor allowed Folkways Records to use his piano roll collection for the LP *The Piano Roll*[70] around 1964. He was recorded live playing solo piano on the *Goldenrod Showboat* in March 1966. *Mississippi Valley Ragtime*[71] had the following ragtime and early jazz tunes along with his own compositions in the ragtime style: "Mississippi Valley Frolic" (a Ragtime & Cake Walk Fantasia), "Naked Dance," "X.L. Rag," "The Favorite" (Ragtime Two Step), "Ham And . . ." (in Ragtime), "'Possum & 'Taters" (a Ragtime Feast), "Show Me Rag" (a Missouri Defiance), "Bowery Buck" (Ragtime Two Step), "Chestnut St. in the '90s," "It's a Long Way Back Home" (a Blue Rag), "Big Fat Ham" (Stomp), "After the 'Possum Hunt" (Cake Walk), "Blind Boone's Southern Rag Medley #2" (Strains from Flat Branch).

Mainstream and Modern Jazz Recordings Made in St. Louis during the Gaslight Era

Vocalist/pianist Ceil Clayton made two albums for the Norman label. The first, titled *I Meet the Nicest People*, featured Clayton with a trio of Ralph DeRousse (bass) and Rich O'Donnell (drums) along with the Russ David Orchestra.[72] O'Donnell went on to a long career with the St. Louis Symphony. The tunes were "I Meet the Nicest People," "What Kind of Fool Am I?," "Ace in the Hole," "Misty," "Bye Bye" (Peter Gunn Theme), "The Sweetheart Tree," "Night Life," "Never Leave Your Sugar," "People," "You Don't Have To Be a Baby To Cry," "I Can't Say No," and "I Want a Little Boy." The second, *Ceil Clayton*,[73] featured Vic Cipponeri (bass), Dave Mortland (guitar), and Rich O'Donnell or Dave Rich (drums). The tunes on *Ceil Clayton* included "You Meet the Nicest People," "Little Girl Blue," "You Don't Have To Be a Baby To Cry," "Never Leave Your Sugar," "Coney Island Washboard," "That's All," "I Want a Little Boy," "I Left My Heart in San Francisco," "A Trout

No Doubt," "Alley Cat," "Bill Bailey Won't You Please Come Home," and "Must You Go." The repertoire on both CDs is a mixture of some standard and contemporary tunes. Both were recorded in the early 1960s.

Pianist Russ David, Art Schieler (bass), and Joe Schirmer (banjo, guitar, tipple) recorded *The Four of Us*[74] for Norman Records in the early 1960s. The tunes were: "One I Love," "The World Is Waiting for the Sunrise," "Take Six," "St. Louis Tickle," "What Is There To Say," "Joe's Jam," "They Can't Take That Away from Me," "St. Louis Blues," "Around the World," "The First Time I Saw Paris," "Cha Cha Joe," "David's Folly," and "Guitar Boogie."

The Quartette Trés Bien recorded for the Norman label in St. Louis before moving to Decca. The Quartette was Jeter Thompson (piano), Richard Simmons (bass), Albert St. James (drums), and Percy James (congas, bongos). Their first album, *Quartette Tres Bien*[75] was recorded in St. Louis around 1962. The tunes were "Lover Come Back To Me," "I Love Paris," "The Breeze and I," "Exodus," "Rhodesian Chant," and "Three O'clock in the Morning." Both "Exodus" and "Three O'clock in the Morning" also were on their Atlantic album, *Bully!*[76] The group also recorded "I Left My Heart in San Francisco" and "Ramblin' Rose" as a 45-rpm single during this time.[77] "Kilimanjaro," the title tune of their first Decca album was also recorded in St. Louis as a single.[78] The remaining tunes on the album *Kilimanjaro*[79] may have been recorded in either St. Louis or New York. They are "Secretly," "I Didn't Know What Time It Was," "My Favorite Things," "My One and Only Love," and "You Came a Long Way from St. Louis." One more tune was recorded in St. Louis as a single, "Boss Trés Bien,"[80] parts 1 and 2, became part of the Decca album, *Boss Tres Bien*.[81] Vocalist Clea Bradford recorded "Someday My Prince Will Come" in two parts with the group in 1963 as a single.[82]

The VGM label released several private recordings made around Gaslight Square in 1961. While the album jackets give various venues, there is a strong certainty that these recordings were made at the Jorgie's Hip Intertainment Club at 4295 Gaslight. *Sittin' in with Johnny Hartman & the Andrew Hill Trio*[83] recorded with Johnny Hartman (vocal), Andrew Hill (piano), John Mixon (bass), and Gene Gammage (drums) contains "Somebody Loves Me," "Stella by Starlight," "Andrew Grooves I" (instrumental), "You Came a Long Way from St. Louis," "Misty," and "Andrew Grooves II" (instrumental).

The Wes Montgomery album *Recorded Live at Jorgies Jazz Club*[84] has Buddy Montgomery (piano, vibes), Wes Montgomery (guitar), Monk Montgomery (bass), and Billy Hart (drums). "All of You," "Heartstrings," "Summertime," and "Back to Bach to Bock" were recorded. The Montgomery Brothers group also played "Stella by Starlight" and "'Round Midnight" with conga player Elvin Bunn. These titles were on another album called *Live at Jorgies and More. Vol. 2.*[85] The *Recorded Live at Jorgies Jazz Club* recording may be the finest recorded example of the Montgomery Brothers work as a group.

Vocalist Nancy Wilson was recorded with The Three Sounds (Gene Harris [piano], Andrew Simpkins [bass], and Bill Dowdy [drums]) on Gaslight Square. VGM released them as *Sittin' in with . . .* The tunes were "Since I Fell For You," "Time After Time," "The Theme," "On Green Dolphin Street," "The Spirit Is Here," "Time After Time," and "Salt Peanuts."[86] This recording represents Wilson's first live recording.

The first recording of vocalist/pianist Shirley Horn titled *Gonna Rain in a Minute*[87] was made in St. Louis with John Mixon (bass) and Gene Gammage (drums). The tunes are "Sometimes I'm Happy," "If I Should Lose You," "Summertime," "Good for Nothin' Joe," "Day In," "Day Out," "'Round Midnight," and "Makin' Whoopee." The record jacket states that the album was recorded at the Village Vanguard in New York, but the bassist and drummer give away the fact that this is a St. Louis record. Joe Schwab of Euclid Records in St. Louis confirms this.[88] The recording was issued on a label called Can-Am International.

The Donald Byrd–Pepper Adams Quintet recorded *Hip-Intertainment* during 1961.[89] The group included Donald Byrd (trumpet), Pepper Adams (baritone sax), Herbie Hancock (piano), Cleveland Eaton (bass), and Teddy Robinson (drums). The tunes were "Jorgie's," "6 M's (Blues in ¾)," "Hush," and "Amen." The rhythm section was recorded on "Like Someone in Love." This recording became part of the LP version of *Miles in St. Louis.*[90]

VGM recorded trumpeter Webster Young on a series of three albums called *Plays and Sings the Miles Davis Songbook, Vol. 1, 2 and 3.*[91] John Hicks, who played piano on what appear to be jam sessions, discussed the personnel on these recordings in a 2003 email to the author.[92]

> Personnel included: Freddie Washington (tenor sax), John Mixon (bass) Joe Charles (drums) and from what I remember we recorded three nights at the same venue (name I don't remember) would have included Hershel Harris (bass) Chauncey Williams (drums) John Chapman (piano). I don't believe Jodie Christian would have been available as he was playing a gig at Jorgies with Paul Serrano (trumpet), Bunky Green (alto sax) on Gaslight Square. Considerable distance from the West End of St. Louis where the VGM Recordings took place.

Because we really do not know who in addition to Webster Young and Freddie Washington played on each tune, the tunes will be noted with no personnel associated with them. They are "Shirley's Horn What's New?," "Whispering," "Stablemates," "Ray's Idea," "When I Fall in Love," "Beautiful Love," "East St. Louis Shoot Out," "When Lights Are Low," "Miles Theme," and "Oleo." Included on *Vol. 2* is an interview with Webster Young called "A Trumpet Player's Town." It was supposedly recorded in 1980. According to Henry Ettman, Webster Young was working a long engagement at Little Nero's, a club on the DeBaliviere Strip, when these recordings were made.

The first live recording of the Miles Davis Quintet with George Coleman (tenor sax), Herbie Hancock (piano), Ron Carter (bass), and Tony Williams (drums) was made in St. Louis at Jazz Villa on Washington in what was listed as June 1963. The VGM recording *Miles in St. Louis*[93] is now issued on a CD that includes an unauthorized release of a KWMU interview with Davis. The tunes were "I Thought About You" (Coleman out), "All Blues," "The Theme," and "Seven Steps To Heaven."

Multi-instrumentalist Don Cunningham worked at the St. Louis Playboy Club on Lindell from 1965 to 1968. He and his group recorded *Something for Everyone* on Exclusive Records. Only five hundred of the LPs were pressed, but this recording has become famous in the jazz-dance world.[94]

> "Of all the tracks on the album 'Tabu' has been the biggest hit with the jazz-dance crowd. That track is the reason many collectors have the album on their wants lists. It remains a tune worthy of heavy DJ play. 'Something for Everyone' has been at the top of my wants list for about ten years now. All my other wants I have managed to track down over the years, but to own an original copy of the Don Cunningham album is as illusionary as driving a Rolls Royce," says producer/DJ Rainer Truby of Compost Records.

The personnel included Don Cunningham (vibes, marimba, sax, conga, bongo, bells, wood logs, boobams, timbales, bird calls, vocal), Marion Miller (piano, orchestra bells, chimes), John Mixon (bass, cello), and Manny Quintero (drums, timbales, birdcalls). It has been reissued on CD.[95] The tunes were "Angelina," "I'm Your Slave," "Quiet Village," "Tabu," "Manha de Carnaval," "Sylvia," and "Samba De Orpheu."

The infamous Frank Sinatra "rat pack" of Sinatra, Dean Martin, and Sammy Davis, Jr., were recorded with the Count Basie Orchestra and Johnny Carson at a Dismas House benefit at the Kiel Opera House on July 20, 1965. The album is called

Goldenrod Showboat Ad, c. late 1960s. © Don Franz.

Sinatra, Basie & Friends.[96]

The Herb Drury Trio recorded two albums that are now on CD. The first, *Keep Your Sunny Side Up*,[97] was recorded in 1965 with Drury (piano) Jerry Cherry (bass), and Art Heagle (drums). The tunes were "Bluesette," "Eleanor Rigby," "Misty," "Keep Your Sunny Side Up," "On Green Dolphin Street," "Why Do You Want To Change Me Now?," "Doodlin'," and "Take Five." The Drury Trio recorded again with Phil Hulsey replacing Heagle on drums with *On the Right Track*[98] in 1967. That recording included "Satin Doll," "Soon It's Gonna Rain," "Close Your Eyes," "My Favorite Things," "Bye Bye, Blackbird," "Tender Is the Night," "Spring Can Really Hang You Up the Most," and "Cherry Street."

The Decline of Gaslight Square

Most commentators put the decline of Gaslight Square as beginning around 1964 or 1965, when some fast-buck operators decided to bring in go-go dancers. Jeter Thompson commented, "With the advent of the go-go girls, which came about in '64, something like that, it seemed to be a breakdown in somethin'. And it deteriorated and a series of events caused people to shy away from Gaslight Square and eventually the downfall came."[99] Others in Crone's book cite pressure put on cab drivers by local hotel owners to not take customers to the Square because it was competition for their own entertainment rooms.[100] Joe Buerger[101] also brought up the possible factor that the newspapers and the media's well-known tactics to frighten people in order to boost circulation.

> The newspapers didn't help us at all, either, because a lot of people didn't want to come down and pay a dollar to park on a lot you had lights and police. So, they would park a block or two over. And they'd hang out of Gaslight Square all night and go back to their car and get knocked over and lose all their loot. And they'd write it up in the paper as being in the Gaslight Square Area. *They wouldn't say that it happened two blocks over*. So everybody was afraid to come on down.

Several interviewees in Crone's book concur with Buerger's assessment. It is interesting to note that the heyday of Gaslight Square lasted from around 1961 to 1964, but the DeBaliviere Strip ran longer as an entertainment district, from about 1952 to 1963 or so.[102] With Leo Gooden's death in 1965, the Blue Note Club began a decline that lasted until it closed in 1967. With the decline of Gaslight Square, the traditional jazz players moved to the *Goldenrod Showboat* and other places on the riverfront. The black players had few places to go.

Endnotes

1 Thomas Crone, *Gaslight Square: An Oral History* (St. Louis: The William and Joseph Press, 2004).

2 Norman Menne, interview with the author, July 10, 1986.

3 Jeter Thompson, interview with the author, May 24, 1986.

4 Charlie Menees, interview with the author, 1986.

5 Jimmy Haislip, interview with the author, June 1986.

6 Charlie Wells Obituary, *St. Louis Post-Dispatch*, July 20, 2002.

7 Crone, *Gaslight Square*.

8 http://www.umsl.edu/%7Evirtualstl/phase2/1950/events/crystalpalace.html.

9 Singleton Palmer, interview with the author, June 1986.

10 Ibid.

11 Ed Thigpen, interview with the author, September 1986.

12 Palmer interview.

13 Joe Buerger, interview with the author, May 24, 1986.

14 Ibid.

15 Ibid.

16 Crone, *Gaslight Square*. p. 60.

17 Ceil Clayton Obituary, *St. Louis Post-Dispatch*, June 25, 1997.

18 Crone, *Gaslight Square*. pp. 56–68.

19 Ibid.

20 Ibid.

21 Jeanne Trevor, *Pow!*, Mainstream Records 56075.

22 St. Louis Jazz Quartet, *St. Louis Jazz Quartet*. ei Productions ei-LP7201.

23 Jeanne Trevor, *Love You Madly*, Catalyst Productions, CP021999.

24 Thompson interview.

25 Lynn Driggs Cunningham and Jimmy Jones, *Sweet, Hot and Blue: St. Louis Musical Heritage* (Jefferson, N.C.: McFarland and Company, 1989), p. 90–93.

26 Ibid., pp. 144–149.

27 Compiled mainly from a Clea Bradford publicity brochure courtesy of Al Becker.

28 Leonard Feather, *Encyclopedia of Jazz in the Sixties* (New York: Da Capo Press, 1986), p. 66.

29 Clea Bradford, *Clea Bradford with Oliver Nelson and Clark Terry*, Prestige New Jazz NJLP 8320.

30 Clea Bradford, *Now*, Mainstream S6042.

31 Thompson interview.

32 Cunningham and Jones *Sweet, Hot and Blue*, pp. 144–149.

33 Thompson interview.

34 Ibid.

35 Compiled from Thompson interview.

36 Cunningham and Jones, *Sweet, Hot and Blue*, pp. 90–93.

37 Crone, *Gaslight Square*, p. 38.

38 Ibid.

39 Ibid., p. 39.

40 Henry Ettman, telephone conversation with the author, February 1, 2006.

41 Kenny Rice and Phillip Wilson, interview with the author, 1986.

42 Compiled from Leo Chears Obituary, *St. Louis Post-Dispatch*, January 3, 2006, and The St. Louis Radio Hall of Fame, http://stlradio.com/halloffame.htm.

43 Freddie Washington, interview with the author, May 27, 1986.

44 John Hicks, interview with the author, October 1986.

45 John Hicks, *John Hicks*, Evidence 22224.

46 Kenny Rice–Richard Martin Quintet with Nat Adderley, *Recorded Live*, Recorded Live Records.

47 Mae Wheeler, *Lady Jazz*, Lady Jazz Records.

48 Hicks interview.

49 Ibid.

50 Scott Yanow, *All Music Guide*, http://www,allmusic.com.

51 Gene Kalbacher, "David Sanborn: R & B Altology," *Down Beat* (August 1986): 18.

52 Ettman telephone conversation.

53 http://www.centrohd.com/bio/bio9/.

54 http://arts.ucsc.edu/faculty/Marsh/pages/home_marsh.htm.

55 Singleton Palmer, *Dixie By Gaslight*, Norman NL-101.

56 Singleton Palmer, *At the Opera House!* Norman NL-106.

57 Singleton Palmer, *Singleton Palmer and His Dixieland Band*, Opera House Records OHR 1001.

58 Singleton Palmer, *Singleton Palmer*, Opera House Records, OHR2002.

59 Singleton Palmer, *The Best Dixieland Band*, Norman Records NL-110.

60 Singleton Palmer, *Singleton Palmer and His Dixieland Band*, Paddlewheel Pwr001.

61 Muggsy Sprecher, *Ah-gah-boo*, Norman NS-214.

62 Muggsy Sprecher, *At Bustles and Bows with Muggsy's Gaslighters*, Marbro P-2479.

63 Muggsy Sprecher, *Silver Dollar Dixie*, Norman NL-301.

64 Muggsy Sprecher, *Silver Dollar Dixie, Vol. 2*, Norman NL-304.

65 Sammy Gardner, *Sammy Gardner*, Norman NL-104.

66 Sammy Gardner, *Circa 1962*, Paddlewheel (Jap) PWR002.

67 Henry Brown, *Barrelhouse Piano and Classic Blues*, Folkways Records FS3815.

68 St. Louis Ragtimers, *Honky Tonk Piano*, George H. Buck GHB-BCD-362 [CD].

69 St. Louis Ragtimers, *St. Louis Ragtimers, Vol. 1*, George H. Buck GHB-BCD-362 [CD].

70 Trebor Jay Tichenor, *The Piano Roll*, Folkways Records RBF 7.

71 Trebor Jay Tichenor, *Mississippi Valley Ragtime*, Ragophile Records.

72 Ceil Clayton, *I Meet the Nicest People*, Norman NL-107.

73 Ceil Clayton, *Ceil Clayton*, Norman NL-300.

74 Russ David, *The Four of Us*, Norman Records NL-109.

75 Quartette Trés Bien, *Quartette Trés Bien*, Norman NL-102/202.

76 Quartette Trés Bien, *Bully!* Atlantic SD1461.

77 Norman 526.

78 Norman 534.

79 Quartette Trés Bien, *Kilimanjaro*, Decca DL (7) 4548.

80 Norman 541.

81 Quartette Trés Bien, *Boss Trés Bien*, Decca 31615.

82 Norman 548.

83 Johnny Hartman, *Sittin' in with Johnny Hartman & The Andrew Hill Trio*, VGM 011.

84 Wes Montgomery, *Recorded Live at Jorgie's Jazz Club*, VGM-Soulard SOUCD1 [CD].

85 Wes Montgomery, *Live an Jorgie's and More, Vol. 2*, VGM 0008.

86 Nancy Wilson, *Sittin' In With …*, VGM 0010.

87 Shirley Horn, *Gonna Rain In A Minute*, Can-Am International 60301 TX.

88 Joe Schwab, private conversation with the author, 2005.

89 Donald Byrd-Pepper Adams, *Hip Intertainment*, VGM 002.

90 Miles Davis, *Miles in St. Louis*, VGM003.

91 Webster Young, *Plays and Sings the Miles Davis Songbook, Vol. 1, Vol. 2 and Vol. 3*, VGM 004, VGM 005, and VGM 006.

92 John Hicks, email to the author, March 5, 2003.

93 Miles Davis, *Miles in St. Louis*, Soulard VGM-SOU CD3 [CD].

94 http://www.ubiquityrecords.com/don_cunningham.html.

95 Don Cunningham, *Something for Everyone*, Luv N' Haight 10038 [CD].

96 Frank Sinatra, *Sinatra, Basie & Friends*, Retrospect 509.

97 Herb Drury, *Keep Your Sunny Side Up*, Victoria Company 4332 [CD].

98 Herb Drury, *On the Right Track*, Victoria Company 4331 [CD].

99 Thompson interview.

100 Crone, *Gaslight Square*.

101 Buerger interview.

102 Menne interview.

7 The Polarization of St. Louis Jazz: Traditional Jazz & BAG (1968–1973)

The period 1968–1973 was one of protest over the war in Vietnam. It was also the period of much experimentation with alternative lifestyles, and a time when the nation was split between those who were forward looking and those who were trying to hold on to what they believed to be traditional values. While there was relative prosperity in 1967, by 1972, the nation was gripped by the recession of 1972–1974. These forces, both external and internal to St. Louis, forced a strong split between traditionalists and experimentalists in the arts, especially when funds began to dry up by 1972. The jazz community in St. Louis was no different; two strong, opposing winds began to blow through it: one group of musicians trying to hold dearly to what they perceived as the jazz tradition; the other group of musicians trying to extend the traditions of jazz into ways that eventually changed the way music was thought about for the next twenty years. The mainstream jazz players were in the middle working quietly, not making waves.

When the music scenes at Gaslight Square, the Blue Note, and the DeBaliviere Strip collapsed by 1967, jazz musicians faced a bleak future, with few places to play. The (mainly white) traditional jazz players found a haven on the riverfront, with the purchase and reopening of the *Goldenrod Showboat* by Frank Pearson in 1964. The Old Levee House and other entertainment venues featured jazz as a way to connect nostalgically to romantic notions about the riverboat era in St. Louis's history. The St. Louis Ragtimers played as the house band on the *Goldenrod Showboat* for twenty years.

Some young black musicians determined that they should develop their own style and organization to present their music. This movement was part of what was known nationally as the Black Arts Movement. The St. Louis organization became the Black Artists' Group (BAG). BAG musicians, along with those from the Association for the Advancement of Creative Musicians (AACM) in Chicago, changed the music in New York when they moved there. The American composer Anthony Davis said, "A lot of the new energy that came into New York in the late seventies was a result of that immigration, I think, and it really changed the music in New York. What was happening, you could see a big difference in the stylistic concerns in the music. You know, more compositional approach, more collective improvisation, music that was less soloistic."[1]

Traditional Jazz: Hanging on Dearly to Keep from Changing

In 1967, pianist/vocalist Jean Kittrell got her start in St. Louis at the Old Levee House on Wharf Street. The *River Queen* was a restaurant on the river, and Jeanne Trevor sang there. The Old Levee House was across the street under the railway overpass and was owned by Frank Pearson. Kittrell was at Southern Illinois University–Carbondale working on her doctorate in English literature.[2]

> Frank Pearson opened that place, and he and Don Franz invited me to come up and perform there as a single. So, that's how I started in St. Louis. I said, "I can't play as a single. I've only played with a jazz band, a couple of jazz bands, and I need to play with the horns so that I can hear the melody." . . . So Don Franz played banjo for the first week. The second week they called me and said, "Oh, you can do it by yourself. You don't need a banjo player." So, I was on my own. It was a good experience for me. . . . I realized that I had never learned many tunes all the way through. . . . I never remembered bridges.[3] . . . So I learned a lot of tunes. As a matter of fact, I had to write out a lot of melodies and put that bridge up in front of me. . . . [There's] nothing like playing in public by yourself to enable you to learn songs quickly. So I worked at the Levee House for two years, two very happy years. It was like giving a party every Friday and Saturday night, to standing-room-only crowds, I might add.

Jean Kittrell, Old Levee House, St. Louis, 1967. Photograph by Ken MacSwan. Photo restoration by Dennis Owsley. © Jean Kittrell.

Kittrell made her first recordings during this period. Here, she describes the recording sessions for Jazzology Records.

> Back in 1967 when I started working at the Old Levee House, I got a call one day inviting me to come to South Carolina and make a record for George Buck of Jazzology Records. And when they said [clarinetist] Tony Parenti would be there, . . . I was thrilled. Mine was one of four records that were cut in that weekend. . . . Mine was the last and by that time, we were all rather punchy. When it came time for my record, Tony said, "Do you have lead sheets for us?" And I said, "Oh, no." "Well, have you got some arrangements some arrangement worked out?" "Well, no." So, that's my first record. I really didn't know that George wanted me to sing every tune on the record.

Gospel singer Mahalia Jackson was one of Kittrell's major inspirations. Here she discusses how she heard Jackson and the differences between black and white traditional jazz bands.[4]

> Mahalia Jackson has been an inspiration to me. I've loved her singing from the time I heard her over the radio singing from a church in Chicago when Ed Kittrell and I were both students at the University of Chicago. . . . She's always been an inspiration to me, even though she never sang secular music. Nevertheless, her singing inspired me as it did Janis Joplin.
>
> "Just a Closer Walk with Thee" is actually a composed hymn; it's not a spiritual as many people think that it is. . . . And [it is] closely associated with New Orleans jazz because it's often played at a jazz funeral. When I lived three weeks in New Orleans and worked at Preservation Hall, I learned that the jazz musicians do not play hymns in Preservation Hall. They don't like to do that in the way that jazz bands here do. They sort of divide that music. And if they do "Just a Closer Walk with Thee," it's not generally as a vocal. . . . On the other hand, most of the white bands have always played hymns and spirituals as part of traditional jazz music.
>
> The first recording [I made] of "Just a Closer Walk With Thee" was with the Old Guys Jazz Band, and it was Charlie Menees' favorite recording. . . . Because it's one of his favorites, I think it's been heard a lot by a lot of people who respond to it.

Kittrell and Dan Havens were part of a band made up of SIU–Edwardsville and SIU–Carbondale musicians. Havens had the idea of the old guys from the Edwardsville campus going to Carbondale for a concert. A tape of the concert was made into an LP. Apparently, the Old Guys Jazz Band functioned for a number of years.

The *Goldenrod Showboat,* by 1964, was one of the two remaining old wooden showboats on the Mississippi and Ohio river systems. Frank Pearson bought it in 1964 and installed the St. Louis Ragtimers of Trebor Tichenor (piano), Bill Mason (cornet), Al Stricker (banjo and vocal), and Don Franz (tuba) as the house band. The band played on the *Goldenrod* for twenty years. By 1965, Tichenor and Pearson conceived the idea of a Ragtime and Traditional Jazz Festival to be held on the *Goldenrod* over the Labor Day Weekend. The first festival was held in 1965, and it continues today. After 1990, the festival was held in St. Charles, and from 2000, at the History Museum in Forest Park. Charlie Booty, a boogie woogie pianist, recalled what

Jean Kittrell

Born in 1927 in Birmingham, Alabama, barrelhouse pianist/vocalist Jean Kittrell[6] began her career in the Southern Baptist Church. She majored in music at Blue Mountain College in Mississippi and began playing jazz in Norfolk, Virginia, where she and her husband, cornetist Dr. Ed Kittrell, organized the Chesapeake Bay Jazz Band. The couple moved to Chicago in 1958 and joined the Chicago Stompers. They took this band to Düsseldorf, Germany, in 1959 and played two months in German nightclubs. She remarked that "people in Germany knew more about American jazz than most Americans did." Don Franz was one of the musicians in the band.

Taking a six-year hiatus from music to study literature, Jean revived her music career when Franz invited her to play at the Old Levee House on Laclede's Landing in 1967. This developed into a two-year engagement on Friday and Saturday nights as a single pianist and vocalist. During this period she developed her large repertoire. She made her first recordings that same year with Tony Parenti. Concurrently, Jean was studying British Literature at Southern Illinois University–Carbondale and completed her Ph.D. in 1973. She took another performing hiatus to complete her dissertation.

Accepting a faculty position at Southern Illinois University–Edwardsville, she began working in Dr. Dan Havens' Mississippi Mudcats and Boll Weevil Jass Band. She has been a favorite in St. Louis since 1967 and currently leads three groups: the Jazz Incredibles, the Old St. Louis Levee Band, and the St. Louis Rivermen. Jean Kittrell continues to work all over the world with her groups.

the festival was about and who played there.[5]

> The St. Louis Ragtime Festival was THE "festival of all festivals" during those early years and those years were certainly "golden years" for me. While it was primarily a ragtime festival, there was not a strict code against playing something other than ragtime. The bands were primarily jazz bands which played some ragtime, and the piano players I heard (over a few short years) covered ragtime, stride and stomps—players such as Eubie Blake, Max Morath, Bob Green, Tom Shea, Dick Wellstood, John "Knocky" Parker, Trebor Tichenor, Terry Waldo, Kjell Waltman, Peter Clute, Robbie Rhodes, Mike Montgomery, to name only a few.
>
> At that time, several ragtime and jazz bands were featured on a relatively loose schedule in the available venues on the *Goldenrod Showboat* and the *Becky Thatcher*, both anchored on the riverfront, just south of the Eads Bridge.
>
> In the main bar—between the theater, the front deck, and the stairway to the smaller upstairs theater—there was a little bandstand with an old upright piano. People sat in folding chairs in the center of the bar area, and because the bandstand was very narrow, the piano player had his back to the audience. To provide eye contact, a relatively large mirror was mounted above the piano, allowing the player and the audience to look each other in the eye.

Jeff Leopold of the St. Louis Jazz Club remembered good times at jam sessions on the levee that lasted until 4:00 A.M. The St. Louis Jazz Club continues today to provide good times for its members with its monthly concerts. But, as time went on, few African American listeners and musicians were associated with the group.

Traditional Jazz Recordings Made in St. Louis (1968–1973)

During the period 1968–1973, ragtime and traditional jazz bands were recorded a total of nine times in St. Louis. In addition, the same St. Louis traditional musicians appeared on six more recordings made at various places. St. Louis Ragtimers recorded a single tune, "Cake Walking Babies from Home," for an International Association of Jazz Record Collectors record. The personnel included Dan Havens (cornet), Frank Powers and Glenn Bower (clarinet), Don Franz (banjo), and Mike Walbridge (tuba) on this 1970 St. Louis recording. Aside from Franz, this was not the longtime lineup of the group as shown below.

The St. Louis Ragtimers recorded three LP's during this period. *Songs of the Showboat Era* (Audiophile AP122)[7] was made in the early 1970s and featured songs associated with St. Louis before World War I. Some of the songs were "Meet Me in St. Louis, Louis," "The Cascades," "St. Louis Rag," "St. Louis Tickle," "Frankie and Johnny," and "There'll Be a Hot Time in the Old Town Tonight." The personnel were Bill Mason (cornet, harmonica, vocal), Glenn Meyer (clarinet), Trebor Jay Tichenor (piano), and Don Franz or Ed McKee (tuba).

The Ragtimers made *Volume 4* for Audiophile (AL116)[8] aboard the *Goldenrod Showboat* in 1973. The personnel remained the same, with McKee out. Some of the highlights of this recording include King Oliver's "Snag It" and "Willie the Weeper"; three tunes associated with Jelly Roll Morton's Red Hot Peppers recordings, "The Chant," "Black Bottom Stomp," and "Sidewalk Blues" along with Tom Turpin's last published composition, "When Sambo Goes to France." The same personnel recorded *Early Portraits* around this time.[9] This recording has now appeared on CD on the St. Louis Ragtimers label (SLR 06007).

Pianist Jean Kittrell was also recorded on the *Goldenrod Showboat* in June 1970 with the Boll Weevils Jazz Band out of Ann Arbor, Michigan. Dan Havens, Kittrell's colleague in the English department at Southern Illinois University–Edwardsville played cornet on this session. The LP, *Tain't Nobody's Business*, was on George H. Buck Records (GHB 51).[10] The *Goldenrod Showboat* hosted two recordings by the New Black Eagle Jazz Band from Boston. A version of "Red Wing" was recorded on June 19, 1973, and appeared on Black Eagle BE (C) 150 (cassette), and a full album called *NBEJB on the River* was recorded for the Dirty Shame (Dsr 2002) label three days later.[11]

Dan Havens's band, the Mississippi Mudcats, recorded *Dan Havens and the Mississippi Mudcats with Jean Kittrell* in St. Louis around 1972, with Havens (cornet, vocal), Leon King and Jimmy Haislip (trombone), Warren Brown (clarinet), Jean Kittrell (piano, vocal), Ray Helsel (bass), and James Hansen (drums) for the Meridian label (Meridian 8).[12] The repertoire included "Someday Sweetheart," "Marching To Richmond," "Basin Street Blues," "Peoria," "1919 Rag," "Just a Closer Walk with Thee," "Sugar Blues," and "Creole Love Call." The Old Guys Jazz Band recorded *Old Guys, Old Jazz* in Manchester, Missouri, for Kesterson, Bradley & Kesterson Custom Records. The personnel included Havens, Brown, Kittrell, Helsel, and Hansen along with Jim Austin (trombone), and Zeke Holden (piano on some cuts). The repertoire for this recording included "Beale Street Blues," "Wild Man Blues," "I Ain't Gonna Give Nobody None O' This Jelly Roll," "Bourbon Street Parade," "Hesitation Blues," "Working Man's Blues," "Cake Walking Babies from Home," "2:19 Blues," and "Canal Street Blues." Much of this repertoire was associated with Turk Murphy and the Yerba Buena Jazz Band out of San Francisco.

Mainstream Jazz Players and Venues in St. Louis during the Period

Mainstream jazz musicians were quietly working in St. Louis and on the East Side, most in private parties and not in clubs. Guitarist Eddie Fisher, born in Little Rock, Arkansas, and 2004 inductee in the Arkansas Jazz Hall of Fame, came to East St. Louis with bluesman Albert King. He was soon working at the Blue Note Club for Leo Gooden in the last years of the club's existence. The sales of a 45-rpm single Fisher recorded for the Tuff label in

Carolbeth True

Born in Nebraska, Carolbeth True[13] began her piano studies with her mother, Carol Miles, at age three. Her mother taught both classical music and pop tunes.[14] True continued her studies with Evelyn Mitchell at the University of Missouri–St. Louis, who helped her with the physical part of playing the piano so that she could play more freely and loosely.[15] She is one of the most in-demand classical and jazz piano teachers in St. Louis and is a long-term member of the Webster University Music Faculty. True was the rehearsal pianist/assistant music director with the St. Louis Muny Opera for twenty years.

Carolbeth is the first call pianist for many visiting jazz musicians, has her own trio, works with trumpeter Randall Holmes's quintet, the Sessions Big Band, the Trinity Jazz Ensemble, and is a part of the cast of the education program, "The Jazz Story," an overview of jazz history at the Sheldon Concert Hall. In 2004, she received the *St. Louis Magazine* Musician of the Year Award in addition to the American Federation of Musicians Local 2-197 Owen Miller Award for service and dedication. She has recorded with Bassist Jay Hungerford (1995),[16] the Sessions Big Band (1999),[17] harmonica player Sandy Weltman (1997),[18] and her own trios (1994 and 2002).[19]

1968 called "Wantu Wazuri, Parts I and II" brought him to the attention of Cadet Records. Fisher recorded two well-received albums for the label, *The Third Cup* (1969) and *The Next Hundred Years* (1970—rereleased on CD in 2006). Since that time, Fisher has toured internationally with his own groups, but has received scant attention in his own community. Currently, his work is in the smooth jazz genre. His latest CD, *42nd Street,* on his own label, Nentu Records, was released in 2001.[20]

The Upstream Lounge at 7th and Pine still continued to employ local St. Louis musicians and continued a jazz policy until 1978. A neighborhood bar in Overland, Mr. C's La Cachet, not only employed local musicians such as tenor saxophonist Bernard Hutcherson, but also they brought in nationally known musicians such as Yusef Lateef, Eddie Harris, jazz bagpiper/saxophonist Rufus Harley, and Gene Harris and his Three Sounds. La Casa (Jefferson between Market and Olive), Helen's Black Eagle (4000 North Florissant), and the Gourmet Rendezvous (3133 North Grand) also employed local musicians and national acts such as Ahmad Jamal. The George Hudson Band worked many private functions during this period, also.

Pianist James "Iron Head" Mathews[21] was born in 1943 in Gloster, Mississippi. He got his nickname for playing football with his head down. His family eventually moved to East St. Louis and owned nightclubs there. He saw a lot of blues musicians performing there as a child. He was first a drummer and switched to piano at age seven. He took lessons at the Ludwig Music Company and later played with "Scrooge" Harris, Raymond Eldridge, Jr., and Rick Bolen. Mathews recorded with Eddie Fisher on his *The Next Hundred Years* LP for Chess in 1970. He also worked with John Mixon and continues working in St. Louis and East St. Louis today. He is an elementary school teacher.

Several St. Louis pianists, including Eddie Fritz, Hugh "Peanuts" Whalum, Herb Drury with Jerry Cherry, Dave Venn, and others, found work in upscale restaurants and in hotel and motel lounges. Another one of these pianists, Carolbeth True, began her long St. Louis jazz career at Schneithorst's Restaurant at Lindbergh and Clayton in 1972. She founded her own trio with bassist Eddie Randle, Jr., and drummer Gary Dinkelkamp (aka Gary Dink) in 1973.

One of St. Louis's musical treasures, saxophonist Willie Akins returned from New York in the spring of 1968 because his father was ill. Akins was born in 1939 in Webster Groves, Missouri. He had worked in St. Louis since he was sixteen with Eddie

Willie Akins, St. Louis, 2001. Photograph by Dennis Owsley. © Dennis Owsley Collection.

Randle and others. His father drove him to New York as soon as he finished his studies at Webster Groves High School in 1957.[22]

> New York was nice, you know. I got a chance to see just what you had to do to make it, so called "make it." I mean you had to be good. Not just good but you . . . had to excel above that. 'Cause from my point of view, they got a lot of mediocre musicians, which would maybe come from somewhere like St. Louis or out west or somewhere they would be considered real good musicians, but you know, there [New York], you know, you had to be more or less exceptional, from my point of view.

While in New York, Akins worked with trumpeter Johnny Coles, tuba player Ray Draper, drummer Roy Haynes, Larry Young, Jack McDuff, Lonnie Liston Smith, and several other organists. He was able to work a lot during his New York sojourn because he took any job he could.[23]

Akins talked about his influences as a saxophone player.[24]

> I used to hear Bird [Charlie Parker] a whole lot, and I heard Coleman Hawkins. But, he didn't impress me as much as Sonny Rollins did, you know. I don't know. I heard a whole lot a' Sonny. Then I started listenin' to the East Coast sound, like Jackie McLean, people like that. But I guess you might say just all the good saxophone players, (I listened to all of 'em) I know when I first heard Benny Golson. I said, "He sound like somebody I know." Then I heard Lucky Thompson and it was kind of a similarity in sound, you know. And then later on, I guess, I was livin' in New York and I got a chance to hear, is it Don Byas, the guy living in France? And I could really see where both styles come from. 'Cause his style was first. And I said, you know, that sounds like where both of these particular styles come from. But I've listened to all of 'em, George Coleman, Joe Henderson. I guess Trane was the biggest, though, you know. After Sonny there was Trane. Then after Trane I started listening to George. George used to mystify me by how fast he was. He could just play so fast and effortless. I got a chance to meet him here in St. Louis, also in New York, too. But, I've never met Joe Henderson, but he's a real favorite too. I like the way he gets into the horn. Also, Wayne [Shorter].

When Akins returned, he began working in a quartet with John Hicks, John Mixon, and drummer Sonny Hamp.[25] Although he was not associated with the St. Louis Black Artists' Group, Akins did work with Julius Hemphill. "I did a thing with Julius one time. We did a thing at Powell Hall and it was, it was kind of nice. We had John Hicks with us that time and I forgot who else. It was about eight or nine pieces. And Julius has always impressed me as bein' a good musician, you know.

He can play, you know."[26] Although he has had to support himself by working off and on as a house painter, Willie Akins has continued to work steadily until the present. He also teaches at Webster University. His first recording as a leader, *Alima*, was released in 1997.[27]

Mainstream Jazz Recordings in St. Louis (1968–1973)

During this period, the scarcity of mainstream jazz recordings made in St. Louis is startling. Two 45-rpm singles were cut: one by Eddie Fisher ("Wantu Wazuri Parts I and II") in 1968 for the Tuff label and the other by the Quartette Trés Bien ("By the Time I Get to Phoenix" and "Voo Doo Man") in the early 1970s for the Royal-tone label.

Only three mainstream jazz albums were made during this period; guitarist Eddie Fisher made two. *The Third Cup* (Cadet LPS828) with Bobby Shelby (piano, organ), Eddie Fisher and Phil Westmoreland (guitar), Paul Jackson (bass), and Kenny Rice (drums, vibes) was recorded in St. Louis in February 1969. The tunes included "Scorched Earth," "A Dude Called Zeke," "Shut Up," "The Third Cup," "Two by Two," "Shoo-Be-Doo-Be-Doo-Da-Day," and "The Shadow of Your Smile." The following year, *The Next Hundred Years* with Fisher (guitar), Richard Nedler (violin), James "Iron Head" Matthews (piano), Raymond Eldridge, Jr. (bass guitar), Johnny Johnson (drums), and Christina Fisher (tambourine). This album was originally recorded for Cadet but has been reissued by GRP/Verve (5955). The tunes were "Jeremiah Pucket," "Land of Our Father," "Either Or," "Another Episode [of the Story of Zeke]," "Beautiful Thing," and "East St. Louis Blues."

The St. Louis Jazz Quartet of Jeanne Trevor (vocal), David Schrage (piano), Terry Kippenberger (bass), and Charles Payne (drums) recorded an album called *St. Louis Jazz Quartet* for ei Productions (LP7201) around 1972. The tunes were "Bridge Over Troubled Water," "Your Sunny Smile Again," "Someone's Knocking at the Door," "Green," "On Green Dolphin Street," "Something Simple," "Fine and Mellow," and "Walk Him Up the Stairs."

The Black Artists' Group and the Human Arts Ensemble: Pushing the Envelope

In 1968, in response to a lack of opportunity, visibility, and community, local black musicians, artist, poets, and dancers organized as the Black Artists' Group (BAG). BAG formally existed for six years and performed a number of multimedia concerts that brought both strong praise and strong criticism.

BAG worked cooperatively with the AACM in Chicago—a major influence on the formation of BAG—as well as the Human Arts Ensemble in St. Louis. They performed regularly at their own facilities, university concert halls, and elsewhere before touring France and relocating to New York and other cities.

This section is not an attempt to write the history of BAG. Benjamin Looker's recently published book, *Point from Which Creation Begins: The Black Artists' Group of St. Louis* does that function admirably. Instead this text is about the music that the group produced. Although the music is intertwined with the other arts in BAG, by separating them we do not have to revisit BAG's entire history.

Most important, BAG musicians were native St. Louisans. During the late 1950s an amazing number of talented musical artists studied at Sumner, Soldan, and Vashon high schools in St. Louis. These artists included trumpeter Lester Bowie; pianist/trumpeter David Hines; trumpeter Floyd LeFlore; woodwind player J. D. Parran; drummers Chuck Carter, Phillip Wilson, Jerome "Scrooge" Harris, and Kenny Rice; and future opera star Grace Bumbry. Saxophonist Oliver Lake had been playing bass drum and cymbals in a drum and bugle corps since age fourteen and started playing saxophone at seventeen to be in the school band. He wasn't serious about the instrument because he was "into clothes and girls and parties."[28] Some of these young musicians went to Lincoln University in Jefferson City and all of them spent much of their musical apprenticeship in local rhythm and blues bands. Lester Bowie described the Sumner High football games.[29]

> Matter of fact, we used to go to the football games and the team was so bad, the football games were nothin' but a big jam session. Mr. [Clarence Hayden] Wilson would let us jam. We'd just go to jammin'; rock and roll, "Shake, Rattle and Roll," and all those sorts of things so all the people would have more fun listenin' to the band than watchin' the team.

Bowie was instrumental in the formation of BAG because of his association with the AACM and his contact with St. Louis musicians.

David Hines worked as a pianist in Bowie's first band. His family did not have a piano, so Eddie Randle allowed him to use their family's instrument.[30]

> That's where I practically grew up in his front room, banging on his piano and stuff before I even knew he was a great bandleader. The only thing I remember is a plaque on the wall. . . . Then one day I talked to him. He pulled out some pictures that they went out to have made at Forest Park right where the fountain is (see Chapter 3).

While at Sumner High, Lester Bowie had problems that a number of gifted children face. He described himself as "somewhat rebellious because I had a pretty high I.Q."[31]

> I was what they call a gifted child. The teachers were very angry with me 'cause I didn't want to be like they wanted me to be. I wanted to relax, have fun. I used to do 'C' work in school because I could do 'C' and 'B' work without even studying, so that's all I would do, but they were disappointed because I was supposed to be working these 'A's and later be some sort of lawyer. I rebelled against that but always got along good with my peers. I was always an organizer, and organized a lot of bullshit, had a lot

David Hines (1942–1991)

Trumpeter/pianist David Hines[32] was born in St. Louis to a nonmusical family. His original instrument was the piano, which he practiced in the parlor of the Eddie Randle and Sons Funeral Home on Natural Bridge. After graduation from Sumner High School, Hines attended the St. Louis Institute of Music (1961), Southern Illinois University (1964), Chicago Conservatory of Music (B.A., 1965), Lincoln University in Jefferson City, Missouri (1966), and Washington University in St. Louis (1978). In the early 1960s, Hines started playing the trumpet, inspired by Lester Bowie and Bobby Danzig. He worked as a pianist in his church in 1960 and, in 1962, worked on Gaslight Square.

By 1963, David was touring on trumpet with Albert King, T-Bone Walker, and Little Milton and, in 1968, with the Ike and Tina Turner Review in both the United States and Europe. In 1968, Hines was the jazz soloist on trumpet with Woody Herman and held the same position with Ray Charles in 1970. David also played in theater orchestras throughout the St. Louis area. He was the leader in halting discriminatory practices in the hiring of musicians for theater work by requiring auditions to be held behind curtains. He taught in various school situations and led the University City High School Jazz Band in the late 1980s. David toured Europe with Lester Bowie's Brass Fantasy in the winter of 1986. Hines was killed in a motorcycle accident a short distance from his home.

David Hines, c. 1985. Photograph by Joyce Hines. © Dennis Owsley Collection.

of fun. But I had a problem with teachers because I could never understand how they could disrespect persons because they were young; we still had minds and in some cases could out-think them.

Bowie described how Bobby Danzig—a prominent but unrecorded St. Louis trumpeter—helped him to become a better musician.[33] He also described the support that musicians had in the St. Louis community.

When I was fourteen, fifteen years old, I used to go over to his house and he used to show me little things and tell me little things that I remember to this day. Bobby would always tell me, "Lester, whatever you do, whatever you end up playing, always be soulful." So it was about having a soulful, personal sound. [That] was our goal. . . . I've never forgotten how to make any sound I've ever learned on the instrument.

In St. Louis, to be a musician was not considered to be an honorable profession, let's say. It wasn't anything to aspire to. . . . The public didn't feel that music was a worthwhile endeavor. And this feeling kind of permeated the whole black community and it permeated the whole community in St. Louis. And the musicians had to do things that were beneath their intellectual capacity

Lester Bowie (1941–1999)

Described as one of the most original trumpeters in jazz, Lester Bowie[34] was born in Frederick, Maryland. His father, Lester Bowie, Sr., was a well-known brass teacher who came to St. Louis to teach music and English at Hadley Technical (later O'Fallon) High School in 1953. Bowie described being taken with the trumpet at age five. Bowie went to Sumner High School and later saw service in the air force as a military policeman. He played trumpet on his first recording at age fifteen, and he led a band that included alto sax, sousaphone, and drums that appeared on a radio show.

Bowie worked with local rhythm and blues bands and married singer Fontella Bass. When Bass had a hit single, "Rescue Me," Bowie moved to Chicago to work with her and found his way to the Association for the Advancement of Creative Musicians (AACM). During this time, Bowie also worked in the Chicago recording studios as a "bootleg musician" (an uncredited musician receiving lower than union scale). He eventually joined the group and began recording with saxophonist Roscoe Mitchell (*Sound* on Delmark[35]), a group that was the forerunner of the Art Ensemble of Chicago.

Bowie was instrumental in inviting St. Louis musicians up to Chicago. This provided the impetus for the formation of St. Louis's Black Artists' Group (BAG). Bowie continued his work with the Art Ensemble and expanded his approach to include the Root to the Source group that included music from blues and gospel sources, his Organ Ensemble with organist Amina Claudine Meyers, and his Brass Fantasy. Bowie described the music of the Brass Fantasy to the author in 1990 as "redoing my teenage music." Both David Hines and trumpeter Sue Beshears described the Brass Fantasy as having some of the most difficult brass writing they had ever heard (or in Hines's case, played). Others have called Bowie "The Cootie Williams of Modern Jazz." Lee Jeske commented, "He commands an exceptionally large stock of effects, including half-valving, bent notes, and a wide vibrato."[36] All these devices come from the St. Louis trumpet tradition. Bowie died of cancer, performing almost up to his death.

to survive. A great saxophonist had to become a house painter to stay in St. Louis. . . . The community didn't think that jazz was important enough to support.

Saxophonist Oliver Lake was another Sumner High graduate who made an impact on jazz once he decided to fully commit. Floyd LeFlore remembered Oliver in high school as wearing capes and having a lot of girlfriends.[37] Lake himself decided he wanted to commit to music at age nineteen.[38]

> I started when I was nineteen. I graduated from high school when I was eighteen. I went to [Harris-Stowe] Teachers College, majoring in Elementary Education, minoring in Biology—flunked out of that school in a year. . . . At that point I decided I wanted to play. I practiced all that summer. . . . When I flunked out of the school I just kind of felt what I really liked and it was the saxophone, so then I started playing it.
> . . . At the year I started to play, Lester had just come out of the service or something and I talked to him about it. He was very influential in getting me to make that decision, saying, "OK, you're nineteen or twenty so it doesn't matter, ten years from now what difference would it make?" I always remembered that. I was thinking I was too old to start, how could I catch up because the players around me at that time were playing and they were my age and they were playing very good. That summer I practiced and then I went to Lincoln University in Jefferson City and stayed in the practice rooms constantly to catch up. To do that, to flunk out of college and I had been making good grades in high school and that whole trip, you know. I realized I had to make some kind of decision of what I wanted to do for the rest of my life.

Lake graduated from Lincoln University with a B.A. in music education in 1968 and taught in the St. Louis Public

Oliver Lake, 1977. Photograph © Anthony Barboza.

Schools while working as part of BAG.

During this time, baritone saxophon-ist Hamiet Bluiett was also in high school in Brooklyn, Illinois, on the East Side. Bluiett started music in the fifth grade and has never stopped playing.[39]

His band director was George Hudson (see Chapters 3 and 4). Bluiett remem-bered what he learned from Hudson.

Without him, I wouldn't have been able to do nothin' that I really do, 'cause he gave me that kind of foundation. For me that was good. I had a high school band director that was already a dance bandleader, a jazz player, and all that kind of stuff. So I already knew about Clark Terry and Ahmad Jamal and guys like that was comin' through with the band, so for me, that was outta sight. I didn't have a band director that was just a teacher, that really didn't have no professional experience. So I started with a guy who was a professional from the beginning; who'd played with Lester Young and Billie Holiday, and etc., all the way back through the line, right? And he taught us different kinds of things that didn't have nothin' to do with what was on the paper. And I really didn't think about it until later on. Like, if a guy makes a mistake, don't look, don't flinch, don't frown, you know, stuff like that. . . . Things that a professional wouldn't do, but kids automatically do. But we were taught that without realizin' that was very special. It was just somethin' that you did.

Bluiett made his first recording with Leo's Five in 1960, on one of his leaves from the navy. When he mustered out of the navy, he worked in rhythm and blues bands but became involved with people like Lester Bowie and Oliver Lake.

Another St. Louis musician involved in BAG was trumpeter Baikida E. J. Carroll (aka Baikida Yaseen). Carroll is the son of tenor saxophonist Jimmie Harris, who worked with Grant Green, Jimmy Forrest, and others. He went to Soldan High School, where his private trumpet and theory instructor was also the band director. During his high school years, he met and played with Lester Bowie, J. D. Parran, and James "Jabbo" Ware. He enlisted in the army as a musician and went to the Armed Forces School of Music. During this time, Carroll became interested in very modern music. He returned to St. Louis in 1968 and resumed the work of his high school years: playing with local rhythm and blues bands. Carroll was also practic-ing in Forest Park when Julius Hemphill asked him to join BAG. He initially performed as an actor in the pivotal production

Oliver Lake

Although saxophonist Oliver Lake[40] was born in Marianna, Arkansas, he grew up in St. Louis and graduated from Sumner High School. He began his music studies on saxophone at age nineteen, attending Lincoln University and graduating in 1968 with a B.A. in music education. Lake was one of the founding members of the St. Louis Black Artists' Group (BAG) and led the Oliver Lake Art Quartet and other groups. He wrote and performed music for an experimental film, *Jazoo* (1968), which provided an interesting look at the St. Louis Zoo. Lake made his first album as a leader, *NTU: Point from Which Creation Begins*, in 1971 with a ten-piece ensemble. The recording eventually appeared on the Arista label.[41]

As BAG began to break up, Lake and other musicians went to Paris in 1972, where they worked as the BAG ensemble for a year. Lake stayed in Paris until 1974 and recorded in other contexts. He then moved to New York, making an impact on the burgeoning "Loft Jazz" scene. He was one of the founding members of the World Saxophone Quartet in 1976, a group that continues into the present. Lake has staged solo saxophone concerts, has presented theatrical pieces in which he wrote both poetry and music, and has written and performed music with a string quartet. He led Jump-Up, a reggae-based ensemble over which he could play his idiomatic free jazz phrasing. Jump-Up toured Africa as part of the United States Information Agency's Arts America Program. In 1987, Lake was part of the US–USSR Composer's Symposium, performing and supervising the performance of chamber music in Russia. Lake has composed commissioned works for the Brooklyn Philharmonic Orchestra and the Arditti String Quartet. He leads his own big band and is the owner/producer of Passin' Thru Records, which issues his recordings and those of others. Lake is a Guggenheim Fellow and is the recipient of awards and grants from the Rockefeller Foundation, Meet the Composer, the McKnight Foundation, Chamber Music America, the Lila Wallace Arts Partners Program, and the Copland Fund, among many others. Lake is also an abstract painter and a poet.

of Jean Genet's play, *The Blacks*. Carroll eventually became the BAG orchestra conductor in addition to teaching trumpet and composition.[42]

Julius Hemphill's wife was from St. Louis and they moved into the city in 1966. Hemphill worked at various non-musical jobs until he became a substitute music teacher in the St. Louis City schools while playing in rhythm and blues bands. J. D. Parran remembered Hemphill's arrival. "I vividly remember the excitement generated by Julius's presence on the scene. Oliver Lake raved about Julius, placing his prowess above all the other saxophonists in town."[43]

Hemphill cited a list of favorite saxophone players. He differed from Lake in that Lake was enamored with Eric Dolphy and Jackie McLean, as well as Coltrane.[44]

> Oh, I have a string of favorite players. . . . You know, John Coltrane. . . . The person that struck me as having the most impact is Charlie Parker, at least you know, recently. And Lester Young had a similar impact, had an impact on Charlie Parker. Sonny Rollins, the regular people, Gene Ammons. I like things about Paul Desmond. I like things about a lot of them, you know. . . . As I became more serious, I started using whatever I could use from whoever it was, you know. So, I don't really have a favorite in that way, you know.[45]

In late 1965, Lester Bowie and drummer Phillip Wilson moved to Chicago, and by 1966, they were interacting with the AACM (founded in May 1965 by Muhal Richard Abrams and others). Bowie described his first musical encounter as "shock-

J. D. Parran

Multi-reed player J. D. Parran[47] was also part of the Sumner High School musicians' cadre in the late 1950s. As a child, Parran learned music theory in a class that Kenneth Billups taught at Washington University for elementary school children. He became a professional musician at age fifteen. Parran was a BAG member and performed on several of the BAG/Human Arts Ensemble recordings in the 1970–1973 period. He went to New York for the first time in 1971 and stayed through 1973. Parran and LeFlore started 3rd Circuit n' Spirit when he returned. Guitarist Marvin Horne worked with them at places like the Orphanage in the Euclid Avenue area and at BB's Jazz, Blues and Soups.

Parran left St. Louis for good in 1977 and has been a first call reed player for many bands, including Anthony Davis and Episteme and Andrew Hill's big band. He has been featured on over fifty recordings in jazz, popular, and classical music. Parran has also recorded with his group Spirit Stage, with Shirley LeFlore on vocals in 1995[48] and in 2005.[49] Parran has received commissions from the New York State Council on the Arts (NYSCA), Jerome Foundation, the National Endowment for the Arts, Meet the Composer, and Helen W. Buckner Foundation. He won the Gerald Oshita Award, has been part of the Djerassi Resident Artist Program, and conducted research in Africa sponsored by the Danforth Foundation. Parran is a lecturer at City University of New York and is a guest lecturer at New York University. He also served as a visiting professor at Mills College in Oakland California. In addition, Parran teaches at Dance Theatre of Harlem and the Harlem School of the Arts. He served the latter organization as music department chair and director of Jazz and African-American Music Studies.

ing, because I hadn't seen that many weird cats in one room before."[46] Bowie became president of the AACM in 1968.

In St. Louis, Oliver Lake, Hamiet Bluiett, Julius Hemphill, J. D. Parran, Scrooge Harris, and others were trying to find work as musicians just as the scenes at the Blue Note Club, Gaslight Square, and the DeBaliviere Strip were in rapid decline. Outside of rhythm and blues gigs, there was no place for them to play and learn their craft. The musicians started playing and jamming any place they could, often outdoors in the summer in Forest Park. Bluiett described the dedication of these musicians.[50]

> We made a commitment. And I found out if you want to play and you want to play the gig, "Let's get a piano and a bass and a drummer and a guitarist." Well, them cats won't always play every day 'cause they can get a job and work. If you just play an instrument, if you're not a piano [player}, bass [player] or drummer, you cain't play. So we said, "Later." So whoever showed up, we'd just play. . . . Our whole thing was just to participate every day. 'Cause it's not the way you're gonna do it anyway. It cain't be the weekend. Maybe the weekend for work, but it's gotta be every day. It's like anything else. If you're gonna be an Olympic swimmer, you don't swim on Saturday and Sunday. You swim every day. And it's forever until you can't swim no more and then you keep on teachin' other people every day. So that's the way we do it.
> . . . We came by some bizarre combinations; and some things I never thought about. . . . If you don't play with a drummer, this happens. If you don't play with a piano, that happens. So we did it and did it and did it and kind of worked it up to where we could actually play and we liked it. Now, the people didn't care for it that much, 'cause it was different. I went to New York and everybody was goin' crazy and it scared me. "These people like this, wow!" I couldn't understand that because St. Louis likes to preservate.

Bluiett also commented on how others got involved in their rehearsals. ". . . A guy might say, 'Well, I'm a poet.' So we find out what to do with the poet. So we just started involvin' everybody. We didn't call it multimedia." Jazz music, poetry, and the

167

Hamiet Bluiett

Born in Lovejoy, Illinois, Hamiet Bluiett[51] is currently the most prominent baritone saxophonist in jazz. His aunt, a choral director, taught him music as a child and by age nine, he began playing clarinet. Bluiett went to Brooklyn High School in Brooklyn, Illinois, and studied under bandleader George Hudson. He began playing baritone sax and flute while at Southern Illinois University at both the Edwardsville and Carbondale campuses. His range on the baritone sax is unusually high; up into the soprano or sopranino saxophone range.

Bluiett served in the navy and returned to St. Louis periodically, recording with the Blue Note Club's group Leo's Five in 1960. He returned to the area in the mid-1960s and became involved with playing with musicians who eventually formed BAG. Leaving St. Louis in 1969, Bluiett moved to New York, where he first joined the Sam Rivers Ensemble. After some freelance work, he joined Charles Mingus in 1972. He described his tour with Mingus as "both a blessing and a curse" because of the music and Mingus's personality. According to Bluiett, "There was no band as powerful as that band during that time." The band included Bluiett, Don Pullen (piano), and George Adams (tenor sax). He remained with Mingus until 1975.

Bluiett was involved in the "loft jazz" scene in New York in 1976. The World Saxophone Quartet began in 1976 with Bluiett one of the founding members. He has recorded for Black Saint/Soul Note and other labels. In addition to conventional ensembles, Bluiett's work has explored some unusual combinations. His *Clarinet Family* recording utilized eight musicians playing clarinets that ranged from soprano clarinet to contrabass clarinet accompanied by bass and drums.[52] His four-baritone band utilizes four baritone saxophones and drums.[53]

visual arts had been sporadically involved with one another since the early 1950s, but not on the scale that occurred in BAG.

Bowie traveled often between St. Louis and Chicago and finally, as Floyd LeFlore relates, "Oliver Lake and myself and a drummer name Leonard Smith, we went up there and got our first dose of the AACM. . . . I guess from that experience, the concept of BAG got into our heads."[54] According to Looker, Hemphill also visited Chicago. Lake formed the Oliver Lake Art Quartet with LeFlore, bassist Carl (later Arzinia) Richardson, and drummer Scrooge Harris and performed at the Circle Coffee Shop in LaClede Town and at the Sheldon Memorial (now the Sheldon Concert Hall) on Washington. This group, with John Mixon in place of Richardson, recorded the soundtrack to an experimental film called *Jazoo* that took first place in experimental film category at the Atlanta Film Festival.[55]

LaClede Town was another in a list of St. Louis urban renewal projects. Initially, it met its goals of integration with a population of 50 percent white, 40 percent black, and 10 percent other minorities. According to Michael Allen, writing on the Urban Review St. Louis website, "Laclede Town was imperfect, but did manage to become a hotbed of radical political and bohemian culture in the late 1960s. People liked the place a lot into the 1970s, when a new manager came on board."[56] Apparently some of the local conservative politicians did not like the atmosphere.[57] The community, the Circle Coffee Shop, and the Berea Presbyterian Church became a focal point for social, political, artistic, and musical activism. One concert at the Circle had a saxophone duo of Julius Hemphill and David Sanborn without a rhythm section. The church congregation was both economically and racially mixed and sponsored a theater group, the Berea Players. Much of the activity in LaClede Town was political and, in some cases, revolutionary, just like such activities in many cities all over the country during the late 1960s.

The spark that united the musical, artistic, and political impulses of the time was an idea of the poet, actor, and stage

Baikida E. J. Carroll

Trumpeter/composer/arranger Baikida Carroll[58] was born in St. Louis. While at Soldan High School, he played in the All-City Jazz Band and All-City Orchestra. During his tenure as an army musician, Carroll was awarded music composition honors at the Armed Forces School of Music. He also led a twenty-one-piece jazz rehearsal ensemble and wrote and arranged music for it. Returning to St. Louis in 1968, Carroll became part of BAG as an actor, leader of the BAG Orchestra, and teacher of composition and trumpet. He also attended Southern Illinois University and took part in Oliver Nelson's jazz master classes at Washington University from 1968 to 1972. Carroll scored his first film, *Billy Goes to Mecca,* for the Metropolitan Community Center for the Arts in 1971. In 1972, Carroll, Floyd LeFlore, Oliver Lake, Joseph Bowie, and Charles "Bobo" Shaw went to Paris and performed as the BAG Ensemble. Carroll remained in Paris until 1975, leading his own band, teaching trumpet and music theory at the American Center for Students, and performing with many musicians all over Europe.

Baikida Carroll, France, 1973. Photographer unidentified. © Baikida Carroll.

Carroll returned from Europe and moved to New York in 1975, performing with Sam Rivers, Hamiet Bluiett, and Julius Hemphill.

He also taught and led the big band at Queens College and was also first-call trumpet for several record producers. He lived and performed in San Francisco for two and a half years, returning to New York in 1978. That year, he moved to Woodstock, New York, to become part of the artistic advisory board and teach at the Creative Music Studio, where he remained until 1984.

Carroll has written music for many plays, including Strindberg's *Miss Julie,* Tennessee Williams's *Cat on a Hot Tin Roof,* Shakespeare's *King Lear,* and Ibsen's *A Doll House.* He composed the score to *Having Our Say* by Emily Mann in 1995. *Having Our Say* was nominated for a Tony Award and continues to tour the world. During this time, he has also continued to lead performing jazz groups and make recordings. Carroll's latest recording is *Marionettes on a High Wire* for Omnitone.[59]

Baikida Carroll has received grants from the National Endowment for the Arts, Meet the Composer, the Musicians' Foundation, and the Southern Illinois University Board of Trustees Academic Scholarship Award. He has been artist-in-residence at Music OMI, the American Center for Students and Artists in Paris, France, and the International Cite des Arts in Paris.

director Malinké Elliott to not only stage Jean Genet's play, *The Blacks,* but also to integrate dance and music into the performance. Dancer and choreographer Georgia Collins, from the Katherine Dunham Arts training center in East St. Louis, provided choreography. The actors came from the Persona Players, the Harlequin Players, and Vincent Terrell's TSOCC. Russell Durgin of St. Louis Country Day School directed the production. Oliver Lake and his Art Quartet, along with Julius Hemphill and two other musicians, provided a series of chamber pieces composed by Lake to accompany the dancers. The performance of *The Blacks* occurred at the Loretto-Hilton Center on the campus of Webster College (now Webster Univer-

World Saxophone Quartet, 1977. Left to right: David Murray, Julius Hemphill, Oliver Lake, and Hamiett Bluiett Photograph © Anthony Barboza.

sity) in Webster Groves, Missouri, on August 1, 1967.[60] The majority of the audience was white. A story in the *St. Louis Globe-Democrat* on August 1, 1967, outlined what Durgin and Elliott hoped to accomplish and listed the names of the cast, choreographer, and musicians. The identical story was found in the *Globe* on August 2 in the West County and South County sections. It is important to note that no review of the production has been found in the *Post-Dispatch*, the *Globe-Democrat,* or the *Argus.* No mention or advertisement of this event was found in the *St. Louis Argus,* although other plays (with white casts) that were at the Loretto-Hilton were discussed around this time.

The group realized that they needed to band together to influence their own destiny. According to Looker, the musicians had considered becoming a chapter of the AACM, but they decided to include all the arts in their group. The group incorporated as a Missouri not-for-profit organization called "The Black Artists' Group, Inc." in August 1968. Julius Hemphill became chairman, Malinké Elliott became the executive and artistic director, and Oliver Lake became treasurer. The group identity was solidified with a performance of *The Third World* at the Art Museum on Sunday August 25, 1967, at 2:30 P.M. The only notice of this production was a one-inch square paid advertisement found in both the *Post-Dispatch* and the *Globe-Democrat* in the Arts sections on Sunday, August 18, 1967.[61] The *Argus* had neither an advertisement nor a story about *The Third World.* LeFlore described the effort, "The very first performance that we did was at the Art Museum. It was a multimedia type thing with dance, music, poetry, acting and the audience was very receptive at that time."[62] Bluiett, Parran, Lake, and drummers Scrooge Harris and Charles "Bobo" Shaw provided the music, along with dancers and poet Ajulé (Bruce) Rutlin. The response apparently was typical: an initially overflow crowd that soon began walking out and newcomers that initially could not get in filling the seats. The remaining audience gave the performers a standing ovation.[63] No review of the concert was found in any of the three papers.

In 1967, due to the Johnson Administration's "War on Poverty," there was a lot of anti-poverty money available. BAG applied

Julius Hemphill

Julius Hemphill[64] was born in Fort Worth, Texas, where he played with local blues bands and jazz groups. After stints at North Texas State (English and a music course one summer), Lincoln University in Jefferson City, Missouri, and the army as a musician, he moved to St. Louis in 1966. Hemphill joined BAG in 1968, serving as their president. In 1972, Hemphill recorded the LP, *Dogon A.D.*, and part of the LP, *Coon Bid'ness*, on his own Mbari label. These recording were later released to a wider distribution on the Arista/Freedom label. Julius moved to New York in 1973 and, in 1976, and was one of the charter members of the World Saxophone Quartet with Oliver Lake, Hamiet Bluiett, and David Murray. Hemphill was the main arranger in the group until he left in 1989. The outstanding performances of the WSQ with Hemphill are *Steppin' With the World Saxophone Quartet* (1978),[65] *Revue* (1982),[66] and *World Saxophone Quartet Plays Duke Ellington* (1986).[67]

Hemphill's "saxophone opera," "Long Tongues," debuted in 1989. This multimedia piece had dancers, actors, slide projections, and the Julius Hemphill Saxophone Sextet. The work was first heard in Washington, D.C., and then at the Apollo Theater in New York in 1990. Another multimedia work, "The Last Supper at Uncle Tom's Cabin: The Promised Land," with the saxophone sextet and the Bill T. Jones/Arnie Zane Dance Company toured the United States and Europe during 1990–1991. Hemphill was the recipient of a "Bessie" Award for both works.

Hemphill made too many recordings over the course of his career to list here. However, special mention should be made of the saxophone sextet's *Fat Man and the Hard Blues* (1992),[68] which was voted one of the top ten CDs of 1992 by *Downbeat* magazine.

Hemphill has received commissions as a composer of classical works. A piano quintet, "One Atmosphere (for Ursula)," was premiered by the Arditti String Quartet and pianist Ursula Oppens in 1992. "Plan B," an orchestral work featuring the Julius Hemphill Sextet and the Richmond Symphony, premiered in 1993. "A Bitter Glory," a music-theater piece collaboration by Hemphill with writer Dalt Wonk, received a workshop performance in Minneapolis in December 1994. Hemphill succumbed to the ravages of diabetes in 1995.

for grants to further their efforts. They were successful with the Rockefeller Foundation and with another program called Artists in Residence that allowed them to rent a performance space and headquarters in an abandoned warehouse. The building, known informally as "the BAG house," was at 2665 Washington. Some groups operating under the BAG umbrella are listed below:

- The Children of the Sun
- The BAG Ensemble (big band)
- Red Black & Green Solidarity Unit
- Fire-Earth-Air-Water
- Omawali Dancers
- Malinque Rhythm Tribe
- BAG Drama Department
- Great Black Music Orchestra of St. Louis
- The Julius Hemphill Quartet
- Oliver Lake's various groups

BAG musicians often performed with the other allied arts. What they didn't do was play in clubs. Their forums were

Black Artists Group and Artists in Residence Building, 2665 Washington Boulevard, St. Louis, 1969. Photograph by Michael E. Emrick. Courtesy of Ben Looker.

concerts at the BAG House, university concert halls, and other concert stages such as the Gateway Theater on the defunct Gaslight Square. In 1969, BAG presented thirty consecutive weeks of concerts with all of their groups.[69]

When the Nixon Administration came to power in 1968, the "War on Poverty" was no longer a priority. Looker makes several references to tensions between the political outlook of the granting agencies and the BAG members. This tension, along with an economy in a worldwide recession by 1970, appear to be factors that led to the eventual withdrawal of BAG funding by these groups.

It is also interesting that, while the Black Arts Movement was political in that it sought both economic and cultural autonomy, the musicians appeared to be less political in their views. Looker expands on this idea.[70]

Like so many other musical groups of the day, BAG was of at least two minds regarding these debates. Although Hemphill mused in a 1970 interview that "unsatisfactory conditions" could affect "your very breathing, let alone your music," the collective's musicians more often denied an explicit connection between the sounds that emerged from their instruments and the sociopolitical winds buffeting the nation. In fact, while stressing their deep commitment to a black aesthetic, they more often saw their artistic work as operating alongside, but not directly with or within, the political thrust of the moment. Decades later, Lake maintained that he "never really thought of [my music] as political. If it makes a political statement, then it does, but I don't consciously think about, 'I'm going to do this political thing.'" In the late 1970s, Hamiet Bluiett put it more starkly, commenting, "I'm not interested in talking about sociology. . . . I'm a musician. The music comes first." And, speaking of the AACM in 1972, Lester Bowie made the same distinction between aesthetic and political realms, saying that the Chicago collective "was purely musical" and "never really had a political orientation." For the musicians of BAG, racial identity was inherent and not always or explicitly political.

Lake made a similar statement in his 1977 interview with Bob Rusch.[71] It should be noted that in human history, several regimes tried to only allow music that was approved politically. In the twentieth century, Communist China, the Soviet Union, and Nazi Germany come to mind. The music produced under these strictures invariably was inferior to the music produced before and after these regimes. The nature of music makes it apolitical.

These political tensions swirled in BAG and became one of the factors for its downfall. In addition, BAG, unlike other Black Arts organizations, was involved with other, allied arts organizations that were either white or multiracial.[72] The Human Arts Association, according to Looker, was a poetry and music organization that was nearly a multiracial twin of BAG. Ajulé Rutlin and white saxophonist James Marshall were two of the founders of the Human Arts Association. Marshall's wife, Carol, soon became a regular member, along with drummer Charles "Bobo" Shaw. The music performance group was called the Human Arts Ensemble. Lake commented in 1977.[73]

> They [the Marshalls] weren't in the Black Artists' Group because they were white (laughter). Not in the Black Artists' in that sense. They were friends of the Black Artists' Group; it was the category we had at that time, 'cause that was a high black power period—'68 and '69. So what happened was the Marshalls started an organization called the Human Arts Ensemble, which included all of us under one umbrella. They were involved with a lot of things we did but it was another level.

KDNA was a fondly remembered community radio station in some quarters of the St. Louis community.[74]

> FM was the wild west of the broadcast world, but two visionary entrepreneurs—Jeremy Lansman and Lorenzo Milam—saw the wide-open spectrum as an opportunity for a new kind of "alternative" commercial radio station. They pooled resources and on February 8, 1969 radio KDNA 102.5 MHz went live.
> Transmitting from Lansman's Bohemian digs in Gaslight Square, KDNA was like nothing St. Louis had ever heard before. The studios had an "open-door" atmosphere, welcoming variety and fostering unpredictability. Broadcasts ranged from Beethoven to Zappa, from Board of Alderman meetings to spectral séances, from interactive political debate (with up to four on-air callers at once) to the occasional appearance by DJ Leonard Slatkin. The only unifying theme was the community connection—passionate programmers (often volunteers) transmitting to a loyal student listener base (who themselves could often just show up at the station and start playing records on-air). It was weird, but it was real; built from the ground up, KDNA was an experiment in what radio could be.

This station became an outlet for the BAG–Human Arts Ensemble music, often presenting their recordings to a wider audience for the first time. BAG poet Michael Castro started a monthly poetry and music show that ran for three years.[75] Saxophonist Marty Ehrlich remembered the importance of KDNA to his development in a 1986 interview on KWMU.[76]

> Let's say, thinking back to that time, I would, I wanna make a plug here, that one really important avenue for me was having KDNA radio, since we're now on the one station that still plays jazz in St. Louis. 'Cause that was the first place I ever improvised in public, with the River Styx Poets. And it was one of the first places I heard, I can remember, you know, hearing *Dogon A.D.* for the first time on the radio station.

Although BAG members appeared sporadically on a KMOX-TV show called *Heads Up*,[77] which started in 1969, print media and the other TV outlets were not so kind toward the BAG–Human Arts Ensemble efforts. Floyd LeFlore recalled the initial indifference.[78]

In terms of the media, they were kind of shy. A lot of people thought we were clowns. You know, these guys don't know anything about music. They don't know anything about art. So the media, when I could see it, was kind of cold to an extent. Later on, I think they warmed up, because we were getting crowds into the place. We were doin' all kinds of different things; so we started getting some help from the media. However, that didn't pick up the audience or anything; the audience stayed extremely small.

Often the point of the group was to challenge audiences. LeFlore commented on audience reaction: "There was one thing about it. When people left a concert they either hated it or loved it. That was the whole point."[79]

BAG also had a community music school that taught anyone who came. Reedman Marty Ehrlich and guitarist Kelvyn Bell are two musicians who went through that school. Trumpeter/pianist David Hines taught there in 1970 and afterward, as did a number of other musicians. Ehrlich stated that his experience in improvisation started with BAG.[80]

Two things, there was a lot of collective improvising and there were a lot of people who were really extending the language on their instruments. You know, people like Oliver and Julius, Lester Bowie, Hamiet Bluiett, etc. . . . So there was this sense of stretching the limits of the music, in ways that people found, you know, interesting creatively, politically, etc. I thought for myself I got a lot of experience playing with other people. I really learned how to improvise with people as opposed maybe just being able to improvise on my own.

David Hines also played in the BAG big band. He recalled the reaction to the BAG musicians from the older musicians.[81]

You didn't get wide acceptance. You only had a handful of musicians who participated in that, 'cause the other guys wanted to keep the other traditions. They don't wanna break with what they had been doing. . . . They [the BAG musicians] stuck to what they started. Nobody was able to make them change their minds. . . . They didn't budge, they stuck to it.

John Mixon played on a lot of their stuff whenever they needed a bass player. He was one of the first people they'd call, John Mixon, Richard Martin (guitarist), a drummer named Johnny Johnson, and also drummer Bensid Thigpen (Ben Thigpen's son) [played with them].

According to Lake, the older musicians started to come around by 1971. He also discusses the "luxury" of not having national media attention on what BAG was doing.[82]

. . . 'cause we had a kind of luxury there. We just got into all kinds of things and that led us to maybe developing a kind of personal sound to what we were doing. Of course we were influenced by what was happening with the AACM because we did exchange concerts and they were influenced by us. 'Cause we had that kind of brotherhood and stuff that was happening and the same kind of spirit and that thing's still happening.

. . . There weren't too many people who knew what we were doing. It seems there were more people who knew what was happening in St. Louis, after we left than they did when we were there . . . it's strange.

To me we were all coming out of the same bag. We were all dealing from all of our experiences that we had in America and all of the experiences that had gone down before us, John Coltrane, Eric Dolphy, everybody, players in St. Louis, players you never heard of. The various experiences we had from playing in blues bands and everything. All that's intertwined.

A lot of it [hostility] came from musicians and from audiences. We started doing concerts in BAG every weekend, and eventually we built a very good audience and it was good. First, we had a lot of hostility from the musicians, so-called bebop musicians, who thought that we were kind of out. I think about '71 we had eventually gotten over to the local musicians, who started using our club, coming to the concerts and checking us out. So it turned around.

Part of the problem in discussing the music of BAG and the Human Arts Ensemble is that the only recordings to have a distribution were made in 1970 and later. We only have oral, not aural, descriptions of the music made before 1970 and thus have no sense of how the music evolved up to 1970. From the recordings, it is apparent that the musicians were affected by the styles current in music at the time: free jazz, jazz-rock, free-bop, minimalism, so-called "world music," rhythm and blues, rock as exemplified by Jimi Hendrix, and the energy music of the mid-to-late 1960s jazz avant garde players like John Coltrane and Albert Ayler. Some of these recordings attempted to fuse all of these disparate elements into a unified whole. Hemphill, Lake, and J. D. Parran "kept up a lively dialogue with St. Louis's classical music world,"[83] in particular with the modernist composers living in the city at the time. A concert celebrating the tenth anniversary of the New Music Circle featured a joint composition between Julius Hemphill and Arthur Custer called "Songs of Freedom, Love and War." The piece incorporated a rock group, Guise, Hemphill's jazz group, a twenty-five-piece orchestra, and a chorus of fifty-five singers. The piece featured Malinké Elliott reading his poetry and taped segments representing war and the tensions on the streets of cities. Apparently, this mélange was hastily put together, not well rehearsed, and did not get good reviews.[84]

J. D. Parran described the experience of collective improvisation and of learning how to do it.[85]

> And that is that the actual spirit of doin', of the collective improvisation, the feelin' of goin' in there, learning to listen to others while you're playing and learn to fit into a context. And, a spirit, there's another sort of a spirit that you can deviate from. . . . These were very important general things that you learned from workin' with the people, and, you had almost a feelin' of relaxation, as opposed to the perfectionist-type approach.
>
> You see what I mean, you move in a way and you see what's gonna happen and you are willing to try something. You're willing to experiment. Of course, every individual will take these experiences and glean different things from them. But you did have that opportunity.

By September 1969, Hamiet Bluiett had made his way to New York and began to make an impression on that scene. A year later, he convinced James "Jabbo" Ware to make the move as well. Bluiett returned to St. Louis periodically and took part in the Hemphill *Dogon A.D.* sessions. Lester Bowie periodically returned to St. Louis as well, and brought the Art Ensemble of Chicago for extended stays. BAG, the AACM, and the Detroit collective also exchanged groups so that there was cross-fertilization between the organizations. In 1971, several members of the Human Arts Ensemble, including the Marshalls, saxophonist Luther Thomas, bassist Arzina Richardson, and Ajulé Rutlin moved to Creswell, Oregon, and tried to set up an artists colony. The group spent their time meditating, eating, living, and working together.[86] Thomas was particularly energized by this experience.[87]

> Played, taught music, slept it, ate it. Mmm, we got so close. It was a communal situation. . . . Oliver Lake had the BAG Ensemble then, living in Paris. We had the music on all sides of the globe. We did some things up in Oregon with the great musicians up there, Alice Coltrane, Sonny Simmons, Sonny King and his wife Nancy, Dave Friesen. It was a family thing! When we came back from out West, we just turned the machines on. We had all the music.

On February 26, 1971, a concert called Images: Sons/Ancestors, a collaboration between Julius Hemphill, poet Michael Harper, and visual artist Oliver Jackson was presented by the African Continuum at Powell Symphony Hall. This concert was advertised in the *Globe* on February 20, 1971.[88] An article in the February *22 Globe* publicized Harper's appearance because he had published a critically acclaimed book of poetry. Scant notice was paid to the St. Louis musician Hemphill and St. Louis artist Jackson.[89] The *Argus* had advertisements of the concert in the February 19 and 26 editions. Despite being interrupted by a bomb threat, the concert went on. Hemphill led a ten-piece orchestra through various jazz styles.[90] The group included Hemphill, Willie Akins, and J. D. Parran (reeds); Zak Diouf and Ishaq Rajab (trumpet);

Black Artists Group, Paris, 1973. Photographer unidentified. © Baikida Carroll. Left to right: Oliver Lake, Joseph Bowie, Baikida Carroll, Charles "Bobo" Shaw, Floyd LeFlore.

Victor Reef (trombone); John Hicks (keyboards); Abdul Wadud (cello); Mor Thiam (percussion); and Phillip Wilson (drums). The piece, with a definite Afro-centric thrust, may have been the high point of BAG's multimedia productions. No review of the concert has been found, but a review of a Max Morath[91] ragtime show was found in the March 2 edition of the *Globe* and in the March 5 edition of the *Argus.* The Morath show had been running Webster College's Loretto-Hilton Center during the time Images: Sons/Ancestors was performed. The concert was not mentioned in the *Post-Dispatch* as an advertisement, story, or review.

By 1972, the funding sources had dried up. BAG began to come apart because of finances and philosophical/political differences between the various parts of the organization and individuals. Oliver Lake, Lester Bowie's brother, trombonist Joseph Bowie, Baikida Carroll, Floyd LeFlore, and Bobo Shaw formed an ensemble that eventually scrounged up enough money to get to Paris, along with two vans for traveling around France to get from gig to gig.[92] They left in late October and got a surprise when they arrived in Paris. Floyd LeFlore remembers their arrival and a recording that the BAG musicians made there.

> It was kind of weird. We didn't have any contacts but this one lady. And from there stuff started happening. I think that two days later we were on French TV [according to Looker, the show was cancelled by a strike] and then we were doing all kinds of concerts. We were workin' out of the French-American Cultural Center and they were turning us on and getting us gigs.
> *BAG in Paris* was a live date at the Grand Palais in Paris, a huge place. I was amazed at how receptive the French people were.

Lake recounted an experience at a festival in the south of France that harks back to LeFlore's comment about audiences either hating or loving the music.

> I think the closest thing we've ever had [to open hostility] was in the south of France where we were doing a festival. We played and half the audience liked it and half didn't. An argument was going on and they started to fight—5,000 people. And we're standing there playing; all fights going on (laughter) we didn't know what was happening. We didn't find out till later.

LeFlore came back to St. Louis first, because he was homesick and he and his wife had a daughter. Bowie and Shaw

Oliver Lake and Baikida Carroll Duo, Paris, 1974. Photographer unidentified. © Baikida Carroll.

eventually returned, but Lake and Carroll stayed in Paris for two more years performing, recording, and teaching. After returning stateside, both went to New York rather than to St. Louis. LeFlore remembered, "When I arrived back in St. Louis there was very little happening. It was kind of a frustrating period for me."[93]

Accelerating the breakup, Malinke Elliott and his wife moved to Sweden in 1972 to join a theater company, followed by actress Portia Hunt, costume designer Darryl Harris and Julius Hemphill. With some Swedish artists, they performed as an improvisatory troupe that traveled around the countryside.[94] Hemphill went to Paris in April 1973 to visit Lake and his colleagues, came back to St. Louis for the summer, and then moved to New York.

There was a final flowering of the BAG–Human Arts musical esthetic in 1973 with a number of recordings made in the studio and at live performances.

One of the prejudices that existed then, and may still exist today, is that black jazz musicians are untutored rubes who just picked up instruments and started to play. Because music was often not on the bandstand, it was assumed that they could not read music. The preceding passages show that such prejudices are unfounded. Since the very beginning of this music, highly trained, highly sophisticated musicians—both black and white—have been the major players who have pushed the music forward. The so-called "free jazz" movement of the sixties that BAG was a part of often had the "untutored rube" charge leveled at it. The reader is asked to consider the biographies of Bowie, Lake, Hemphill, Carroll, Bluiett and LeFlore above and to consider that the best-known free jazz group of this period, the Art Ensemble of Chicago, would often rehearse for two months[95] before starting a tour. Can the people who started BAG be characterized as the untutored and undedicated clowns[96] that the majority of the St. Louis community thought they were?

Other St. Louis Musicians Associated with BAG and the Human Arts Ensemble

James and Carol Marshall were important in the formation of the Human Arts Association along with Ajulé Rutlin and Charles "Bobo" Shaw. A dropout from Southwest High School, James Marshall was hanging around the Washington University area trying to get his saxophone playing together. He was active in the Congress of Racial Equality (CORE). Carol Lowenstein was from Charleston, West Virginia, and was a student at Washington University who was acting with the Alan

177

Nichols Theater Company. The couple went to India on a spiritual quest in 1971 and brought back instruments from the region that were used on several of the Human Arts Ensemble Recordings. Carol had some money from a trust fund and insurance policies, and she paid for the Human Arts Ensemble recordings at Technisonic Studios. Although Bobo Shaw was involved, Universal Justice Records was her project and her company. Carol financed the move to Oregon for several of the Human Arts Ensemble members. After their return from Oregon, the Marshalls remained in St. Louis and had two children. They divorced in 1979. James Marshall moved to Tucson in 1980 and has remained there, working in a performance art group and practicing saxophone. Carol eventually moved to Florida.[97]

Drummer Phillip Wilson[98] (1941–1992) was born in St. Louis and attended Sumner High School. His grandfather, Ira Kimball, was a percussionist who played on the riverboats. He started his training on violin at age eight and played for the Tom Powell Post Drum and Bugle Corps from age ten until he was fifteen. James Meredith, drum teacher for the Powell Post, played a crucial role in Wilson's development. Wilson was part of a group with Oliver Lake and Scrooge Harris when he was in high school. He began playing professionally with organist Don James and Freddie Washington at the Toast of the Town when he was fourteen. He joined organist Sam Lazar when he was sixteen and went on the road with him for four years, eventually ending up at Minton's in New York with Lazar. Wilson played with rhythm and blues bands up to 1964. While he was in St. Louis, he played with Lester Bowie, practicing in the park with him. He moved to Chicago in 1965 and became active in the AACM and was the drummer with the Roscoe Mitchell Art Ensemble, eventually the Art Ensemble of Chicago. Wilson also worked with the Paul Butterfield Blues Band (1970) and other rock groups and as a studio musician for Stax Records in Memphis (1975–1976). He eventually moved to New York in 1976, where he played with bands led by Lester Bowie, Anthony Braxton, and other major free jazz players. He was the original drummer with Lester Bowie's Brass Fantasy and Organ Ensemble. Wilson was killed in New York near Central Park.

Trumpeter Floyd LeFlore was born in St. Louis and attended Sumner High School. LeFlore's uncle was Clarence "Bucky" Jarman, a professional guitarist. His father was a jazz fan and Floyd was exposed to the music from an early age. He played the mellophone in the high school band and describes his playing as being "not very good."[99] LeFlore was drafted in 1963 and began to get serious about the trumpet. He was discharged in 1965, saw how dedicated Bowie, Lake, and his classmates were, and decided to get serious about music. LeFlore remained in St. Louis except during the sojourn in France in 1972–1973. He worked in St. Louis from 1973 to 1977 with J. D. Parran in 3rd Circuit n' Spirit. He also worked with saxophonist John Norment and had a group with saxophonist Freddie Washington. LeFlore recorded a CD titled *City Sidewalk Street Song Suite* in 1998.[100]

Drummer Charles "Bobo" Shaw was born in 1947 in Pope, Michigan. He moved to St. Louis and studied drums with Ben Thigpen. Shaw was an original member of both BAG and the Human Arts Ensemble, taking part in most of the recordings made by the groups. He went to Paris with the BAG Ensemble in 1972, but returned to St. Louis in 1973 and soon moved to New York with Joseph Bowie.[101] They soon found a place to perform, the Children's Workshop Theater, and began organizing music workshops and classes for children. One of their efforts was a Sunday morning "free jazz church service." Shaw and Bowie started a popular concert series featuring advanced musicians in New York and activated the Human Arts Ensemble name for their combo, which had a repertoire that ranged from modal pieces to free jazz and rock inspired by Miles Davis's 1970s bands.[102] The two musicians started Defunkt,[103] a hybrid of punk rock and free jazz.[104]

Trombonist Joseph Bowie (born 1953) is a brother of Lester Bowie. Joseph joined BAG at age seventeen and traveled to

Paris with the BAG Ensemble. Bowie and Oliver Lake recorded an album of free jazz duets in 1976 for Sackville Records in Toronto.[105] Joseph worked with Bobo Shaw during his early days in New York and now leads his band Defunkt all over the world. In 1995, Bowie recorded with Don Pullen.

Saxophonist Luther Thomas[106] is from St. Louis and was given a saxophone when he was fourteen years old. He soon was playing in his school's band, marching band, and a top 40 band that played at dances and parties in East St. Louis and Brooklyn, Illinois. This cover band backed many rhythm and blues artists working in the area. While still a teenager, he began hanging out with Oliver Lake, Hamiet Bluiett, and Julius Hemphill. Originally a baritone sax player, Thomas was inspired first by Oliver Lake and Oliver Sain. An unlikely source of inspiration, alto saxophonist Vi Redd caused him to change to alto. Lester Bowie was also an early mentor. Thomas became involved in BAG and the Human Arts Ensemble and soon moved to Oregon with the Marshalls and others. Returning to St. Louis, he made two recording as Luther Thomas and the Human Arts Ensemble (see below) and then moved to New York. He became involved in the "loft jazz" scene there. Thomas eventually moved into hip-hop and rap music and in 1996 moved to Christiana, Denmark.

Saxophonist James "Jabbo" Ware[107] was born in 1942 in Rome, Georgia. After his family moved to St. Louis, he began the study of alto saxophone under Harry Winn, a tenor saxophonist who led a sweet band in St. Louis during the 1930s through the 1950s. Ware, like most St. Louis musicians, served his apprenticeship in local rhythm and blues bands and in George Hudson's Orchestra. In the late 1960s, Ware worked with BAG, composing and performing with their ensembles. Hamiet Bluiett's sound on baritone sax intrigued him and he switched to that instrument. He followed Bluiett to New York in 1970. In New York, Ware studied improvisation and composition with George Coleman. He played in the Collective Black Artists Band, the Frank Foster Band, and the Sam Rivers Orchestra. He founded his own Me, We and Them Orchestra in 1973. His orchestra's latest recording is *Vignettes in the Spirit of Ellington*.[108]

Saxophonist Marty Ehrlich (born 1955)[109] was born in St. Paul, Minnesota, but raised in University City, Missouri. When he was in the ninth grade, he took a theater class from Malinké Elliott. Elliott played records of musicians like Ornette Coleman, John Coltrane, and Albert Ayler and began loaning Ehrlich records. Around that time, Ehrlich met James Marshall, who introduced him to some of the BAG musicians like Bobo Shaw, Oliver Lake, and Lester Bowie. Ehrlich eventually became part of the Human Arts Ensemble and made his first recordings on *Under the Sun* in 1973. Ehrlich went to the New England Conservatory of Music that same year. He moved to New York in 1978 and has led many of his own groups and worked with most of the advanced musicians in the city. Ehrlich's 1999 recording, *Malinké's Dance*, commemorates the association with one of his early mentors.[110]

St. Louisan Richard Martin (1948–1984) was a guitarist of uncommon talent.[111] He began taking lessons at age nine, apparently becoming obsessed with the instrument. By sixteen, he was a guitar instructor in the Ludwig Music Store. Martin worked in a variety of contexts with such musicians as Buddy Rich, Gene Ammons, Jimmy Smith, Jimmy McGriff, and others. He played on two BAG recordings in 1970. In 1977, he recorded with Freddie Washington, the Kennedy Brothers, and Nat Adderley in a concert at SIU–Edwardsville.[112] He and drummer Kenny Rice worked around St. Louis for several years. In 1983, he toured thirty-two countries and performed before Queen Elizabeth II in London. Martin was better known in Europe than in the United States.

Guitarist Marvin Horne was born in 1953 in St. Louis. He attended the University of Missouri and went on to play with the Human Arts Ensemble, recording *Funky Donkey, Parts 1 and 2* that same year. Horne left St. Louis and toured with Chico

179

Richard Martin, location unknown, c. 1980. Photograph by Roscoe Crenshaw. © Roscoe Crenshaw.

Hamilton (1973–1979) and Elvin Jones (1979–1983). His playing career has taken him from jazz to soul music to Latin bands. He lives in New York.

Drummer Jerome "Scrooge" Harris[113] was born in St. Louis and attended both Soldan and Sumner high schools. Harris, like Kenny Rice and Phillip Wilson, is a graduate of the Tom Powell American Legion Post Drum and Bugle Corps. Harris also played bass. He hung out with drummer Bensid Thigpen, pianist James "Iron Head" Matthews, bassist Raymond Eldridge, Jr., pianist Rick Bolden (who Kenny Rice[114] remembered as being highly talented), and a young Baikida Carroll. Bolden left St. Louis early, but before he left, he, along with Harris and Eldridge, were called for gigs with John Mixon and Freddie Washington. Harris was a member of BAG and cites it as "overall just a good experience—being involved with all the genres of the arts. The quality of musicians was high."[115] Harris has continued to work in St. Louis and is currently the artistic director of the Institute for the Advancement of Jazz Study and Performance, an educational program of the human services organization, Community Women Against Hardship.

Trumpeter Rasul Siddik[116] was born in 1949 in St. Louis but now resides in Paris. He is the uncle of drummer Ronnie Burrage. Siddik was around the Black Artists Group in its early days but soon went to Chicago to study, where he became a member of the AACM. He worked with the groups Soul Emotions, the Temptations, and Gladys Knight. Siddik moved to Los Angeles in 1975 and founded the Now! Artet. He was a part of the Watts Towers Creative Musicians group and worked with Pharoah Sanders and Julius Hemphill. Moving to Oakland, California, he became part of the Loft, a community-based association of musicians producing concerts and teaching music to underprivileged children. Returning to New York ten years later, he has played and recorded with many of the major players in the New York scene.

Trumpeter George Sams spent his formative years in St. Louis.[117] He was a bugler in the American Woodmen Drum and Bugle Corps that was sponsored by the Tom Powell American Legion Post. Sams went to Sumner High School and played trumpet in the band. He later transferred to Beaumont High School but did not play in the band. Sams worked in blues clubs in East St. Louis and while in high school hung out with musicians like Oliver Lake, Julius Hemphill, and Bobby Danzig. Trumpet player, Rozwell Darby (Ishaq Rajab), was an early influence. Sams hit the road at age nineteen and did not come back to St. Louis until the late 1980s. He worked and toured with pianist Andrew Hill and others before leading his own group, The United Front, based in San Francisco. This group introduced players who later became well known with pianist/composer Jon Jang. Sams also taught at a college in San Francisco for six years. He is now a consultant for the National Jazz Service Organization and lives in St. Louis.

Music Recorded by BAG and Human Arts Ensemble Musicians (1968–1973)

BAG and Human Arts Ensemble musicians made a total of twelve recordings between 1970 and 1973. This book will comment only on the works that the author has heard. The other recordings will only receive comment in the form of reviews from other sources, if they exist. These recordings have more comments than previous recordings because they are rare and hard to find.

The primary record label making these recordings was Universal Justice, which was the brainchild of the Marshalls and Charles "Bobo" Shaw. Carol Marshall funded the recordings and acted as the business manager for distribution. Julius Hemphill's Mbari label was very small and most of his music was heard in a wider context on the Arista/Freedom label. Lake's recording was not made into an LP during the BAG years. It was issued on the Arista/Freedom label in 1976.

As these recordings are being discussed, note the propensity for small percussion instruments (in common with the AACM) and unusual ensembles. No wonder that three original members of the World Saxophone Quartet, which plays mainly without bass and drums—Hemphill, Lake and Bluiett—were from BAG.

The Children of the Sun recording, *Ofamfa*, was recorded live in the fall of 1970 and featured both poetry and music that accompanied dancers. The personnel consisted of Ishaq Rajab (trumpet), Floyd LeFlore (trumpet, small instruments), Oliver Lake (soprano sax, alto sax, flute, poems, small instruments), Arzinia Richardson (bass, small instruments), Charles "Bobo" Shaw (drums, small instruments), Rashu Aten (conga, small instruments), Vincent Terrell (cello), and Ajulé (poet, arranger, small instruments, drums). The recording was on Universal Justice Records (29105/29106). The works were "Sweet Street Song," "Uu-Twee," "After Jeremiah'swed," "Sounds Of Scorpio," "Trane Song," "Rent Man," "A Little Tom Is a Dangerous Thing," and "Echoes" [O Susannah].

Rutlin's speaking voice is unusually high and uses cadences that sometimes tumble over one another. Sometimes he draws syllables out into long sounds. He uses silence, which is sometimes filled by the instrumentalists. While the message is clearly political, there is a lot of broad humor in the references and the poetry, especially in "A Little Tom Is a Dangerous Thing" and "Echoes." There are several fierce, unaccompanied solos by Lake. This recording is the debut of Lake and Shaw.

The BAG Solidarity Unit, Inc., made a recording titled *Red Black and Green* on September 18, 1970. The personnel included Bobo Shaw (percussion), Richard Martin (guitar), Oliver Lake (alto sax, flute), Floyd LeFlore (trumpet), Joseph Bowie (trombone), Arzinia Richardson (bass), Clovis Bordeaux (piano), Danny Trice (conga), Baikida Carroll (trumpet), and Kada Kayan (bass). The tunes were "Something to Play On," "Floreto," and "Beyond the New Horizon." The recording was issued on a BAG Live Concert Series. It marks the recording debut of Martin, Carroll, and Bowie.

Poet K. Curtis Lyle and Julius Hemphill (alto sax, flute) made a delightful recording, *The Collected Poems of Blind Lemon Jefferson*, for Hemphill's Mbari label in 1971. This recording marks the debut of Hemphill. Malinké Kenyatta is added on one of the selections. Lyle uses his voice to stretch and bend words and syllables to almost sing and sometimes to chant. Some of the poems are almost surreal. Hemphill's contributions mainly support the words, but they also are in opposition to the rhythms of the poet. The works are "Lemon's Holy Blues," "Lemon's Warm Life Blues," "Lemon's at the Shore of the World Blues," "Lemon's Etched in Halved Moons Blues," "Lemon's Comin' on Strong Blues," "Lemon's Born at a Bad Time under a Lemon Sign Blues," "Lemon's Revised Birdman Blues," "From Sun to Sun Blues," "Lemon's Dance," "Lemon's Easy Riding Skyboat Too Late Earth Moving Blues or a Dozen Different Blues," "Lemon's Brand New Shiny Skyboat Blues," "Lemon's Whistle Blowin' Heart Pealin' Blues," "Lemon's New World Blues," "Lemon's Fixin' to Die Blues," "Lemon's New Shot Between Planets Blues," "Lemon's Last Ditch Harmonize My Black Mule Blues" [with Kenyatta added], "Lemon's New Everclear Blues," and "My Own Blues." The recording is now available on CD on IKEF Records (IKEF 05)

Oliver Lake's recording, *NTU: Point from Which Creation Begins*, was not issued initially in St. Louis due to business problems. It was finally released on Arista/Freedom (AL1024) in 1976. The personnel was: Baikida E. J. Carroll, Floyd LeFlore (trumpet, percussion), Joseph Bowie (trombone, percussion), Oliver Lake (flute, soprano sax, alto sax, percussion), John Hicks (piano), Clovis Bordeaux (electric piano), Richard Martin (guitar), Don Officer (bass), Famoudou Don Moye (conga), and Bobo Shaw (drums). Oliver Lake wrote the tunes, which were "Africa," "Tse Lane," "Electric Freedom Colours," "Eriee," and "Zip." The music is clearly influenced by Miles Davis's recording, *Bitches Brew*, with its brew of twin keyboards and twin percussionists. "Africa" is almost a sonic exploration of a walk through a jungle, while "Tse Lane" is a fairly standard bossa nova. "Electric Freedom Colours" features a wonderful guitar solo by Richard Martin that becomes more and more distorted as the piece moves forward. "Eiree" is what the title sounds like: eerie and atmospheric. "Zip" features free improvisations over rock-like rhythms. The density of the sonic landscape in this recording is not overwhelming so that the solos stand out clearly.

In the author's view, Hemphill's *Dogon A.D.* recording with Baikida E. J. Carroll (trumpet), Hemphill (alto sax , flute), Abdul Wadud (cello), and Phillip Wilson (drums) is the masterpiece of the recordings that came out of BAG/Human Arts Ensemble musicians during this period. It was recorded in February 1972 and was engineered by Oliver Sain. The quartet is unusual in that a cello is used in lieu of a bass, a practice Hemphill continued throughout his career. The recording has a bluesiness that, for example, the AACM recordings of this period do not have and the solos, while having free jazz characteristics, do not fall into the trap of furious scale running that free jazz players sometimes fall into. The tunes are "Dogon A.D.," "Rites," and "The Painter."

Hemphill explained the inspiration for *Dogon A.D.*[118]

> I was interested in African culture, various African cultures and one of them was the Dogon tribe that lives in Upper Volta and Mali . . . parts of Mali. So, I read an article in a very beautiful color magazine, put out by, published by UCLA, I think, just called African Arts. And I read an article in that that said that the Dogon, who are fairly mysterious people in that they are fairly isolated, had decided to tap the tourist trade. And by revealing some of their sacred dance rituals for tourists, I guess they, you know, elected to, they said, "O.K., we'll do number 31, but we won't do 35." You know, it's just, I don't know . . . I'm just joking. But from that, I just got this notion of doin' a kind of a dance rhythm, you know. Actually the full title of it is "Dogon Adaptive Dance," that's what the AD really stands for. But, you know, it could also be "After BC," whatever, you know, (laughs). It all ties in I guess. But that was the . . . the influence behind doing such a piece.

Looker notes that Hemphill was attracted to the static quality of the accompaniment to the Dogon's dances. The riff played by Wadud and Wilson's drum accompaniment varies little during the performance. Malinke Elliot told the author in

2005 that the rhythm in the drum part comes from a tune played by an Appalachian fiddle player. Hemphill is like a Texas blues player in his solo parts. Carroll is very Freddie Hubbard–like in his playing. "The Painter" is a tribute to artist Oliver Jackson with Hemphill on flute. "Rites" is a collective improvisation reminiscent of Albert Ayler.

On the same recording date, Hemphill added baritone saxophonist Hamiet Bluiett to his ensemble for "The Hard Blues." This tune later appeared on Arista/Freedom AL 1012 as the second side of an LP called *Coon Bid'ness*. The other titles were recorded in New York with different personnel. "The Hard Blues" is a down home finger snapping blues with some free jazz touches and collective improvisation. *Coon Bid'ness* was reissued as *Reflections* (Freedom 741012).

The first Human Arts Ensemble recording, *Poem of Gratitude* (Universal Justice POG), was made in St. Louis in October 1972. It has some of the Tibetan and Indian instruments brought back to St. Louis by the Marshalls. The personnel was Ajulé, (tenor radong, poetry, drums, small instruments), Luther Thomas (tenor sax, tenor radong, small instruments), James Marshall (alto sax, tenor radong, small instruments), and Carol Marshall (vocal, bass-radong, small instruments). The tunes were: "Introduction," "Out to Lunch," "Sophisticated Lady," "Imagination-1," "Imagination-2," "Imagination-3," "Funny Things," "Poem of Gratitude," "Strange Autumn Tree Shapes," "Upbeat Feeling," and "God Bless the Child." *Downbeat* magazine awarded the recording three stars (out of five).[119]

> . . . It contains fine horn work by Marshall and Thomas. The problems lie in the space granted Rutlin's poetry and singing, and the inclusion of Ms. Marshall's vocals. Marshall's alto and Thomas' tenor either singularly or in emphatic duets reveal brilliant and beautiful conceptions. Thomas is more straight ahead, while Marshall's approach makes a bit more use of energy (though he doesn't rely on it as a replacement for ideas). Rutlin's drumming is okay, though his poetry is merely ultra-hip black relevance stuff (and often will have little meaning for those outside the St. Louis milieu). His singing on Ellington's *Sophisticated Lady* is disastrous, even if he was intending it as a parody. Ms. Marshall is okay on one track, but is a bit too "free" in her relationship to the music most of the time.

The second Human Arts Ensemble recording, *Whisper of Dharma*, had Floyd LeFlore (trumpet, small instruments), Joseph Bowie (trombone, conga, small instruments), J. D. Parran (bass clarinet, soprano sax, tenor sax, small instruments), James Marshall (alto sax, radong, wooden-flute, small instruments), Oliver Lake (soprano sax, tenor sax, flute, small instruments), Gene Lake, Bobo Shaw (drums, small instruments), and Baikida Yasseen (gong, small instruments). The tunes were "Whisper of Dharma" and "A World New." The recording was first issued on Universal Justice (WOD) and then on Arista/Freedom (AF1039). *Downbeat* assigned a rating of four stars for this recording.[120] The title track is clearly trance music, slow moving and elegiac. J. D. Parran's bass clarinet stands out on this piece. The interplay between all of the horns is also a highlight. The other side reveals a problem with free jazz ensembles of this type. The sonic landscape is so dense that it is difficult to follow. The *Downbeat* review points out that this is not pleasant music and cites Lake's tenor and soprano solos as bristling with "power, emotion and excitement."

The third Human Arts Ensemble recording, *Under the Sun* (July 1973) featured Lester Bowie (trumpet), Victor Reef (trombone), J. D. Parran (bass clarinet, soprano sax, piccolo, flute, harmonica , small instruments), Marty Ehrlich (alto sax, tin flute, small instruments), Oliver Lake (alto sax, tenor sax, flute, small instruments), James Marshall (alto sax, wooden flute, punji, small instruments), Kwame Graham (electric piano), Butch Smith (bass), Bobo Shaw (drums), Vincent Terrell (cello), Abdulla Yakub (percussion, small instruments, vocal), Alan Suits (tambourine), and Carol Marshall (vocal, small instruments). The two sides of the LP were "A Lover's Desire" and "Hazrat, the Sufi," and it first appeared on Universal

Justice (TS73-776) and then on Arista/Freedom (AL 1022). The melody line of "A Lover's Desire" is an Afghan folk song transcribed from Radio Kabul. "Hazrat, the Sufi" appears to be a continuation of the initial piece, with a variation of the Afghan melody. Both pieces feature Ayler-like solos over a bass vamp and a very dense sonic landscape that makes it difficult to follow the solos and collective improvisations. The solo accompaniment is very reminiscent of Miles Davis's early 1970s electronic work. *Downbeat* awarded the album a five-star rating.[121] It is possible that the problem of separating the solos from the sonic landscape lies with poor recording techniques.

The Black Artists Group Expatriates recorded *In Paris, Aries 1973* with Baikida E. J. Carroll (trumpet, flügelhorn, bass, percussion), Floyd LeFlore (trumpet, vocal, miscellaneous instruments), Joseph Bowie (trombone, conga, miscellaneous instruments), Oliver Lake (saxes, flute, miscellaneous instruments), and Bobo Shaw (drums, miscellaneous instruments). "Echo's," "Something To Play On," "Recreation," and "Olcsjbflbc Bag" were recorded in a live concert. Only around one hundred of the records were pressed, making this recording extremely rare. A CD issue was promised[122] but never released by early 2006.

The Luther Thomas Human Arts Ensemble recorded *Funky Donkey Volume 1 & 2* live at the Berea Presbyterian Church in St. Louis in September 1973. The group included Lester Bowie, Floyd LeFlore, Harold "Pudgy" Atterbury (trumpet), Joseph Bowie (trombone), J. D. Parran (soprano sax), Luther Thomas (alto sax), Marvin Horne (guitar), Eric Foreman (electric bass), Bobo Shaw (drums), and Abdulla Yakub and Rocky Washington (percussion). The tunes were "Funky Donkey," "Una New York," and "Intensity." The LP was first issued on Creative Consciousness (CC1001T) and has been reissued on CD on Atavistic/Unheard Music Series (UMS/ALP 215). The CD release was reviewed at Jazzreview.com.[123]

> The title is most accurate because this is one Funky Donkey indeed. Released as part of Atavistic's Unheard Music Series, this is an interesting blend of funk, fusion and free jazz. Think of one of Ornette Coleman's harmolodic funk ensembles with the Ayler brothers thrown in and you have an idea of what's going on here. This was recorded live and the musicians bring a lot of energy to the table taking brief themes and blasting them into the stratosphere.
>
> Thomas is joined by a great band, with Lester and Joseph Bowie on trumpet and trombone, J.D. Parran on reeds, Marvin Horne on guitar and Clerence [sic] "Bobo" Shaw on drums. The funk involved in the music is of a very organic, bluesy, electric-Miles nature, and All Music guide compares it to going to a stomping gospel church.
>
> Regardless, labels don't really do this music proper justice. It may not be the most immaculately played or cleanly recorded, but it's music with heart and soul, and it's a lot of fun.

The Luther Thomas Human Arts Ensemble also recorded an LP that was never released. This is known as *Banana: The Lost Session.* The personnel includes Luther Thomas (alto sax, piano, slide whistle, finger chimes) James Marshall (alto sax, tenor sax, soprano sax, flute, small instruments), Abdulla Yakub (alto horn, small instruments), Carol Marshall (vocal, accordion, small instruments), and Bobo Shaw (drums). It was recorded in St. Louis in 1973. The tunes were "Three Seven," "B Natural," "Headhunter," "Banana," "Out," and an alternate take of "B Natural." The music was released as a CD on Atavistic/Unheard Music Series (UMS/ALP 227).

In the end, what did BAG and the Human arts Ensemble bring to St. Louis and the world? Speaking in terms of music only, there is a chance that without this special period in the jazz history of St. Louis, the world might not have heard of Lester Bowie, Julius Hemphill, Oliver Lake, J. D. Parran, and Baikida E. J. Carroll. Without the Midwest musicians' collectives, jazz music might not have taken the course it has. Shirley LeFlore summed up what BAG meant to her.[124]

[The St. Louis Organization] reached some of the goals it didn't even know it had: the collective voice; a place to be somebody; a place to develop your craft. Because, ultimately, whether it's the Black Arts Movement or the human arts movement, artists need a place to work on their craft. And not just art for the sake of art, but art that can be appreciated, art that can be shared.

Lester Bowie sums up what has happened in St. Louis in jazz from way back and even up to the present time.

The thing about growing up in St. Louis was at that time, if you could survive that, you could survive anywhere. . . . And since then, I've been all over the world, I've lived in the Caribbean; I've lived in Africa; I've lived in Europe. And the lessons I learned right here in St. Louis have enabled me to live in New York like it's nothing, because it was so hard on the musicians there. I hope that the St. Louis people have begun to realize the importance of the creative musician and the artist in the community and to do something more now than to just pay lip service to it. Saint Louis is a great breeding ground for musicians. And if it is acted upon, it could be more than that. It could be a center for music.

Endnotes

[1] Anthony Davis, J. D. Parran, and Marty Ehrlich, interview with Jim Wallace, KWMU radio 1986.
[2] Jean Kittrell, interview with the author, April 2, 1986.
[3] A "bridge" is a contrasting section in popular song forms. A 32-measure form is usually broken down into four eight-measure segments. The first two have the same or similar harmonies. The third section (the "bridge") has contrasting but related harmonies and/or rhythm and leads to the fourth section of the form, which is nearly identical to the first two sections.
[4] Kittrell interview.
[5] Rent Party Echoes: The Role of the Louisville, Dallas, Fort Worth, Evansville Piano Parties in the History of Boogie Woogie Piano—As Seen by Charlie Booty, http://www.colindavey.com/BoogieWoogie/articles/booty.htm.
[6] Compiled from Kittrell interview. and http://www.jeankittrell.com/Bios.html
[7] Tom Lord Discography, version 3.3.
[8] Ibid.
[9] Ibid.
[10] Ibid.
[11] Ibid.
[12] Ibid.
[13] Compiled from information on Carolbeth True's website, http://carolbethtrue.com.
[14] Carolbeth True, interview with Jim Wallace, KWMU radio, 1985.
[15] Ibid.
[16] Jay Hungerford, Keys to the City, MusicMasters MM-20148
[17] Keith Ellis/Sessions Big Band, Softly as in a Morning Sunrise, Sessions Productions; and Keith Ellis/Sessions Big Band, Tribute, Sessions Music.
[18] Sandy Weltman, New World Harmonica Jazz, Wildstone Audio WSA 0981.
[19] Carolbeth True, Carolbeth Trio, Diamond Note SNS-0016; and Carolbeth True, True, Victoria Company VC 4349.
[20] Compiled from correspondence from Eddie Fisher with the author, 2003.
[21] Compiled from Lynn Driggs Cunningham and Jimmy Jones, Sweet, Hot and Blue: St. Louis Musical Heritage (Jefferson, N.C.: McFarland and Company, 1989), pp. 118—122.
[22] Willie Akins, interview with the author, July 10, 1986.
[23] Ibid.
[24] Ibid.
[25] John Mixon, interview with the author, July 1986.
[26] Akins interview.
[27] Willie Akins, Alima, Catalyst Productions CP011998.
[28] Oliver Lake, interview with Bob Rusch, Cadence (February 1977): 3.
[29] Lester Bowie, interview with Jim Wallace, KWMU radio, May 1986. This interview was the first interview Bowie ever had with any members of the St. Louis media.
[30] David Hines, interview with the author, January 14, 1986.
[31] Lester Bowie, interview with Bob Rusch, Cadence (December 1979): 3.
[32] Compiled from David Hines interviews with the author, January 14, 1986, and March 24, 1986; and Cunningham and Jones, Sweet, Hot and Blue, pp. 88–89.
[33] Bowie, interview with Wallace.
[34] Compiled from Bowie, interview with Wallace; Bowie, interview with Rusch; and Lee Jeske, "Lester Bowie," The New Grove Dictionary of Jazz, Barry Kernfield, ed. (New York: St. Martin's Press, 1995), pp. 140–141.
[35] Roscoe Mitchell, Sound, Delmark DE-408.
[36] Lee Jeske, "Lester Bowie," The New Grove Dictionary of Jazz, Barry Kernfield, ed. (New York: St. Martin's Press, 1995), pp. 140–141.
[37] Floyd LeFlore, interview with the author, June 1986.
[38] Lake interview.
[39] Hamiet Bluiett, interview with the author, fall 1986.
[40] Compiled from Lake interview; Barry Kernfield, "Oliver Lake," The New Grove Dictionary of Jazz, Barry Kernfield, ed. (New York: St. Martin's Press, 1995), p. 673; the Oliver Lake website (http://www.oliverlake.net); and The European Jazz Network, http://www.ejn.it/mus/lake.htm.
[41] Oliver Lake, NTU: Point from Which Creation Begins, Arista AL1024.
[42] This information excerpted from Baikida Carroll's website, http://www.baikida.com/bio2.html.
[43] J. D. Parran, quoted in Benjamin Looker, Point from Which Creation Begins (St. Louis: Missouri Historical Society Press, 2004), p. 14.
[44] Lake interview.
[45] Julius Hemphill, interview with the author, fall 1986.
[46] Looker, Point from Which Creation Begins, p. 16.
[47] J. D. Parran, Press Release, December 2005.
[48] J. D. Parran, J. D. Parran and Spirit Stage, Y'all of New York YALL-002.
[49] J. D. Parran, Omegathorpe: Living City, Y'all of New York.
[50] Bluiett interview.
[51] Compiled from Bluiett interview; Chris Kelsey, "Hamiet Bluiett," All Music Guide.

http://allmusic.com.

52 Hamiet Bluiett, *The Clarinet Family*, Black Saint 120097-2.

53 Hamiet Bluiett, *Bluiett Baritone Saxophone Group Live at the Knitting Factory*, Knitting Factory KFR 217.

54 Bluiett interview.

55 Looker, *Point from Which Creation Begins*, p. 17.

56 Michael Allen, "Urban Review St. Louis," http://www.urbanreviewstl.com/archives/000239.php.

57 Looker, *Point from Which Creation Begins*, p. 23.

58 This information excerpted from Baikida Carroll's website, http://www.baikida.com/bio2.html.

59 Baikida Carroll, *Marionettes on a High Wire*, Omnitone 12101.

60 *St. Louis Globe-Democrat*, August 1, 1967.

61 *St. Louis Post-Dispatch*, August 18, 1967; *St. Louis Globe-Democrat*, August 18, 1967.

62 LeFlore interview.

63 Looker, *Point from Which Creation Begins*, pp. 31–32.

64 Compiled from information from Subito Music, http://www.subitomusic.com/hemphill_bio.htm.

65 World Saxophone Quartet, *Steppin' with the World Saxophone Quartet*, Black Saint BSR 0027 CD.

66 World Saxophone Quartet, *Revue*, Black Saint 120056.

67 World Saxophone Quartet, *Plays Duke Ellington*, Nonesuch 9 79137.

68 Julius Hemphill, *Fat Man and the Hard Blues*, Black Saint 120115.

69 Looker, *Point from Which Creation Begins*, p. 70.

70 Ibid., p. 179.

71 Lake interview.

72 Looker, *Point from Which Creation Begins*, pp. 89–90.

73 Lake interview.

74 Dylan Hassinger, "A Brief History of the Double Helix," progressiveSTL.com. http://www.progressivestl.com/?p=62.

75 Looker, *Point from Which Creation Begins*, pp. 90–92.

76 Anthony Davis, J. D. Parran, and Marty Ehrlich, interview.

77 Looker, *Point from Which Creation Begins*, p. 84.

78 LeFlore interview.

79 Ibid.

80 Ibid.

81 Hines interview.

82 Lake interview.

83 Looker, *Point from Which Creation Begins*, pp. 176–177.

84 Ibid., p. 177.

85 Davis, Parran, Ehrlich interview.

86 Looker, *Point from Which Creation Begins*, pp. 190–191.

87 Funky Donkey, ttp://www.organissimo.org/forum/index.php?showtopic=21272&mode=linear.

88 *St. Louis Globe-Democrat*, August 20, 1971.

89 Ibid., August 22, 1971.

90 Looker, *Point from Which Creation Begins*, pp. xvii–xix, 263.

91 *St. Louis Globe-Democrat*, March 2, 1971.

92 Looker, *Point from Which Creation Begins*, pp. 195–197.

93 LeFlore interview.

94 Looker, *Point from Which Creation Begins*, pp. 190–191.

95 Bowie, interview with Rusch.

96 LeFlore interview.

97 Compiled from Carol Loewenstein, interview with Benjamin Looker, November 6, 2003; and James Marshall, interview with Benjamin Looker, August 11, 2003, in Looker, "Interviews on the Black Artists' Group (BAG) of St. Louis," unpublished collection, 2004, held at Special Collections, Washington University in St. Louis.

98 Compiled from Kenny Rice and Phillip Wilson, interview with the author, 1986; Bruce Eder, "Phillip Wilson," All Music Guide. http://allmusic.com.

99 LeFlore interview.

100 Floyd LeFlore, *City Sidewalk Street Song Suite*, Vid Recordings (Music Masters MM-34612).

101 "Charles "Bobo" Shaw," The New Grove Dictionary of Jazz, Barry Kernfield, ed. (New York: St. Martin's Press, 1995), p. 1109.

102 Human Arts Ensemble, *P'NKJ'ZZ*, Muse MR5232.

103 DeFunkt, *DeFunkt*, Hannibal/Island 6313 125.

104 Looker, *Point from Which Creation Begins*, pp. 222–224.

105 *Joseph Bowie-Oliver Lake*, Sackville 2010.

106 Compiled from information Luther Thomas's website, http://www.lutherthomas.com.

107 James "Jabbo" Ware biography, http://www.yallnewyork.org/James_Ware.html.

108 James "Jabbo" Ware, *Vignettes in the Spirit of Ellington*, Y'all of New York.

109 Compiled from an interview on the Omnitone Records website, http://www.omnitone.com/malinkesdance/ehrlich-interview.htm, and Marty Ehrlich.com, http://www.martyehrlich.com/marty.html.

110 Marty Ehrlich, *Malinké's Dance*, Omnitone 12003.

111 Cunningham and Jones, *Sweet, Hot and Blue*, p. 117.

112 Kenny Rice–Richard Martin Quintet with Nat Adderley, *Recorded Live*, Recorded Live Records.

113 Roscoe Crenshaw, "Living It," *St. Louis American*, July 20, 2005.

114 Rice and Wilson interview.

115 Crenshaw, "Living It."

116 Rasul Siddik, http://moments-of-jazz.skynetblogs.be.

117 Compiled from information in *Lift Every Voice and Sing—St. Louis African Americans in the Twentieth Century*, Doris A Wesley, Wiley Price and Ann Morris, eds. (Columbia: University of Missouri Press, 1999), p. 217.

118 Hemphill interview.

119 *Downbeat*, March 28, 1974, p. 29.

120 Ibid.

121 *Downbeat*, June 6, 1974, p. 27.

122 Joe Schwab, Euclid Records, St. Louis, private conversation 2004.

123 Jazzreview.com. http://www.jazzreview.com/guestreview.cfm?ID=751.

124 Looker, *Point from Which Creation Begins*, p. 249.

Epilogue
Jazz in St. Louis, 1974 to the Present: Flying Below the Media Radar

Since 1974, with few exceptions, there has been little change in the working conditions, public recognition, and media recognition of St. Louis's jazz musicians. In St. Louis, the jazz scene is split along stylistic, neighborhood, and unfortunately, racial lines. The stylistic split is between a (mostly white) traditional jazz audience and an (racially mixed) audience for other styles of jazz. St. Louis is a conservative place. Some people rarely leave their neighborhood to attend a cultural event. At many venues in St. Louis, the audience will be mixed racially if the jazz performer is black. If the jazz performer is white, the audience will be mainly white.

Currently, Grand Center is the only St. Louis locale where all types of people congregate to hear music. At venues such as the Sheldon Concert Hall and Jazz at the Bistro, mixed audiences are found, no matter the race of the performer. With the Fox Theater, the Black Repertory Theater, the Symphony at Powell Hall, and the Cabaret Series, world-class music and theater are found in this one central location.

Since the 1920s, jazz musicians in St. Louis have always made the bulk of their income in the world of commercial music (wedding bands, theater orchestras, corporate receptions, etc.) rather than in clubs or on concert stages. Still, this is usually not enough to live on, and most musicians must have other non-performing day jobs. Another outlet for many jazz musicians has come with the rise of jazz education in high schools, colleges, and universities.

This more "legitimate" music making and teaching still flies below the radar of the main media. The only local musicians to gain continuous recognition are the symphony musicians. For example, the Webster University Jazz Series has been ongoing since 1980, with outstanding concerts. The *Globe-Democrat* ran previews and reviews of these concerts by Tom McDermott and John McGuire until it went out of business in 1986. At least one or more concert per year by local musicians at the Webster series is at the performance level of nationally known musicians that come to St. Louis. Currently, a preview article will run one or two times a year in the *Post-Dispatch*, but there has never been a review of any of these concerts. In the past two years, preview articles have produced nearly standing-room only attendance at these concerts. The Crusaders for Jazz have presented nearly a dozen nationally known jazz artists at the Sheldon Concert Hall with little media coverage.

Why is sparse attention paid to local artists? It seems that a healthy community would revel in its local artists and the contributions they make to the fabric of the community. However, for reasons that the author has never understood, St. Louis has a civic inferiority complex. This issue is discussed sporadically in the media, most lately in a Bill McClellan column on January 16, 2006, in the *Post-Dispatch*.[1] If St. Louis is inferior in the eyes of its inhabitants, nothing or no one working in it will be equal to or better than what is outside the region. This applies not only to local musicians, actors, visual artists, photographers, and writers but also to scientists, educators, and institutions of higher learning. How demoralizing is that attitude on the psyches of these people? Is it any wonder that the saying goes that "it is better to be a jazz musician from St. Louis than to be a jazz musician in St. Louis" holds true for most of our musicians?

Currently, the *St. Louis Post-Dispatch* has a full-time music critic who writes only about classical music and reviews every concert by St. Louis Symphony musicians whether it takes place at Powell Hall or another venue. But for other music, including jazz, freelancers write most reviews. But the freelancers do not review performances of local artists. Only nationally known artists are reviewed. There are few exceptions. Both Kevin Johnson and Calvin Wilson review nationally known artists and jazz recordings.

It seems that St. Louis audiences need some sort of validation of a performer's worth. Roscoe Crenshaw has been writing stories about local jazz musicians for the *St. Louis American* for years, but the readers of this paper are African Americans, a minority in the St. Louis area. Terry Perkins, writing in an online discussion on St. Louis Jazz Notes on jazz festivals said, "But freelancer reviews—the lifeblood of that system—have dried up almost completely. I used to review every major concert at Jazz at the Bistro . . . and I haven't been able to do that in over a year. I agree with Dennis regarding reviews—they are an essential document of musical culture. You can write all the previews you want. But if there's no record of what actually went down . . . it could all just be 2084 (updated for Bush) speak. There's no record it ever happened."[2]

Social and artistic conservatism has been the norm in St. Louis. Some conservative ideas from the Victorian era are against praising children, lest they get swelled heads. Does this apply to how St. Louis treats its own musicians? Is this Victorian idea the genesis of Missouri's "Show Me State" slogan? In Chapter 7, Lester Bowie stated that being a musician was not an honorable profession in the eyes of the St. Louis community when he was growing up. Conservatism in the arts means sticking with the known, the tried and true. Thus, a little-known national musical act has a difficult time. A new and untried repertoire can present problems for some St. Louis jazz musicians. These musicians are more comfortable with playing the repertoire made popular by Miles Davis and others during the 1950s and early 1960s than they are learning newer methods and tunes.

In addition to the lack of media, jazz musicians are not supported by the local musicians' union. Presently, the only overt union support has been for the symphony musicians and those who work at the Fox Theater, the Municipal Opera, and other theaters. Nearly all other jobs are non-union. Although the practice seems to have disappeared by the early 1980s, some musicians used to arrive for a job at a club only to find another band in residence, because the other band had offered to play at a lower price than the resident band. This practice of "job knocking" was prevalent in St. Louis from the 1920s. Those that currently work weddings have had the problem of not being paid by the band booker for as long as three months after a gig (shades of Charles Creath in the 1920s gambling his proceeds away).

This lack of union support, however, does not mean that musicians cannot find work. The Black Music Society acts as a clearinghouse for black musicians playing in many styles. The St. Louis Jazz Club used to act as a clearinghouse for local traditional jazz musicians. The author suspects that the Crusaders for Jazz recommends players for functions. Local media people are often asked for recommendations. But, in the main, musicians are independent contractors and therefore need to market themselves. The late David Hines made a good living in St. Louis because he marketed himself well and always insisted on top dollar. Musicians now have the internet to aid them in getting name recognition with their own websites, email to fans, and like endeavors. Many local musicians, however, are not business savvy and are at a disadvantage. In 1988, Frankie Richardson tried to get many black players under contract as the Lakeside All-Stars. He put on two concerts; the first concert was somewhat successful while the second was a financial disaster for both Richardson and the musicians. Richardson put ads in the media and put up handbills in the black community for the first concert. The second concert received little or no publicity anywhere because Richardson could not make up his mind as to what to do, even though he had discussed his venture with professional publicists.

Even with such a lack of support, the period from 1974 to the present has seen a steep rise in the amount of jazz education for both aspiring musicians and fans alike. Steve Schenkel started teaching jazz history at Forest Park Community College in the 1970s. Webster University and Southern Illinois University–Edwardsville all possess robust, healthy jazz studies departments. The University of Missouri–St. Louis has also begun a jazz program in recent years. Washington University music majors can have a minor in jazz. This has allowed many St. Louis musicians to teach young players and pass along their knowledge. Although "stage bands" have been present in public and private high schools nationally since the mid-1950s, jazz education in these schools today is more problematic, with funding cuts and, in some cases, academic musicians who have never played professionally trying to teach jazz techniques.

Charlie Menees gave a talk on jazz education in schools to a meeting of the St. Louis music teachers at University City High School in 1950.[3] Menees's lifelong commitment to jazz education led him to teach short courses on jazz and big band music to adults at the University of Missouri–St. Louis, Meramec Community College, the Jewish Community Association, Elder Hostel, and other venues. Several of his students, including the author, have also taught short courses in similar venues. Don Wolff specializes in jazz films. Robert Carlock specializes in big bands. The author specializes in general jazz history, St. Louis jazz history, Duke Ellington, Count Basie, and modern and avant-garde jazz.

The Young Audiences program has brought jazz to children all over the St. Louis area as far back as 1972, when Jeanne Trevor and the St. Louis Jazz Quartet began presenting for the organization. For a while during the 1970s, pianist Jimmy Williams presented jazz history programs over the public television station, KETC. The Sheldon Concert Hall presents "The Jazz Story" several times a year for school children. Vocalists Jeanne Trevor and, more recently, Mardra Thomas along with pianist Carolbeth True and her group introduce jazz to about 7,500 young people every year. In addition, Jazz St. Louis has an education component, taking nationally known musicians working at its primary venue, Jazz at the Bistro, into the schools to introduce children to the music.

University City High School during the late 1980s and early 1990s had jazz bands that produced nationally known musicians. John Brophy directed the band when it performed at the Montreux Jazz Festival in 1986. Later, David Hines directed the band. These nationally known musicians include trumpeter Jeremy Davenport, pianist Peter Martin, bassists Chris Thomas and Neal Caine, and saxophonist Todd Williams.

Ron Carter directed East St. Louis Lincoln High School's music program that won many regional and national honors. This program produced musicians such as pianist Reggie Thomas, Tony Suggs, trumpeter Russell Gunn, saxophonist Andre Roberson, and drummers Terreon "Tank" Gulley and Montez Coleman. Thomas now teaches in the jazz department at Southern Illinois University–Edwardsville. Gunn is one of the more innovative mainstream trumpeters. Both Gulley and Coleman are now working in New York. Suggs is the pianist for the Count Basie Orchestra. Roberson records in the "smooth jazz" genre.

Another component of jazz education is the radio. In the 1950s and 1960s, Charlie Menees, Harry Frost, and Spider Burks had jazz shows that were well received. In 1959 and 1960, the Jazz Central group broadcast regularly from KMOX. Toward the middle of the 1960s, Leo Chears began broadcasting jazz. His career lasted on several stations until his death in early 2006.

Charlie Menees kept traditional jazz and swing styles alive during the jazz-rock fusion years of the 1970s with his show on KWMU. His show proved to be so popular that Bob Hyland of KMOX hired him for Saturday nights. KMOX is a clear channel station and is heard across the country. Don Wolff has hosted that program since Menees's death in 1993, playing mainstream swing and traditional jazz styles.

Currently, there is one station in the St. Louis region that broadcasts jazz most of the time, WSIE at Southern Illinois University–Edwardsville. WSIE has been broadcasting jazz for over twenty-five years. Ross Gentille, Bob Bennett, Bob Pelc, Adam Tracey, and Buddy Moreno are currently heard live, while a subscription service provides music the other times. Pat Graney, Don Wolff, and the late Jim Bolen were also heard on this station during the 1980s and 1990s. WSIE also broadcasts "Jazz at Lincoln Center," "Jazz at the Smithsonian," "Riverwalk," and "Marian McPartland's Piano Jazz." Most of the jazz heard on WSIE is mainstream swing with a high concentration on the hard bop style of the 1950s and 1960s.

KDHX has some jazz programming: "All Soul, No Borders" with Joshua Weinstein features avant-garde jazz, while "Voices in the Dark" with Al Becker features female jazz and blues vocalists. KWMU has only one locally produced music program, "Jazz Unlimited," the author's show, which has been on the air under various names since 1983. The show covers all styles of jazz from Louis Armstrong to John Zorn. Previously, KWMU had Walter Parker with "Jazzstream," playing traditional and mainstream jazz. In the 1980s, KWMU had a jazz music format in the evenings and overnight. For several years, there was a "smooth jazz" station in St. Louis, WSSM. A similar music style can be heard on KCLC in St. Charles. The Washington University station, KWUR, also broadcasts jazz, but at such a low power that it is not heard except in the immediate area.

Two other components of jazz education are visual and archival. The Sheldon Art Galleries hosts a permanent "History of Jazz" gallery, with rotating, far-ranging exhibits. Both the Southern Illinois University–Edwardsville Foundation and the Western Historical Manuscript Collection at the University of Missouri–St. Louis have collections of memorabilia and transcriptions of interviews with local jazz musicians. Don Wolff created an archive at Harris-Stowe State College by donating his large jazz LP collection.

The growing presence of jazz education to the broader community shows that there is a strong interest in the music. Education is one thing, but appreciation is a whole different matter that needs to be grounded in the community if jazz is to thrive in St. Louis. And how best to appreciate jazz than to hear it live in a club? The current club scene for local musicians includes Cookies Jazz and More and the Crossings Taverne and Grill in Webster Groves and Brandt's and Riddle's Penultimate Café in the Delmar Loop. Steady club work for modern jazz musicians has been sporadic. Currently, five-night-a-week jobs are nonexistent. If a musician wants to work five nights a week, he or she usually must find work in five different venues. Traditional jazz musicians have it even harder; they must tour or rely on the St. Louis Jazz Club for work. Here is a list of a few venues that offered live jazz in the 1970s and 1980s. Mr. C's La Cachette in Overland in the late 1960s and early 1970s presented both local and national musicians, as did La Casa on Jefferson in the mid-1970s. Gino's and Helen's Black Eagle flourished for a time in the 1970s and early 1980s. The Moose Lounge hired local and some national musicians for years, but has since closed. On Laclede's Landing, Marquette's and the *Admiral* presented jazz in the 1980s. Other clubs that have come and gone are Ice's Jazz Plus on Natural Bridge, Connors Jazz House, and Major Beaux. Spruill's on Jefferson and Washington University's Holmes Lounge Jazz Series present local and occasionally national jazz musicians.

A component of a successful presentation of any event is publicity, a major ingredient for the success of Jazz at the Bistro (now in its tenth year). No other club in St. Louis promotes their shows as intensely as Jazz at the Bistro. Instead of taking note of Jazz at the Bistro's success, most other club or bar owners where music is performed cannot even bother to inform the media about who is playing at their establishments. The author remembers a 1970s La Casa performance by the great jazz vocalist Carmen McRae with ten people in the audience.

St. Louis has a number of big bands that work sporadically:

- The Gateway City Big Band (primarily swing arrangements)
- The Sessions Jazz Band, working every Monday night (primarily Woody Herman, Stan Kenton, and Maynard Ferguson–based charts)
- The Gary Dammer Band (primarily swing arrangements)
- The Jazz Edge Big Band (Basie-style charts)
- The Kim Portnoy Big Band (original music)
- The Genesis Jazz Project (mainstream jazz)
- The Jim Widner Jazz Band (mainstream jazz and original music)
- The Bob Coleman Big Band (primarily swing arrangements)
- Student bands in all college and university jazz departments

Currently, there are several organizations presenting jazz in St. Louis. They are:

- The Webster University Jazz Series presents faculty concerts with both local and national guests.
- The St. Louis Jazz Club presents monthly traditional jazz concerts.
- The Crusaders for Jazz presents mainly local hard bop and mainstream players, along with some nationally known players.
- Jazz at the Bistro and now its parent organization, Jazz St. Louis (second incarnation), presents top national and local jazz groups of all styles except Dixieland.
- The Sheldon Concert Hall presents both local and national jazz musicians in a variety of styles.
- The Pageant presents some jazz along with all genres of music except classical.
- Finale Fine Music and Dining presents mainstream jazz and jazz influenced pop music.
- The Blanche M. Touhill Center for the Performing Arts at the University of Missouri–St. Louis presents jazz of all styles.
- The St. Louis Symphony sporadically presents national jazz performers. The Black Music Society also acts as an umbrella organization for all forms of black music.

Historically Trebor Tichenor and Frank Pearson started the National Ragtime Festival in 1965 on the *Goldenrod Showboat*. It continues today at the Missouri Historical Society. In 1969, a St. Louis Jazz Day was held on Lenore K. Sullivan Boulevard featuring the Oliver Lake group, Odell Brown and the Organizers, Tom Scott and Oliver Nelson with Duke Pearson, Mickey Roker, Bob Cranshaw, Stanley Turrentine, Clea Bradford, Big John Patton, and Clark Terry. Later, the St. Louis Jazz Society (1970s) and Jazz St. Louis (first incarnation under JoAnn Collins—late 1980s to around 1995) produced jazz festivals and other concerts featuring local and nationally known musicians. The Mid-America Jazz Festival ran for eighteen years from 1981, presenting mainly traditional jazz but including some swing musicians. An astounding lineup of jazz musicians performed at the 1989 Fair St. Louis, including the Lester Bowie Brass Fantasy, the Tony Williams Group, the St. Louis Jazz All-Stars, the Phillip Wilson Big Band, Emily Remler, Tania Maria, and the Timeless All-Stars. Cecil Taylor was scheduled to perform but missed his airline connections and ended up at the Moose Lounge. Chris Mullin and Phillip Wilson booked these musicians. With the exception of 1989, jazz has been underrepresented at Fair St. Louis.

Barbara Rose started a jazz concert series called "Just Jazz" at the Hotel Majestic in the early 1990s that featured both local and national musicians. When the Majestic was sold, Rose moved her concert series to the Bistro on Washington Boulevard in 1995. She was able to convert Jazz at the Bistro into a non-profit organization. Rose lost a battle to breast cancer in 1998, but Jazz at the Bistro continues under the leadership of Gene Dobbs Bradford. Diana Krall, John Pizzarelli, Ahmad Jamal, James Carter, the World Saxophone Quartet, and Nicholas Payton have all performed at Jazz at the Bistro.

The Sheldon Concert Hall in Grand Center, under the direction of Paul Reuter, created a subscription series beginning with the 1995–96 season called "Jazz at The Sheldon" and featuring artists such as Ramsey Lewis, Dave Brubeck, Cleo Laine, George Shearing, Arturo Sandoval, Jim Hall, Dee Dee Bridgewater, Jane Monheit, Dianne Schuur, Marian McPartland, James Moody, and Terence Blanchard. The weekly "Notes from Home" series, now in its thirteenth year, often features local jazz musicians.

Webster Groves presented its first jazz festival with mainly traditional jazz bands in 2001. The festival is now a jazz and blues festival. The St. Louis Jazz Festival, an annual two-day event begun in 2001 with a naming sponsorship from Firstar Bank (now U.S. Bank), brings in a range of mainstream, smooth, Latin, and crossover artists. Included in the festival have been Wynton Marsalis,

Nicholas Payton, Dee Dee Bridgewater, Branford Marsalis, Regina Carter, Joe Lovano, Marlena Shaw, Dianne Reeves, Dave Douglas, Larry Coryell, Arturo Sandoval, George Benson, David Sanborn, Aaron Neville, Al Jarreau, Poncho Sanchez, and the Afro-Latin Jazz Orchestra of Lincoln Center. It is interesting to note the number of local jazz artists featured at this festival: 2001 (three local groups); 2002 (six local groups); 2003, 2004, and 2005 (four local groups). For 2006, Denise Thimes and the Craig Russo Latin Jazz Project will be on the main stages. In addition, more local artists will be presented under a tent in continuous performance.

A major local jazz label, MAXJAZZ, was started by Richard McDonnell in 1998. MAXJAZZ records and markets jazz recordings nationally and internationally by both local and nationally known artists. Vocalist Carla Cook's *It's All About Love* CD was nominated for a Grammy Award. *The Penguin Guide to Jazz on CD* named *Vertigo*, by vocalist René Marie, as a Recording of Special Merit. Catalyst Productions, a company started in St. Louis by pianist Simon Rowe, recorded Willie Akins, Jeanne Trevor, Kansas City vocalist Luqman Hamza, and Indiana vocalist Jenice Jaffe. Bill Becker's Victoria Company records local artists such as pianists Herb Drury, Kim Portnoy, and Carolbeth True, along with other mainstream jazz musicians. Dan Warner's Gaslight Records records both local swing and traditional musicians. This label recorded pianist Ralph Sutton in solo and trio contexts and in piano duets with his sister Barbara Sutton Curtis. Because the technology to record digitally is so affordable, many St. Louis musicians are recording compact discs to market at their performances.

Some of the jazz vocalists working in St. Louis from 1974 to the present include Asa Harris (now a chaplain in a hospice in Seattle), Erin Bode, Valerie Tichachek, Sherry Drake, Christine Hitt, Mae Wheeler, Mardra Thomas, Denise Thimes, Jeanne Trevor, Elaine Donohue, Hugh "Peanuts" Whalum, Tom Heitman, Maury Jannett, Ron "Scratch" Wilkinson, Danita Mumphard, and Gene Lynn. Tichachek recently won a national *Downbeat* competition.

A few of the jazz trumpeters working in St. Louis up to the present are the late David Hines, Michael Parkinson, Randy Holmes, Sue Beshears, Keyon Harold, Bob Ceccarini, Floyd LeFlore, Brian Casserley, Danny Campbell, Keith Moyer, Dan Smith, Lee Hyde (also piano), and Jim Manley. Trombonists include Brett Stamps, Kevin Ward, Brad Bobsick, John Wolf, Jim Martin, Pat Arana, John Covelli, and Norman Menne.

While St. Louis has been known as a trumpet town, it could also be classified as a pianists' town in this latter period. The list of these artists is long: Herb Drury, Dave Venn, Ray Kennedy, Carolbeth True, Ed Nicholson, Reggie Thomas, Kim Portnoy, James "Iron Head" Matthews, Eddie Fritz, David Parker, Carol Schmidt, the late Charles Fox, Curt Landes, Pat Joyce, Jay Oliver, the late Max Potts, Mike Silverman, Jeter Thompson, Tony Simmons, Chris Walters, Leslie McLean, Karen Baldus, Ptah Williams, Nick Schleuter, Pete Ruthenberg, Leslie McLean, and Elizabeth Hutcherson. Organist Terry Williams works in East St. Louis. Reggie Thomas also plays organ and has a working group called OGD. The late Richard "Groove" Holmes lived with his wife Renee in St. Louis but worked and recorded in other cities.

St. Louis has many excellent reed players working from 1974 to the present: Freddie Washington, Willie Akins, Paul DeMarinis, the late Gerald DeClue, David Stone, the late Jimmy Sherrod, James Warfield, Sid Rodway, Jason Swagler, Chad Evans, Jeff Anderson, Scott Alberici, Hugh Jones, Larry Smith, Mike Karpowicz, Chuck Tillman, Stan Coleman, the Bosman twins, the late John Norment, Jerry Greene, Rob Hughes, Hugh "Peanuts" Whalum, Brett Spainhower, Freddy Del Gaudio, Michele Isam, the late O'Hara Spearman, the late Charles "Little Man" Wright, the late Bob Gibson, and the late Bernard Hutcherson.

St. Louis jazz guitarists working since BAG days include the late Richard Martin, Steve Schenkel, Chan Johnson, Dan Rubright, Rob Block, Marvin Horne, Tom Byrne, Bill Linehan, Rick Haydon, Scott McCloud, Bill Mamer, Tommy Moore, Corey Christianson, Farshid, and Dave Black. St. Louis bassists include the late John Mixon, Bob Stout, the late Jerry Cherry, Kent Miller, Darrell Mixon (John's son), Gus Thornton, Kim LaCoste, Tom Kennedy, Raymond Eldridge, Jr., Dan Eubanks, Ric Vice, James Forman, Eddie Randle, Jr., Jon Thomas, Jay Hungerford, Willem von Holmbracht, Eric Foreman, Eric Markowicz, Pat Murphy, Mark Turlina, Ben Wheeler, Eric Warren, Jim Widner, Glenn Smith, Zeb Briscovic, and Dave Troncoso.

Since 1974, St. Louis has been blessed with several world-class drummers and percussionists. Gary Sykes, Jerome "Scrooge" Harris, the late Clarence "Sonny Hamp" Hamilton, and the late Joe Charles fit this category. Other drummers and percussionists working in St. Louis include the late McClinton Rayford, Kenny Gooch, Jimmy Merity, Kenny Rice, Kevin Gianino, Joe Buerger, Kyle Honeycutt, the late Tony Saputo, Miles Vandiver, Moldon Pickett, Matt Kimmick, DeMarius Hicks, Al St. James, Percy James, Emanuel Harrold, Maurice Carnes, Kim Thompson, John Gillick, Clarence "Clancy" Newell, Tommy Crane, the late Chuck Carter, and the late Michael Tyree. Vibraharpists include the late Jim Bolen, Gordon Lawrence, Jonathan Whiting, Tom Rickard, Ernie Douglas, and Don N. Parker.

Pianist David Parker worked with and financially supported recordings by the Jimmy Sherrod group for his VID label in 1992. This group included Jimmy Sherrod and David Stone (tenor sax), Sue Beshears (trumpet), Parker, Eric Markowicz (bass) and Joe Charles (drums). These recordings were made under the name, *The Joe Charles Collective*, and are prized by collectors because of the presence of Charles. They are the only recordings of Charles and Sherrod.

St. Louis has continued to supply highly trained jazz musicians to the national and international scene. Quite a few of these musicians have come out of University City High School in recent years. Reed player Marty Ehrlich went to University City High School and came up during BAG days. His recording debut was on a BAG record. Drummer Ronnie Burrage is also a University City High School graduate who went on to New York. His career has taken him into many different forms of the music with many different artists, including pianist McCoy Tyner. Guitarist Kelvyn Bell also trained at the BAG community music school and has been involved in the M-Base collective in New York and other avant-garde music pursuits. Pianist/composer Harry Miller is now working in New York in a wide variety of contexts. Todd Williams (reeds) played with the Wynton Marsalis Septet and the Lincoln Center Jazz Band. He now teaches at a college in New York. Jeremy Davenport (trumpet, vocal), Peter Martin (piano), and bassists Chris Thomas and Neal Cain are all University City High graduates who moved to New Orleans and are using it as a base for national recognition with their own groups, Harry Connick, Jr., Joshua Redman, Elvin Jones, and many others.

Others who are now nationally known musicians from St. Louis are below.

- Saxophonist/composer Byron Bowie is the brother of Lester and Joseph Bowie. He has been a part of the Chicago music scene since 1980 and leads the Defunkt big band with Joseph.
- Pianist/vocalist Johnny O'Neal is from Detroit, but has lived for long periods in St. Louis. He made his debut at Carnegie Hall in 1984 on a program with Oscar Peterson and Cecil Taylor and has recorded with Art Blakey in Japan and for the Concord and Justintime labels.
- Dave Weckl studied drums with Joe Buerger and others in St. Louis. He worked with Simon and Garfunkle and is a very busy studio musician. Weckl was part of Chick Corea's Elektric Band and has worked off and on with St. Louis pianist Jay Oliver.
- Russell Gunn (trumpet) from East St. Louis Lincoln High School now leads his own groups and is in the forefront of combining hip-hop beats with jazz improvisation.
- Trumpeter Keyon Harold is now working in New York with a wide variety of bands.
- Eric Person (reeds/composer) is a Normandy High graduate who has worked for over twenty years on the international scene with Chico Hamilton and others.
- Greg Tardy (reeds) has his own groups and also works with Tom Harrell, Russell Gunn, Dave Douglas, Andrew Hill, Nicholas Peyton, and Elvin Jones.

- Bruce Purse (trumpet, composer, arranger) is best known for his arrangements for Lester Bowie's Brass Fantasy.
- Pianist Tony Suggs works with the Count Basie Band.
- Saxophonists Conrad "Butch" Thomas and Chris Cheek are Webster University graduates who have made reputations for themselves in New York in both the jazz and rock worlds.
- Steve Kirby is one of the first call jazz bassists in New York and is director of jazz studies at the University of Manitoba, Canada.
- Saxophonist Greg Osby was also part of the M-Base music collective in New York and has made many recordings under his name and as a sideman.
- Drummer Steve Davis is an active clinician and touring musician with many groups, most recently with the Lynne Arriale Trio.
- Drummers Montez Coleman, Terreon "Tank" Gulley, Kim Thompson, and Jim Orso are now working in New York. The first three have worked with many major musicians, including Kenny Barron and Stefon Harris.
- Vocalist Zelphia Otis from East St. Louis Lincoln High School has performed and recorded in Dubai, Singapore, and Indonesia.
- Vocalist Denise Thimes has performed and recorded in Singapore.
- Ray Kennedy is the pianist for guitarist John Pizzarelli.
- Tom Kennedy (bass) lives and works mainly in St. Louis but tours with nationally known musicians several times a year.
- The Mayer brothers, Peter (guitar) and Jim (bass), have distinguished themselves in both the rock and jazz worlds.
- Bill Linehan (guitar) teaches at Washington University but spends six months a year touring in Italy and Europe.
- Pianist Ptah Williams continues to work in St. Louis but has toured abroad with drummer Ed Thigpen, saxophonist Lou Donaldson, and vocalist Fontella Bass.
- Bassist Kent Miller studied with Wendell Marshall and then moved to Maryland, working in the Washington, D.C., area.
- Trombonist Mike Vlatkovic works on the Los Angeles free jazz scene.
- Vocalist Erin Bode also works around St. Louis but has achieved national and international fame with her MAXJAZZ recordings.

This book was written to show the wealth of jazz talent that has been in St. Louis since the beginnings of the music. Since the 1920s, the list of highly trained St. Louis jazz musicians succeeding on the national scene is very long. Currently a vibrant, if mainly unrecognized, jazz scene exists in St. Louis, but the city's jazz musicians and other local artists must still continuously fight for survival and recognition in their own hometown. In spite of (or because of) this lack of recognition of local artists throughout its history, St. Louis has played a vital role in the history of jazz and will continue to do so by training players and building audiences for the future of the music.

Endnotes
[1] *St. Louis Post-Dispatch*, January 16, 2006.
[2] *St. Louis Jazz Notes*, http://stljazznotes.blogspot.com/.
[3] Charlie Menees interview with the author, October 1986.

Charter Members of
the St. Louis Jazz Club (Chartered October 1951)

Musician

Carter, Robert
Diringer, Skip
Eckhardt. Wally
Koppe, Marllyn
Koppe, Betty
Lambert, Chas. B.
Lankford, Harvey M.
Mason, Norman
Nathan, Einil
O'Connor, Rick
Palmer, Singleton N.
Reece, William
Saunders, Vertna L.
Shaw, Alexander
Shaw, Lige
Smith, George L.
Sutton, Barbara L.
Thompson, Charles

Active

Abkemeier, Mary Ann
Alumbaugh, Maryanne
Austin, Mary Frances
Barkowski, Ronnie
Bash, John H.

Berger, E. Dexter
Berger, Joyce
Bishop, Eugene
Bishop, Rosalie
Cashlon, Eileen
Chronlster, Betty
Codemo, Donald J.
Codemo, Jerry
Crowder, Eaward
Dailey, Tom
Deibel, George
Donaldson, George
Donelly, Ed
Donovan, Jerry
Dorrin. Mike
Edison, Lydia
Edison, William
Edwards, John P.
Farrow, Robert W.
Fend, W. J.
Fischer, Hans H.
Fister, Ronald B.
Foster, Joan
Futhey, Jack
Garrison, Hollis L.
Gruetzmacher, W. H.

Harrlson, Richard G.
Hartzog, G. Harley
Herzberg, Dolores
Hintze, John L.
Hocutt, George
Jessie, LeRoy
Johnson, Oliver W.
Koester, Robert
Lambert, Hattie
Lawton, Don
Layton, Ruth
Lodge, Frances
Lodge, R. L.
McWeeny, Robert
McDonald, Marian L.
Menees, Charles
Moore, Pat
Murray, George R.
Nantz, Udell
Niemoellezr, A. F.
Noe, Patricia J.
Olegschlaeger, Pauline
Oswald, Robert C.
Oswald, Vivian
Pearlmutter, Morris
Pearlmutter, Stella

Pessen, Richard
Poll, Connie
Reese, Lloyd E.
Rives, Roland
Roessler, LaVerne
Ruth, E. Dorsey
Ruth, Mary C.
Sankus, Helene
Schenk, Joseph T.
Shaw, Georgia
Sheltler, Dorothy
Sneed, Raymond
Trotwein, Sybil
Trotwein, W. Cecil
Walz, Bob
Winhelm, Harold
Youngdahl, James E.

Corresponding

Crosby, Barney
Curtis, Harold E.
Menville, Myra
Randolph, John
Shorter, Madge

Index

Adam Lambert's Six Brown Cats, 86
Adams, A. W., 16
Adams, Pepper, 139, 143, 150, 158
Adderley, Cannonball, 82, 89, 116
Adderley, Nat, 126, 145, 179
Adkins, William, 95
Admiral, The, 70, 109, 190
Akins, Willie, 59, 88, 115, 159–161, 175, 192
Almac Hotel, 44
Allen, Dick, 30
Allen, Ed, 19, 33–34, 38, 41–44
Allen, Henry "Red," vii, 20, 34, 39, 44, 71
Allister Wylie Orchestra, 16, 25
Alphonso Trent Orchestra, 32, 39, 62. See also Alphonso Trent.
Ambassador Bellhops, 24, 30
American Federation of Labor (AFL), 11, 47
American Negro Music Festival, 92
Ammons, Gene, 121, 166, 179
Anderson, Buddy, 86
Anderson, Jeff, 192
Anderson, Joe, 56
Anderson, Ivy, 77
Apollo Theatre, 89–90, 93, 141–142, 171
Arcadia Ballroom, 9, 22–24, 26–31, 47, 75
Arcadia Peacock Orchestra of St. Louis, 15
Arcadian Serenaders, 15–16, 22, 27–28
Argo label, 123
Argus Hall, 31
Arista/Freedom label, 166, 171, 181–184
Armstrong, Lil, 71
Armstrong, Louis, vii, 5, 10, 12–13, 15, 17, 19, 21, 29, 32–33, 40–42, 44, 54, 57, 75, 81, 101–102, 190
Arnold, John, 7, 38, 58
Ashby, Irving, 102
Ashenbrenner (Ash), Paul, 25
Association for the Advancement of Creative Musicians (AACM), 111, 155, 161–162, 164, 166–168, 170, 172, 174–175, 178, 180–182
Atkins, Boyd, 17, 31, 37
Atlantic, 142, 149
Atterbury, Harold "Pudgy," 184
Auld, Georgie, 100
Austin, Willie, 8, 67–68

BAG House, 171–172
Baker, Frankie, 2
Baker, Harold "Shorty," 52–53, 56–57, 79, 95
Baker, Josephine, 101
Baker, Winfield, 52–53, 56–57, 79
Baquet, George, 8
Barker, Danny, 80
Barlow, James, 32, 68
Barnet, Charlie, 67, 99
Barrel, The, 49, 107, 112–113, 129
Baskerville, William "Bede," 55–56
Bass, Fontella, 164, 194
Batchman, Clifford, 66, 92–93, 95
BB's Jazz, Blues and Soups, 167
Beard, James, 68
Bechet, Sidney, 39, 102
Beiderbecke, Bix, 22–23, 26–30
Bell, Kelvyn, 174, 193
Bell, Robert, 51, 68
Belle, Jewel, 117
Bellson, Louis, 118
Bennet, Theron C., 5
Benny Washington's Six Aces, 16
Benson Orchestra, 26
Berger, Herbert, 16, 23–25
Berigan, Bunny, 72
Beshears, Sue, 164, 192–193
Bess, Druie, 33, 59–60, 71
Bibb, Theodore, 94–95
Bierman, Rolla, 25
Billings, Dale, 115

Billups, Kenneth, 9, 167
Bismark Hotel, 48
Black Artists Group (BAG), 1, 154–185
Black Arts Movement, 155, 172
Black migration, see Great Migration
Blacks, The, 166, 169–170
Bland, Jack, 27
Blanton, Jimmy, 17, 36, 40, 56, 59, 70, 74–80, 88, 102
Blue and Harmony Band, the, 8
Blue Devils. See St. Louis Blue Devils
Blue Flame Club, 15, 113, 129
Blue Note Club, 107, 118, 125–127, 146, 151, 155, 158, 167–168
Blue Note Records, 125–126, 146–147
Blue, William, 8, 41
Blue, William Thornton, 8, 36–37, 41
Blues, and St. Louis jazz, 15
Bluiett, Hamiett, 94, 102, 126, 165, 167–177, 179, 181, 183
Bogg's Café, 9
Bohlen, Movel, 88
Bolen, Jim, 95, 112–113, 189, 193
Bolen, Rick, 159
Bolo Club, 100, 113
Booker T. Washington Theater, 2, 7, 23, 29, 31, 49, 54
Boots on the Levee, 15
Bose, Sterling, 22
Bosman, Dwayne, 102, 192
Bosman, Dwight, 102, 192
Bowden, Len, 92, 95–96
Bower, Glenn, 158
Bowie, Joseph, 176, 178–179, 181–184
Bowie, Lester, 33, 162–169, 173–186, 188, 191, 193–194
Bowie, Sr., Lester, 9, 164
Bradford, Clea, 115, 138–141, 149, 152, 191
Bradshaw, Tiny, 86, 90, 102
Brass Fantasy, 163–164, 178, 191, 194
Brazier, George, 58, 88
Brazier, Jessie, 58, 60, 88
Britt, Albert, 2
Brooks, Dudley, 95
Brown, Armand "Red," 32
Brown, Andrew, 9, 30
Brown, Henry, 148
Brown, Les, 128
Brown, Porter, 25
Brown, Vernon, 24, 27, 30
Brubeck, Dave, 7, 191
Brunswick label, 15–16, 25, 40
Buchanan, Elwood, 9, 82–83
Buckner, Milt, 102
Buerger, Joe, 137–138, 152, 193
Bumbry, Grace, 162
Burks, Jesse "Spider," 97, 102, 122–123, 126, 130, 140, 143, 189
Burnside, Vi, 100
Burton, Bob, 100
Bushell, Garvin, 35
Bustles and Bows, 133–134, 138, 153
Butler, Albert "Peanuts," 51
Butler, Charlie, 16
Byrd, Donald, 139, 147, 150

Calloway, Cab, 31, 39, 42–43, 54, 61, 80, 101
Calloway, William, 32
Campbell, Brun, 4, 72
Campbell, Danny, 192
Campbell, Floyd, 19, 32, 36–39, 43, 68
Campbell, Paul Guydner, 93, 95, 120
Capitol, 17–19, 21, 33, 38, 41–43, 54
Carnegie Hall, 30, 57, 102
Carroll, Baikida E. J., 165–166, 169, 176–177, 180–185
Carruthers, Earl, 66, 68
Carter, Benny, 39, 71, 86, 129
Carter, Sr., Charles, 92, 140, 162, 193
Carter, Emmett, 144
Carter, Robert, 70, 95–96, 108–109
Carter, Ron, 82, 150, 189
Casa Loma Ballroom, 75, 103

Casey, Bob, 25
Castle, the, 1, 3, 36, 50, 67, 75, 84, 88, 100–101
Castro, Michael, 173
Catlett, "Big" Sid, 63
Chambers, Paul, 82, 115, 122
Chapman, John "Albino Red," 113, 115, 128, 145, 150
Charles, Joe, 124, 145, 150, 193
Chase Hotel, 75, 80, 103, 114, 128
Chaudet, Bob, 25
Chauffeurs Club, 9, 31, 34
Chauvin, Louis, 2, 4
Chears, Leo, 126, 144, 189
Cherry, Jerry, 112–113, 116, 147, 151, 159
Chestnut Valley, 1–2, 5
Chet Baker Quartet, 122
Childers, Buddy, 75, 128
Christian, Charlie, 63, 71, 124
Circle Coffee Shop, 168
City of Providence, 10
Clark and Lovere, 7
Clarke, Kenny, 63, 102
Clay, Shirley, 9
Claybrooks, Albert "Pee Wee," 51, 60
Clayton, Ceil, 138, 148
Club Villa Valencia, 60
Cobb, Jimmy, 82
Cobb, Oliver, 33, 40, 50, 52, 111
Coffey, Father, 5
Cole, Cozy, 80
Cole, Eddie, 72
Cole, Nat King, 101, 112
Coleman, George, 122, 147, 150, 160, 179
Coleman, Ornette, 23, 179, 184
Coltrane, John, 23, 82, 87, 122, 139, 143–145, 166, 174–175, 179
Columbia, 64, 82, 102, 115, 122, 142, 147
Comet Theater, 92
Condon, Eddie, 23, 27, 39, 43, 81
Confrey, Zez, 7
Conley, Larry, 24–25, 28, 44
Connors, Babe, 1, 3
Cornwell, Blaine, 97
Coronado Hotel, 24–25, 48, 75, 77–78
Cotter, John, 89, 92, 109, 112, 115
Cotton Club, 30–31, 39, 101
Cotton Club Orchestra, 30, 33, 36, 39, 42
Count Basie, 40, 54, 58, 63, 71–72, 89, 92, 95, 99, 101–102, 108, 114, 117, 119–120, 189
Covington, Ike, 64, 70
Cox, Ida, 67
Crawford, Forrest, 72
Creath, Charles, 7, 15, 19, 21, 23–24, 29, 31, 33–45, 48–50, 54, 68–69, 71, 111, 188
Crenshaw, Louis, 10, 54, 180, 187
Creole, 1
Creole Band, The, 8, 13
Creve Coeur Lake, 24, 34
Crystal Palace, The, 133–134
Cunningham, Don, 141, 146, 150
Custer, Arthur, 175

Dabney, Elisha "Bartley," 95, 114
Dameron, Tadd, 63, 91
Daniels, Charles N., 6
Danzig (Danzie), Bobby, 84–86, 88, 145, 163, 181
Dark Side, The, 133, 139–142
Davey Bold's Celebrity Club, 113–114
David, Russ, 128, 148–149
David Silverman Orchestra, 16, 24
Davis, Leonard "Ham," 9, 33–34, 36, 39, 43, 56
Davis, Miles, 9, 34, 56, 59, 75, 80–81, 88, 91, 100, 112, 118, 122, 126, 129–130, 139, 144, 147, 150, 178, 182, 184, 188
    In St. Louis, 81–86
Dean, Tommy, 59, 85, 88, 98, 100, 116–117, 120, 124
DeBaliviere Strip, 107, 112, 129, 137, 150–151, 155, 167
Decca, 56, 94, 141–142, 147, 149
DeClue, Gerald, 101, 192
Deep Morgan, 5